Turning the Power

Critical Studies
in the History
of Anthropology

SERIES EDITORS
Regna Darnell
Robert Oppenheim

TURNING THE POWER

Indian Boarding Schools,

Native American

Anthropologists, and

the Race to Preserve

Indigenous Cultures

NATHAN SOWRY

University of Nebraska Press | Lincoln

The University of Nebraska Press is part of a land-grant institution with campuses and programs on the past, present, and future homelands of the Pawnee, Ponca, Otoe-Missouria, Omaha, Dakota, Lakota, Kaw, Cheyenne, and Arapaho Peoples, as well as those of the relocated Ho-Chunk, Sac and Fox, and Iowa Peoples.

Publication of this work was assisted by the Murray-Hong Family Trust, to honor and sustain the distinguished legacy of Stephen O. Murray in the History of Anthropology at the University of Nebraska Press.

Library of Congress Cataloging-in-Publication Data
Names: Sowry, Nathan, author.
Title: Turning the power: Indian boarding schools, Native American anthropologists, and the race to preserve Indigenous cultures / Nathan Sowry.
Other titles: Indian boarding schools, Native American anthropologists, and the race to preserve Indigenous cultures
Description: Lincoln: University of Nebraska Press, [2025] | Series: Critical studies in the history of anthropology / series editors, Regna Darnell, Robert Oppenheim | Includes bibliographical references and index.
Identifiers: LCCN 2024026896
ISBN 9781496241924 (hardback; acid-free paper)
ISBN 9781496242846 (epub)
ISBN 9781496242853 (pdf)
Subjects: LCSH: Off-reservation boarding schools—History. | Indian children—Relocation—United States—History. | Indians of North America—Education—History. | Indian students—United States—Social conditions. | Indians of North America—History. | Indians of North America—Ethnic identity. | Indians of North America—Government relations. | Indians, Treatment of—United States—History. | Ethnology—Research—Methodology.
Classification: LCC E97 .S69 2025 | DDC 973.04/97—dc23/eng/20250108
LC record available at https://lccn.loc.gov/2024026896

Set in Arno Pro by Lacey Losh.

For Leslie, who has patiently listened to me, aided me,
and supported me throughout this entire process.

And for our felines Pierogi and Paprika. Since day one they both
kept me company, assuring me that the best seats in the house
were somehow always on my keyboard and notes.

Contents

Illustrations

Acknowledgments

This book grew out of my dissertation research, and for that I need to thank Dan Kerr, Kate Haulman, and Malgorzata Rymsza-Pawlowska (MJ). Thanks are also due to a number of professors whose mentorship guided me along this path. Among many others, these include Paula Kane, Heather Salter, and Michelle Caswell.

I visited many different archives during this research, often accompanied by my patient wife, Leslie. I wish to acknowledge the help of staff from the following repositories: the American Museum of Natural History, Field Museum, Harvard University Archives, the Manuscript Division at the Library of Congress, Milwaukee Public Museum, National Archives and Records Administration in Washington DC, Peabody Museum of Archaeology and Ethnology, Penn Museum, Smithsonian Institution's National Anthropological Archives, and Yale University's Beinecke Library.

Numerous family members, friends, and colleagues supported and encouraged me while writing this book, and I can't thank them enough. I received thoughtful advice and helpful criticism from more than a few of them. Among that long list are Dave Beck, Trevor James Bond, Rose Buchanan, Philip Deloria, Armand Esai, Curtis Hinsley, Ira Jacknis, Benjamin Kracht, Rosalyn LaPier, Kristen Mable, Nancy Parezo, Alex Pezzati, Sam Redman, and Jen Shannon. Matt Bokovoy and Taylor Martin at the University of Nebraska Press also deserve a special thanks for guiding me through this new world of academic publishing. Their support and kind words have made it all possible.

Finally, I also need to acknowledge the wonderful work of the staff of the Archives Center at the Smithsonian Institution's National Museum of the American Indian: Jeremy Gardner, Rachel Menyuk, Emily Moazami, and honorary member Maria Galban. I consider myself fortunate every day that I get to work and learn from such a great group of people who are not only my colleagues but also my friends. Their efforts to process, digitize, and make accessible the collections in their stewardship made my research that much more successful, rewarding, and enjoyable.

Turning the Power

Introduction

What Happened Before (Bellevue, Nebraska Territory, 1862)

Immediately upon entering the doors of the Presbyterian Mission School, the young girls and boys met the school's staff. Stepping forward, one of the more stern-faced missionaries informed the children that their language would no longer be spoken. To emphasize his point, he repeated that only English was permitted, all the while holding a large hickory rod aloft. Although their English wasn't that good, all of the incoming students quickly comprehended the point being made: speak Omaha, and get the rod. Speak English, and the rod would be spared.

In the coming days, many of the young Omaha children found that to keep from being struck by their teachers, it was better to simply say nothing at all. Despite wanting to speak with their fellow students, to discuss the confusing rules of this school, or to commiserate about their shared sadness of being away from their families, it was easier, at least physically, to remain silent.

Along with their language, religion, and culture, the Omaha pupils soon learned that their names, too, were to be discarded. To continue to use such heathenish names was sinful, their teachers told them, a reminder of their savage past. They were to receive new names, Christian names, which would be more fitting as they left their supposedly barbaric ways behind them and became productive members of the Euro-American capitalist society. Of course, many of the young Omaha girls and boys found a variety of ways to resist this enforced assimilation. Some physically fled from the school, even though they knew that doing so risked increased punishment if and when they were caught. Others outwardly accommodated themselves to the racist teachings of their classroom, while inwardly accepting or rejecting those aspects that they felt they could best adapt to their own lives.[1]

These childhood memories of the abuse and cultural arrogance experienced in an Indian mission school belong to Francis La Flesche, probably the most recognized Native American anthropologist at the turn of the twentieth century. Importantly, the imposed erasure of La Flesche's Omaha language and culture while a student at the Presbyterian Mission School in Bellevue, Nebraska, in the early 1860s was hardly unique. The ostensible purpose of religiously affiliated mission schools and federally sanctioned Indian boarding schools was to educate and assimilate Native American youths into the dominant Euro-American Christian society. More nefariously, though, in practical terms this meant the eradication of distinct Native identities, languages, religions, and cultures. The oft-quoted maxim of Carlisle Indian Industrial School founder and assimilation advocate Richard Henry Pratt summed up this practice quite simply: "Kill the Indian in him, and save the man." For the teachers, religious instructors, and staff of the scores of mission schools and Indian boarding schools that sprung up in the latter half of the nineteenth century, the charge before them was clear. The burden of "civilizing" the supposedly incorrigible Native youths of the United States fell solely upon their shoulders. And they would do all in their power to cancel any semblance of their students' Indigenous pasts.[2]

Francis La Flesche and the Life of a Native Anthropologist

Published half a lifetime later in 1900, La Flesche's *The Middle Five: Indian Schoolboys of the Omaha Tribe* recalled the alien world he entered as a child when he and his fellows first walked through the doors of the Presbyterian Mission School, located on the Omaha Reservation in the Nebraska Territory. La Flesche, born in 1857 to a distinguished Omaha chief, and his sisters were notable for their education and activism on behalf of their people. An older sister, Susette, advocated for Native land rights and participated in speaking tours for reform efforts, while a younger sister, Susan, pursued her medical degree and later ministered to her Omaha community in Nebraska. Francis himself went on to receive his bachelor's and master's of law degrees in Washington DC, and by the time he published his recollections of the Indian mission school of his youth in 1900, he was working as a clerk in the Bureau of Indian Affairs (BIA). Ten years later he secured a position at the Smithsonian's Bureau of American

Ethnology (BAE), one of the premier institutions outside of academia then doing anthropological research and collecting work. There he joined Tuscarora community member J. N. B. Hewitt as the second permanent Native American anthropologist on staff.[3]

La Flesche's career was unique and groundbreaking as one of the first Native American professional anthropologists. Although he did not formally enter the profession until later in life, from his earliest years he worked as an interpreter and collaborator with many non-Native luminaries in the field, most notably Alice C. Fletcher, with whom he developed a close working and personal relationship. By 1881 the two began their initial fieldwork together on the Omaha Reservation, acquiring cultural heritage objects and information from La Flesche's community for deposit in Harvard University's Peabody Museum of American Archaeology and Ethnology, where Fletcher was employed. The following year he aided her in overseeing the allotment of Omaha tribal lands after the U.S. Congress passed the 1882 Omaha Act and appointed Fletcher a "special agent" to conduct such work. Eventually, in 1911, La Flesche and Fletcher published together their massive anthropological study on his people simply titled *The Omaha Tribe*.[4]

When La Flesche became a member of the BAE staff in 1910, then director Frederick Webb Hodge requested that the fifty-three-year-old Omaha man immediately proceed to Oklahoma to pursue ethnological studies among the Osage and any neighboring Native communities. Hodge later wrote that La Flesche's Native ancestry and fluency in English, the latter attained in his youth at the Presbyterian Mission School in Nebraska, perfectly qualified him to procure Native objects and information. And La Flesche did just that, undertaking fieldwork with the Osage, Omaha, and Ponca peoples and, in his words, making a special study of their histories, their traditions, and their social customs. In particular, La Flesche worked with a number of Native collaborators who helped him in securing sensitive information and acquiring sacred objects. To be sure, though, many Osage community members feared human or divine punishment for revealing sacred information to anthropologists, even to Native anthropologists such as Francis La Flesche, and consequently refused to work with him. As discussed in following chapters, community mistrust and skepticism toward the collecting work of anthropologists, Native or non-Native, remained constant across nearly all Indigenous communities in the United States at the time. Not surprisingly, such mistrust continues to persist to this day.[5]

As a Native American anthropologist, La Flesche sympathized with the plight of contemporary Indigenous peoples, but he simultaneously also advocated for policies of assimilation and allotment in these nations. While always passionate about documenting his community's culture, his views on what aspects were worthy of preserving and what should be abandoned gradually changed over his lifetime. Because he came from a family who early on championed Native American assimilation into Euro-American society, readers should not be surprised to learn that La Flesche once described his fellow community members as existing in the shades of superstition. In this he was no doubt echoing the pronouncements of missionaries he had heard in his youth.[6]

At the same time, though, he was also critical of the colonizing Euro-American society that surrounded him, telling Native students in an address at the Carlisle Indian Industrial School that although he had met "a great many white people" who were good, the same could not be said for a great many of their actions. As readers may already know, La Flesche aired some of his more direct criticisms of Euro-American society in the recollections of his school days. In his 1900 publication *The Middle Five*, for example, he exposed at an early date the abuse, racism, and cultural arrogance rife in mission schools and Indian boarding schools.[7]

La Flesche remained in his position as a leading Native American anthropologist at the BAE in Washington DC for nearly two decades. Throughout those years he collected tangible and intangible materials from the Osage, Omaha, and Ponca communities, supplementing the vast holdings of Native American material culture at the Smithsonian. If he ever felt conflicted about his role in removing Native material culture from the communities that created it, he, like many of his fellow Native anthropologists and collaborators, did not address it publicly. By 1929 La Flesche retired from his position at the Smithsonian's BAE due to poor health. He soon after moved back to the Omaha Reservation in Nebraska where he was born; surrounded by members of his family, he died there in 1932 at the age of seventy-four.[8]

La Flesche's life and work in the early days of U.S. anthropology were in many ways quite like those of the Indigenous anthropologists and collaborators readers will meet herein. All of them confronted Euro-American colonialist rhetoric in the mission schools and Indian boarding schools of their youth. All of them inhabited the dynamic, interconnected field of U.S. anthropology in its infancy. All of them faced daily racism from their colleagues and others for being members of a supposedly lesser race. The main difference is that La Flesche's story has already been told, but these other stories have not. For many people knowledgeable about the history of anthropology or Native American and Indigenous studies, Francis La Flesche is already a familiar name. Probably without question he was the most famous Native American anthropologist at the turn of the twentieth century. Numerous books and dozens of articles have been written about him. Very few, on the other hand, have been written about the subjects of *Turning the Power*.

Although this has not been largely explored, La Flesche also interacted with a handful of these Native anthropologists and collaborators, their lives and work often overlapping in anthropology's early days when the field was small and before it made a major transition from museums to universities. Like the people whose life stories are portrayed in this book, La Flesche was a product of his Native heritage and a Euro-American education gained in mission schools and Indian boarding schools. As such, he strove not only to represent Indigenous peoples accurately to a largely Euro-American public, but also to document Native cultures and histories for future generations. He acted in the way that he thought best to preserve the unique lifeways of his people before they eventually disappeared, as he believed they inevitably would.[9]

In many ways, La Flesche's life mirrored that of his Native contemporaries who were also involved in the fledgling field of anthropology. Importantly, though, while La Flesche's story is a familiar one, their stories are not. Few people a century ago and fewer today know the names of Tichkematse, D. C. Duvall, Cleaver Warden, or Florence Shotridge. But each of these Native individuals was instrumental in the development of early anthropology in the United States, and all of them directly or indirectly represented their Indigenous communities in museum exhibitions, in publications, and on a variety of public stages to a world eager to learn about "the vanishing Indian." Despite their disparate origins from across North America, two major factors shared by these individuals were their attendance at Indian boarding schools and a desire to take the English knowledge they learned there to preserve their cultures. In greater or lesser degrees, then, each found ways to confront settler colonialism and undermine federal assimilation policies that sought to eliminate their unique Indigenous identities, languages, and histories.[10]

The Advent of Mission Schools and Indian Boarding Schools

From the earliest days of the European invasion of North America, colonizing powers strove either to eradicate the continent's Indigenous inhabitants or to convert them to Christianity. Nor did these efforts lessen with the founding of the United States. By the time this young nation was less than a century old, scores of religiously affiliated mission schools had sprung up across the country. Their purpose was clear—"the speedy evangelization of pagan tribes." Each school was in direct competition with the others to accomplish this mission, battling among themselves to "save souls" and convert Native communities to various sects of Protestantism and, slightly less often but with equal religious fervor, to Catholicism. These mission schools were operated by ardent missionaries certain in the correctness of their actions and funded by church groups hoping to spread the Christian gospel, and the goal of the schools was to compel Native Americans to become members of Euro-American Christian society. Of course, soon finding that adults were less likely to abandon ingrained cultural beliefs and practices handed down from their ancestors, missionaries began to instead indoctrinate Native youths as a more pliable group of potential converts. In the schools that these missionaries created, young girls and boys lived and worked for months or years at a time. Recruiting agents physically removed students from their families, hoping to sever any connections between these Native youths and their communities.[11]

By the final quarter of the nineteenth century, though, something had begun to change. Many Euro-American reformers started voicing their criticisms of the mission school system. Its critics argued that there had to be a better way to convince or compel Native peoples to assimilate into Euro-American ways of thought, dress, and belief rather than simply meeting them on their own territory. These reformers pointed out that the mission schools, situated as they often were on Native reservations, did not do nearly enough to separate Indigenous children from the supposedly backward and negative influences of their communities. What the children needed, reformers argued, was complete physical removal from their families and their lands. As one early BIA agent noted, the communal nature of the Indigenous nations of the United States represented barbarism; only by forcing individualism upon them would these people be led to civilization.[12]

The solution eventually arrived at was the creation of federally funded off-reservation Indian boarding schools. These were often located hundreds and even thousands of miles from reservations. Richard Henry Pratt, founder of the Carlisle Indian Industrial School and a staunch advocate of assimilation, summed up the responsibility that motivated him and others to lay out the off-reservation boarding school system. "There is but one plain duty resting upon us with regard to the Indians," he declared. "That is to relieve them of their savagery and other alien qualities. . . . Help them, too, to die as helpless tribes, and to rise up among us as strong and capable individual men and American citizens." Echoing the death metaphor of his more popular slogan, "Kill the Indian in him, and save the man," Pratt believed his solution to the "Indian problem" was clear—eradicate everything that was Native about Native peoples. He theorized that once they were successfully cast in the mold of Euro-American Christians, their "Indianness" would cease to be a problem, as it would simply no longer exist. By the final decade of the nineteenth century many reformers, missionaries, and BIA agents began to take up Pratt's call to help Native Americans assimilate into the broader society rather than being made to stand outside it. Through the Indian boarding school system, they believed, Native children's reliance on their communities would be eliminated as each of them assimilated into mainstream Euro-American society.[13]

And thousands upon thousands of Native children did go to these schools, though the degree to which they reached the level of anticipated assimilation is debatable. From their homes they traveled in every direction. Indian boarding schools continued to pop up like weeds, ultimately surrounding reservations by the final years of the nineteenth century. Native children attended these racist and abusive factories of enforced assimilation for a variety of reasons. Clearly many were forced to do so; they were rounded up like cattle and sent via train, boat, and wagon to distant towns and cities far from their families and their homes. But some also chose to go voluntarily. A young Shawnee man who attended the Carlisle Indian Industrial School in its opening year of 1879 indicated that he made the decision to go because his community elders wished him to. As he later recalled, there had been a consensus then among his people that some of the adolescent members of the Shawnee Nation should be educated in the ways of Euro-American society. It was hoped that by learning to read and write in the language of the colonizers, these young Shawnee pupils could return to their people better equipped to defend and direct their community in its communications with the U.S. government. Whether they were dealing with treaties, land claims, or enforced allotment policies, a better knowledge of English, and thus the ability to negotiate on a more level playing field, became a major source of power for those deemed powerless. In the final decades of the nineteenth century, countless courageous young women and men from Indigenous nations across the United States answered this call of their communities. In droves they traveled hundreds or thousands of miles to Indian boarding schools where they armed themselves with knowledge to bring back to their homes and families in Indian Country.[14]

Of course, a great many Indigenous parents and Native nations simply refused to send their children away from them, regardless of any supposed benefits. While Indian boarding schools in their earliest years were at least nominally entered into on a voluntary basis, by 1891 the U.S. Congress authorized the commissioner of Indian affairs to issue regulations that would secure the attendance of Native children in schools established and maintained for their supposed benefit. Not seeing the results they hoped for, in 1893 Congress further authorized the commissioner and his staff at the BIA to withhold rations, clothing, and other annuities from those Indigenous parents who refused to send their children to one of these schools. While physical violence was not explicitly condoned in this authorization, the threat of starvation nevertheless became an accepted motivator on the part of the U.S. government to enforce policies of compulsory education and assimilation.[15]

Perhaps surprisingly, given the explicit racism, violence, and cultural arrogance that pervaded all aspects of mission schools and Indian boarding schools in the United States, the experiences of the ten Native anthropologists and collaborators depicted in this book did not follow the expected pattern. Unlike a great many of their peers, none of the ten individuals portrayed here were compelled to attend Indian boarding schools. Arguably their reasons for attending may have had more to do with their parents' wishes rather than their own, but nevertheless none of them were physically forced to attend. Further, once they were there, whether at Hampton, Carlisle, Haskell, or the other institutions, none of them attempted to flee, as far as the records show. Importantly, this does not in any way mean that they did not suffer horrendous racism during their time there, as well as daily experiencing physical, verbal, and emotional abuse in these institutions. Nor does it show that they agreed or accepted the assimilationist doctrines forced upon them. What it does show is that these ten individuals, or in many cases their parents, had a desire for their children to learn about and be able to respond to the settler colonial world that had insinuated itself into their everyday life, oppressing them and controlling their actions.

Between the years 1878 and 1909 all ten of the Native individuals portrayed in this book attended either a religiously affiliated mission school, a federally sanctioned Indian boarding school, or, for some, both. Tichkematse, William Jones, and James R. Murie were all alumni of the Hampton Institute in Virginia. Richard Davis and Cleaver Warden were among the first and second class to attend the Carlisle Indian Industrial School in Pennsylvania. And Amos Oneroad graduated from the Haskell Institute in Kansas after many previous years at mission and Indian boarding schools in his home state of South Dakota. D. C. Duvall, John V. Satterlee, and Florence and Louis Shotridge all attended smaller, less well-known, yet no less severe Indian boarding schools and Christian-run mission schools in Montana, Wisconsin, and the Alaska Territory, respectively.

While they were students in the above-named colonial institutions, their teachers taught these young Native women and men that their cultures were backward, their histories primitive, their languages barbaric, and their religions blasphemous. But in addition to the heartrending racism and abuse these children endured, they also learned lessons from each other that their teachers did not anticipate. They learned that their cultures were rich, their histories a source of pride, their languages beautiful, and their religions something to be honored, not discarded. Each of these ten individuals learned to use the English language forced on them during their school days as its own source of power. Through their fluency and ability to read and write in the language of the colonizers, each of these Native women and men later chose to join the nascent field of anthropology, using it as a platform from which they could document, preserve, correct, and expand upon what was known about their cultures.[16]

Salvage Anthropology

Emerging from the avocational pursuits of earlier generations of armchair enthusiasts, U.S. anthropology's race to preserve all aspects of Indigenous cultures began roughly in the 1870s and 1880s. Responding to the federal policy of enforced assimilation and compulsory abandonment of Native cultures in Indian boarding schools, a reactionary movement by anthropologists emerged to save, salvage, or capture everything they could about the Indigenous peoples of North America before they supposedly disappeared or assimilated into mainstream Euro-American society. By the late nineteenth century these claims of "the vanishing Indian" were everywhere. The Smithsonian Institution's assistant secretary Spencer Baird even said as much to members of the U.S. Congress in 1876. Baird argued that in his scientific opinion the Indigenous peoples of the United States would soon cease to present any distinctive characters of their own, completely merging into the dominant Euro-American culture within the next hundred years. Therefore, the onus was clearly on the nation's anthropologists to get collecting.[17]

The competitive nature of the anthropological museum field being what it was—exhibiting Native material culture objects for museum-going audiences eager to gawk, admire, and scorn the lifeways of the supposedly vanishing American Indians—ushered in a scramble for budding anthropologists, predominantly non-Native men and sometimes women, to visit Indigenous communities across the country in search of the pure, the authentic, the "real Indian." The salvage anthropology ethos that resulted was not limited to collecting sacred objects and secret ceremonial information, either, but rather encompassed everything relating to Indigenous cultures. Everyday objects, songs, and trickster stories were commonly sought out. Many anthropologists even pilfered Native human remains, digging up graves and mounds in their thirst for more knowledge. Sadly, these latter actions illustrated the contradictory nature of salvage anthropology, in which practitioners of the field exhibited a passion for learning about Indigenous cultures while simultaneously disregarding the feelings or beliefs of the people whom they studied.

Of course, for anthropologists to accomplish their mission of "saving" Native cultures, they would also need help from actual Native peoples. As recent scholars have wisely noted, by themselves non-Native anthropologists were highly imperfect conduits between Indigenous nations and the rest of the United States. What they needed were Native individuals willing to collaborate with them. It was this need and desire to preserve Indigenous cultures that suddenly placed such a high value on people who formerly were seen as valueless in the eyes of the American government—Native Americans. The mission schools and Indian boarding schools that had been created with the express goal of assimilating Native American youths into Euro-American Christian society and away from their supposedly benighted pasts had the unintended consequence of creating ideal anthropological collaborators. Those same individuals forced to attend these racist institutions almost overnight discovered that they were in demand, with their cultural knowledge a highly valued commodity.[18]

This book, then, is about the Native women and men from across North America who willingly chose to collaborate with non-Native museum anthropologists in their documentation and collecting work. It is a book about how these individuals provided anthropologists, museum professionals, and other curious outsiders with an enormous amount of cultural information and objects in the form of rare, sacred, and everyday items. But the story is not so simple as nefarious anthropologists and willing or naive Native collaborators who worked to steal Native cultures. All involved believed they were preserving these tangible and intangible items, saving them from inevitable erasure.

Ironically, perhaps more than any other factor, salvage anthropology separated and alienated Indigenous peoples from their tangible and intangible cultural heritage materials. These items ultimately ended up in museums, far from their creators and users. Although well-intentioned and with an eye on preserving the beauty and uniqueness of Native cultures, this collecting work on such a massive scale directly led to Indigenous cultural and identity loss that remains to this day. In a significant way, then, this book is also about how these Native anthropologists and collaborators unintentionally brought about their own culture loss.

Turning the Power

The through line that connected the ten disparate characters in this book was not simply their Native heritage or their compulsory attendance in mission schools and Indian boarding schools. While they all had these two factors in common, they shared something greater as well—the desire to embrace, promote, and preserve their Native cultures rather than succumb to the dominant rhetoric of racism and assimilation. Ultimately, this is the story of ten Native individuals who worked to preserve Indigenous cultures against the onslaught of enforced Euro-American assimilation and colonization. They accomplished this feat by "turning the power" against a settler colonial world that used every weapon in its arsenal to change them into something other than who they already were.[19]

The phrase "turning the power" is here borrowed from Native scholar Clifford E. Trafzer, who has identified how Indian boarding school students used their negative experiences in these institutions to produce positive results, including the preservation of their Native identities, cultures, communities, and languages. Of course, not every former student chose to join the anthropological field to turn the power. Many used their English language skills in other ways, including becoming interpreters, negotiators, and official delegates for their Native nations in dealings with representatives of the federal government. Related to Trafzer's "turning the power" as a means for Native people to confront the power imbalance inherent in settler colonialism is Ho-Chunk (Winnebago) anthropologist Renya K. Ramirez's notion of "doubling." According to Ramirez, Indigenous peoples learned to juggle two realities, their own Native perspectives with those of the Euro-American settler colonizers surrounding them. In this way, Native peoples, most clearly illustrated in the example of Indian boarding school students, confronted racist assimilation policies by camouflaging or masking their Native identities in order to be accepted into the dominant power structure, yet importantly without ever truly abandoning their own cultures.[20]

Regarding terminology for those Native peoples employed in the anthropological field, the labels "anthropologist" and "collaborator" are used throughout this book. While related and sometimes overlapping, anthropologist and collaborator are not interchangeable, though the distinction between them is slight. Anthropologist was a term most often used solely for those individuals, Native or non-Native, who attained the requisite amount of schooling to warrant this title. Occasionally, too, the term anthropologist was used for those without higher-level schooling, but who were still employed in museum settings. For all others engaged in this work, the term collaborator is applied. Though at the time the anthropological establishment chose to label this latter group "informants," today this term is avoided in favor of the still problematic label of collaborators. The latter term importantly has two meanings. The first and most direct is a willingness to work jointly with others. But the term collaborator also describes an individual willing to cooperate with an enemy or an occupying force. In this case the colonizing power was that of the U.S. government.

These Native women and men, whether labeled anthropologist or collaborator, actively worked in the field gathering intangible linguistic, ceremonial, and religious information. All of them also collected tangible material culture items from their own people as well as from other Native communities whom they studied. While many of these Native collaborators lacked the official title of anthropologist, all of them performed the work that made them anthropologists in everything but name. Native anthropologists and Native collaborators were Indigenous peoples who worked "in the field" among Indigenous communities and on reservations to gather both information and objects that they would later sell to museums. Often these individuals carried on months or yearslong correspondence with non-Native anthropologists based in museums in faraway cities. They compared notes through a back-and-forth process with their non-Native museum anthropologist colleagues, resulting in anthropological publications and museum exhibitions geared toward the public. Although power structures clearly existed in which the Native American anthropologists and collaborators played a subordinate role, they nevertheless held a considerable amount of power in providing access to Native communities and in gathering cultural information and objects in the first place.

Related to these ideas of power and information gathering, there is also a glaring omission in this book that must be acknowledged from the outset. Women, specifically Native women, are virtually absent from this story. Of the ten individuals we meet, only one, Florence Shotridge, is a woman. Notably, too, while she was an anthropologist and museum employee in her own right, she was also the wife of another Native anthropologist. Due to this relationship, she gained a status unattainable by many of her female peers.

So the question arises—why aren't more Native women represented in this book or more generally in the field of early U.S. anthropology? Women were undoubtedly present, playing integral roles and providing a great deal of information. In addition to Florence Shotridge, three Native female collaborators we meet herein include Cleaver Warden's first wife, Eva, Louis Shotridge's second wife, Elizabeth, and Alanson Skinner's second wife, Esther. All three women accompanied their husbands on anthropological collecting trips, often gathering valuable information from other women they met in the field. In fact, as Margaret Bruchac notes in her article "My Sisters Will Not Speak," many Native men regularly turned to their wives, mothers, sisters, and other female relatives as sources of information otherwise unavailable to them. Not surprisingly, these men often would then provide this information to non-Native anthropologists as it if were their own, rarely ever crediting or acknowledging their female sources. Thus, there remains a huge gap in how we understand anthropological information to have been gathered and interpreted before it ever even made it into the hands of non-Native museum anthropologists and later to the public.[21]

Locating Forgotten Voices and Pathways of Resistance

Much of the history of early anthropology in the United States abounds with the deeds and misdeeds of the non-Native men and occasional women who shaped the field in its infancy. Most everyone who has an interest in the early years of the anthropological discipline knows the names of Franz Boas, John Wesley Powell, and Alice C. Fletcher. Occasionally the lives of Native American anthropologists and collaborators are also discussed in the scholarly literature. Individuals such as Francis La Flesche, whom we already met, Gladys Tantaquidgeon, George Hunt, and Ishi, though perhaps less well-known than their non-Native contemporaries, are still spoken of and written about by anthropologists, historians, and others who maintain an abiding interest in the history of this field.

However, there are countless other Native women and men, anthropologists in everything but name, who also shaped the field of U.S. anthropology in the late nineteenth and early twentieth centuries. This book is about those people. It is about Tichkematse, a former Southern Tsitsistas/Suhtai (Cheyenne) prisoner of war who conducted anthropological fieldwork in Florida, Arizona, and New Mexico but who also guided tours through the Smithsonian's Ethnological Hall in 1879, thus becoming one of the institution's first Native American employees. It is about Florence Shotridge (nee Scundoo), a Tlingit woman from Alaska who conducted anthropological fieldwork among Northwest Coast communities in 1915, while simultaneously playing the role of an "Indian princess" as she educated groups of schoolchildren who visited Philadelphia's University Museum where she worked. This book is also about former Carlisle Indian Industrial School student Cleaver Warden, a Southern Inunaina (Arapaho) man who, in addition to collecting material culture items from among the Indigenous nations forcibly relocated to the Oklahoma Territory, was also a lifelong advocate for his community's rights. In 1918 Warden even testified before a congressional subcommittee in the U.S. House of Representatives for the freedom to use Peyote as a sacrament in religious ceremonies.

These ten representatives of their Indigenous nations in the Indian boarding schools of their youth became so much more once they entered the anthropological field. All of them became in practice, if not in name, anthropologists and historians. Their job was to observe, interpret, and preserve their cultures. But their other responsibilities also included becoming salespeople, often haggling and cajoling to acquire material culture objects and information at low prices. They became linguistic experts and diplomats, able to seamlessly work within the bureaucracies of their own communities on western reservations as well as in museum hierarchies in Midwest and East Coast cities. They became technology experts, learning the skills to operate and repair cameras, phonograph machines, typewriters, and even boats in the most adverse of weather conditions. When cameras were unavailable due to lack of funds, these Native anthropologists and collaborators opted to instead draw illustrations to preserve a record of their cultures.

Each of these individuals worked within the confines available to them as colonized peoples to promote their cultures and preserve their histories in the face of unrelenting racism and assimilation. Richard Davis, for instance, advocated for his community through vaudeville performances, Wild West shows, and the early film industry. William Jones, a Sac and Fox man and the first Native American to receive a PhD in anthropology, used academia as a path to highlight his rich cultural heritage and language. Their contemporary, Amos Oneroad, a member of the Sisseton Wahpeton Oyate people of South Dakota, struck a balance between preserving his Indigenous culture as a Native anthropologist and spreading his Christian beliefs as a Presbyterian minister. Thus, while *Turning the Power* examines the individual lives of these Native peoples, each of their lives also serves as a window through which we can view how Native peoples at the turn of the twentieth century confronted, responded to, and worked within a settler colonial world bent on either their assimilation or annihilation.

Connections and Influence beyond Themselves

Central to this book is the idea of the interconnected lives of many of these Indigenous figures in early U.S. anthropology. In this young field with only a few score primary movers and shakers at the time, many of the Native and non-Native women and men knew each other. Working for the handful of newly emerging anthropology and natural history museums across the country, many had studied and lived with each other in the radically different environments of Columbia University, the Hampton Institute, or the Carlisle Indian Industrial School. Some became mentors and teachers, as Franz Boas was to William Jones and Louis Shotridge. Some developed familial bonds, such as Alanson Skinner with John V. Satterlee and Amos Oneroad.

Working for different museums with competing collections goals, several of these individuals developed friendly, and at times not-so-friendly, strategies to "salvage" information and material culture objects from Native nations throughout Indian Country. Echoing the language used by some of his non-Native anthropologist colleagues, for instance, Chaticks si Chaticks (Pawnee) collaborator James R. Murie even wrote of "opening up" and "draining" his fellow community members in order to acquire their cultural knowledge. Such phrasing well describes the salvage anthropology ethos in which Native and non-Native anthropologists intended to gather all that they could from a people believed soon to vanish into oblivion either through death or assimilation.[22]

Importantly, too, the influence of these Native anthropologists and collaborators was profound, even if their names come up rarely if at all in the anthropological literature. Many non-Native anthropologists' celebrity and income depended to a great extent on their contacts, their collaborators in the field. If it weren't for individuals like Tichkematse, Florence Shotridge, and Cleaver Warden, for instance, the careers of well-known non-Native anthropologists may not have existed. Just a few of the careers that these three Native collaborators helped to create included Frank Hamilton Cushing, George Byron Gordon, James Mooney, Alfred L. Kroeber, and George A. Dorsey.

As Indigenous collaborators and museum professionals, the women and men portrayed in *Turning the Power* updated, expanded, and continually corrected non-Native anthropologists' inaccurate and racist depictions of their cultures. Most importantly, they inserted Native voices into records that had formerly been written solely by non-Native peoples and were intended for non-Native audiences. These Native American museum professionals observed, documented, and preserved their cultures not for the edification of a non-Native audience, but as a lifeline to future generations of their own communities who hopefully wouldn't live in a world in which their histories and cultures were constantly under attack.

But none of them worked in a vacuum. When retelling their lives, it is also necessary to look at the museums that employed them and the non-Native anthropologists who worked alongside them. Important to this larger context, too, is inclusion of the many Native and non-Native individuals who were opposed to anthropological work in general. People such as Carlisle Indian Industrial School founder Richard Henry Pratt, numerous Bureau of Indian Affairs staff, and many Indigenous members of the Society of American Indians (SAI). All of them made up the world in which salvage anthropology took place at the turn of the twentieth century. And each of them become recurring characters in this book.

Whether working toward the aims of salvage anthropology or in opposition to it, none of the individuals we meet herein are simply one-dimensional stereotypes, heroes, villains, or martyrs for their people. While retelling their life stories highlights their many individual contributions to the field of anthropology, all were also complicated human beings whose lives and actions were often contradictory. It is important to keep in mind that despite the intentions of Native anthropologists and collaborators, at its very core, anthropological collecting resulted in the confiscation of massive amounts of cultural heritage from Indigenous communities around the globe.

Finally, although this book is organized following a historical timeline covering the fifty-year period from approximately 1875 to 1925, it is not a story of linear progress or advancement for the people we meet. Although Native Americans successfully transitioned from "wards" of the federal government to U.S. citizens by the tail end of this half century, neither then nor now does the average Native person live in a state of equality with their non-Native, specifically Euro-American, fellow U.S. citizen. Hopefully books such as *Turning the Power* will help chip away at the systemic inequalities upon which our society was founded. By retelling the life stories of these largely unrecognized Native anthropologists and collaborators, we humanize them and acknowledge the work they did to preserve their cultures. It is only a little step perhaps, but it is a step in the right direction.

I

A Great Favorite at the Smithsonian

Tichkematse (Zuni, New Mexico Territory, 1881)

It was a scorching hot day in June 1881 when Tichkematse arrived in the New Mexico Territory. Forcibly relocated by the U.S. government repeatedly throughout his youth, the young Southern Tsitsistas/Suhtai (Cheyenne) man was accustomed to change. Over the past six years he had already lived as a prisoner in Florida, a student in Virginia, and a museum employee in Washington DC. And now, as the twenty-four-year-old Tichkematse arrived in an A:shiwi (Zuni) village in the New Mexico Territory, he was again traveling at the insistence and direction of Euro-American men who tried to control him.

It was there among the A:shiwi peoples that Tichkematse was to reunite with his anthropologist friend and fellow Smithsonian employee Frank Hamilton Cushing. The two intended to collect as much ethnographic data as they could on the Indigenous nations of the U.S. Southwest, including the A:shiwi and their relatively unknown neighbors of the Grand Canyon region, the Havasupai (Coconino). Like all of the Native American anthropologists and collaborators who would follow him in later decades, Tichkematse possessed two highly favorable qualities for anthropological work at the turn of the twentieth century—first, he was Native, possessing both language skills and cultural knowledge of his own and other Indigenous communities. Second, due to his Indian boarding school education, he was also fluent in English and a capable interpreter. As such, he was the ideal candidate for this type of anthropological fieldwork.

Capture

Also known in the historical record as Squint Eyes or John Squint Eye, Tichkematse was born in 1857 among the Tsitsistas/Suhtai territorial lands of present-day Colorado. Due to unceasing Euro-American encroachment on Native lands, the years surrounding Tichkematse's birth were calamitous for the Tsitsistas/Suhtai and their neighbors. A few short years before he was born, eight Plains communities signed the Fort Laramie Treaty of 1851 with the U.S. government, designating Indigenous territorial borders that the U.S. agreed not to cross. Agreeing to cease hostilities against the federal government and to live in peace, the Tsitsistas/Suhtai and Inunaina (Arapaho) consented to remain on lands that today make up large portions of Wyoming and Colorado. But greed for land and resources, accompanied by a population boom in the east, made short work of these supposedly permanent treaty agreements.[1]

By the time Tichkematse was ten years old, Southern Tsitsistas/Suhtai and Southern Inunaina leaders agreed to define new territorial borders with the U.S. government, this time signing the Medicine Lodge Treaty of 1867. This new treaty stipulated that these Plains communities would abandon all claims to former western lands in exchange for 7.3 million acres in the Indian Territory in present-day Oklahoma, along with the guarantee of food, clothing, and tools provided by the U.S. government. Additionally, reservations were to be created and staffed with school teachers, doctors, carpenters, blacksmiths, and farmers, all sent by the federal government to help usher Native peoples into assimilating into Euro-American life.[2]

Not surprisingly, given the history of U.S. treaty relations with North American Indigenous communities, the U.S. Congress delayed ratification of this latest agreement. No provisions were sent to the Native parties involved. As available hunting lands rapidly dwindled due to land theft, local Native communities transitioned from a state of prosperity and self-reliance to one of destitution. They resented their newfound dependence on an indifferent federal government for support. Hungry Southern Tsitsistas/Suhtai and Southern Inunaina people, unable to find enough buffalo to feed their families, directed their anger against Euro-American surveyors, hunters, farmers, and ranchers, indeed on anyone seen to be an agent of the U.S. government. Violence erupted on both sides over the ensuing years, eventually culminating in the Red River War of 1874–75.[3]

Determined to put down any further attacks by Native peoples against U.S. military personnel or civilians, army troops under the command of General Philip Sheridan sought out all Plains individuals and groups not on reservations. Throughout late 1874 and early 1875 Sheridan summarily destroyed the supplies and killed the animals of those parties he located off-reservation. According to a young soldier named Richard Henry Pratt, later to become the founder and first superintendent of the Carlisle Indian Industrial School, Pratt and his fellow soldiers under Sheridan's command pursued Native southern plains peoples throughout the western part of the Indian Territory from July 1874 to April 1875. There the U.S. soldiers captured hundreds of Native individuals whom they held as prisoners at nearby Fort Sill. Defeated, demoralized, and suing for peace, the remaining Kiowa, Niuam (Comanche), Southern Inunaina, and Southern Tsitsistas/ Suhtai peoples eventually returned to western Indian Territory, turning themselves over to the mercy of the U.S. government in return for food and a cease to military harassment.[4]

Despite the weakened state of many Native communities in Indian Territory, the U.S. federal government wished to make an example. The Justice Department determined to go one step further by forcibly exiling all supposed agitators and unrepentant community leaders to a prison in Florida. That way, so the thinking went, those with unwanted influence were removed, and those remaining in the Indian Territory would prove more pliable to U.S. control. There was an additional hope among federal authorities that by removing the prisoners from their own lands and placing them in greater proximity to Euro-American communities in the east, so-called civilized ways might rub off on them.[5]

All that was left was to determine the undesirables who would be shipped eastward. Two army officers divided this responsibility among themselves. Lieutenant Colonel Thomas Neill selected from among the Southern Tsitsistas/Suhtai prisoners confined at the Darlington Agency in western Indian Territory, while Lieutenant Richard Henry Pratt selected from the Kiowa and Niuam prisoners at Fort Sill. The two men couldn't have been more different in their selection process and in weighing the available evidence, however. While Pratt attempted to be methodical, using witness reports from other Native peoples, Neill randomly selected prisoners from among a group not known to have committed any crimes. According to other soldiers who witnessed Neill's actions, the lieutenant colonel evidently grew impatient with the tedious protocol of selecting prisoners, and as nightfall loomed, he made the snap decision to add eighteen innocent men's names to his list. Regardless of the lack of any evidence of their involvement in the Red River War, these men were grouped with the others selected. Young eighteen-year-old Tichkematse was among those whom Neill arbitrarily identified for exile and imprisonment in Florida.[6]

With no charge listed against him, in April 1875 Tichkematse joined the seventy-one other Native men and a few women accused or suspected of committing crimes against the United States. These individuals represented a number of southern plains communities, including the Caddo, Kiowa, Niuam, Southern Inunaina, and Southern Tsitsistas/Suhtai. While the prisoners were primarily men, there were also a few women who demanded to accompany their husbands rather than be separated from them. They were imprisoned without trial, and military personnel forcefully loaded all seventy-two Native people into eight army wagons. Placed ten to a wagon, five people on each side, the prisoners wore iron handcuffs around their wrists and ankles. An additional iron chain connected each prisoner to another as well as to the wagon itself.[7]

On departing Fort Sill on the morning of April 26, 1875, the wagons met heartbroken family members upset over the forced removal of their sons and daughters, their brothers and sisters, and, for some, their fathers and mothers. The soldiers set to guard the prisoners kept a tense watch on the crowds surrounding the wagon route eastward. With loaded guns the soldiers marched to the front, rear, and sides of the wagon train. Although no physical confrontation occurred, Pratt and others who witnessed the event recalled Native women wailing and cutting themselves with knives in their grief at their loved ones' forced departure. Although no definitive evidence remains to verify this, it can be assumed that Tichkematse's family members were also there among the crowd, venting their frustration at the injustice heaped upon them and their innocent son.

After a wagon journey of 165 miles, at Fort Leavenworth the prisoners were corralled onto a train to take them the rest of the way to St. Augustine, Florida. Few of the prisoners had even seen a train close-up before, let alone ridden on one. While initially in awe of the train cars, the majority of the prisoners soon grew afraid, covering their heads with blankets as the train continued to gain speed. Stopping in cities that included St. Louis, Nashville, and Atlanta on their way east, Pratt recorded that each stop had its own crowd of curious onlookers, eager to catch a glimpse of the

Native prisoners. Although not among this group of prisoners, a Southern Inunaina man recorded his own similar experience of taking the train for the first time a few years later from his home in the western Indian Territory to the East Coast. At once both awed and frightened by the towns and cities he passed along the way, he noted that few of his people had ever seen more than the simple forts and trading posts located near their agency. Such sights must have been frightening for anyone unaccustomed to them, especially for prisoners unable to fully comprehend the fate that awaited them at the end of their journey.[8]

By the time their train arrived at the station in Jacksonville, Florida, the Indigenous prisoners finally approached the end of their harrowing ordeal by train. Yet there was still more to come. Deboarding, they then traveled by steamer and railroad again for the last twenty-five miles to Fort Marion, a U.S. Army prison in St. Augustine, Florida. Arriving there in late May 1875, Tichkematse and his fellow prisoners had already traveled across half a continent, covering nearly 1,300 miles. But once in Florida they faced not only the intensity of the southern summer heat and the immensity of the Atlantic Ocean. They also saw for the first time the seventeenth-century Spanish prison that would be their home and prison for the next three years.[9]

Life at Fort Marion

Despite all the new experiences confronting them on their arrival in Florida, one thing that remained constant since their days as prisoners at Fort Sill was the presence of U.S. Army soldier Richard Henry Pratt. A lifelong military man born in New York in 1840, Pratt served in the Civil War and later the Indian Wars of the 1860s and 1870s throughout the American West. As noted above, Pratt was one of the soldiers during the Red River War whom General Sheridan directed to track down those Native individuals who saw themselves as freedom fighters, but whom U.S. Army and government authorities deemed criminals, worthy of prison time.

It was during his military service among Indigenous nations of the west that Pratt first recognized what he considered the untapped potential of Native Americans. Arguing against the scientific racism of his day that classified Native peoples as backward and primitive, Pratt believed that if afforded the same opportunities of education and assimilation, Native

Americans could compete on the same level as anyone in the rest of the country. Selected by his superiors to escort and oversee the care of the prisoners once in Florida, Pratt believed this the ideal opportunity to implement his experiment of "Americanizing" those in his care.[10]

Immediately upon arrival at Fort Marion, Pratt began efforts to press upon his captives Euro-American standards of life. His goal, of course, was to assimilate the prisoners into the broader society, relieving them of what he believed were their savage, alien, and barbarous ways. He wanted to help Native Americans "die as helpless tribes" and rise up as strong and capable individual American citizens. Individualism was the key to his plan, as Pratt believed that an Indigenous emphasis on the tribe or the community stifled creativity and individual thought.[11]

Certain that Native peoples were just as intellectually capable as anyone else, Pratt sought to prove this by initiating his own educational program soon after the prisoners arrived at Fort Marion. Spending one- to two-hour sessions each day, Pratt, his wife, and their interpreter introduced the English alphabet, gradually transitioning to simple reading and writing exercises. Soon after, Pratt boasted to his military superiors of the captives' success, noting that they were well-behaved and were cheerfully and industriously attending classes.[12]

As word spread of Pratt's attempts to educate the Native prisoners, like-minded individuals from the local community rallied to support him. Several women from Christian uplift organizations volunteered their time as teachers at Fort Marion. Perhaps most notable of these was Harriet Beecher Stowe, the abolitionist and author of *Uncle Tom's Cabin*. Having moved to Florida soon after the Civil War, Stowe visited the prisoners regularly. She donated not only her time but also her name to championing Pratt's experiments in assimilating and Americanizing Tichkematse and the other prisoners. Writing in the popular New York magazine the *Christian Union* in 1877, Stowe strove to humanize American Indians to a non-Native reading audience, declaring that these fearful beings whom most people viewed only as wild beasts truly had the hearts of men.[13]

Schooling was hardly Pratt's only objective in his assimilation campaign. He also believed that labor would make the prisoners enjoy the feeling of a hard day's work. As such, he hired out the prisoners for various projects in the St. Augustine area. The money the prisoners made was rightly their own to keep, which Pratt encouraged them to either save or use to purchase objects in the town, believing such financial payments would induce the prisoners to embrace capitalism and the Protestant work ethic. Notably, as Pratt correctly believed that many of the Southern Tsitsistas/Suhtai prisoners, such as Tichkematse, were unjustly chosen for imprisonment in exile, he tended to treat them better than the other prisoners, offering greater kindness and less grueling hard labor projects. Conversely, Pratt had little sympathy for the Kiowa and Niuam prisoners whom he believed fully deserved punishment for their actions in the Red River War.[14]

One of the first large-scale labor projects Pratt assigned the prisoners was excavating Native burial mounds in the vicinity of St. Augustine. Working in partnership with Spencer Baird of the Smithsonian Institution, Pratt directed the prisoners to first sketch the mounds before removing massive amounts of earth. Within the burial mounds they located shell implements, pottery, stone axes, and even human skeletal remains, all of which they sent to the Smithsonian in Washington DC for study and exhibition. How the Native prisoners themselves felt about disturbing the resting place of other Indigenous peoples is not recorded in Pratt's notes, but it can be surmised that such actions would have been frowned upon, to say the least.[15]

On a much smaller scale, Pratt also encouraged the Fort Marion prisoners to make and sell those handicrafts with which they were most familiar. Within weeks of their arrival in Florida, an industry raged of Native-made bows, arrows, and painted shields. Pratt invited the public to come to the prison to view the progress of its inhabitants, and at the same time to purchase the goods they produced. Native dances and archery displays became a regular spectacle for the curious onlookers at the fort to enjoy, with some of the events even advertised in the local St. Augustine newspapers. As Henry Roman Nose, one of Tichkematse's fellow Southern Tsitsistas/Suhtai prisoners, would later recall, he and many of his fellow captives regularly fashioned bows and arrows for sale to an unending stream of visitors. In even greater demand than bows and arrows, though, were the ledger art drawings that the Native prisoners made.[16]

Ever desirous of keeping the Fort Marion inhabitants occupied, Pratt early on acquired ledger books and colored pencils for their use. As the Native poet and novelist Diane Glancy has noted, these ledger book drawings were in a sense a way for the prisoners to reconnect to their families, their cultures, and the homes they had lost. Detailing the lives they had known before being uprooted to their new prison home in Florida, the prisoners' drawings often depicted tipis, battles with other Native groups, buffalo hunts, and even illustrations of their long cross-country train journey.[17]

Demand among the public to acquire these illustrations grew rapidly, with tourists regularly purchasing individual drawings and even entire sketchbooks. Not surprisingly, Pratt lost no time in using this popular demand for ledger drawings to his advantage. He not only sent a series of drawings to be kept in the collections of the Smithsonian Institution, but he also sent drawings to several high-ranking U.S. military personnel to better illustrate the industry and creativity of the Native prisoners under his command. Pratt likewise sought to curry favor, and no doubt to prove his assimilation theories correct, by shipping books of these drawings to both his commanding officer, General Philip Sheridan, and to General William Tecumseh Sherman, the highest-ranking officer of the U.S. Army at the time. Although the total number of drawings made by the prisoners during their three years at Fort Marion is unknown, nearly eight hundred of these drawings still exist today, several dozen created by Tichkematse.[18]

An interesting corollary to the production of ledger art among the prisoners was the arrival in 1876 of a large picture letter from the Northern Tsitsistas/Suhtai, cousins to Tichkematse and his Southern Tsitsistas/Suhtai brethren. Sent soon after the Battle of the Little Bighorn or the Battle of the Greasy Grass that June, Tichkematse's northern relatives sent this picture letter containing an account of the battle and utter defeat of General George Armstrong Custer and his troops. The drawing was on a blank army muster roll and detailed the battle itself, as well as the departure of the Hunkpapa Lakota (Hunkpapa Sioux) leader Sitting Bull and his people from the Northern Tsitsistas/Suhtai days after the battle. Perhaps more importantly than the drawing itself, though, is what it tells us about the lines of communication between Native communities spread out across a continent. While the prisoners languishing in St. Augustine, Florida, almost certainly received some accounts of battles and events from their captors, the existence of this picture letter also illustrates that the prisoners received word directly from their friends and relatives, apprising them of continued Native resistance to colonial land theft.[19]

Another important event during Tichkematse's confinement in Fort Marion was the fabrication of plaster life masks of himself and his fellow prisoners. Soon after first hearing of their incarceration in St. Augustine, Florida, Spencer Baird of the Smithsonian recognized the potential benefit these individuals could have on the Smithsonian in particular, and on the field of science more generally. As mentioned, Baird and Pratt previously worked together using convict labor to desecrate and remove Native remains from local burial mounds in Florida. Now Baird wanted something only the prisoners could provide.

In a letter from May 1877, Baird told Pratt he was hoping to acquire not only linguistic information from these prisoners but, more importantly, plaster casts of the individuals' faces for the Smithsonian's collections. Baird hoped to use these life masks to aid him and his staff in constructing human-sized Native figures that would feature Indigenous clothing already in the Institution's holdings. A journalist for *Harper's Weekly* later commended Baird's idea after it was made public, noting that there would be much value in attaining accurate physical representations of the world's Indigenous peoples while they still existed.[20]

Baird surmised that with approximately six dozen captive Native Americans confined in one location and under the control of the U.S. Army, he could gather important biological information not otherwise readily available. Seeking to expand upon the prevailing racist cranial studies of the 1850s that supposedly proved the physical and mental superiority of Europeans, Baird sought to also acquire accurate measurements of the shape of Native faces and bodies. Up until this point, the Euro-American scientific community had only been able to make plaster face masks of Native peoples already dead, but with the Fort Marion prisoners, Baird had a study group at his disposal and was eager to take advantage of this.[21]

The man assigned to make the life masks of the prisoners was Clark Mills, famous at the time for creating the sculpture of President Andrew Jackson displayed prominently today across from the White House in Washington DC. Pratt, as the prisoners' jailor and overseer, elected to have his own life mask made first by Mills, in order to convince the prisoners that there was no harm in the procedure. Once his process was complete, the Fort Marion prisoners gladly acceded to the same process, at least according to Pratt. Baird also requested that Mills and Pratt record vital statistics of each prisoner for the Smithsonian's records. Because of this, we know that Tichkematse stood at just over 5 feet 8 inches tall, weighed 134 pounds, and was approximately twenty years old when his life mask was made. His own and the other prisoners' life masks were subsequently placed on display in the Smithsonian Institution, where they would remain for many years afterward.[22]

Notably, the procedure of obtaining life masks of the Fort Marion prisoners was not Baird and Pratt's only foray into such scientific information gathering. The two would repeat the same process eighteen months later in Virginia, again with Clark Mills facilitating, though this time with Indian boarding school students. As with the Fort Marion prisoners, how much choice Native youths had in the ultimate decision to have their likenesses captured in plaster remains uncertain.[23]

One of Pratt's most important innovations at Fort Marion, and one that would have the longest-lasting impact on future generations of Native students, was his implementation of military-style discipline among the Florida captives. Mirroring the regimented life Pratt had come to revere in his own days as a U.S. Army soldier, Pratt introduced similar military uniforms among the Fort Marion prisoners. Along with the uniforms came military drills, marching, and even formal inspections of all prisoners, their clothing, and their sleeping area. All of this Pratt would carry with him when he opened the Carlisle Indian Industrial School a few years later in 1879. Pratt's innovations in introducing military discipline first to Native prisoners in Florida and later to Native students in Pennsylvania would be copied again and again with every new Indian boarding school established in the following half century.[24]

As discussed, Pratt made many uses of the Native prisoners under his control during their captivity at Fort Marion. He introduced compulsory English language classes, initiated labor projects including Native burial mound excavations, advertised dances and archery contests for the public's enjoyment, volunteered the prisoners as objects of scientific and anthropological study for the Smithsonian, and, finally, encouraged the production of Native artwork for sale and as gifts. Pratt's ostensible purpose for these projects was for the uplift of the men and women under his command. He believed that the only way they could successfully compete and survive in the new United States was to completely assimilate into the broader Euro-American society. A savvy public relations expert, Pratt promoted the success of his experiments widely. And over time, not just the public but also his superiors began to take notice.

Hampton Institute

After nearly three years of imprisonment, in 1878 the Department of War transferred the care of Tichkematse and the other Fort Marion prisoners to the Bureau of Indian Affairs (BIA), though notably with Pratt still in charge. While all were now free and able to return home, before they left the confines of the Fort Marion prison, each of them was given the choice of remaining in the East to continue their schooling or to return to the embrace of their families and friends out west. Nearly two dozen prisoners ultimately opted to stay. Always an advocate for greater "mingling" between Native and non-Native peoples, Pratt then arranged for seventeen of his most promising students, Tichkematse among them, to attend the Hampton Norman and Agricultural Institute in Virginia.[25]

Traveling by an excursion steamer ship up the St. John's River, Pratt and his cohort of Native pupils arrived at Hampton in the dead of night in mid-April 1878. There they were warmly received by Hampton's principal, General Samuel C. Armstrong. Originally founded for the education of Black youths in the years immediately following the Civil War, Hampton also began accepting Native American students in 1878 with Tichkematse and the other ex-prisoners' arrival.[26]

Pratt and Hampton's principal, General Armstrong, were of like minds when it came to assimilation. Both men believed that all peoples, Black and Indigenous included, should become an integral part of the melting pot society of the United States. Armstrong and his Hampton staff prided themselves on the belief that they were ushering Native peoples from barbarism to civilized conditions. At Hampton, the staff proclaimed, Tichkematse and his fellow former Fort Marion prisoners would learn the self-reliance adequate to prepare them to resist the degrading charms of savage life. Of course, what Pratt, Armstrong, and the wider Hampton staff failed to consider was that not everyone desired simply to become assimilated into the Euro-American way of life. Furthermore, few students at Hampton, Black or Indigenous, were willing to fully abandon their own peoples' cultures, histories, and languages. To maintain their own cultural identities, though, all students, regardless of background, camouflaged or masked themselves when in the presence of those in power. Native author Renya K. Ramirez refers to this act as "doubling," in which Indigenous peoples would try to make themselves appear unobjectionable to colonizers, yet without betraying or letting go of their own cultures on the inside.[27]

One of the first and most powerful tools that the Hampton authorities used to promote Native students' assimilation was the rule forbidding the speaking of any language other than English. Punishments for speaking Native languages were meted out with regularity. An early Hampton publication put the matter succinctly when it declared, "there is no Indian talk here." A second tool in the arsenal of the assimilationist-minded school authorities was the balance struck between the need for physical labor and the need for a classroom education. To be sure, vocational schools of this nature were already in existence, but this was one of the first times that Native American students also took part.[28]

Classroom education took up half of each day, with the other half given over to labor consisting of farm work, carpentry, printing, blacksmithing, or some other trade. The thinking behind this balance was the racist assumption that few Black or Native students would ever actually need much more than an elementary education in English, math, geography, or history to participate in the broader society. What was necessary, Hampton staff stressed, was a good knowledge of farming, a regular trade or skill, or both. With experiences such as these, it was believed, American Indian students would return to their reservations after their schooling to teach others about the many opportunities awaiting them once they fully assimilated into the Euro-American mainstream.[29]

The mere fact that Hampton was originally and primarily a vocational school for Black youths raised some concerns among the staff about possible racial admixture of Black and Indigenous students. To remedy this, a policy of semi-segregation was introduced. Although the largely younger Black students and slightly older Native students did attend class together, they lived in separate dormitories and ate in separate dining areas.

A Hampton teacher at the time noted that while there was not intimacy between the two groups, there was nevertheless the best of good feelings. In later years when Native American girls and young women were also admitted to Hampton, an even greater caution was given to keeping them and the young Black men apart.[30]

In addition to its strict rules regarding language, vocational training, and racial segregation, Hampton also prided itself on being a Christian institution. Though nondenominational in terms of Protestant or Catholic doctrine, the school still required all students to attend Sunday school, church, and other religious services held in the Hampton chapel. For Tichkematse and his fellow American Indian pupils, this was nothing new. The endless parade of Christian ministers and well-meaning women teachers at Fort Marion had certainly done their best to indoctrinate the Indigenous men with their own belief system. How much the Native students genuinely accepted this is of course up for debate, but what is clear from the historical record is that in March 1879 eleven of the seventeen Native students received baptism by the Hampton school chaplain. Tichkematse was among this group.[31]

Not much is known specifically about Tichkematse's personal experiences at Hampton. We are left with a few dates to mark his time there but know next to nothing of how he actually felt about what was done to him and to those around him. Was he curious and excited at the opportunity to learn new things, to be able to speak English and be understood by others? Was he angry at the constant efforts of Hampton staff not only to denigrate but also to obliterate all traces of his Tsitsistas/Suhtai culture? Sadly, we are only able to put together what pieces are available to us, and the rest is largely conjecture.

What we do know, though, and what readers will see in succeeding chapters, is that Tichkematse was only the first among many Native Americans educated at Hampton to later embrace the nascent field of anthropology. James R. Murie, of the Chaticks si Chaticks (Pawnee) community, and William Jones, of the Sac and Fox, soon followed in his footsteps. While pupils at Hampton, Tichkematse and these other Native American young men received instruction in English and training in vocational skills and trades. Such a skillset made each of them highly desirable as anthropological collaborators and as anthropologists in their own right. Indeed, as his first year at Hampton came to an end, Tichkematse was to receive a whirlwind introduction to anthropology just as the field was coming into its own in the nation's capital.[32]

At the Smithsonian

By the spring of 1879 Richard Henry Pratt's dream of creating his own boarding school was coming to fruition. The school was modeled on Armstrong's Hampton Institute, though with a sole focus on assimilating and educating Native American youths as opposed to Black children, and Pratt had already found his ideal location at an old U.S. Army barracks in Carlisle, Pennsylvania. His Native students already at Hampton, Pratt determined, would transfer to Carlisle as well. There they would help usher in new classes of Indigenous students, guiding them through the intricacies of Euro-American etiquette and language, as well as serving as mentors to the younger pupils. For Tichkematse, though, Pratt had other plans.

As noted, Pratt and Spencer Baird of the Smithsonian had maintained a friendship of correspondence since soon after the Fort Marion prisoners' arrival in St. Augustine in 1875. Both men worked on a number of scientific projects that relied on Native input, knowledge, and labor, if not necessarily on Native willingness. These collaborative endeavors resulted in the recording of Indigenous vocabularies, the acquiring of grave goods and human remains from Florida burial mounds, and the creation of plaster life masks of the Fort Marion prisoners' faces. All these materials were eventually deposited in the Smithsonian's collections, becoming the permanent property of the federal government. But in the spring of 1879, Baird wanted something else. He wanted an American Indian man who was both literate and fluent in English, who had a good disposition, and who showed an aptitude toward creating and maintaining natural history collections.

Whether Baird and Pratt selected Tichkematse for this type of museum work or if he personally volunteered to fill this position is unclear. But what is known is that in early 1879, Tichkematse, freshly plucked from his schooling at Hampton, found himself at the Smithsonian to begin his taxidermy and natural history collections training under Secretary Baird. Although we don't know if Tichkematse necessarily enjoyed the work or even wanted to do it, we can infer from the historical record that he certainly had other interests that he pursued there as well. Indeed, in addition to the rather mundane work of taxidermy, Tichkematse soon took on other responsibilities at the institution that were more anthropological in nature.

At the time that Baird wrote to Pratt in 1879 requesting a Native employee to work with the institution's collections, the Smithsonian was already a leading scientific and educational institution that had recently passed its thirty-year anniversary. In fact, anthropological collections relating to the Indigenous inhabitants of North America played a conspicuous role in the institution since its very beginning in 1846. In that year Congress established the Smithsonian Institution from a bequest of the Englishman James Smithson, a wealthy scholar who had never actually visited the United States.[33]

As early as December 1846, the Smithsonian Board of Regents passed a resolution requesting that the secretary of war and the commissioner of Indian affairs collect objects from Indian Country. Specifically, the agents sought materials illustrating the physical history, manners, and customs of North America's original inhabitants. These material culture objects would complement those previously acquired by the federal government and held in the U.S. Patent Office in Washington DC. At least five thousand ethnographic objects had already been collected during the Wilkes Exploring Expedition of 1838–42, and these were in addition to C. B. King and George Catlin's American Indian paintings housed in the National Institute in Washington since 1840.[34]

Joseph Henry, first secretary of the Smithsonian and Spencer Baird's predecessor, though opposed to the concept of the institution serving as a museum, nevertheless understood the importance of anthropology and anthropological collections to the development of science in the United States. In the Smithsonian's 1857 Annual Report, Secretary Henry even declared that it was the country's sacred duty to collect everything related to the history of the original inhabitants of North America. And with that, the Smithsonian quickly became the nation's most prominent repository of Native American material culture, regardless of the feelings of Native peoples themselves, of course. In the same year that Secretary

Henry made his sacred duty declaration, all of the materials stored in the Patent Office were transferred to the Smithsonian, forming what would become the institution's first anthropological museum exhibits.[35]

This was the Smithsonian that Tichkematse came to know in 1879. As mentioned, Baird wanted the young Southern Tsitsistas/Suhtai man to learn the trade of taxidermy, including collecting, creating, and labeling the institution's natural history collections. But Tichkematse's work responsibilities soon grew. Within months of starting at the Smithsonian, Tichkematse and another Indigenous man, George Tsaroff, an Alaska Native of the Aleutian Islands, also took on the role of guiding visitors through the institution's Ethnological Hall. There the two men worked with Native object collections in the museum's galleries, interpreting them to the public, and correcting inaccurate descriptions written by non-Native Smithsonian staff. According to contemporary newspaper accounts, the public regarded Tichkematse as a great favorite, praising his knowledge of American Indian life. Secretary Baird likewise acknowledged Tichkematse's skill in attracting much attention to the Native American holdings in the Smithsonian, as well as his ability to explain intelligently the functions of many of the Native American items in the collection.[36]

That same spring of 1879, Tichkematse even had the opportunity to meet the president of the United States. Ever eager to promote the success of his assimilation project, Richard Henry Pratt's supervisors arranged a meeting for him with President Rutherford B. Hayes. Pratt brought along several former Fort Marion prisoners as showpieces, including Tichkematse. As a former prisoner, Indian boarding school student, and now federal employee of the Smithsonian Institution, Tichkematse was one of Pratt's most notable success stories, and one that Pratt never failed to show off. Although not a former prisoner or student of Pratt's, Tichkematse's fellow Smithsonian colleague George Tsaroff also accompanied this group to the White House. President Hayes reportedly received the party graciously, complimenting the Indigenous men on their hard work, and heaping praise on Pratt for his assimilation efforts. The group then remained in Washington DC for a few more days, taking in the sights, and even visiting the Smithsonian with Tichkematse and Tsaroff as their guides.[37]

The young Tsitsistas/Suhtai man was not just a favorite of museum visitors; he was also in high demand among his fellow Smithsonian staff. In April 1879, for instance, he helped Bureau of American Ethnology (BAE) linguist Albert Samuel Gatschet create a Tsitsistas/Suhtai vocabulary. As he and his fellow Fort Marion prisoners had done a few years earlier with members of Spencer Baird's staff, Tichkematse provided valuable linguistic information from his own people that had not previously been recorded.

Two months after that, in June, Pratt again requested Tichkematse's aid in a different venture. Pratt's superiors directed him to travel to Florida and investigate conditions among the Seminole peoples. His goal was to determine if they could be "civilized" by government authorities and placed under the control of the Bureau of Indian Affairs. Pratt requested that Tichkematse accompany him on this errand. Pratt was ostensibly there to gather natural history collections for the Smithsonian, but it is clear that his true reason in bringing the twenty-two-year-old Southern Tsitsistas/Suhtai man was to exhibit Tichkematse as an example of the success that Seminole peoples could attain if they assimilated to Euro-American society.[38]

The two men, former captor and captive, teacher and student, left Washington DC on June 11, 1879, stopping for a few days in St. Augustine, Florida, on their journey south. Although little mention is made of this part of their trip, it must have been an odd experience indeed for Tichkematse to travel through the city where he had been a prisoner for three years, and from which he had emerged as a free man only one year before. By early July Pratt and Tichkematse had visited a handful of Seminole villages in the region of the Caloosahatchee River of southern Florida, all with the same result. According to newspaper accounts at the time, Pratt was unsuccessful in his efforts to persuade the Seminole peoples to join in greater intimacy with the rest of the U.S. public. Desiring to be left alone and aggressively opposing any further attempts at their forced removal, Seminole leaders also refused Pratt's suggestion of erecting a school building for the education of their local youths. Pratt eventually realized the futility of any further attempts at wooing the Seminole peoples and, with Tichkematse, returned northward, stopping at Virginia's Hampton Institute for a brief visit on their way back to Washington, DC.[39]

Collaboration with Cushing

Clearly 1879 was a very busy time for Tichkematse, but it was also during his first year at the Smithsonian that he met anthropologist Frank Hamilton Cushing. Their collaborative work in the coming years forever stamped Tichkematse's name in the annals of early anthropology. Not only one of the first Native American collaborators to work at a museum, Tichkematse, more importantly, conducted anthropological fieldwork among Native communities not his own. To understand how Tichkematse and Cushing came to work together, we must go back a few years to Cushing's early days and his first entrance into professional anthropology.

Considered by many to be a prodigy of late nineteenth-century anthropology, Frank Hamilton Cushing was born in 1857 in Pennsylvania. Like many anthropologists of his day, his only schooling at the collegiate level consisted of a matter of months spent at Cornell University as a geology student in the spring of 1875. That summer, however, Spencer Baird of the Smithsonian Institution selected Cushing to help prepare the Smithsonian's "Indian Collections" exhibit destined for the U.S. Centennial Exposition in Philadelphia in 1876. One year prior, in 1874, President Ulysses S. Grant had called upon government departments, including the Smithsonian Institution, to prepare displays illustrating the functions and administrative faculties of the federal government for an international exposition scheduled to take place on the nation's centennial, 1876, in Philadelphia. Baird, at the time the Smithsonian's assistant secretary under Joseph Henry, was overjoyed at the prospect of increasing the institution's holdings. The collected materials, including those related to North American archaeology and ethnology, would ultimately be housed in the nation's repository, the Smithsonian's National Museum.[40]

As he did with Richard Henry Pratt in acquiring Native American life masks, Baird reached out to those familiar with Native American cultures to locate objects of Native manufacture for the Centennial Exposition's much anticipated opening. Notably, though, he chose not to reach out to Native peoples themselves. Rather, Baird hired former soldiers, surveyors, and geologists, one of whom, John Wesley Powell, would later head the Smithsonian's Bureau of American Ethnology. These men then worked throughout the western U.S. territories, from Alaska and the Puget Sound down through California and the Southwest, collecting Native clothing, weapons, utensils, and other items for eventual display in the Philadelphia World's Fair exhibits.[41]

Baird was not content with the collections of Native American physical objects alone, however. He also wanted the Philadelphia Centennial Exposition to include an exhibition of living representatives from various American Indian nations throughout the country. He envisioned a handful of individuals from each major Indigenous community throughout North America, who would travel to Philadelphia with their clothing, weapons, crafts, and even their dwellings. Once there, these handpicked individuals would reside on the exposition grounds, living in Native-constructed homes while manufacturing their crafts and practicing their "aboriginal arts" for the education and entertainment of the visiting public.

Acknowledging that the cost of transportation and subsistence for the selected Native individuals would be enormous, in March 1876 Baird went before the congressional House Committee on Indian Affairs to plead for funds. Despite Baird's requests, though, Congress ultimately decided not to allocate more funding, thus ending any further discussion of Native participation at the Philadelphia exposition. Because of this decision, a significant anthropological exhibit of Native American living representatives would not take place at a world's fair until the 1893 Chicago World Columbian Exposition under the direction of Frederic Ward Putnam and Franz Boas.[42]

With the planning, collecting, and Baird's unsuccessful pleading complete, in May 1876 the Philadelphia Centennial Exposition officially opened to the public. As Congress had denied Baird's request for the inclusion of Native peoples in his "Indian Exhibit," he instead substituted several hundred life-size lay figures, or mannequins, dressed in the clothing and ornaments of various American Indian nations. In addition, Baird also displayed photographs of Native peoples alongside the thousands of North American objects collected by John Wesley Powell. Such a vast assemblage of American Indian materials had not been displayed before at a world's fair, and, according to fairgoers, the outcome was less a coherent exhibit than an oversize cabinet of curiosities.[43]

Although not terribly successful with his intended displays at the Philadelphia exposition, Baird did find success in kickstarting Frank Hamilton

Cushing's anthropology career. Like Tichkematse, Cushing was born in 1857 and had little formal schooling. There the similarities of their early days end. By the summer of 1875 Tichkematse entered his prison cell in St. Augustine, while Cushing entered the world of anthropology as Baird's assistant at the Philadelphia exposition. Having been personally selected to work for the Smithsonian at the 1876 World's Fair, it was not a big surprise to Cushing when Baird subsequently asked him to continue as a Smithsonian employee after the Philadelphia exposition concluded the following November. The younger man readily agreed and soon thereafter accompanied the anthropological collections on their journey back to Washington DC. Once there he began his new position as curator of the Ethnological Department of the Smithsonian's National Museum.[44]

Not long after Cushing started his new role in the nation's capital, only a couple hundred miles to the south in Virginia the young Tichkematse commenced his schooling at the Hampton Institute. Tichkematse began his own employment at the Smithsonian in the spring of 1879, consisting of taxidermy work, overseeing the Ethnological Hall with George Tsaroff, and even traveling to visit the Seminole peoples with his former captor and teacher, Pratt.

Soon after returning to Washington DC from his Florida trip in July 1879, Tichkematse and Cushing initiated their first collaborative project. The two studied American Indian sign language, ultimately compiling 161 detailed cards analyzing the ubiquitous hand gestures common on the plains, with which Tichkematse was quite familiar. Clearly impressing Cushing with his cultural knowledge and work ethic, Tichkematse was awed by Cushing's passion for everything Native American. More importantly, this first collaborative venture proved that the two could work well together.[45]

The BAE and the 1879 Expedition

While Tichkematse and Cushing commenced their collaborative study of American Indian sign language, something else also occurred at the Smithsonian. The director of the institution's newly created Bureau of American Ethnology, John Wesley Powell, announced that year that he intended to send an anthropological collecting expedition to the U.S. Southwest. Worried that Native peoples were losing their distinct cultures due to an increased Euro-American presence in their homelands, Powell organized the first BAE anthropological expedition within months of taking office. Its mission was to acquire ethnographic data and material objects from the little-known Pueblo communities of the U.S. Southwest before they supposedly vanished.[46]

Powell ordered James Stevenson, accompanied by his anthropologist wife Matilda Coxe Stevenson, to lead the expedition. Baird, as Smithsonian secretary, directed Frank Hamilton Cushing to accompany the Stevensons and to find out all he could about a "typical" Pueblo community. According to Cushing, Baird provided great leeway in this assignment, instructing him simply to make his own choice of field site or village and to use his own methods, but with the end goal of acquiring as much cultural heritage information as he could. Baird also encouraged Cushing to communicate with him freely, advice Cushing closely followed, providing Baird frequent updates from the field.[47]

In 1880, only a matter of months after arriving in the New Mexico Territory, Cushing wrote to Spencer Baird and broached the idea of sending Tichkematse to aid him in the Southwest. Cushing wrote that he highly valued the prospect of having him as an assistant, adding that Tichkematse himself was a very important study to him. Cushing's phrasing makes it clear that he desired Tichkematse to serve not only as a field assistant but also as an object of study. In this way Cushing hoped to continue to expand his knowledge of Southern Tsitsistas/Suhtai culture. Throughout the remainder of 1880 Cushing continued to write to Baird, stating that he was extremely desirous of Tichkematse joining him in the field. Importantly for Cushing, he believed that Tichkematse's knowledge of American Indian lifeways would no doubt aid him in his anthropological fieldwork and allow him to better achieve his goal of learning about Southwest Native cultures. After much back and forth between Cushing and Baird, the Smithsonian secretary eventually acquiesced, agreeing to send Tichkematse to join Cushing in the Southwest.[48]

Tichkematse himself, meanwhile, had since returned to his family and friends in the Indian Territory of present-day western Oklahoma. Leaving Washington DC, in late January 1880, Tichkematse continued his association with the Smithsonian Institution from afar. Sources note that he collected natural history specimens including birds and deer antlers, as well as headdresses, shields, and other cultural heritage materials from his own Tsitsistas/Suhtai community. These he sent to Baird to help build the museum's Native American holdings.[49]

Tichkematse became a bit of a hometown celebrity after his return to the Indian Territory in early 1880. Although many of his fellow Fort Marion prisoners had returned to western reservations as well, very few of them had the months of additional schooling that Tichkematse gained at Hampton. And none of the returnees could boast of employment at the Smithsonian in Washington DC or of Tichkematse's continuing work for the institution collecting items of Native manufacture. The local *Cheyenne Transporter* newspaper reported on Tichkematse's activities at home and in Washington DC, naming him a great favorite at the Smithsonian due to his knowledge of all things Native American. In fact, the February 25, 1881, issue of the *Cheyenne Transporter* even reported on his impending travel to the New Mexico Territory, highlighting that he would be working with a noted scientist and would conduct research into the wilds of the southwestern lands.[50]

In the New Mexico and Arizona Territories

So it was that Tichkematse arrived on a June day of 1881 in the New Mexico Territory, ready to begin a new chapter of his Smithsonian-affiliated anthropological work. Escorted by two U.S. Army soldiers from nearby Fort Wingate, he soon reached the A:shiwi village Cushing had adopted as his new home. Within days of Tichkematse's arrival, the two men departed on their anthropological expedition westward to visit the Havasupai peoples who inhabited the Grand Canyon region.[51]

The expedition's purpose, with Tichkematse as both Cushing's companion and assistant, was to take vocabularies and a census of the Havasupai communities, while also collecting as much ethnographic material as possible. In a lively series of articles published in *Century Illustrated* and *Atlantic Monthly*, Cushing wrote of his anthropological adventures traversing the U.S. Southwest alongside Tichkematse. Though written in Cushing's romanticized and exaggerated style, his articles "My Adventures in Zuni" and "The Nation of the Willows" nevertheless popularized the anthropological field to a wide audience in the profession's early years.[52]

From the Havasupai villages, Tichkematse and Cushing traveled south to explore the archaeological sites near Fort Whipple and present-day Prescott, Arizona. Cushing's journal entries from this period laud Tichkematse's abilities hunting antelope for their meals, as well as withstanding the privations of the local climate. Cushing continually noted the Tsitsistas/Suhtai man's adeptness at camping, riding stoically, and dealing with hunger and thirst along the journey. Although surely meant to be complimentary, Cushing's patronizing words reveal more of his own Eurocentrism than anything about Tichkematse. The latter, readers will remember, had spent the first eighteen years of his life living on the southern Great Plains where hunting and living out of doors were commonplace. Cushing, on the other hand, had only recently experienced such hardships, having spent all his life living in East Coast cities and towns.[53]

Another event of note during Tichkematse and Cushing's travels through the Arizona Territory that is surprisingly absent in Cushing's journals was the Battle of Cibecue Creek. Taking place in late August 1881, this conflict occurred between U.S. Army soldiers and members of the White Mountain Apache Tribe. In a newspaper interview given months later, Tichkematse recalled being suddenly attacked while he was traveling along with a company of soldiers. Defending himself, he reportedly killed one of the White Mountain Apache in the battle, whose scalp he often exhibited with pride on returning to the Indian Territory. Incidentally, this is one of the only definitive sources of Tichkematse's participation in a battle, though some of his ledger art drawings from the 1870s do suggest that he may have participated in battles with Osage and Ute neighbors before his 1875 imprisonment.[54]

After returning from their expedition through the Hopi and Havasupai lands in the Arizona Territory, Tichkematse chose to remain with Cushing among the A:shiwi people, continuing to work alongside his fellow Smithsonian colleague for several more months. Along the East Coast, word began to spread about the unprecedented work Tichkematse was doing as a Native American anthropologist in the field. Spencer Baird, for instance, wrote favorably of the young Southern Tsitsistas/Suhtai man's very important service on behalf of the National Museum. Tichkematse's former captor Richard Henry Pratt at Carlisle, too, learned of the younger man's anthropological work in the field, as John D. Miles, U.S. Indian agent for the Cheyenne and Arapaho Agency, updated him on Tichkematse's success in making collections for the Smithsonian while in the Arizona and New Mexico Territories.[55]

Tichkematse learned much about the Indigenous communities with whom he lived and visited in the Southwest. Unfortunately, little is left in his own words about these experiences. John Bourke, a soldier, writer, and amateur anthropologist passing through the area in the latter months of 1881, however, did mention Tichkematse by name in his journal. Bourke recorded Tichkematse's attendance at an A:shiwi festival in which the latter took part as a participant rather than just an observer. Cushing also recorded a final collecting expedition westward among the Hopi peoples that Tichkematse took with BAE staff member James Stevenson that December, shortly before returning to his home in the Indian Territory. In addition to living among the A:shiwi, then, this young Southern Tsitsistas/Suhtai man also conducted anthropological work with the Havasupai and Hopi, interacted with neighboring Diné (Navajo) peoples, and fought against members of the White Mountain Apache Tribe.[56]

In early 1882, after more than six months of living side by side with Cushing and his A:shiwi neighbors, Tichkematse bid farewell to the Southwest and his anthropological fieldwork and returned to the embrace of his Southern Tsitsistas/Suhtai friends and family in the Indian Territory. The *Cheyenne Transporter* newspaper didn't waste any time in reporting on the celebrity's return, quoting Tichkematse as saying that he had explored New Mexico to his entire satisfaction and was now content to be back at home.[57]

Return to Indian Territory

Tichkematse did not leave a written account of his life to explain why he made the decisions he made, or how he felt about the work that he and Cushing did together. In fact, from retelling his story it is evident that few of the major decisions during the first several decades of his life were even his own to make. Questions of choice and control were out of his hands. The U.S. government, for example, branded him a criminal and incarcerated him 1,300 miles from his family and home. Richard Henry Pratt decided that he should attend the Hampton Institute in order to better assimilate into Euro-American society. Smithsonian secretary Spencer Baird decided that Tichkematse should take up the trade of taxidermy. And Frank Hamilton Cushing then decided that he should travel to the U.S. Southwest to document the lives of the Indigenous peoples there.

But while all of these actions illustrate the varying power structures in which Euro-American men controlled or tried to control Tichkematse's life, none of them relegate him to the role of a merely passive victim. He chose to learn English under Pratt's racist tutelage in Fort Marion, Florida. After his release from the St. Augustine prison, Tichkematse had the choice of returning to his family out west or staying in the East to continue his schooling at the Hampton Institute; he ultimately opted for Hampton. In addition to working as a taxidermist while a Smithsonian employee, he also chose to collaborate with several BAE anthropologists in documenting Tsitsistas/Suhtai grammar and recording American Indian sign language. When Cushing asked Spencer Baird to send Tichkematse to the New Mexico Territory to serve as his companion and assistant, the twenty-four-year-old Southern Tsitsistas/Suhtai man chose to go. And finally, when their anthropological fieldwork among the Havasupai, Hopi, and A:shiwi was complete, Tichkematse chose to return to his people in the Indian Territory, ending his anthropological career.

Without his own words to account for the decisions he made, we are left with conjecture. Why did Tichkematse choose to end his anthropological work, a role that garnered him a celebrity status across the United States? Perhaps he had had enough of non-Native anthropologists and museum professionals who simultaneously romanticized and denigrated his culture and his history. Perhaps he no longer wanted to be an example of Pratt's assimilationist project that called for the eradication of Native culture to "save" the Native individual. Or maybe much more prosaically, after six years spent in prisons, Indian boarding schools, and the federal capital, he simply wanted to live among his family and friends again. Maybe after so many years of being on his own, he was just looking for a partner with whom to spend his life.[58]

Shortly after returning to the Cheyenne and Arapaho Reservation, Tichkematse married a Southern Tsitsistas/Suhtai woman named variously Vick-e-a, Hairy Face, or Little Woman. The two had at least one son, who bore Tichkematse's anglicized name of Squint Eyes Jr. but who sadly died young. In 1884 the twenty-three-year-old Vick-e-a was listed as an employee at the local Indian boarding school, though her exact position and duties are unclear. The following year, in July of 1885, Tichkematse enlisted as an Indian scout in Company B at nearby Fort Reno.[59]

Tichkematse's decision to join the U.S. Army as an Indian scout, though possibly a difficult one for him to make, was not atypical. Southern Tsit-sistas/Suhtai and Southern Inunaina men in the later decades of the nineteenth century regularly served as Indian scouts, including several of the returned Fort Marion prisoners. Those like Tichkematse who could speak, read, and write in English were in demand. Enlistments of three or six months' duration provided a reliable income and guaranteed an old-age pension. Tichkematse served for six months at Fort Reno as an Indian scout and then later for an additional three years as a sergeant at Fort Supply, approximately a hundred miles to the northwest. While their responsibilities varied, many of the Indian scouts accompanied non-Native cavalry units in their monitoring of the surrounding areas. This included ensuring that Native camps were made only on designated reservation lands and maintaining the peace between Native peoples and settler colonizers.[60]

Tichkematse also worked as a guide for military personnel visiting Fort Supply, regularly showcasing the Indian Territory's flora and fauna. In April 1887, for instance, he led a hunting expedition in honor of Colonel Zenas R. Bliss and Major John Dunlop. The gathered men hunted antelope, deer, turkeys, and even a skunk. What is so significant about this particular hunt is that in addition to leading the expedition, Tichkematse was also the group's artist. The drawings he made, now in the collections of the Smithsonian Institution, depict his fellow Indian scouts, non-Native soldiers, and the numerous animals they hunted and even include a few self-portraits of Tichkematse hunting a bear and several turkeys. In total he made a series of twenty-one illustrations of the hunt, thus recording the event for future generations, just as he had been doing since his days as a Fort Marion prisoner a dozen years earlier.[61]

Sometime around 1891, after less than ten years of marriage, Tichkematse's wife died. The cause of her death is unknown. Sadly, any children resulting from this union had also already passed by 1891. Soon thereafter Tichkematse departed the Indian Territory in the company of several prominent Oglala Lakota men on their way to Pine Ridge in South

Dakota. Due to his language abilities Tichkematse served as the group's interpreter as well as their guide on the nearly six-hundred-mile journey. A non-Native rancher in the vicinity of Dodge City, Kansas, recalled them passing through the area and noted particularly the cheerful nature and keen intelligence of Tichkematse.[62]

Life in South Dakota and Montana

Tichkematse's 1891 trek from Fort Supply in the Indian Territory to Pine Ridge in South Dakota was more than just a simple departure. It represented a significant end to one chapter in his life and the beginning of another. Although he remained in contact with his Southern Tsitsistas/Suhtai friends and family, he never again lived in the Indian Territory. Rather, after his first wife's death he moved north to South Dakota and later to southeastern Montana, living among his Northern Tsitsistas/Suhtai relatives. There he created a new life for himself, no longer under the control of men like Richard Henry Pratt, Spencer Baird, or Frank Hamilton Cushing.

Less than a year after arriving at Pine Ridge, Tichkematse married a Northern Tsitsistas/Suhtai woman named Nellie Wolf. The two spent a few years in South Dakota before he again enlisted with the military, this time with Troop L of the U.S. Cavalry at Fort Keogh, Montana. That same year of 1893, Tichkematse and Nellie sent their eight-year-old-daughter Minnie, technically Tichkematse's stepdaughter, to the Indian boarding school in Fort Shaw, Montana. Like many students at the time, Minnie's enrollment at the school required a minimum commitment of three years. There is little information about Minnie's experiences at this school, but just short of three years later, in May 1896, Tichkematse learned of Minnie's poor health. Penning a personal letter to the commissioner of Indian affairs in Washington DC, he requested his daughter's immediate return to her family for recovery. The school's superintendent, W. H. Winslow, flatly refused this request.[63]

The case of Minnie's attendance at an Indian boarding school, her poor health there, and the superintendent's refusal to abide by her parents' wishes brings up two major issues common to Native peoples at the time: control and choice. How much control did Tichkematse, Nellie, or Minnie have in their own lives or in the decision to send Minnie to school away from her family? We know that only a few years earlier in 1891 Congress authorized the commissioner of Indian affairs to enforce such rules and regulations that would secure Native American youths in attending Indian boarding schools for their supposed benefit. By 1893, the same year that Minnie entered the Fort Shaw Indian Boarding School, the commissioner of Indian affairs directed his staff to withhold rations, clothing, and other annuities from parents who refused to send their children to these schools. As was the case with Tichkematse and his daughter Minnie, Indian boarding school authorities frequently ignored the concerns of parents worried about their children's mental and physical health while attending schools far from their families.[64]

What we don't know, however, is how Tichkematse felt about all of this. Although federal authorities exerted control over Indigenous peoples, we don't know how much choice Native peoples such as Tichkematse had. Was Tichkematse forced into sending his stepdaughter over three hundred miles away? Or did he and Nellie instead think that such an education would benefit their daughter's future, as Tichkematse believed his own education had? Did Minnie wish to attend this school, or was she forced to go with tears in her eyes? Minnie's health recovered, at least enough for her to return to her family sometime around 1896, and she was still living with them a decade later.[65]

By 1901 we find Tichkematse employed as the official interpreter for the Tongue River Indian Agency at Lame Deer in southeastern Montana. In this position he received $150 per year. By 1902 he had changed his employment and was instead a private with the agency's Indian police. Tichkematse maintained this position for several more years, continuing through 1904 at least. While the pay was a little less, at $10 per month, it was steady employment that guaranteed food for himself, Nellie, and their daughters Minnie and Cora, the latter born in 1892.[66]

In September 1906 Tichkematse held a ceremony for the recovery of his youngest daughter's health. Approximately fourteen years old at the time of the ceremony, Cora had been suffering from tuberculosis for months, with her health deteriorating rapidly. An amateur anthropologist working among the Northern Tsitsistas/Suhtai was permitted to observe the healing ceremony, which he later described in the journal *American Anthropologist*. Cora lived another three years after the ceremony before eventually succumbing to tuberculosis. When her death did come, as per her request, her dog and her saddle pony were killed at her grave, accompanying young Cora into the afterlife.[67]

Ever since moving among his Northern Tsitsistas/Suhtai relatives in South Dakota in 1891 and Montana in 1893, Tichkematse considered himself a farmer. Although also employed as a member of the U.S. Cavalry, as an agency interpreter, and as an agency policeman, at heart he wanted to work the land. After living for a while in Lame Deer, Tichkematse moved to his own ranch a few miles outside of town. Although none of his children were still living in 1911, he and Nellie continued to run the considerable property they had accumulated over the years. More than just land alone, their material wealth also included five dozen cattle and more than three dozen horses on their property. Despite the assimilationist doctrine Richard Henry Pratt had drilled into him and despite his material success, Tichkematse never completely embraced the trappings of Euro-American society. Although clearly possessing the financial means to build a modern house in the early decades of the twentieth century, he reportedly always preferred a tipi. The agent of the Tongue River Indian Agency described Tichkematse as extremely competent and industrious, fully capable of handling his own affairs. Given the explicit racism of many reservation agents of the time, such a statement is surprising, even ignoring the patronizing language used.[68]

In 1924 Nellie, Tichkematse's partner and wife for over three decades, died. Nearly seventy years of age, Tichkematse suddenly found himself alone. His children from his first and second marriages had not survived into adulthood, and now his second wife was also gone. In 1929 Tichkematse married another Northern Tsitsistas/Suhtai woman, Josie Whistling Elk. Unlike his previous two marriages performed by "Indian custom," his 1929 marriage to Josie was officiated by a local Montana justice of the peace. Perhaps due to Josie's wishes, Tichkematse also received baptism at the same time as a member of the Mennonite Church. Tichkematse and Josie had no children, and their marriage was a short one, lasting little more than three years. He died on the former Tongue River Reservation in Rosebud, Montana, in November 1932, at approximately seventy-six years of age.[69]

Born to Crooked Arm and Crooked Nose Woman in 1857 on the lands of the Tsitsistas/Suhtai in the Colorado Territory, Tichkematse spent the next seven decades in a life that few women or men, Native or non-Native, could equal. His experiences with Native peoples were vast and covered much of the North American continent. He battled against Osage, Ute, and White Mountain Apache peoples on the southern plains, was imprisoned alongside Caddo, Kiowa, Niuam, and Southern Inunaina men and women at Florida's Fort Marion, and attended school at Virginia's Hampton Institute with A'aninin (Gros Ventre), Lakota (Sioux), Numakiki (Mandan), and Sahnish (Arikara) students. At the Smithsonian he worked alongside an Unangan (Aleut) man, explaining North America's Indigenous cultures to the public. In his anthropological fieldwork Tichkematse studied Seminole culture in the country's southeastern tip and learned about A:shiwi, Havasupai, Hopi, and Diné peoples in the southwestern region. And all of this before the age of twenty-five, and before moving among his Northern Tsitsistas/Suhtai relatives, where he worked as a member of the U.S. Cavalry, an agency interpreter, an agency policeman, a farmer, and a rancher.[70]

Tichkematse and Anthropology Today

As an Indigenous museum employee during U.S. anthropology's infancy, Tichkematse is rarely mentioned today, if remembered at all. This book strives to change that fact. Although his work in the field of anthropology was short-lived, it straddled the discipline's subfields of linguistics and ethnology and encompassed traveling across vast regions of the United States collecting work for his museum. Whether he sought material culture items with Pratt among the mangrove swamps of Florida, with Cushing among the deserts, cliffs, and canyons of the Southwest, or even among his own Tsitsistas/Suhtai relations in the Indian Territory, Tichkematse collected items including shields, headdresses, and moccasins from Indigenous communities. These objects he later sent to the Smithsonian Institution, where he hoped they would enhance the Native American collections already there.

Finally, and perhaps most compellingly, Tichkematse represented American Indian cultures in a way that few of his anthropological peers could—through his art. Beginning during his confinement in the U.S. Army prison in St. Augustine and continuing for many years afterward, Tichkematse documented his culture and those of the people around him through his drawings. While at the Smithsonian between 1879 and

1881 he produced nearly two dozen pieces of art depicting everyday life, dances, buffalo hunts, and battles between southern plains communities. Later, after ending his employment with the Smithsonian and returning to the Southern Tsitsistas/Suhtai and Southern Inunaina lands in what is now western Oklahoma, he continued this art form while employed as an Indian scout, with many of his works ironically ending up in museums after his death. Taken altogether, these drawings are just one more example of Tichkematse's lifelong efforts to document and preserve his Southern Tsitsistas/Suhtai culture.

While not definitively the first Native American museum professional in the United States, Tichkematse was one of the earliest to conduct anthropological fieldwork and collect objects from communities other than his own, as well as to provide interpretation within a museum's Ethnological Hall. He entered the field during U.S. anthropology's infancy and before its rapid professionalization in the early twentieth century. The salvage anthropology movement then sweeping the nation created a niche that Native women and men such as Tichkematse, fluent in English and with a passion to preserve their cultures, could fill. Along with these new anthropological positions also came newfound levels of power, status, and celebrity formerly out of reach for many Native peoples.

Although Tichkematse's work in the profession was brief, in many ways he made it easier for other Native peoples to also enter the anthropology museum field. Once there, he and those who followed in his footsteps began the massive undertaking of dismantling, updating, and correcting the anthropological record that portrayed American Indians as either bloodthirsty savages or romantic children of the forest soon to disappear. Many Native peoples today continue the much-needed decolonizing and Indigenizing work that Tichkematse began 150 years ago.

2

One Who Clearly Understands the
Thoughts and Ideas of the Indians

William Jones (Cambridge, Massachusetts, 1897)

His meeting having just finished, William Jones tried to control his excitement as he left the Harvard University professor's office. His mind raced with the possibilities as he walked/ran from the Peabody Museum of American Archaeology and Ethnology back to his dorm. As only the best professors can, Professor Frederic Ward Putnam had opened a new world to the twenty-six-year-old Sac and Fox student. Putnam had spoken eloquently and passionately about the opportunities that a career in the new field of anthropology offered.

And Putnam knew what he was talking about, Jones thought, slowing his pace to a more acceptable speed as he passed his fellow Harvard pupils walking across campus. Four years ago Putnam had directed the Anthropology Department at the acclaimed Chicago World's Fair, and now, in 1897, he was the undisputed leader in the academic field. He had conferred only the second PhD in anthropology granted in the United States, and under his direction Harvard's graduate program in archaeology and ethnology had doubled and then tripled in size over the past few years.[1]

By the time Jones reached his dorm room, his excitement had ebbed, and doubts began to creep in. For as far back as he could remember, his plan, and his family's plan, had been for him to become a medical doctor. With that degree in hand, Jones envisioned returning to the West to aid his people in Indian Country. A career in anthropology would change all of that.

Over the coming days and weeks, Jones confided to friends of the two career paths pulling him in opposite directions. Troubled by the nagging thought that rejecting a career as a physician meant rejecting his Sac and Fox community, one night he suddenly struck upon a new way of looking at the problem. As an anthropologist, Jones mused, maybe he could help his people in an even bigger way. By observing and documenting Native American languages, ceremonies, and everyday practices, perhaps he could create permanent records of Native cultures currently under attack. Also, as a Native person himself, he could add his own perspective and voice as a needed corrective to the anthropological literature on Native Americans written almost completely by non-Native men.

And with that, Jones's mind was made up. The twenty-six-year-old Sac and Fox first-year student who had met Putnam in his office that March day in 1897 was now committed to becoming an anthropologist. He threw himself into his schoolwork, taking classes under Putnam and Roland B. Dixon. When not in class or serving as an editor of the *Harvard Crimson* student newspaper, Jones pored over his books and wrote papers in his Stoughton Hall dorm room. In the coming years he pursued his chosen course relentlessly, receiving his bachelor's degree at Harvard, followed by a master's degree and then PhD in anthropology from Columbia University in 1904. Not only was Jones the first Native American at Columbia University to hold this degree, but he was also the first Indigenous man in the country to do so.[2]

After eighteen years of schooling, at age thirty-three Jones had attained the highest terminal degree possible in the field. Beginning with a Quaker-run Indian boarding school in Indiana and culminating in Ivy League graduate universities in Massachusetts and New York, these years shaped Jones's career as well as his outlook on the world. Although he regularly expressed sympathy for the deplorable conditions of Indigenous peoples on and off U.S. reservations, Jones's view of the world's other colonized peoples tended to fall more in line with mainstream American imperialist rhetoric. Indeed, his surety in the correctness of things Euro-American combined with his colonial swagger eventually proved to be his undoing while conducting fieldwork in the Philippines five years later in 1909.

Youth

Nearly four decades earlier, in 1871, William Jones was born on the Sac and Fox Reservation in the Indian Territory of what is today western Oklahoma. Historically two separate communities, the Sac and Fox peoples originally neighbored each other in the areas around Lake Michigan and Lake Huron. Banding together to repel attacks from European invaders in the eighteenth century, the two communities gradually began to move southward and to be seen as one people. Due to increased Euro-American encroachment in the first several decades of the nineteenth century, Sac and Fox leaders agreed to treaties ceding their lands along the Mississippi River in the present-day states of Illinois, Iowa, Missouri, and Wisconsin to the U.S. government.

By 1867 the Sac and Fox peoples were again pressured to leave the lands of their most recent displacement in Kansas. That year several community leaders signed a treaty relinquishing their rights to all lands in Kansas in exchange for approximately 750 acres in what is today Oklahoma. The physical removal of the Sac and Fox peoples from their lands in Kansas did not actually take place until two years later, though, in 1869. This delay was due to failure on the part of the U.S. Congress to appropriate the necessary funds for transporting everyone and their belongings hundreds of miles away. Incidentally, many Sac and Fox peoples remained steadfastly opposed to removal to the Indian Territory. Refusing the terms of the treaty stipulations, these groups instead settled alongside their relatives in Iowa and Nebraska, where many of their descendants still live today.[3]

Williams Jones's family members were among those who relocated to the Indian Territory in 1869, and it was there that Jones was born on March 28, 1871. His father, Henry Clay Jones, was of Fox ancestry, and his mother, Sarah Penny, was non-Native. Henry was the son of a non-Native man and a Fox woman named Katiqua, the daughter of a Fox chief. After William's mother died while he was still an infant, his Fox grandmother Katiqua took him in and raised him for the next decade. He later described her as his poor, simple-minded, and possibly pagan grandmother. While Jones no doubt loved and fondly remembered this woman, such loaded language in describing Native peoples was typical of him for the remainder of his life. Although Jones was sympathetic to members of Indigenous communities, he was also a Western-educated Native man, influenced by the dominant Christian assimilationist and imperialist ideologies taught in the Indian boarding schools of his youth.[4]

Schooling: From Indiana to New York

Beginning at a young age, Jones attended numerous boarding schools and educational institutions, the first a Quaker-run Indian boarding school in Wabash, Indiana. Founded by the Indiana Yearly Meeting of Friends in 1861, White's Manual Labor Institute was named for Quaker Josiah White and conceived as a manual labor school for all children, regardless of race. After several years of financial difficulty, in 1882 the school received a federal contract to educate Native American students. By this agreement the U.S. government paid an annual amount to the school for each Native student enrolled. While various American Indian communities were represented in the student population at White's Institute over the years, two of the most prominent were Sac and Fox and Ihanktonwan (Yankton Dakota) children.[5]

Lamentably, we today lack records of Jones's three years at White's Institute. He arrived in 1882, at the age of eleven, soon after the death of his Fox grandmother. He and his fellow students referred to the elderly Quaker man and woman who ran the school as "Maw" and "Paw" and were likewise made to see themselves as part of a large multiracial family. Similar paternalistic language was employed at other Indian boarding schools of the time, perhaps most notably at Carlisle, where the staff encouraged Indigenous children to view Richard Henry Pratt as a father figure and even as a Moses to American Indians.[6]

Although records of Jones's days at White's Manual Labor Institute are sparse, we do have documentation of another former pupil's first recollections on entering this school. A few years younger than Jones, Ihanktonwan child Gertrude Simmons, later known as Zitkála-Šá, arrived at the Wabash, Indiana, school in 1884 when she was eight years old. Writing many years later, Simmons recalled reaching the school grounds at night with snow blanketing all in sight and icicles hanging from the trees. She remembered trembling more from fear than from the snow. Upon entering the large house where she was to live, she remained close to the wall, dazzled by the bright lights and the sound of hard shoes upon the wooden floors. Led upstairs to a quiet hall lined with matching beds that contained sleeping Native children, Simmons likened herself to a small animal driven by a herder. Although impossible to know for certain, Jones's experiences on first entering White's Institute were probably not that different than those of Simmons.[7]

Begun as a manual labor institute, this Quaker school followed a pattern common at Hampton, Carlisle, and many other Indian boarding schools of the time. Students devoted half of their day to classroom education, while the remainder was spent farming or working at some trade. The school itself was a working farm of over six hundred acres, with students learning to take care of the crops and animals. While boys were instructed in trades of carpentry, blacksmithing, and broom making, female students learned dressmaking, dairy work, canning of food, and all forms of housekeeping. All of this was directed toward preparing Native youths to supposedly compete in a Euro-American society swiftly surrounding them. Assimilation was the name of the game, and Indian boarding school teachers lost no time in indoctrinating Indigenous youths into the preferred Euro-American division of labor.[8]

There was no division between students in the classroom. All received instruction in reading, writing, mathematics, and, of course, Christian education. As in other Indian boarding schools, speaking in Indigenous languages was forbidden, with only English tolerated. Gertrude Simmons in her later writings noted the countless misunderstandings, unjustifiable frights, and severe punishments experienced by young Native children on account of simple miscommunication from the teachers, who spoke only in English.[9]

By 1885, at the age of fourteen, William Jones had completed his three-year commitment at White's Manual Labor Institute. He thereafter returned to his father's home in the Indian Territory, working for several years as a cowboy and ranch hand. However, William's father, Henry, wanted something more for his son, and he believed that access to a Euro-American education was the best way for Native American youths to compete in this new society. So when Cora Folsom from the Hampton Institute arrived on a recruiting trip in the autumn of 1889, Henry was adamant that William should go with her. How much say William had in this decision is unclear, but he and ten other Native youths accompanied Folsom on her journey back to Virginia a few days later.[10]

Jones arrived at the Hampton Institute on October 1, 1889. Although he would not learn of their achievements until years later when he became a full-fledged anthropologist himself, two prominent Native American collaborators had preceded him as Hampton students. As described in chapter 1, Southern Tsitsistas/Suhtai (Cheyenne) student Tichkematse, who went on to work for the Smithsonian Institution, attended Hampton from 1878 until 1879, and Chaticks si Chaticks (Pawnee) student James R. Murie, who subsequently became one of the most prolific Native American collaborators of the early twentieth century, attended Hampton from 1879 until 1883.[11]

A Shawnee student named Thomas Wildcat Alford, who attended Hampton around the same time as Jones, spoke of his fondness for the school, but also of its semi-military nature, with strict rules and regulations that required promptness in their execution. Alford recalled rising each morning at five o'clock with the days broken down into a series of minutes—so many minutes to prepare oneself before breakfast, for roll call, twenty minutes for meals, and so on. Daily inspections included ensuring that uniforms were properly brushed and shoes shined. As Alford phrased it, "We dressed, we ate, we drilled, we studied, and we recited our lessons with a precision that left not even one minute without its duties."[12]

In addition to becoming accustomed to the military rigor of the school, Jones also worked on the farm, learned the carpenter's trade, and proved himself to be an above average student. Excelling at his studies, during his third year at the school in 1892 he won two prizes for his scholarship. Like Shawnee student Alford, Jones's education opened him to a broader understanding of the world and, contrary to the assimilationist doctrines of his teachers, an appreciation for his own people and culture. Though not yet pursuing the field of anthropology, Jones knew that by furthering his education he wanted to help Native peoples throughout Indian Country.[13]

After graduating from Hampton in 1892, Jones aggressively pursued more schooling, determined to become a medical doctor and serve his community. From Hampton in Virginia Jones eventually traveled to the Phillips Academy in Andover, Massachusetts. There he studied for four years, preparing himself for university life and graduating from Phillips in 1896. Before entering Harvard though, Jones returned to his father's home, now renamed the Oklahoma Territory. William's father, Henry, fluent in English, had worked as an interpreter for many years for the Sac and Fox peoples and believed Euro-American education a positive influence for Native children. In addition to sending William to Hampton, Henry also sent three of William's siblings to the Haskell Institute in Lawrence, Kansas, one of whom later taught there as a Native instructor.[14]

In the summer of 1896 Henry recruited students to attend Pennsylvania's Carlisle Indian Industrial School. William, a recent product of both White's Manual Labor Institute and the Hampton Institute, was happy to help his father in his recruitment efforts. The two spent several weeks traveling throughout the Oklahoma Territory persuading parents to send their children eastward to attend Carlisle. In addition to recruiting among their Sac and Fox community, William and Henry also visited the neighboring Kickapoo, Potawatomi, and Shawnee Nations. William's journal documents their successes securing students. Importantly, the journal also records several leading women and men refusing to part with their children, despite William and Henry's best efforts to persuade them otherwise. By the end of August 1896, William and his father had convinced the parents of eight Native children to allow them to travel east for their education. William even accompanied the girls and boys, delivering the children to Richard Henry Pratt at Carlisle before traveling north to begin his undergraduate career at Harvard University.[15]

Jones and his father's work as Native recruiters for Indian boarding schools was not as unusual as it sounds. Gertrude Simmons, who attended White's Manual Labor Institute in Indiana alongside Jones, also worked for Richard Henry Pratt as a recruiter for the Carlisle Indian Industrial School. Simmons, though, unlike Jones, later looked upon her recruiting days with regret, dismayed that parents entrusted their children to strangers for their upbringing.[16]

Following William and Henry's recruiting work in 1896, William went on to Harvard to continue his education. It was during his first year as a Harvard student that he had that life-altering meeting with Professor Putnam on March 8, 1897. From that day forward Jones was under the spell of anthropology, pursuing the study of his own and other Native American cultures with an intense passion.

Anthropological Influences

An integral player in the spread of professionalized anthropology across the country, Frederic Ward Putnam was born in Massachusetts in 1839. Although entering Harvard University as a student at age seventeen, he never completed his studies there. Nevertheless, due to his intelligence and talent, at the age of thirty-six Putnam became the curator of the Peabody Museum of American Archaeology and Ethnology, and in 1887 he became the Harvard professor of ethnology. With his dual roles in both the museum and the classroom, Putnam represented the changing nature of anthropology, contrasting with the career path of his self-taught and government-funded contemporaries such as John Wesley Powell at the Smithsonian's Bureau of American Ethnology (BAE). It was a younger generation of students and colleagues including Franz Boas, Alfred L. Kroeber, and Frank G. Speck, however, who followed in Putnam's footsteps and transitioned the field away from museums, solidifying anthropology's place in academia.[17]

Of Putnam's many students who later became influential leaders in the field, two of the earliest were George A. Dorsey and George Byron Gordon. Dorsey received his PhD in 1894, later directing the Field Museum's Anthropology Department in Chicago, while Gordon graduated in 1903 and subsequently directed what is now the University of Pennsylvania Museum of Archaeology and Anthropology in Philadelphia. Both men illustrated the changing world of U.S. anthropology, where graduate degrees were becoming a necessity by the early years of the twentieth century. William Jones, too, would come to represent this transition in the professionalization of the field.[18]

Along with his directorship of the 1893 Chicago World's Fair, Putnam is now also remembered in the history of anthropology for his archaeological work, institution building, and mentorship to leading anthropological figures of the following generation, including Franz Boas, George A. Dorsey, Alice C. Fletcher, M. R. Harrington, Alfred L. Kroeber, and, of course, William Jones. In addition to serving as curator and later professor at Harvard University, Putnam's leadership of the Anthropology Department at the 1893 Chicago Exposition not only was a success but also laid the foundation for what became the Field Museum of Natural History. In coming years he also directed the Anthropology Department at the American Museum of Natural History (AMNH) in New York, from 1894 to 1903, and chaired the Anthropology Department and Museum at the University of California, Berkeley, from 1903 until his retirement in 1909. In this way Putnam played an integral role in spreading academic museum anthropology across the country from east to west in less than a quarter century.[19]

Based on Putnam's stellar résumé, it was no surprise that William Jones was eager to begin his studies under this man. Jones continued at Harvard under Putnam's tutelage for the next several years, writing a thesis on the "Massachusetts Indians" and graduating with his bachelor's degree in 1900. Directly after receiving his undergraduate degree, and at Putnam's urging, Jones moved to New York to begin his graduate work at Columbia University. There he studied anthropology under Franz Boas, receiving his master's degree and PhD. Leaders in the anthropological field, both Putnam and Boas assumed the role of mentor and ersatz father for the younger Sac and Fox man. Their collective correspondence, especially that between Boas and Jones, displays a level of warmth and friendship in which Boas continually encouraged and supported Jones first during his academic years and later in his professional career.[20]

As the second great influence on Jones's future anthropology career, Franz Boas hardly requires an introduction. Probably the most well-known figure in U.S. anthropology, Boas was born in the province of Westphalia, now part of modern-day Germany, in 1858. There he attended Heidelberg University, Bonn University, and the University of Kiel, receiving his doctoral degree in physics from the latter in 1881. Six years later, in 1887, Boas immigrated to the United States and that same year married American Marie Krackowizer in New York City.[21]

For much of the first decade of his life in the United States, from 1887 until approximately 1895, Boas struggled to find a solid footing where he could truly begin his anthropological career. In January 1887 he accepted the position of assistant editor with the New York–based weekly periodical *Science*, compiling an Ethnological Notes column in many issues. Two years later he quit this position to work as a docent in the Psychology Department at the newly opened Clark University in Worcester, Massachusetts. Although he retained this position less than three years, resigning in 1892, Boas still managed to train and confer the first PhD in anthropology in the United States to one of his students, A. F. Chamberlain. The following year Boas traveled to Chicago to work as Frederic Ward Putnam's chief assistant in organizing the Anthropology Department at the Columbian

Exposition of 1893. When the world's fair ended, Boas stayed on to direct the transfer of the anthropological collections to the recently created Field Museum of Natural History, the successor institution and inheritor of Putnam and Boas's exposition work. Feeling slighted and overlooked by the museum's board of directors, however, Boas did not remain long in Chicago, later resigning in the spring of 1894.[22]

Meanwhile Boas's friend and mentor Putnam secured for himself the position of chair of the Anthropology Department at New York's AMNH, and in 1895 he brought Boas on board as well. There Boas remained for the next decade, increasing the museum's object collections through expanded ethnographic fieldwork and further developing the country's anthropological field. Alongside his work at AMNH, in 1896 Boas also accepted the position of lecturer in anthropology at Columbia University, later becoming a professor in 1899. Although he terminated his AMNH curatorship in 1905, Boas remained a professor at Columbia for more than four decades. There he wielded the largest influence on the future of U.S. anthropology, instructing students in the four-field approach of academic anthropology: cultural anthropology, physical anthropology, linguistics, and archaeology. As recent scholars have noted, Putnam at Harvard and Boas at Columbia trained most of the succeeding generation of anthropologists. In addition to notable non-Native students who studied under him, Boas also replicated Putnam's approach, encouraging Indigenous women and men like William Jones to enter the field of anthropology.[23]

One major distinction between Boas and the generation of anthropologists who directly preceded him, men such as Daniel Garrison Brinton, Lewis Henry Morgan, and John Wesley Powell, was Boas's dismissal of social evolutionist thought and scientific racism pervading much of these men's work. Boas argued the social evolutionary themes that divided the world's peoples into savage, barbarian, and civilized categories were artificial constructs claiming universal, scientific validity. This broadmindedness was something Boas returned to again and again throughout his long career, and something he drilled into his students and the public.

While a curator at the AMNH, Boas labored to illustrate to museum visitors that Europeans and Euro-Americans were not the only carriers of civilization, but rather that humankind had been creative everywhere. In his publications he delivered a similar message, arguing that anthropology and the intensive study of foreign cultures broadened the view of humankind, freeing people from cultural prejudice. In other words, anthropological exhibits, lectures, and publications offered insight into the world's shared humanity instead of focusing on physical differences, as previous generations of anthropologists had done. While Boas clearly advocated for his version of liberal anthropology and for the physical and mental equality of the world's peoples, he nevertheless remained shockingly silent about the suffering, racism, and oppression experienced by the Indigenous peoples whom he studied.[24]

Although advocating for immigrants' rights and African American equality in scientific journals, Boas effectively took no stand to ameliorate the living conditions of contemporary Native peoples. As historian Douglas Cole has written, Boas's emphasis was on the urgency of work, of salvaging Native cultures before they supposedly disappeared, not on aiding actual American Indian communities. Instead, Boas represented the individuals he studied as a vanishing people, frozen in an ethnographic present, and thus outside the temporal bounds of modern society. This influence and mindset, though tempered in the work of Boas's student William Jones, nevertheless persisted in the latter as well.[25]

Jones as an Anthropologist

As the first academically qualified and professionally trained Native American anthropologist, William Jones was unique among both his Native and non-Native peers. Unlike his contemporary Native anthropologists J. N. B. Hewitt, Francis La Flesche, Florence and Louis Shotridge, and Amos Oneroad, all of whom possessed Indigenous ancestry and a passion for ethnological work, Jones also attained the requisite doctoral qualification to fit the professionalizing anthropological world of the early twentieth century.

Among non-Native anthropologists, Jones was seen as possessing unique access into the so-called Native American mindset. His Euro-American colleagues frequently remarked on the clearness of his understanding of the thoughts and ideas of American Indians, which they attributed to his Native heritage. This false assumption that an Indigenous person intrinsically better understood all other Indigenous peoples was common among leading anthropologists at the time. Boas, for instance, noted that in addition to his learning and special training, Jones also reportedly carried unusual sympathetic insight and understanding toward Native peoples. From Jones's published and personal writings, however, it is evident that he never wished to be considered different on account of his Sac and Fox ancestry.[26]

Repeatedly throughout his life Jones objected to receiving special treatment due to being American Indian. This was because he always felt conflicted about his identity and how to reconcile the Euro-American and Native American parts of his heritage. In the spring of 1892, for instance, when about to be named valedictorian of his graduating class at the Hampton Institute, Jones declined this honor on the grounds that he was "more white than Indian," having at best only a one-fourth title to any such distinction. He felt that other students with a greater claim to Native heritage were more deserving of this accolade and the scholarship prize that accompanied it. The Hampton school newspaper of that year even identified Jones's reluctance to accept awards when competing against other Native students. The newspaper noted twelve students in the running for highest grades, with Jones notably absent. According to sources, Jones refused to enter the lists, and the school's faculty reluctantly accepted his decision.[27]

While attending the Phillips Academy and applying to Harvard a few years later, Jones sought a scholarship to defray the costs of attending the expensive institution. However, he declared that he would not "pose as an Indian" to receive financial help. He would not take a cent on that score, he told his friends. It wouldn't be fair to other Native applicants, he believed, and it would be uncomfortable for him, too. Jones clearly wrestled with issues of Native and non-Native identity. Pursuing a profession that shone a spotlight on and at times aggrandized these differences only exacerbated this very personal issue. In the end Jones knew that whichever career he chose, whether as a physician or as an anthropologist, he would help his fellow American Indians.[28]

His career took Jones across North America, working with Indigenous communities in the U.S. Midwest, upper Great Lakes, New England, parts of Canada, and eventually the recently acquired U.S. territory of the Philippines. While he did not definitively decide on anthropology as a profession until meeting with Putnam at Harvard in 1897, he nevertheless displayed an interest in the field years earlier. While still a student at the

Phillips Academy in Massachusetts, Jones sent correspondence to John Wesley Powell in 1895 and again in 1896, attempting to secure work at the Smithsonian's BAE in Washington DC.

With help from Cora Folsom, Jones's former recruiter and teacher at Hampton, the young Sac and Fox man reached out to Powell at the BAE in early 1895. Interested in gathering all the information he could from Jones, Powell arranged funding for the younger man to travel to Washington DC that summer. That July, during a break from his classes at the Phillips Academy, Jones and BAE employee Albert Samuel Gatschet documented the closely related Sac and Fox languages. Jones supplied as much linguistic information as he could, though he noted that he had already forgotten much in the years since being away from his community. Readers may recall that sixteen years prior, Tichkematse worked on an almost identical linguistic project with Gatschet at the BAE, writing out a vocabulary of the Tsitsistas/Suhtai peoples.[29]

Excited about the linguistic work he and Gatschet had done over the previous summer, in April 1896 Jones wrote to Powell again, eager to take on similar work. Jones asked if Gatschet planned to be out in the field, conducting fieldwork and taking down Native vocabularies, and if so, if Jones would be able to accompany him. Being sure to highlight his Native heritage, Jones reminded Powell that his home was among the Mississippi River Band of Sacs and Foxes in the Oklahoma Territory, and that he was eager to undertake anthropological work among his own people. Despite his apparent passion and knowledge, no linguistic fieldwork was forthcoming for Jones in 1896. However, by the following year he had begun his anthropological studies under Putnam at Harvard. Nearly every summer season thereafter, Jones worked among North America's Indigenous communities, conducting fieldwork, sharpening his linguistic skills, and preserving information for future generations.[30]

Fieldwork

Jones undertook his first true anthropological fieldwork in the summer of 1897, only a few months after his consequential meeting with Putnam. Given Jones's Native heritage, he and Putnam decided that he should visit members of his own community, with whom he might have a little more influence and who might be more willing to answer an anthropologist's questions. Traveling to Tama, Iowa, Jones remained three months with his relatives in the Meskwaki Nation (Sac and Fox Tribe of the Mississippi in Iowa). There, he lived with an elderly couple distantly related on his father's side. He observed daily life among the Meskwaki, happily listening to and jotting down the stories and tales the old men were willing to share with him.[31]

In addition to some of the more innocuous notes Jones gathered during this summer, he also wrote up his own account of sacred information that was never meant to be made public. This included Jones's sketches, diagrams, and interpretation of Meskwaki religious ceremonies he witnessed. After Jones's death in 1909, his father, Henry, successfully kept these materials from the public eye. Henry insisted that much of this information was made available to William only due to his ancestry, not because of his profession as an anthropologist. Therefore, it should not be published or made public, at least during the lifetime of those who provided William with the information. Regrettably, Jones's 1897 manuscript was later published posthumously by the Smithsonian Institution. It reputedly included descriptions of the sacred ceremonies never meant for public reading.[32]

Years later during the summer months of his Columbia University graduate education, Jones traveled again to Iowa and the Oklahoma Territory, continuing his work among the Meskwaki, Sac and Fox, and related Kickapoo peoples. Laboring under the joint auspices and funding of the AMNH in New York and the BAE in DC, Franz Boas directed Jones to collect as much information on the language and customs of the Sac and Fox as he could and to obtain as many objects as possible illustrating the ethnology of his people. While linguistic information and narratives were sent to the BAE, material culture objects Jones collected were sent to the AMNH. Following the dictates of salvage anthropology in its race to preserve Indigenous cultures before they supposedly disappeared, Jones collected nearly everything he could get his hands on, with wooden bowls, leggings, moccasins, and other items he acquired still residing in the AMNH collections today.[33]

Referring to the items he collected as "plunder," Jones was typical of the salvage anthropologists of his time. But he also did something a little unusual among museum collectors. When he couldn't find a particular example of an object he wanted to acquire—a buckskin dress, for instance—he requested that it be made by Native people for museum acquisition. The notion behind this was that while anthropologists believed older objects were objectively better for collecting work, sometimes the old objects simply were not available. When this was the case, some anthropologists such as Jones paid skilled elders in the community to make the object in question, thus resulting in new, yet still "authentic" items. Using this method, Jones acquired a series of buckskin outfits made for women, men, and children to adorn museum mannequins. He not only paid for the final products himself, but he also supplied the materials, including the buckskin and sinew, which ironically came from Chicago.[34]

As these examples show, fieldwork for Jones was never a solitary pursuit. He not only lived with the people he studied, but he often collaborated with other Native and non-Native anthropologists. While living among Plains Indigenous nations in the Oklahoma Territory, for example, Jones also had the good fortune to briefly work alongside another Native collaborator and fellow Hampton alumni, Chaticks si Chaticks man James R. Murie. As with many of the individuals in this book, Jones's and Murie's willingness to work together illustrates the interconnectedness of the anthropological profession at the time.

In addition to gathering Native cultural material from Plains Indian communities in the Midwest, Jones also worked among the Anishinaabe (Chippewa/Ojibwa) near Lake Superior. There he collected a large amount of information on their beliefs and customs, acquired a thorough knowledge of the "Ojibway dialect," and recorded a vast amount of material in its Indigenous language. In collecting linguistic information, Jones also did something quite unique among anthropologists. When unable to travel long distances due to scarcity of funds, he regularly journeyed the shorter route to the Carlisle Indian Industrial School in Pennsylvania, there collecting stories and information from Native students. In February 1903, for instance, he wrote that he had a pleasant time with the Sac and Fox and Kickapoo youths, recalling them as extremely cordial and supplying him with volumes of things he had not previously known.[35]

Carlisle's student-run newspaper, the *Red Man and Helper*, publicized Jones's visit in the March 6, 1903, issue. The paper noted his anthropological work at the school, in which he researched the derivation of Sac and Fox words. Surprisingly, despite his constant denunciations of the field of anthropology, Richard Henry Pratt, superintendent of Carlisle during Jones's frequent visits, nevertheless permitted such linguistic work to occur.[36]

Job Searching

Despite Jones's collecting success, securing stable employment as an anthropologist proved quite challenging. As early as 1901, Boas sought a place for his young Sac and Fox protégé. Writing to a colleague, Boas noted that if Jones continued along his current path, he would no doubt be offered a position within the BAE at the Smithsonian in the not-too-distant future. Two years later as Jones prepared to receive his PhD, Boas wrote to another colleague in the museum field, trumpeting Jones's achievements. Boas highlighted Jones's linguistic work, identifying him as the best person for any thorough study of Algonquian languages. Clark Wissler, Boas's successor as head of the Anthropology Department at the AMNH, also sought to locate a promising position for Jones. Writing to the AMNH director, Wissler urged that he offer Jones a permanent assistant job in the museum's Anthropology Department. Wissler stressed that not only was Jones fully qualified for the work, but he had already collected nearly the entirety of the museum's material culture from eastern and Great Lakes Native communities in North America.[37]

Despite his colleagues' best efforts, by 1905, one year after receiving his PhD from Columbia University, Jones continued to face disappointment in the job market. Jones hoped to retain his focus on Algonquian languages and earn a sufficient living to marry his fiancée, Caroline Andrus, a non-Native employee at the Hampton Institute he met several years earlier. Not much is known about their first meeting or their later romance, but what is clear is that Jones and Andrus met during their early days at Hampton. Four years younger than William, Caroline arrived at Hampton in 1885 at the age of ten. Originally planning to assist her elder sister in her teaching responsibilities, Caroline remained at the school as an employee in the Indian Records Office when her sister fell ill soon after arriving. Sometime during their three-year overlap between 1889 and 1892, with William a Native student and Caroline a non-Native employee, the two fell in love. Continuing their relationship from afar during William's undergraduate and graduate years, they became engaged in late 1901. However, an actual wedding date was postponed again and again by the couple until Jones located gainful employment. By November 1905 he opined optimistically to a friend that with his education, experience, and cultural knowledge a job was bound to open up for him. Unfortunately, no such position was forthcoming.[38]

Writing to Boas in the fall of 1905, Jones spoke of his love for anthropological fieldwork, but also his discouragement over the lack of a suitable position in the discipline. While recording linguistic information among the Fort William First Nation of Canada, Jones wrote that he wanted to continue this work for as long as possible, but if there was no guarantee of making a reasonable living at it, he would need to go into another field of work. Both the AMNH and the BAE, although willing to fund fieldwork of a short duration, were unable financially to hire on another anthropologist position. It was at this time that George A. Dorsey entered the picture.[39]

Dorsey, curator of anthropology at Chicago's Field Museum of Natural History, played a recurring role in the lives of many of the major actors in the early years of U.S. anthropology. Illustrative of the interconnected nature of the discipline at the time, Dorsey previously studied at Harvard, receiving his PhD there in 1894 under the tutelage of Frederic Ward Putnam, instigator of Jones's initial foray into the anthropological field. An assistant under Putnam at the 1893 Chicago World's Fair, Dorsey also worked alongside such disparate characters as the cantankerous yet intellectually gifted Franz Boas and the charming yet duplicitous Antonio Apache. Finally, by 1906, when Dorsey offered Jones an opportunity to join him at the Field Museum, Dorsey was already simultaneously conducting anthropological work with a number of prominent Native American collaborators including Richard Davis, James R. Murie, and Cleaver Warden.

So it was that after all his schooling—the Quaker-run Indian boarding school in Indiana, the Hampton Institute in Virginia, the preparatory academy in Massachusetts, the undergraduate and graduate degrees at Harvard and Columbia Universities—and after two additional years of cobbling together part-time contract work, Jones found no permanent employment in the field of anthropology. Some scholars have posited that Jones's position remained marginal due to his race, asserting that as an American Indian, he had little hope of receiving permanent employment at either a university, a museum, or a federal institution such as the BAE.

While a seemingly plausible argument, however, there is no evidence Jones failed to secure a position simply because of his race.[40]

Undoubtedly race and gender influenced many peoples' decisions about hiring at the time, just as they unfortunately continue to today, but there were still numerous Native Americans who secured these positions. A few of Jones's Native contemporaries, all conspicuously male, who did so included J. N. B. Hewitt, Tuscarora ethnologist hired on full-time at the BAE in 1886; Francis La Flesche, Omaha ethnologist hired on full-time at the BAE in 1910; Louis Shotridge, Chilkat Tlingit assistant curator hired on full-time at Philadelphia's University Museum in 1915; and Amos Oneroad, Sisitonwan Dakota (Sisseton Sioux) assistant anthropologist hired on full-time at the Museum of the American Indian, Heye Foundation (MAI) in 1918. The more likely reason for Jones's difficulties was not his race, but rather that such positions were few and far between during professional anthropology's infancy.[41]

These points aside, it was no doubt due to poor job prospects that Jones accepted, not without some reservations, the peculiar job offer George A. Dorsey made to him in 1906. Somewhat inexplicably, given Jones's experience in Native North American fieldwork, Dorsey offered him the choice of working in one of three places: Africa, the southern Pacific, or the Philippines. The reason for these geographic locations was that by 1906 and 1907 the Field Museum's Anthropology Department began to transition from a focus on U.S. Plains Indian communities to a broader global emphasis, primarily collecting among the Indigenous peoples of Africa and Asia. Therefore, while anthropologist positions focusing solely on North American Indian cultures were not in the offing, Dorsey still wanted to employ the talented and accredited Jones.[42]

At the Field Museum

Jones, with few options, eventually accepted Dorsey's offer, agreeing to travel to the recently acquired U.S. territory of the Philippines in late 1907. Ever Jones's mentor and friend, Boas, learning of the younger man's decision, expressed his surprise and disappointment in a series of letters. Writing in September 1906, Boas urged Jones to reconsider, stating that such fieldwork in the Philippines was not right for him. A resigned Jones replied a few days later that his only reason for entering upon this new field of research was due to the lack of opportunities for him to continue his linguistic work in Algonquian languages. He soon after relocated to Chicago in the latter part of 1906, working long, busy hours in the Field Museum, near to which he had his lodgings.[43]

While anthropological fieldwork in the Philippines had never been Jones's motivation in entering the field, the contract that Dorsey offered him was one few could turn down. This contract stipulated that the expedition's duration was two years but could be extended based on Jones's findings in the field. The nature of his work included investigating local cultures, documenting Indigenous languages, and collecting and shipping material culture items back to the museum in Chicago. Dorsey also noted in the contract that any scholarly publications resulting from Jones's collected Philippines fieldnotes would be published by the Field Museum but left open the opportunity for Jones to publish in book form any of his own results deserving of a more popular audience.[44]

In addition to the contract's stipulated work, Dorsey suggested that after completing his Philippines expedition, Jones could also pursue further anthropological work in South Asia and the Pacific. Though not a requirement, Dorsey encouraged Jones to conduct similar anthropological investigations and collecting work in southern India, Borneo, and what are today the island nations of Kiribati, Palau, and sections of the Federated States of Micronesia. While Jones never had the chance to take on this additional work, Dorsey's suggestion to do so was ahead of its time. His recommendation to visit Pacific Island nations preceded Bronislaw Malinowski's work in the Trobriand Islands by nearly a decade and Margaret Mead's studies in Samoa by two decades. Dorsey's only miscalculation in this larger scheme to collect tangible and intangible culture from Indigenous peoples throughout the Eastern Hemisphere was in sending Jones to do the fieldwork. Not that Jones was unqualified, but rather that the entire expedition ignored Jones's linguistic talents and knowledge of Native American cultures specifically suited for North America, but wholly out of place in the Philippines. Nevertheless, after some back and forth Jones looked upon the venture as an opportunity, and a well-paid one at that, and he agreed to Dorsey's contract.[45]

After almost a year of preparations, in July 1907 Jones bid goodbye to friends, family, and his fiancée and left Chicago, taking a train toward the Pacific Coast. He stayed briefly with fellow anthropologist and former Boas student Alfred L. Kroeber in San Francisco before continuing on his way to Seattle. From there he boarded the *Aki Maru* and sailed west in August 1907, never again to return to his native land.[46]

Reconciling himself to think of the Philippines expedition as an opportunity to learn more about the world's cultures, Jones delighted in the layovers on the way to his destination. Undoubtedly his favorite of these was his visit to Tokyo. Penning a quick letter to Dorsey back in Chicago, Jones wrote of sitting comfortably by the window in his inn in Japan's capital, watching the locals walk the city's rainy streets. There they hurried to and fro, carrying large umbrellas and going about their daily business, so like and unlike his own experiences of U.S. cities. Waxing poetic, Jones wrote to his Field Museum colleague Stephen Simms, comparing himself to the Greek hero Ulysses and Japan to the island of the enchantress Calypso, where Jones hoped to remain forever. Confiding to Simms, Jones admitted he found the Japanese women utterly bewitching. Less besotted was he with his stops in China. Shanghai and Hong Kong overwhelmed Jones with China's antiquity and solidity, but also, he wrote, with its filth and stench. Of course, all his visits amounted to not much more than a handful of days on the way to his actual destination of Manila, capital of the recently acquired U.S. territory.[47]

In the Philippines

After Spain's defeat by the United States in the 1898 Spanish-American War, the United States "acquired" several of the former European superpower's overseas colonial possessions including Cuba, Puerto Rico, and the southeast archipelago known as the Philippines. Unsurprisingly, formal declarations transferring control of these territories from Spain to the United States were made between the colonial powers themselves, without permission or input from the actual inhabitants of these lands. As with Cuba and Puerto Rico, following formal annexation of the Philippines, U.S. Army troops, adventure seekers, scientists, and even anthropologists flooded the new colonial possession, eager to salvage or otherwise make a profit from what they found.[48]

Soon after arriving in the Philippines, Jones began his investigation of the diverse peoples of this massive island chain. Fortunately for him, he was not completely alone in this venture. Another of his Field Museum colleagues, Fay-Cooper Cole, had been in the Philippines conducting anthropological fieldwork for several months before Jones's arrival. Cole and his wife, Mabel, introduced the Sac and Fox anthropologist to members of the local constabulary and invited him to travel with them into the northern reaches of the largest island, Luzon. There, in Abra province, Jones met the Itneg (Tinguian) peoples with whom the Coles lived and studied.[49]

While his experiences with the Coles were encouraging, Jones met disappointment when venturing to get information out of the U.S. military personnel who occupied the Philippines Territory. Complaining to Dorsey about the lack of knowledge of Luzon's inland Indigenous communities, Jones wrote the situation was one with which anthropologists were already familiar in the United States. Army personnel, despite living near Native American communities for decades, knew virtually nothing factual or positive about them, Jones wrote. So, apparently, was the case with U.S. military personnel living near Indigenous communities in the Philippines. In particular, Jones wished to learn more about the Bugkalot (Ilongot) peoples in the island's landlocked center and east. From everything he had learned, he wrote Dorsey, these people would prove to be a promising and fruitful anthropological study.[50]

Over the succeeding months, Jones, accompanied by his dog, Dona, traveled regularly into the interior of the island of Luzon, venturing north from his base of operations in Manila. On each venture, he questioned locals about the Bugkalot peoples, and each time the response was the same—a warning not to go. Jones's diary entries from early 1908 teem with cautions that he was taking too great a risk in his travels farther east and north. There, the locals warned, he was sure to be slain, meeting certain death as soon as he crossed into the Bugkalot lands. Such forewarnings only further motivated Jones, however, with the danger of the undertaking thrilling him.[51]

Ever the anthropologist, Jones sought what many of his colleagues also strived for—the opportunity to observe, study, and document cultures believed to be virtually unknown and exotic to Western science. And with publication of these observations, of course, came fame within the anthropological discipline. By mid-1908 Jones was nearing his success. He finally ventured into the territory of the Bugkalot in the Nueva Vizcaya province, an area surrounded on three sides by mountain chains, making it virtually isolated from the rest of the island of Luzon. In letters home Jones wrote of his joy in observing "the wild men" inhabiting the hills and jungles surrounding him. He described these people as picturesque, the very model of the timeless "primitive" that anthropologists tirelessly pursued.[52]

Notwithstanding his joy at finding the "wildest," that is, most pure or unassimilated people in northern Luzon, Jones's cultural arrogance was never far removed. As an anthropological observer, Jones regularly wrote in his diary with condescension about the Bugkalot community. He remarked again and again on their hygiene and biological functions. Unable to recognize that he maintained the same colonial gaze toward the Bugkalot peoples that U.S. anthropologists maintained toward Native Americans, in an October 1908 diary entry Jones described the Bugkalot with distaste, labeling their physical aspect repellent. Depicting them with disheveled hair and dirt-covered hands, faces, and bodies, Jones likened the Bugkalot people more to beasts than human beings.[53]

Despite his use of imperialist and racist language to describe the peoples he studied, Jones eventually began to consider himself a member of the Bugkalot community, even taking on some of the collective responsibilities. For instance, he regularly served as a medical doctor of sorts, doling out his limited supplies of medicine to aid ailing children and elders. Within a few weeks of his arrival, the men even invited him to accompany them on hunts for game and on at least one occasion to defend their community against rivals. Notably, though, in his description of Bugkalot battle tactics, Jones couldn't help comparing them with those of Native Americans, noting that the Bugkalot exposed themselves too much and disgracefully even allowed women to accompany them in their collective defense.[54]

As in his ethnographic studies of North America's Native peoples, Jones captured all the information he could in the Philippines, even taking photographs and sketching illustrations of Bugkalot houses. He intended these illustrations to aid him in constructing models of Bugkalot houses and place them on exhibit in the Field Museum, but such plans never came to fruition. In addition to gathering information on religion, warfare, agriculture, sexuality, and other topics important to anthropologists, Jones collected material culture items. By early 1909 he let his colleague Simms know that while he had made some object collections, few were very good, "but as good as these naked people have." What became of critical importance to Jones in February and March 1909 was securing enough balsa rafts to float himself and these collected objects down the river to Echague and from there to Manila. It was this steadfast emphasis on demanding these rafts that led to his death soon after.[55]

After spending more than a year among the Bugkalot communities of the Cagayan River valley in northern Luzon, Jones was prepared to ship himself and the Bugkalot objects he had gathered out of the territory. Using the same high-handed colonial tactics that became commonplace to him in his interactions with the Bugkalot peoples, Jones ordered a series of balsa rafts made to transport these materials downriver. Delay after delay arose in the construction of these rafts, however, and over the weeks Jones's frustration grew and his patience diminished. In his final letter to Dorsey dated March 19, 1909, Jones complained about the lack of adequate rafts preventing him from leaving the area. What happened next was not recorded in letters but rather was presented in official Philippines court hearings the following month after Jones's death.[56]

Seeking to force the Bugkalot men into delivering the required fifteen balsa rafts, Jones reportedly resorted to verbal abuse and intimidation of community members. In late March Jones physically detained the local Bugkalot leader, Takadan, informing the other men that until the rafts were delivered, Takadan would remain in Jones's custody. On the afternoon of March 28, 1909, Jones attempted to force Takadan into his own raft on the Cagayan River, confining him until delivery was made. By laying hands on a community leader, Jones overstepped his bounds, acting as an agent of U.S. imperial control and crossing a line that no Bugkalot person could let go unanswered. A party of approximately twenty Bugkalot men, armed with bolos and spears, immediately surrounded Jones, and three of them, Palidat, Magueng, and Gacad, quickly delivered fatal blows, wounding Jones in the head, chest, and arms. Court hearings later reported that both Jones and his interpreter, Romano Dumaliang, fired a pistol on the gathered Bugkalot men, with the two of them eventually reaching the safety of a raft and floating downriver. However, the damage was already done, and Jones would succumb to his wounds approximately four hours later. According to Palidat, one of the men who had delivered a fatal blow to Jones, they attacked the Sac and Fox anthropologist because he was guilty and deserved death for his actions. As far as they were concerned, Jones brought about his own demise by trying to remove the local Bugkalot leader, Takadan. William Jones died on March 28, 1909. It was his thirty-eighth birthday.[57]

The Aftermath of Jones's Death

News of Jones's death shocked the U.S. public. The *New York World* newspaper published an account of his murder with the headline "Tribesmen Kill Noted Scientist in Philippines." Within days of his death, accounts of Jones reached his family, and his brothers and father wrote hurriedly to Dorsey at the Field Museum, seeking assurance that the newspapers had somehow gotten it wrong. Henry, William's father, penned Dorsey a short letter, expressing his hope that the reporting was a mistake. "This is hard," Henry wrote with emotion, ending his missive abruptly. After accepting his son's death, Henry asked Dorsey a few days later if it would be possible to have William's body returned to the United States, where it could be buried in Oklahoma next to his mother's grave. In response, Dorsey informed the Jones family that it would be impossible to embalm the body. Further, health authorities in the Philippines would not permit the removal of Jones's remains, as they were already interred at Echague, in the Isabela Province. Having developed a close bond with Jones during their work together, Dorsey shared his grief with members of the Jones family, noting that the Sac and Fox man was like a brother to all of them.[58]

For reasons unknown Jones never told his family about his engagement to Caroline Andrus at the Hampton Institute. So Henry was understandably shocked when he received several letters from Andrus in the wake of William's death, informing him of their 1901 engagement and her wish to be involved in any decision about William's personal effects. Sadly, Henry chose to lash out rather than cooperate with his son's fiancée, informing Dorsey that he would make all decisions about his son. He added that if Andrus came to the Field Museum in Chicago, he did not want her to touch any of William's things still stored there.

In spite of Henry's demands, Andrus, as William's fiancée, still worked to preserve her betrothed's memory, funding the erection of an Episcopal chapel named in honor of William near Echague in the Philippines. Lamentably for us today, Caroline Andrus destroyed hundreds of letters of personal correspondence between William and her, preventing a fuller understanding of William's experiences before and during his Philippines expedition.[59]

Soon after learning of Jones's demise, members of the U.S. anthropological community also commiserated over the young man's tragic death. Ever the salvage anthropologists, Boas and Dorsey wrote each other of the need to find someone with equal familiarity with Anishinaabe language and culture to continue collecting this material before it supposedly vanished. According to Boas, the individual whom the AMNH selected for such work, Alanson Skinner, simply wasn't capable of being Jones's successor in this field, perhaps in part because he lacked Native ancestry. Dorsey also ordered Stephen Simms at the Field Museum to immediately travel to the Philippines and there transport Jones's fieldnotes and remaining object collections back to Chicago.[60]

The U.S. government in the Philippines lost little time in responding to Jones's death. According to recent scholars, U.S. colonial authorities used the incident as a pretext for vigorously pursuing a pan-Philippines pacification policy. In a letter to Jones's aggrieved family, Dorsey reassured them that U.S. soldiers in the Philippines had been dispatched into the Bugkalot territory to inquire into the circumstances of Jones's death and, more importantly, to punish those responsible. Just weeks after news broke of Jones's death, Lieutenant Wilfrid Turnbull of the U.S. colonial authorities in the Philippines led a punitive expedition to burn Bugkalot houses and crops in retribution for Jones's killing. Turnbull's actions were not focused on destruction alone but were also an attempt by the U.S. colonial administration to pacify and supposedly civilize non-Christian Indigenous communities in northern Luzon.[61]

By the end of May 1909, just two months after Jones's death, the three men directly responsible for his killing, Palidat, Magueng, and Gacad, were arrested and presented before a local magistrate in a court in the province of Nueva Vizcaya. The judge pronounced all three guilty, sentencing them to death. However, in less than a year, the Supreme Court of the Philippine Islands commuted their death sentences, instead confining the men to life imprisonment.[62]

William Jones and Anthropology Today

William Jones's life and career were both tragically cut short when he died at age thirty-eight thousands of miles from his friends, his family, and his fiancée, with the Philippines' Municipal Cemetery of Echague as his body's final resting place. Having accepted an assignment he had never envisioned nor fully embraced, he left his home and his country on the other side of the world, never to return. Given his intelligence, his tenacity, and his academic pedigree, if Jones had lived another two or three decades he may have become one of the most prominent people in the field of U.S. anthropology, rather than simply one of its footnotes.

Although his death at the hands of Bugkalot community members was undoubtedly tragic, it was also easily preventable. Some scholars have argued that Jones's cultural arrogance and affected superiority, combined with his quick temper, were the ultimate cause of his death. Jones's certainty of the correctness of his views and those of his society over the customs and social mores of the people whom he studied ultimately forced the Bugkalot men to retaliate and right the wrong done to their chief.

Interestingly, if Jones had possessed the wherewithal to view his own situation from a broader vantage point, he might have noted some striking similarities between his own work as a representative of a colonial power and that of the countless missionaries, federal agents, and anthropologists who had likewise observed and denigrated the lifeways of his forebears in the United States. According to oral histories given by Bugkalot community members decades later, Jones manipulated the people he studied into trading cultural objects for beads, wire, salt, and cloth that he carried for just these exchanges. By voicing his dissatisfaction at the state of objects he received, Jones shamed Bugkalot villagers into gathering higher-quality items, regularly threatening to leave and work with neighboring Indigenous communities to acquire objects. Such actions, though arguably commonplace practice among anthropologists of his era, nevertheless illustrate the gross asymmetries of power foundational to Jones's imperial enterprise.[63]

While sympathetic to the plight of his fellow Indigenous peoples in the United States, Jones did not extend such sympathy toward other colonized individuals in the Philippines and elsewhere. No doubt such views were due in part to his upbringing and education in the Indian boarding schools of his youth. Throughout his life Jones was influenced by and espoused the language of assimilation and Christian reform for Native Americans. While still a student in Massachusetts in the mid-1890s he composed a letter to his former Native classmates at the Hampton Institute discussing current reform efforts on reservations. Though appreciative of reform-minded non-Native Christians hoping to aid American Indians, Jones stressed that he and his fellow Western-educated classmates knew best. They knew, Jones wrote, echoing the words of his boarding school teachers, that it was their responsibility as products of Indian boarding schools to help uplift their fellows in Indian Country. He hoped that they could show their parents, cousins, and distant relations on reservations how to live better. In other words, he hoped to show those in Indian Country how to assimilate into Euro-American Christian society.[64]

As his fellow Hampton alumni Thomas Wildcat Alford noted after his return from Indian boarding school in the East, his education had instilled in him a desire to impart some of the "good and pleasant things" learned under his Christian assimilationist schooling. Likewise, Jones desired to proselytize to his Sac and Fox family members, working as a missionary of sorts to disseminate the knowledge he had gained. Despite his passion to document and preserve the beliefs, languages, and histories of his Sac and Fox people and numerous other American Indian Nations, Jones nevertheless believed that the best way to combat the ills that befell Native peoples was to assimilate into the broader Euro-American society. Clearly, the doctrine of assimilation he received in the Indian boarding schools of his youth remained with him for the rest of his life.[65]

Like many of his fellow Native American anthropologists and collaborators, William Jones was a complicated individual. He was conflicted by his identity, hesitant to fully embrace or completely abandon either his Native or non-Native ancestry. In the end, he opted to try to balance the two. He fought to preserve a record of his people's words, thoughts, and deeds, while simultaneously trying to separate Native Americans from their past.

3

We as a Race Cannot Be Wiped Out in a Short Time

Richard Davis (Colony, Oklahoma Territory, 1905)

After discussing the idea at length with his fellow Southern Tsitsistas/
Suhtai (Cheyenne) leaders in the Oklahoma Territory town of Colony,
Richard Davis returned to his house that May night and began penning
a letter. Writing to his colleague and employer Dr. George A. Dorsey,
curator of anthropology at Chicago's Field Museum, Davis tried to find a
middle ground between begging and demanding that his people be able to
practice their religious beliefs. Community leaders wished to hold a Sun
Dance ceremony, he informed Dorsey, something local missionaries and
Bureau of Indian Affairs staff deemed savage and barbarous, and therefore
illegal. As far back as 1882 the federal government established the Courts
of Indian Offenses, banning the possession of Native religious objects and
the performance of dances or ceremonies. Although some reservation
agents were more lax than others about these "offenses," the official ban
still stood in 1905 when Davis sat down to write his letter.[1]

Davis knew all of this, of course. And he also knew that Dorsey and
numerous other anthropologists would jump at the chance to witness
such a rare ceremony. Not that most anthropologists were exactly champions of Native peoples' religious freedoms, but a few of them, such as
Dorsey at the Field Museum and James Mooney at the Smithsonian's
Bureau of American Ethnology, were at least sympathetic. Perhaps they
were motivated more out of intellectual curiosity and potential fodder
for their publications and exhibitions than out of pure altruism. But that
didn't mean Dorsey wouldn't go to bat against the reservation agents,
missionaries, and other federal representatives who tried to control every
detail of Native Americans' daily lives.

And that was just what Davis was counting on as he began writing.
Playing on Dorsey's desire to document all aspects of his peoples' reli-

gious and ceremonial life, Davis entreated Dorsey to witness the event. A prominent member of his community had pledged to perform the "Most Holy Lodge" or Sun Dance ceremony on June 30, 1905, Davis wrote, which was less than six weeks away. "All Indians desire your assistance," he urged, for with Dorsey and other leading anthropologists in attendance, Davis and his community members would not need to fear any interference on the part of reservation agents. Davis stressed this was a special invitation given from Southern Tsitsistas/Suhtai priests and chiefs to Dorsey, and that they required his protection to make it happen.[2]

Davis knew that he was using Dorsey, but such a thought didn't trouble him in the least. The way he figured it, anthropologists used Native peoples to get access to sacred information, and Native peoples likewise occasionally used anthropologists for their protection or as a mouthpiece in a Euro-American world that ignored or silenced non-Euro-American voices. In a way their relationship was symbiotic, though with a clear power imbalance that favored non-Natives. But sometimes such a relationship also paid off for Indigenous peoples. Davis also knew that Dorsey was never one to back down from a fight. The Field Museum anthropologist had previously encouraged members of the Northern Inunaina (Arapaho) Nation in Wyoming to hold their religious ceremonies, without waiting for permission from reservation agents and BIA officials. Aware of Dorsey's views on such matters, Davis hoped that the young anthropologist's presence at the Tsitsistas/Suhtai Sun Dance ceremony in the Oklahoma Territory that summer would have a similar effect.[3]

Stretching back from the table that doubled as his desk, Davis read his letter one more time, smiled to himself, and decided that the following day he would get the other leaders' signatures before mailing the request to Dorsey in Chicago. Although a member of a colonized group, Davis was by no means powerless. He knew how to work within the system and how to take advantage of the few paths to freedom open to him. This was simply one of those paths. At age thirty-eight that May night in 1905, Davis had spent nearly four decades walking the fine line between being pro- and anti-assimilationist. Sometimes he supported and sometimes he challenged the doctrine of Euro-American Christian assimilation touted in the halls of the U.S. Congress and enforced in Indian boarding schools. By 1905, though, over fifteen years removed from his Carlisle Indian Industrial School indoctrination, Davis had begun to embrace the culture and history of his early youth once again. No longer under the spell of Richard Henry Pratt and other assimilation advocates, Davis found that one of the best ways to embrace his Tsitsistas/Suhtai culture was through the performance and celebration of the Sun Dance.

Youth and the Agency School

Although ten years younger, Davis was from the same Southern Tsitsistas/ Suhtai community as his fellow Native anthropologist and collaborator Tichkematse. As discussed earlier, several Plains Indian communities including the Tsitsistas/Suhtai and Inunaina signed the Fort Laramie Treaty of 1851, agreeing to remain on lands that make up present-day portions of Wyoming and Colorado. Sixteen years later, in 1867, Richard Davis was born in Sand Creek on the Colorado Territory, only a short three years after U.S. Army troops massacred several hundred of his community members there. Not surprisingly, Davis carried a distrust of the federal government for the entirety of his life. Nevertheless, the same year of Richard's birth, his father, Bull Bear, a noted war chief of the Dog Soldiers, signed the Medicine Lodge Treaty of 1867. This treaty abandoned all claims to former western lands in exchange for over seven million acres in the Indian Territory of present-day Oklahoma.[4]

During the mid-1870s unrest grew among members of Native nations living in the Indian Territory due to the failure of beef contractors and others on the federal payroll to fulfil their obligations in delivering food to Indian reservations. By 1874 and 1875 the Red River War broke out between Native communities and U.S. Army soldiers, with Tichkematse one of the many innocent victims of colonial injustice. As when he signed the 1867 Medicine Lodge Treaty, in 1875 Richard Davis's father, Bull Bear, sought to avoid further conflict and again do what was best for the safety and well-being of his people. In March of that year, Bull Bear, along with several other Southern Tsitsistas/Suhtai leaders, surrendered to U.S. Army personnel. They were placed under guard, and their weapons were taken from them, as were their ponies, which were later sold by the army. According to the agent of the Cheyenne and Arapaho Reservation, by 1875 the Southern Tsitsistas/Suhtai had lost their former strength and been reduced to a half-starved and poverty-stricken people.[5]

Despite their wretched condition, Davis's family acknowledged that to survive and succeed in their changing world, they needed to learn the ways of Euro-Americans. Thus, when the U.S. government established the Arapaho Manual Labor and Boarding School on the reservation in early 1876, Bull Bear decided that Richard, his youngest son, should attend. Bull Bear stated that although he had raised his older sons to be warriors, he would give his youngest son to Washington for his education. According to Davis, it was at this point he left behind his blanket and his paint, becoming a student of those who sought to erase his culture. On his arrival at the reservation school, authorities there cut young Davis's hair and required him to dress "like a white-boy." Sadly, we don't know Davis's own thoughts from this time, whether he enjoyed or hated his attendance at the school. And even if he didn't want to attend the agency school, it is doubtful that nine-year-old Davis could successfully challenge his father's wishes. But in the coming years, Davis often remembered his boarding school days as something more akin to an opportunity rather than a hardship.[6]

Attending school irregularly between 1876 and 1879, Davis was surrounded by friends and family at the agency school. Among these was a young Southern Inunaina boy named Cleaver Warden, who would also go on to become a Native anthropologist and collaborator. As previously discussed, Indian boarding schools of this period combined classroom education and manual or vocational training, usually relating to the practice of agriculture. The Arapaho Manual Labor and Boarding School was no different, with the young students working a one-hundred-acre plot of land to grow corn and other vegetables for their meals. The boys also cut, chopped, and hauled wood for the school, while the girls received training in domestic arts. For their classroom education, the students learned reading, writing, and arithmetic. Their teacher, John Seger, encouraged friends from the East Coast to send him magazines, newspapers, and books to support Native youths in their reading and writing exercises. In this way, the Tsitsistas/Suhtai and Inunaina school children learned of events taking place in the wider world beyond their reservation.[7]

At Carlisle for the Long Haul

In the autumn of 1879 Richard Henry Pratt made the first of many recruiting trips to the Indian reservations of the West. There he sought to encourage

Native parents to entrust their children to his care in far-off Carlisle, Pennsylvania. At the school he promised that the children would receive an education in English reading and writing as well as learn a practical trade. His plan to systematically eradicate Native languages, beliefs, and practices was left unsaid. Writing later of his recruiting efforts, Pratt recorded that he had gathered fourteen girls and thirty-eight boys from Chaticks si Chaticks (Pawnee), Kiowa, and Southern Tsitsistas/Suhtai communities in the Indian Territory. Notably, all these early students were recruited to attend Carlisle with their parents' permission. More than a few of the children even volunteered to go, thinking that the experience would be a grand adventure. Of course, neither children nor their parents had a fair conception of what really awaited them at the far-off Indian boarding school in Pennsylvania. Few understood that Pratt's educational program was based on the complete eradication of all things Native.[8]

Like many parents who sent their children to Carlisle in its early years, Davis's father Bull Bear was a self-proclaimed follower of "the white man's road." He believed that it was beneficial for not just Richard to attend Pratt's Indian boarding school in the East, but for all of his children to do so. Subsequently, not only was thirteen-year-old Richard Davis packed off but so too was his twenty-year-old brother, Oscar. Although Richard's sisters Emma and Elsie remained on the reservation to attend the Arapaho Manual Labor and Boarding School, Elsie later joined Richard at Carlisle. Accompanying Richard and Oscar on their journey eastward were twenty-four other youths from the Cheyenne and Arapaho Agency, including the fifteen-year-old younger brother of Tichkematse. Departing October 9, 1879, the Southern Tsitsistas/Suhtai children journeyed by wagon 160 miles to the railroad, following the same route Tichkematse and the Fort Marion prisoners traveled only four years earlier.[9]

Although Richard Davis's thoughts on his departure are unknown, one of his contemporaries among the first class at Carlisle recorded his memories of leaving his family. Lined up on the shore of the Missouri River in the Dakota Territory, Luther Standing Bear recalled many Sicangu Lakota (Rosebud Sioux) parents crying, immediately causing the children to also cry. Despite volunteering to go to Carlisle, Standing Bear and the Native youths traveling with him still vented their fears and sorrow along the banks of the Missouri River that day. He later wrote that he thought their hearts might break at the overflow of tears on departing their homeland.[10]

The Carlisle Indian Industrial School officially opened on November 1, 1879. There were 147 Native students in attendance, thirteen-year-old Richard Davis among them. Davis's memories from these first days and nights in Carlisle are unknown, but his contemporary Luther Standing Bear again provided a vivid recollection of the struggles many children faced. Standing Bear wrote of the loneliness he felt, wishing he was back with his mother and father and riding free on his ponies. The thought of returning to his home in the West was ever present, as he constantly wondered how long he had to remain away. At home with his family young Standing Bear could eat when he wanted, sleep when he wanted, do what he wanted. But at Carlisle students had to comport themselves like U.S. Army soldiers. All male students received an issue of "western" clothing, had their hair cut, and received Anglicized first names to assimilate them into Euro-American society. Each day they wore their uniforms and had an inspection of their clothing, their hygiene, and their sleeping quarters. Punishments followed for those who rebelled against the strict military regimen Pratt demanded. The speaking of Native languages was foremost on the list of punishable offenses.[11]

One of the first Native Americans to enter the school's doors, Davis was also one of its longest-lasting students, spending much of the next fifteen years of his life there. Only one year after sending his children to Carlisle, Bull Bear wrote a letter to Pratt, complimenting him on the progress his sons had made. Bull Bear reminded Pratt that when the latter asked for children to attend his school, Bull Bear was the first to volunteer his own. Since that time his elder son Oscar had become a leader among his fellow students, and young Richard was learning fast—reading, writing, and speaking English well.[12]

Bull Bear further told Pratt he was happy he and his children were taking up "the white man's road." He thought it would be good for the Southern Tsitsistas/Suhtai people to send all their children to Carlisle for their education. He even suggested that his older son Oscar, a current student of Pratt's, could recruit more of the youths in their community. Though we are lacking Davis's feelings on attending both the Arapaho Manual Labor and Boarding School and later the Carlisle Indian Industrial School, this letter from his father shows he at least had some Euro-American assimilationist ways. Seeking to please his father, it is not surprising that within a short time of being at Carlisle Richard Davis too began to espouse the need for Native peoples to assimilate into Euro-American society.[13]

In early 1882 many of Davis's friends who accompanied him to the school in 1879 departed for their homes in the Indian Territory. Their three-year terms were up, and they were eager to return to their families. Davis, on the other hand, desired more schooling. He "turned his face toward the east instead of the west." When Bull Bear sent his children to Carlisle under Pratt's care, he wanted them to receive an education on "the white man's road." English language skills and Euro-American attitudes were his primary desire. But he also expected his children to return in approximately three years' time, as Pratt had promised. Because of this, in 1883 Bull Bear ordered Davis to return to the Cheyenne and Arapaho Agency. Though he wished to remain at Carlisle, sixteen-year-old Davis acceded to his father's demands, departing soon after receiving his father's letter. Accustomed to many of the niceties in Carlisle, Davis was discouraged to see the lack of so-called progress on the reservation. Depressed over the state of affairs in the Indian Territory, he begged his father to let him return to Carlisle to continue his education. Bull Bear eventually acquiesced to his son's wishes. After little more than a month away, Davis returned to Pratt's Indian boarding school.[14]

Back at Carlisle Davis excelled at his studies, becoming a star pupil. Nor was he alone in his good marks. Cleaver Warden, the same Southern Inunaina boy who studied alongside Davis at the Arapaho Manual Labor and Boarding School years earlier, soon joined him in Pennsylvania, arriving at Carlisle in September 1880. An article in the *Carlisle Weekly Herald* mentioned both young men participating in the school's annual examination, illustrating their mathematical skills with fractions and their oratorical abilities through public presentations. Savvy at advertising his assimilation success stories to the public, Pratt proudly pointed to Davis and Warden as examples of what Native peoples could accomplish after casting off the yoke of their Indigenous pasts.[15]

Integral to Pratt's assimilation program at Carlisle was the outing system. The genesis of this system arose years earlier when Pratt served as the jailor of Tichkematse and the Fort Marion prisoners. As described earlier, Pratt hired out the Native prisoners for labor projects in the St. Augustine area, encouraging the prisoners to keep the monetary proceeds of their work. Pratt's prison labor projects had the additional benefit of introducing the Indigenous prisoners to Euro-American social mores and practices. Thus, Pratt hoped the prisoners would become accustomed to the broader, largely non-Native, society, gradually assimilating into it.

In 1881 Pratt introduced this system to Carlisle students, literally hiring children out to local Pennsylvania farmers. There students lived and worked several months a year, performing manual labor on farms and in households. The students were out of school, away from the corrupting influence of other Native children who might cause them to backslide into their previous ways. In the overwhelmingly Euro-Christian Pennsylvania countryside Pratt hoped students would replace their Native languages and cultures with the languages, cultures, manners, and beliefs of those with whom they lived and worked. It is an understatement to note that the possibilities for physical and mental abuse of the children in this situation were rife.[16]

Native students were not compelled to be a part of the outing system at Carlisle in its early years. Rather, those interested made a formal request to Pratt for placement. When requesting placement in the outing system, students swore to obey their employers, termed "patrons." They also agreed to bathe regularly, to refrain from drinking, gambling, smoking, and to uphold themselves in a moral manner, even attending their patrons' churches. Fully aware of potential problems arising in these living situations, Pratt also interviewed patrons before placement. Additionally, Pratt required both the patron and the child laborer to send monthly reports, updating him on any problems. At the end of the term, which was usually three months in duration, the patron submitted a final report to Pratt on the child's "worth and conduct."[17]

Richard Davis fully embraced the outing system while at Carlisle. After Pratt first implemented this system in 1881, Davis requested and received placement six times during the seven summers he was eligible to do so. In fact, the only time he did not request an outing was during the summer of 1886 that he spent with family in the Indian Territory. Placed among a farmer by the name of Henry Kratz in Bucks County, Pennsylvania, for his first outing from June until September 1881, Davis received a stellar report by his patron. According to Kratz, Davis gave perfect satisfaction in every particular, with conduct deserving the kindest regards and highest praise. By age fifteen Davis was a vocal advocate of Euro-American Christian assimilation. According to his own account, he even voluntarily accepted baptism, becoming a member of the local Presbyterian church in Carlisle in 1882.[18]

In following years Davis again requested placement in the outing system, working as a laborer on various farms in Bucks, Montgomery, and Schuylkill Counties. He didn't work only on farms, however. In the summer of 1884 Davis worked for several months as a coachman in Philadelphia, exploring the large city at his leisure during his off-hours. At Carlisle during the school year he worked in the student printshop, setting type for the monthly student newspaper the *Morning Star* half of the day while attending classes the other half. By late 1887 Davis finished his classes, though didn't technically graduate, and continued working as an assistant disciplinarian under Pratt at Carlisle. In this role he mentored younger Native children, encouraging them to conform to Pratt's call for assimilation. He later proudly noted that he attained the rank of sergeant major in the school's student cadet battalion, enforcing compliance with Carlisle's military rigor.[19]

Sometime during his eight years of study at Carlisle, Davis met and pursued a romance with a young Chaticks si Chaticks woman named Nannie Aspenall. The daughter of John Aspenall, Nannie grew up in the Indian Territory and arrived at the school only a few years after Davis, in August 1882. Like Davis, she too requested placement in the school's outing system, doing domestic work on farms in rural Pennsylvania for three summers. Little exists in the school records of their early days together, but by March 1888 the two married at Carlisle. Feted by fellow students, the school's newspaper *Indian Helper* also celebrated their union.[20]

West Grove, Dairy Work, and Demands for Citizenship

Immediately after their wedding, Nannie and Richard moved to a farm in West Grove, Chester County, Pennsylvania. According to Davis, he and Nannie did not want to return to their reservations in the Indian Territory and instead stayed in the East among "civilized people." There in West Grove the two obtained room and board with a Quaker farmer named

William Harvey. Harvey raised cattle and pigs and maintained a dairy on his property, with Davis in charge of the latter. Davis rose each morning at four a.m., and his work was arduous but something he fully enjoyed. Over the three years from 1888 until 1891 the Davis family grew to include two daughters—Richenda and Mary. Despite the larger family, all four of them continued to live on William Harvey's property in West Grove.[21]

During these years Davis kept in close contact with Richard Henry Pratt back at Carlisle. The Davises even visited their former boarding school on a few occasions, including attending the 1889 commencement ceremonies. On his end Pratt regularly held the Davis family up as the ultimate example of what assimilation could do—and Nannie and Richard were quick to agree with him. As Davis wrote Pratt in a December 1890 letter, they were glad to be seen as representatives and were anxious to demonstrate to the public the good results of Carlisle.[22]

Echoing the assimilation doctrine Pratt instilled in his students, Davis often gave public talks about the good that assimilation and citizenship could do for Native peoples. According to Pratt, Davis spoke knowingly of his "former savage habits" but despised these practices. Davis said as much himself in the Carlisle student newspaper when he returned from his 1886 visit to the Indian Territory. To fellow students he wrote how the inhabitants of the Cheyenne and Arapaho Reservation were pulled down by their religion and their medicine dances. He optimistically opined, however, that they would soon see the way, noting he and his fellow Carlisle students would help guide them through assimilation on "the white man's road."[23]

Consumed by thoughts of citizenship and striving to separate himself from being a dependent ward of the United States government, Davis wrote in 1888 of never wanting to draw rations on a reservation. Working for Harvey in West Grove instilled a great deal of confidence in himself and his abilities. Davis wrote of wanting to support his family independent of government support. During this same period Pennsylvania newspapers lauded him for his many calls for the abandonment of Indigenous sovereignty and communal ownership of Native land. His words and actions here echo almost word for word Pratt's own assimilation pronouncements from his office in nearby Carlisle.[24]

Learning about Davis's pro-assimilationist rhetoric during these years is undeniably troubling to read today. Clearly he was under the spell of Pratt, whom the younger man saw as a charismatic ersatz father figure. The arrogance of youth also played some role. Davis was proud of his accomplishments at Carlisle—his good grades, his work on the student newspaper, his fluency in English, and his rank in the school's cadet battalion. These things separated him from the bulk of other Native youths living in Indian Country. They made him feel better and smarter. Importantly, though, perhaps Davis was also displaying a form of "doubleness," passing among Euro-American Christian society by repeating the words he knew his audience wanted to hear.[25]

Back to Carlisle

While the Davis family was generally happy at West Grove, they also missed the companionship they had come to know during their boarding school days. And after more than three years away, they desired to go back. Davis wrote to Pratt in May 1891, informing the older man that if Carlisle produced a dairy and creamery on a larger scale, he wanted to be the one to run it. Davis continued, telling Pratt he was willing to do anything for the Carlisle Indian Industrial School—the institution that had already given him so much. Eager to reunite with his star pupil, Pratt moved some things around, and by November 1891 the Davis family returned to Carlisle.[26]

Starting in late 1891 and continuing until 1894, Richard, Nannie, and their growing family lived and worked on the Carlisle property. Davis was the school's dairy manager, starting at a monthly pay of $36 his first year and gradually increasing to $48 per month or $576 annually by 1894. While little money comparatively, the pay at Carlisle was considerably more than he had initially received under William Harvey in West Grove. Further, as far as Richard and Nannie were concerned, at Carlisle they had the benefit of again being surrounded by their friends and family. Pratt later wrote to the commissioner of Indian affairs that Davis was well fitted to the work and that his management of the school's large dairy herd was most gratifying.[27]

So enamored was Pratt with Davis that the older man invited the twenty-four-year-old former student to accompany him and the Carlisle children to perform in the Columbus Day Parade festivities in New York in October 1892, despite the fact that Davis was no longer a student at Carlisle and had not been one for the past four years. The parade commemorated Columbus's 1492 voyage and "discovery" of the Americas. Lacking sources, we don't know the Native participants' feelings on being involved in this event. Were they upset that they had to take part, or perhaps ashamed to be involved in such a celebration? Already indoctrinated into Pratt's belief system, no doubt many of these students spouted the benefits of assimilation, just as Davis was doing at this time.

On October 10, 1892, 322 students from the Carlisle Indian Industrial School marched New York City's parade route, beginning at Fifty-First Street and culminating near Washington Square. Included in this number were 52 Native girls and 270 Native boys. The boys were dressed in standard dark blue military-style uniforms, with each child carrying a small American flag to display their patriotism. At the head of the Carlisle contingent were three representatives with a large banner—Davis at the lead, flanked by two young Native boys. The banner proudly proclaimed the name of the school, accompanied by the motto "Into Civilization and Citizenship." Davis and over three hundred Carlisle students, all boys, would repeat this same procession ten days later in Chicago. Invited to be part of the Windy City's own Columbus Day Parade, Pratt, Davis, and the selected students agreed to go. Davis again marched at the head of the group, proudly holding the Carlisle banner aloft for all to see.[28]

Of course, not all Native Americans took the same pro-assimilationist stance that Davis did during the Columbus Day celebrations of 1892. When the Chicago World's Fair opened the following year to commemorate Columbus's voyage, Simon Pokagon, chief of the Pokagon Band of Potawatomi people of Michigan, was one of the most vocal of the numerous individuals upset by the fair's representation of the Indigenous peoples of North America. He was an elder by the time of the 1893 World's Fair, and Chicago newspapers labeled him the only man who had seen the Columbian Exposition and didn't approve of it. As a form of protest, Pokagon published a short work titled *Red Man's Rebuke* printed on birch bark that he sold to fair visitors. Styling himself the spokesperson for American Indians everywhere, Pokagon wrote in his *Rebuke*, "I hereby declare to you, the pale-faced race that has usurped our lands and homes, that we have no spirit to celebrate with you the great Columbian Fair now being held."[29]

In scathing language, Pokagon declared Columbus's "discovery" of America, what non-Native peoples considered a joyous event, to be the collective funeral of American Indians. "Your hearts in admiration rejoice over the beauty and grandeur of this young republic," he chided his readers, reminding them their success had been at the sacrifice of Indigenous homes and "a once happy race."[30] Lamenting the absence of Native voices included in the world's fair, in October 1893 Pokagon wrote a letter to Chicago's mayor that was later published in city newspapers. In this letter he stated that American Indians wished to speak for themselves, not to have their cultures and lifeways represented by non-Native outsiders. Though many Chicago fairgoers knew nothing of his protest, Pokagon's forceful language sounded an early call for equality for the diverse and underrepresented peoples of the United States.[31]

After a few days spent in Chicago admiring the grandeur of the Columbus Day celebrations of which they were a part, Davis, Pratt, and the gathered boarding school students returned to Pennsylvania. It was also during these years living back at Carlisle from 1891 to 1894 that Davis reunited with old friends as well as his young sister Elsie, who came to Carlisle as a student in 1890 while Davis was living in West Grove. Though further information is lacking, we know Elsie died in July 1893 at age sixteen from tuberculosis. Her remains were buried in the school cemetery rather than returned to her family. According to school records, Elsie's body and those of all the other 185 Carlisle students who died at the school between 1880 and 1918 were dug up and reinterred in a new cemetery in the early twentieth century to make way for a building project. At present, Elsie's remains still rest in Carlisle, more than 1,300 miles from those of her family. How Davis reacted to his sister's death away from her homeland is unknown.[32]

Return to the Oklahoma Territory

Less than a year after his sister's death, Davis received a job offer taking him and his young family back to the Indian Territory, now renamed the Oklahoma Territory. Three years prior, in 1891, the U.S. government introduced allotment to the people living on the Cheyenne and Arapaho

Agency. The goal of the allotment system was to "civilize" Native peoples, forcing them to embrace small-scale subsistence agriculture through the dismantling of communal land ownership. The results were disastrous. After twelve months of living under the allotment system, the Southern Tsitsistas/Suhtai and Inunaina peoples retained only about 6 percent of their former reservation lands. The rest was held in trust by the federal government and U.S. military. In 1892 colonial authorities opened the former Cheyenne and Arapaho Reservation territory to a public land rush. Thirty thousand non-Native settler colonizers invaded and claimed the land within hours. Additional land seekers, eager to swindle Native peoples out of their remaining territory, followed soon after. This is the scene Richard, Nannie, and their young family encountered on their return home.[33]

Relocating to the small town of Arapaho in the Oklahoma Territory in the summer of 1894, Davis happily began his new career as a Bureau of Indian Affairs–appointed "additional farmer" of his former agency. He saw himself as an advocate for change, hoping to teach fellow community members the good things learned during his years away in the East. However, disillusionment with Carlisle's teachings about assimilation and allotment quickly set in. For years Christian educators, reformers, and missionaries championed such policies in the halls of Congress. They argued allotment would civilize American Indians by eradicating communal ownership of land, thus transforming everyone into successful individual farmers. Instead of benefits, however, Davis saw only the greed of Euro-American settler colonizers eager to cheat Native peoples out of their federally allotted acreage.[34]

One year after taking on his role as additional farmer, Davis wrote Pratt at Carlisle complaining that many of his people were in a lower and poorer condition than before allotment. Still reticent to criticize the federal government's policies, Davis instead charged that "certain whites" in the local area were the problem. These men feigned friendship, Davis wrote, but ultimately sought to cheat Southern Tsitsistas/Suhtai people out of their lands. What Davis saw were land seekers metaphorically "skinning Indians to the bones," while the federal government simply turned a blind eye. Witnessing such a charade only further fanned the flames of Davis's resentment against a blatantly racist and unjust system.[35]

Although his role as additional farmer was short-lived, Davis nevertheless still saw himself as a voice for his people. In his immediate post-Carlisle years in particular, he considered himself a progressive voice, pushing assimilation and Western-style education over community traditions. Writing Pratt in November 1895, Davis informed him that many of the leading chiefs of the community wanted Davis and other "educated Indians" to lead the rest, teaching them what was best for their people. How much Davis's community actually accepted him is difficult to ascertain, but certainly not all Southern Tsitsistas/Suhtai agreed with his push for assimilation.[36]

Notwithstanding his optimistic messages to Pratt, as time passed, Davis's disillusionment grew. Lack of job prospects and practical use of the skills learned at Carlisle only increased these feelings. By 1901 Davis accepted a position as a gardener and night watchman at the local agency school. This job not only paid little but made no use of Davis's education and skills. Nevertheless, Davis still refused to deviate from many of the Carlisle teachings drilled into him in his youth. For instance, in 1900 Davis and his family chose to live in a permanent Western-style house rather than a moveable tipi like many of their neighbors. Additionally, he refused to speak the Tsitsistas/Suhtai language with his family, even compelling his young children to speak only in English. Such actions mirrored his own experiences at Carlisle years earlier. So entrenched was Davis in the assimilationist mindset that around this same time he wrote a letter to Pratt, seeking the older man's aid in finding appropriate schooling for his daughters. Davis specifically noted that he wished for them to attend an English-speaking school like Carlisle, congratulating himself on thus far keeping them from learning their Native language.[37]

Beginning of Anthropological Fieldwork

Despite his stubborn refusal to abandon the racist and assimilationist teachings received at Carlisle, there was also a growing tendency during these years for Davis to embrace his culture and the beliefs of his people. As early as 1898 Davis attended the Omaha World's Fair, where he worked as an interpreter for other Southern Tsitsistas/Suhtai peoples on exhibition. At this time Davis was not yet a "Show Indian," the name Native peoples called those who performed in Wild West shows and similar venues. Nevertheless, Davis agreed to pose for a series of photographs taken by Smithsonian Institution employees and the general public at the Omaha fair. Changing out of his normal wear, he posed in buckskin clothing and received a small amount of money for doing so. Although such an action does not sound overly scandalous, it was certainly taken that way by Davis's Native and non-Native peers out east. Word of his actions spread quickly through the Carlisle student newspaper. Therein Davis and other former pupils were called out for attending the Omaha fair's Indian Congress and participating in its related sham battles. While not under the name of Buffalo Bill's Wild West, the Indian Congress and associated battles were of a similar nature. For Pratt, who held Davis up as a shining example of an assimilated, educated Native product of the Carlisle Indian Industrial School, it was a damning blow. Even worse, it was a sign that Davis was slipping back into "primitive" ways.[38]

Lacking Davis's perspective on why he chose to be a part of the Omaha World's Fair, we can surmise that it was partly based on financial need. The real-world applicability of skills learned in Indian boarding schools for former students returned to western reservations was virtually nil. Many of the trades they had learned were either irrelevant or already filled by settler colonizers who flocked to these areas. Davis tried again and again in Pennsylvania and later in the Oklahoma Territory to make a good living at his agricultural skills, all to little avail.

It is not surprising then that when opportunities arose that promised decent pay, even those antithetical to the assimilationist rhetoric of his boarding school days, Davis eventually agreed to take such positions. And one of the leading fields that was willing to pay was anthropology. Museum anthropologists eagerly sought individuals such as Davis to work with them as collaborators, employing Native men, and sometimes women, to provide information and collect objects from their communities. Recent Indian boarding school students were ideal candidates for these positions, provided they could disregard the anti-Native sentiments drilled into them at school. Former students possessed fluency in English, and because they were Indigenous people, they could often gain access to cultural information that non-Native anthropologists could not. As Davis was one of these ideal collaborators, anthropologists lost little time in snatching him up once he was on their radar.[39]

As early as 1901 Davis took on anthropological fieldwork, interpreting for George A. Dorsey from the Field Museum and James Mooney from the Smithsonian's BAE. Both men had an interest in southern plains Native communities and, in particular, Sun Dance ceremonies. Whether motivated simply by money or by a desire to document his own culture, Davis located knowledgeable elders to share information and for whom he would interpret. According to Dorsey and Mooney, Davis worked for both men, collecting information on the Sun Dance beginning in 1901 and continuing to do so through at least 1905.[40]

In the summer of 1903 Davis provided vocabulary information on the Tsitsistas/Suhtai language to Mooney, while simultaneously creating richly colored illustrations of the Sun Dance for Dorsey. While working with anthropologists to document his community's language, Davis ironically prevented his daughters from speaking their own Native language at home. Examples like this illustrate the contradictory world many Native anthropologists and collaborators inhabited. Although they often gravitated toward anthropological work, many of them like Davis struggled to balance their appreciation for their own cultures with assimilation doctrines that encouraged them to abandon everything that made them Native.[41]

Around this time Davis learned about WJ McGee's appointment as the Anthropology Department chair at the upcoming 1904 St. Louis World's Fair. For years McGee was the deputy director of the Smithsonian's BAE, nominally reporting to Director John Wesley Powell, but in reality serving as the bureau's ultimate decision-maker during the older man's final years of ill health. Born in 1853, McGee gained prominence in the late nineteenth century as a leader in the rapidly professionalizing field of anthropology. His wife, no less than himself, also played a major role in popularizing anthropology. Anita McComb McGee was one of the first women in the nation's capital to earn her medical degree and in partnership with BAE anthropologist Matilda Coxe Stevenson founded the Women's Anthropological Society. Due to McGee's experience in the anthropological field and his connections to high society, Missouri governor David R. Francis selected the BAE anthropologist as chair of anthropology at the St. Louis fair. When Davis learned of McGee's new role, he lost no time in writing to the older man and requesting a paid position at the event.[42]

As Davis was well aware, world's fairs at the turn of the twentieth century were huge money-making endeavors. They offered temporary work for many people who couldn't otherwise find gainful employment. For Native American women and men barely able to eke out a living on reservations, exhibiting oneself at a world's fair became an alternative source of income. Playing on this idea, Davis penned a letter to McGee in March 1902. His letter began with a simple inquiry into the possibility of including a few American Indian nations as part of the exhibit. Using language he knew appealed to McGee's pro-assimilationist worldview, Davis wrote of the benefits that Native peoples would experience by bringing them into contact with the latest that Euro-American society had to offer. Davis argued that at a world's fair they would learn more in a few months' time than in fifty years spent on an allotment or reservation, where Native peoples were confined by reservation agents and did not see much of the world. Davis's ever-savvy words echoed McGee's often-repeated statements that "less advanced" peoples such as Native Americans greatly benefited from association with those "more advanced." As he had in the past and would continue to do in the future, Davis used the means at his disposal to help himself and his people. If he had to humble himself to leave the reservation and earn some money at the fair, then so be it.[43]

In beautiful handwriting that belied his anger, Davis also wrote McGee about his resentment toward those who sought to erase his culture and history. After recounting the accolades of his father, Bull Bear, leader of the Southern Tsitsistas/Suhtai Dog Soldiers, Davis lamented to the BAE anthropologist that he and a few elderly men were the last surviving members of this society. If certain missionaries, educators, and BIA officials had their way, Davis argued, his way of life would soon be over. Some of these people thought it better if Native Americans simply went extinct, Davis posited, rather than allow Indigenous nations to compete with Euro-American society. Responding to this attempted cultural genocide, Davis declared that although U.S. politicians and religious leaders might succeed in eradicating tribal laws, Native American peoples as a race could not be wiped out in such a short time. In a way, Davis figured, even though anthropological exhibits at world's fairs reproduced many racist stereotypes of American Indians typical of the day, they also provided the opportunity for him and other Native leaders to assert their own voices, ultimately exhibiting the beauty and resilience of their people.[44]

Despite being fully aware that bigoted interactions such as these surely awaited him at the fair, Davis nevertheless appealed to WJ McGee to be included. His stratagem worked, and when the St. Louis World's Fair opened to the public in April 1904, Davis and many of his family and friends were there. Of the more than three hundred Native Americans who took part in the fair's Indian Village, members of Davis's Southern Tsitsistas/Suhtai community were included, as were the friends and relatives of a few of his fellow Native collaborators. Cleaver Warden, Davis's former Southern Inunaina classmate from Carlisle, attended with his wife Eva and son George, as did James R. Murie, a Chaticks si Chaticks collaborator already well-known among anthropologists, accompanied by his wife Mary and their four children. And, of course, Davis was there too, escaping at least temporarily the ever-watchful gaze of the reservation agents and BIA staff in the Oklahoma Territory. With him were his wife, Nannie, their five daughters, and their two young sons, Roy and Henry. Alongside members of fifteen other Indigenous nations from across North America, these women, men, and children sought more than simply a change of scenery from reservation life and a small bit of money. They each strove to represent the beauty and complexity of their unique cultures against a concerted national effort to eliminate the very things which made them unique.[45]

Despite their willingness to put their lives and their families on display for the edification of fairgoers, by the time the St. Louis World's Fair closed in December 1904, much of the U.S. public continued to view Native peoples as savage, ignorant, and lazy. His experiences at the St. Louis fair and in the years since Carlisle made Davis angry. He was angry at a world where men with landed interests cheated Native peoples out of the pitiful plots of earth left to them. And in the spring and summer of 1905 he was angry at missionaries and BIA staff who arbitrarily determined that his religious practices and the religious practices of his Tsitsistas/Suhtai ancestors from time immemorial were now considered illegal. And so he wrote his letter that May night of 1905 to George A. Dorsey.

Unfortunately, Dorsey was unable to attend the Southern Tsitsistas/ Suhtai Sun Dance in the summer of 1905. However, the Sun Dance itself still took place, despite a host of threats from reservation agents and missionaries. Davis, as he had done over the past several years, documented this sacred ceremony of his people.

Working alongside Dorsey in the Midwest's preeminent natural history museum, Davis collected stories from community elders. Like other Native anthropological collaborators of his day, he also purchased material culture objects for museum acquisition and witnessed, participated in, and wrote about his people's ceremonies and secret societies. In 1905 the Field Museum published his collaborative research with Dorsey in two parts, *The Cheyenne: Ceremonial Organization* and *The Cheyenne: Sun Dance*, complete with color illustrations of ceremonies drawn by Davis.

From today's vantage point it is difficult to determine Davis's reasons for agreeing to make public his community's sacred beliefs and practices. Assuredly some of it was based on financial need to help care for his large family. But no doubt a greater motivating factor was his desire to provide accurate and reliable information from an actual Southern Tsitsistas/Suhtai person rather than relying solely on non-Native anthropologists' partial understandings. Interestingly, several decades later Davis explained why he aided non-Native anthropologists in this type of work. Writing a book manuscript left unpublished at the time of his death, Davis wrote that he never explained to Dorsey and Mooney the full meaning of the rites they witnessed. According to him, he did this because he was adhering to tribal law that any non-Tsitsistas/Suhtai person seeking knowledge of these ceremonies must first go to a priest-chief. This Dorsey and Mooney did not do, and they did not know to do so. Davis argued that though the two men ate with the Southern Tsitsistas/Suhtai, slept in their tipis, and learned their songs and language, when it came to the meaning of sacred ceremonies, they did not follow protocol but instead offered money to gain information. Because of this, Davis offered only partial facts, not full explanations. These teachings were sacred to him and his community. They were not meant for the eyes and ears of non-Tsitsistas/Suhtai people and thus were withheld from the anthropologists. According to Davis, while he and his fellow community members appreciated the valuable contributions these anthropologists made in recording and preserving their culture and history, the two men were little more than welcome guests, and by that designation, they were privy to only partial knowledge.[46]

Transition to "Show Indian" and Performer

By 1906 the Field Museum's Anthropology Department began to change the focus of its collecting activities. For Dorsey and the museum's board of directors, American Indians weren't as much of a draw as they formerly had been. This is the same period Dorsey hired Sac and Fox anthropologist William Jones, directing him to fieldwork in the Philippines rather than the United States. Whether museum audiences in Chicago were still interested in Native Americans didn't really matter, at least for Davis. What mattered was that his employer unceremoniously ended their working relationship. Now Davis needed to find a new source of income.

In the months following the 1905 Sun Dance ceremony, Davis wrote Dorsey seeking additional anthropological fieldwork and advice. He noted that he currently had no gainful employment. His individual allotment was improved and rented to German American farmers, which fortunately provided some income. With that money, he told Dorsey, he could choose to simply lay around, as many of his fellows were doing, but Davis didn't want that. He wanted to do something besides "just drawing lease money" on his property. He was interested in any anthropological work that Dorsey might be able to offer, but if there was none, he did have another prospect—working as a "Show Indian" with a traveling group of Native performers.[47]

An unnamed gentleman from England had recently visited several Native reservations, Davis informed Dorsey, recruiting specifically among Oglala Lakota (Oglala Sioux) and Tsitsistas/Suhtai communities to join him in London the following year. All expenses and travel would be paid, the man had promised, along with a standard contract rate of $65 per month. With no other offers forthcoming, Davis was interested in the opportunity, but he wanted to hear back from Dorsey first regarding further anthropological work. Responding a few days later, Dorsey informed Davis that unfortunately there was no fieldwork for him in the immediate future due to the change in the Field Museum's priorities. Because of this, he encouraged Davis to take the opportunity to travel to England as a Native performer. Dorsey, having recently traveled to Europe himself, thought it would be a great undertaking for the thirty-eight-year-old Tsitsistas/Suhtai man to see wonderful things away from the Oklahoma Territory. While it is unclear if

Davis accepted the offer to travel to England the following year, this was the start of his life as a performer and Show Indian. Such work consumed the next several years of his life, eventually leading him to the West Coast, where he pursued a career in the nascent film industry.[48]

By the second decade of the twentieth century, the written record of Davis's life becomes a bit muddied. He signed on as a Show Indian for the 1911 season of the Miller Brothers 101 Ranch Real Wild West, a competitor of Buffalo Bill's more popular Wild West show, where his performances mirrored those of the originator and are worth a brief mention. No stranger to entertaining the public, William F. "Buffalo Bill" Cody opened the first Wild West show in Omaha, Nebraska, in 1883. Within four years the fame of the Wild West grew so great that Cody took his fellow performers on an international tour of Europe in 1887. Throughout its more than thirty-year existence, Cody's Wild West again and again promoted inaccurate views of Native Americans, defining "real Indians" as only those who lived in tipis, rode horses, and wore feather headdresses. Due in part to the large number of individuals Cody hired out of Pine Ridge, South Dakota, Wild West audiences grew to identify the Oglala Lakota as the "prototypical" American Indians.[49]

Along with their stereotyped portrayal of Native Americans, Cody and his partners also maintained that they gave the public a remarkably accurate idea of life on the plains. Whether accurate or not, though, for millions of people around the world Cody's representations of the American West became a reality. Seeking to legitimate their performances through an association with the scientific field, Cody's Wild West also billed itself as an "Ethnological" and "Anthropological Congress," just as P. T. Barnum had done in the previous half century.[50]

Building on the popularity of Cody's Wild West, the Miller Brothers 101 Ranch Real Wild West imitated these stereotyped portrayals. Operating from 1906 to 1931, the Miller Brothers outlasted Cody's show by more than a decade. Beginning in the Oklahoma Territory, the Ranch Real Wild West toured the globe, employing a staff of more than 150 Native American performers recruited primarily from South Dakota and Oklahoma. Native performances included buffalo hunts, dances, battle scenes, and, when they were not performing, an "Indian Village" for the public to walk through. The latter was something Davis and many of the

Show Indians were already familiar with from their days on display in world's fairs.[51]

In January 1911 Davis sent a letter to the Miller Brothers, recommending himself and Walter Battice, a Sac and Fox man and former Hampton Institute boarding school student, to join the show's coming season. According to Davis, they were both prepared with the finest Indian outfits and Indian wigs, with Davis even owning an eagle feather headdress he had worn years earlier in performances in Chicago and at New York's Coney Island. The eldest of the Miller Brothers, Joseph, agreed to sign them on. By April Davis and Battice were marching in the opening-day parade in Washington DC. The following September they performed in the Oklahoma Territory with their friends and family members watching.[52]

Although we lack Davis's own words from his days with the Miller Brothers 101 Ranch Real Wild West, other Show Indians often left recollections of their experiences. Luther Standing Bear, for instance, the same Sicangu Lakota man who attended Carlisle alongside Davis, also worked as a Show Indian. He recalled that in their free time he and other Show Indians often talked of home, particularly how much they missed the foods they loved. They spoke nostalgically of wild peppermint tea, fry bread, and chokecherry soup. Standing Bear noted that while they had plenty to eat as performers, none of it was prepared "Indian style," the way they were used to. No doubt Davis, too, missed food from home and the companionship of his family while traveling with the Miller Brothers.[53]

What Davis received in abundance during these years was criticism. As always, there were many who disapproved of Native peoples performing in Wild West shows and at world's fairs, seeing it as a backward step on the road to supposed progress and assimilation. Carlisle's Richard Henry Pratt, ever eager to voice his displeasure, complained of Western-educated American Indians such as Davis misrepresenting Native peoples. In the press Pratt attacked anthropologists and Wild West show leaders such as Buffalo Bill Cody and the Miller Brothers. He argued any events wherein American Indians received money to paint their faces and dress in "primitive costumes" brought discredit upon their educated counterparts, deceiving the public regarding Native Americans generally. Both Davis and Cleaver Warden, as former students of Pratt at Carlisle, incurred his enmity for participating in such performances.[54]

Illustrative of the larger debate over Native assimilation into Euro-American society was the ongoing war of words between Pratt and BAE anthropologist WJ McGee. Firing the initial salvo on July 4, 1902, Pratt penned an editorial in Carlisle Indian Industrial School's newspaper, the *Red Man and Helper*. Pratt argued anthropologists studied Native Americans because they were different from non-Native peoples. If American Indians assimilated into mainstream society, Pratt posited, they would lose their Native identities, and anthropologists their source of income. McGee, never one to back down from a slight, responded with a repudiation of Pratt's charge. He argued he and other anthropologists did not oppose the education of American Indians but simply wished to document the old arts, beliefs, and customs of Native peoples before they disappeared.[55]

Two years later the two irascible opponents were at it again. In the February 12, 1904, issue of the *Red Man and Helper*, Pratt claimed anthropologists persuaded Native Americans to adhere to and exaggerate their former lifeways. McGee responded with a detailed list of his and other anthropologists' efforts to raise American Indians to the lofty place of U.S. citizenship. However, calling into question the educational methods of BIA agents, Indian boarding school teachers, and Christian missionaries, McGee retorted that anthropologists preferred to do so constructively rather than destructively, through knowledge rather than ignorance, through sympathy rather than intolerance. Finally, in scathing language McGee declared that if Pratt did not print a retraction of his most recent libel, McGee would deem him a pusillanimous slanderer. No further correspondence exists between the two men, and there is no evidence that Pratt ever issued a retraction.[56]

Non-Native critics such as Pratt were hardly the only ones upset over Native American participation in world's fairs and Wild West shows. Many Western-educated and primarily non-reservation Native American women and men who formed the Society of American Indians (SAI) also voiced their displeasure. This organization was notable as the first national Native American advocacy group in the United States. Among others, its members included Arthur C. Parker and Gertrude Simmons Bonnin, the latter a former employee of Pratt's at Carlisle. In addition to challenging BIA domination of Native American life on and off of reservations, many SAI members were highly critical of anthropologists and

Wild West performers. They believed the latter two groups perpetuated stereotypes of American Indians as backward, rather than individuals worthy of citizenship.[57]

Chauncey Yellow Robe, an SAI member and Carlisle graduate of Sicangu Lakota heritage, was notable for his denunciation of Wild West shows. He wrote in the SAI's *Quarterly Journal* of the degrading, demoralizing, and degenerating aspects of these performances. Expounding on the commercializing of American Indian peoples, Yellow Robe accused Wild West showmen of representing Native Americans as "savage" beings. Arthur C. Parker, a Seneca museum anthropologist who formerly worked with the Peabody Museum's Frederic Ward Putnam, likewise railed against Wild West shows for deceiving the public. In addition to compelling Native peoples to "act the white man's idea of an Indian," Parker believed such performances lumped all North American Indigenous nations into one monolithic group, deluding the public into believing that every American Indian, regardless of Native community, "wears the Sioux war bonnet." None of these criticisms were new to Davis during the early years of the twentieth century. He had already heard them during his days with various world's fairs and the Miller Brothers 101 Ranch Real Wild West, and he would soon hear them again as he took a new direction as a Native performer on stage and screen.[58]

Mademoiselle Toona's Indian Grand Opera Company

Equally displeasing to both his Native and non-Native critics, in the years following his Miller Brothers work Davis moved ever further from the assimilationist doctrines taught at Carlisle in his youth. While a clear paper trail is difficult to locate, we know that by 1913 Davis was working for a traveling American Indian Grand Opera Company. Embracing the name Chief Thunder Bird, Davis toured the country under the management of a non-Native woman named Mathilde A. Coutts-Johnstone, also known as Mademoiselle or Madame Toona in the press. Coutts-Johnstone was born in Colorado half a century earlier and, along with her younger sister Mary, had worked as a music, piano, and voice instructor with limited financial success. By the second decade of the twentieth century, though, Coutts-Johnstone hit upon a new marketing idea that promised great success. She hired talented Native Americans, gave them voice lessons, and had them perform Italian operatic pieces on stage dressed in Native clothing. Audiences went crazy for it.

Letters from Davis record the frenzied pace of the opera company staff. Traveling back and forth across the country, they regularly performed in Los Angeles one week, and then Chicago, Pittsburgh, or Baltimore only days later. Newspaper reviewers applauded the novelty of Indigenous peoples singing opera, variously referring to the show as instructive, artistic, interesting, and extraordinary. In addition to operatic pieces, Toona's Indian Company performed pieces more common to Native vaudeville troupes at the time, namely American Indian songs and dances.[59]

Odd as it may sound today, the distinction between anthropology and show business often blurred for Native American collaborators in the early twentieth century. As Davis's situation illustrates, it was not much of a leap between interpreting for Native peoples at a Sun Dance and interpreting at world's fairs or even Wild West shows. From there, Davis discovered he had a knack as a Show Indian and stage performer. He subsequently pursued such work—one of the few jobs in his entire life that promised a decent income. Nor was Davis alone among Native anthropologists and collaborators in choosing this work. As previously discussed, both Cleaver Warden and James R. Murie also exhibited themselves and their families in the Indian villages constructed at world's fairs.

Approximately the same time Davis performed with Mademoiselle Toona's act, another notable anthropological couple soon followed in his footsteps. Chilkat Tlingit wife and husband anthropology team Florence and Louis Shotridge also walked the fine line between Native stage performers and anthropologists. In the years before they officially began as employees of the University of Pennsylvania Anthropology Museum, the Shotridges worked with a Los Angeles–based Indian Crafts Exposition and later also worked for Mademoiselle Toona's Indian Grand Opera Company. Definitive records are difficult to locate, but the Shotridges and Davis may have even briefly overlapped in their work for this touring company.

With so many Native individuals willing to become entertainers during these years, questions of representation and intent inevitably arise. How much of a role did Richard Davis, Cleaver Warden, James R. Murie, the Shotridges, and other Native performers have in constructing or perpetuating stereotyped images of Indigenous peoples? As some scholars have noted, we also need to ask to what extent were Native people in show business actively pushing back against these negative stereotypes? Lamentably, many Wild West shows and theater performances of this era promoted the idea of manifest destiny and the conquest of North America's Indigenous nations by Euro-American settler colonizers. All too often the options for Native entertainers were either perform or not get paid. Importantly, though, many within the scholarly community have wisely pointed out that Native entertainers should not be viewed as helpless victims. In many cases these individuals found ways to resist the racism and oppression daily confronting them. In fact, for Davis, Luther Standing Bear, and other survivors of Indian boarding schools, the very act of performing in Native dress in Wild West shows, in world's fairs, and on stage was a form of resistance against the assimilationist doctrines forced upon them in their youth.[60]

As noted, Davis and other Native collaborators sought to work alongside non-Native anthropologists in documenting their cultures and preserving their tangible and intangible information for future generations. Through their anthropological fieldwork, Davis and other Native collaborators worked to show the complexity, diversity, and beauty of their histories and cultures. In so doing they battled against racist and monolithic views of Native peoples as primitive or savage. In many ways, too, their performances with vaudeville troupes, at world's fairs, and in Wild West shows literally served as stages on which they could do more of the same, publicizing to the world at large the beauty of their own communities.[61]

California and the Transition to Film

By 1913 Davis's stage and film career began to take off. He had already been involved with some of the biggest names in Wild West–style entertainment, and with Mademoiselle Toona's Indian Company he toured the nation as an in-demand singer and entertainer. His personal life and relationship with Nannie and the children back in Oklahoma, however, did not fare as well. What occurred between Nannie and Richard to end their twenty-five-year marriage is not recorded. But by 1920 Nannie was divorced and still living in Oklahoma raising their three youngest children. Davis, on the other hand, lived in Long Beach, California. In the census of that year he listed himself as an actor, boarding in the home of his former employer, Mathilde A. Coutts-Johnstone or Mademoiselle Toona. Living alongside Davis and Mathilde in the house on East First Street in Long Beach was Mathilde's younger sister Mary. Within months Mary Johnstone and Richard Davis married. The two would spend the rest of their lives together in Pasadena, California, with Mathilde living only streets away. The two sisters, admirers and champions of Davis, encouraged him as he pursued his entertainment career, transitioning from the stage to the screen.[62]

Though of a different medium, Wild West shows such as Buffalo Bill Cody's or the Miller Brothers' were actually a great entrée into the film industry for hundreds of Native Americans. The Miller Brothers 101 Ranch Real Wild West, for example, maintained winter quarters in Inceville, in the Santa Ynez Canyon of Southern California. As early motion picture companies moved to the area in the 1910s, they found a constant supply of Native actors ready to perform in films highlighting the American West and settler colonial life. In many ways Native performers and the film companies who employed them told the same story the Miller Brothers and Buffalo Bill had been championing for the past several decades, except now with the addition of movie cameras.[63]

In 1914 Davis made his film debut with an uncredited role in *The Perils of Pauline*. Nearly two dozen films followed over the next three decades, with his last film appearance in *The Falcon Out West*, released in 1944, only two years before his death. Nearly all these works were Westerns, depicting Davis and other Native actors as taciturn, violent, or both. Native entertainers such as Davis, even with their long lists of Wild West, stage, and screen roles, nevertheless still received only minor parts as supporting characters. But just as he had done with his anthropological work, Davis used his platform as an actor to work toward celebrating and highlighting his rich Tsitsistas/Suhtai culture.[64]

Advocacy

Beginning in the 1920s and continuing until his death two decades later, Davis lectured on Native cultures and advocated for Indigenous causes, using his celebrity to reach the public. His home in Pasadena became a gathering place and salon for Native and non-Native performers. In 1931 he even founded a national Native organization known as First Americans.

Their mission was to unite American Indian entertainers in the greater Los Angeles area and celebrate Indigenous art and music in the United States. Davis later wrote that he undertook this type of work because he wanted non-Native people to understand Native cultures. If there was more understanding in the world, Davis hoped, there would be less push by Euro-American Christians to convert or forcibly assimilate Native peoples. Reflecting on the violent history of the federal government's interactions with Native Americans, Davis wrote optimistically that no matter what mistakes had been made in the past, it was still possible to do right in the future.[65]

Newspaper articles from this time record numerous lectures Davis gave throughout Southern California. At times his wife Mary joined him as he spoke of Tsitsistas/Suhtai culture, history, and religion. His repertoire grew, too, after his many years as a resident of the West Coast. This is evident in his many speaking engagements on the history of the Indigenous peoples of California, including the theft of their land and the rape and murder of countless individuals first by the Spanish and later by Euro-American settler colonizers in the nineteenth century. Many considered him an expert on American Indian arts and cultures, relying on his knowledge to aid them in their own work. In 1931, for instance, the New York–based Exposition of Indian Tribal Arts requested Davis's help to determine "authentic art and dances" from those that were simply sensational or spurious. Clearly Davis had come a long way in re-embracing his own Native culture. It was not too many years earlier that he blamed his fellow community members' supposed backwardness on their religion and would not allow his children to speak the language of their ancestors.[66]

Determined until the end to present his culture as he believed it should be seen, in 1929 Davis began writing a book about Tsitsistas/Suhtai culture and history. He desired to focus on the lives of women and men of his parents' generation. That April he sent a letter to the staff of the Smithsonian's BAE, requesting photographs of his family members. He intended to add these images to his book, tentatively titled "Secret Rites and Ceremonies of the Ancient Cheyennes." Sadly, he left this important work unfinished at the time of his death.[67]

In the later years of his life Davis re-embraced not only his culture but also his immediate family. Despite his leaving his wife and children in

Oklahoma to move to California and marry a non-Native woman, three of his four adult daughters eventually moved out to the West Coast to be close to him. His second eldest, Mary, moved to Laveen, Arizona, and wrote to her "dear Papa" often. In 1942 she informed him that despite the persistent racism and enforced assimilation they encountered, two of his grandsons attended the Gila Crossing Day School and St. John's Catholic Mission School and were happy there. Closer to home, two of Davis's other adult daughters lived in Southern California, with Nannie, also known as Nellie, only five miles away in the larger Los Angeles area. The only daughter who remained in Oklahoma was his eldest, Richenda. She and her brother Roy chose to stay there, not far from where Nannie and Richard lived as a young married couple after returning from Carlisle. Davis died in his Pasadena home in 1946 with his wife Mary by his side. His remains were laid to rest in Forest Lawn Memorial Park in California.[68]

Richard Davis and Anthropology Today

Richard Davis was a Western-educated Native American man interested in anthropology and in illustrating the richness of his culture. Sometimes he did this quite literally by producing drawings himself, much as his fellow Southern Tsitsistas/Suhtai member Tichkematse had also done years earlier. Davis was willing to humble himself to make a living and to put food on the table for his wife and children. To do so, he seized any opportunity he could to earn a few dollars, whether collecting narratives and ceremonial objects from his Southern Tsitsistas/Suhtai neighbors, posing for photographs in the Indian Villages of the Omaha and St. Louis World's Fairs, or playing the part of a Show Indian in the Miller Brothers 101 Ranch Real Wild West performance. Despite his willingness to fit the stereotype expected of him, Davis was also proud of who he was and where he came from.

Davis's place in anthropology today is largely forgotten, like that of many of his fellow Native collaborators and anthropologists. Like them, Davis was a survivor of Indian boarding schools. As a child Richard Henry Pratt indoctrinated him into assimilationist doctrines calling for the wholesale abandonment of Native cultures. Davis not only swallowed these racist pronouncements but even became an outspoken advocate of allotment and assimilation before realizing the irreparable harm they did to American Indian nations. One of the first students to enter the doors of the Carlisle Indian Industrial School, he ultimately spent more time there than any other student, first as a student and later as an employee. It was only after becoming an anthropological collaborator that Davis "turned the power" of his education. Working with George A. Dorsey and James Mooney, Davis used his fluency in English to document and preserve the rich cultural heritage he had been taught to be ashamed of during his school days.

In later decades when signing his name as Thunder Bird, he added the appellation Richard Davis in parentheses, as an afterthought. Eventually he dropped the name Richard Davis altogether and became known only as Thunder Bird. Ever since the day thirteen-year-old Davis entered the doors of Carlisle he was surrounded by the policies of assimilation. By the time he was a sixty-year-old man known only as Thunder Bird, he had left both that previous name and any thoughts of assimilation behind him. A more apt metaphor for resilience in the face of racism and settler colonialism is hard to find.

4

All the Information There Is to Be Got

D. C. Duvall (Browning, Montana, 1911)

He was ecstatic. After nearly five years of interviewing elders from his community, D. C. Duvall found the man who had all the answers, or at least more of them than anyone else. Since 1903 Duvall had been working with Clark Wissler, head curator of anthropology at the American Museum of Natural History (AMNH) in New York, to collect Pikuni Blackfeet (Piegan) stories, songs, dances, and ceremonies. Throughout this time Duvall worked with many elders willing to share what information they could. A number of these women and men told him what they knew of the old ways and beliefs, but it often wasn't that much. In fact, Duvall began to fear that all of those who possessed the older knowledge had already passed away.

Now, though, in early January 1911, the situation had rapidly improved. Duvall happily wrote a letter to Wissler to share with him the good news. He wrote that he was staying with a Pikuni Blackfeet elder in the latter's home on the Two Medicine River, a few miles from where Duvall lived on the Blackfeet Reservation in Browning, Montana. This man was a veritable font of wisdom, Duvall continued, knowing nearly all of the ceremonies and even having a sacred medicine bundle in his care. Almost as an afterthought, Duvall asked Wissler if there was any way the museum could send him a phonograph machine. This elder knew many of the old songs, and Duvall wanted to record all he could on wax cylinders. As he had told Wissler when he began collecting anthropological material from his people, he wanted to "get all the information there is to be got."[1]

After several years of unfulfilling work at odd jobs on and off the reservation, Duvall was happy to now do something he believed truly mattered. He considered the preservation of his people's tangible and intangible cultural heritage to be his most important work, and he subsequently strove to become the most accurate translator of his people's language into

English. Like his contemporary William Jones, the prominent Sac and Fox anthropologist, Duvall sometimes felt he was on the outside of his community and not exactly sure where he fit in. Because of these feelings he was proud to create an anthropological record, ensuring Pikuni Blackfeet culture and history would continue after he was gone.

Youth and Schooling

The Blackfoot Confederacy, of which the Pikuni Blackfeet of Browning, Montana, are one part, is a union of four linguistically and culturally related Native American and First Nation communities straddling the international boundary of Canada and the United States. The four distinct communities of this larger confederacy consist of the Siksika, the Kainai, and the Apatohsi Pikuni, concentrated in Alberta, and the Amskapi Pikuni or Pikuni Blackfeet in Montana. As was true for many Indigenous nations throughout North America, the carving up of Native lands by present-day settler colonial boundaries wreaked havoc on the Blackfoot Confederacy's ability to govern its lands and communities.[2]

Historically the peoples of the Blackfoot Confederacy lived a semisedentary lifestyle, remaining in one geographic place in the colder months of the year and traveling across the northern Great Plains for food during warmer months. They hunted large game animals including bison, deer, and elk and gathered roots, plants, berries, and fruit for their subsistence. By the late nineteenth century, however, the U.S. government issued a number of executive orders creating the Blackfeet Reservation in western Montana and confining the Pikuni Blackfeet peoples to the far western edge of their ancestral lands.[3]

The decades surrounding the turn to the twentieth century were a time of dramatic change for the Pikuni Blackfeet. No longer able to hunt for their livelihood and daily resources, community members depended on a distant and explicitly racist colonial government for their survival. Non-Native soldiers, fur traders, settlers, and anyone eager to make money off the Pikuni Blackfeet people flooded into the Montana Territory during these years. D. C. Duvall's father, Charles Duvall, was one of these men.

Charles Duvall arrived in the northwest section of the Montana Territory around 1870. Despite various sources listing his ancestry as either Métis or French Canadian, Charles Duvall identified himself as having been born in Louisiana to a non-Native mother from Mississippi and a father from Scotland. Regardless of his origins, by 1880 the elder Duvall moved to the town of Fort Benton, in the Montana Territory, not far from the Blackfeet Reservation. There Charles worked as a drayman, transporting goods by wagon to those living in Fort Benton. Sometime after arriving in the area, Charles began a relationship with a Pikuni Blackfeet woman named Yellow Bird or Louise Big Plume. The two had four children together, three girls and one boy, with the latter, D. C. or David Charles, born in 1877. Yellow Bird and Charles's relationship was a tempestuous one by all accounts. In approximately 1881 Yellow Bird left Charles and returned home to the Blackfeet Reservation in Browning, taking her young children with her. Charles died of unknown causes soon after her departure.[4]

D. C. Duvall was raised on the Blackfeet Reservation during his formative years, and much of his early life and schooling remain unclear. Multiple sources provide conflicting accounts of Duvall attending either the Carlisle Indian Industrial School in Pennsylvania or the Fort Hall Indian Boarding School in Idaho. Neither of these seem likely, however. It appears Duvall received his earliest classroom education from Catholic clergy on the Blackfeet Reservation at the St. Ignatius and St. Peter's Catholic Boarding School. According to missionary records, in 1885 there were two hundred Pikuni Blackfeet students enrolled at the school. Attending this Catholic-run reservation boarding school between approximately 1885 and 1890, Duvall remained close to his mother's family during his adolescence. Young Duvall received instruction in English, math, and related subjects. Simultaneously, he was also taught that his Pikuni Blackfeet culture was backward and primitive. Catholic clergy at the school encouraged Duvall to abandon his Native language and his past and instead embrace Euro-American Christianity.[5]

While records of his attendance are spotty, it seems that after finishing his primary education at the Catholic mission school on the reservation, Duvall then entered Montana's Fort Shaw Indian Boarding School. A military fort since 1870, the U.S. Army transferred control of the Fort Shaw complex to the Department of the Interior in April 1892. In June of that year the commissioner of Indian affairs sent a letter informing Indian reservation agents throughout Montana of the opening of the school and encouraging them to send Native youths to the new Fort Shaw school.

Ideal children, the commissioner's letter continued, would be above the age of twelve and already familiar with English. Such requirements fit D. C. Duvall perfectly. He was fifteen years old in 1892 and educated in English and other fundamental subjects from the Catholic mission school on the Blackfeet Reservation.[6]

In 1892 W. H. Winslow, a physician and the former principal teacher of the Chilocco Indian Boarding School in the Oklahoma Territory, became Fort Shaw's first superintendent. The school officially opened that December, with fifty-two students in attendance. Nearly all of them came from the Pikuni Blackfeet Nation, Duvall most likely among them. Although this community had the greatest representation at the school due to Fort Shaw's proximity to the Blackfeet Reservation, other Native children attended from the Apsáalooke (Crow/Absaroke), Inunaina (Arapaho), Nakota (Assiniboine), Salish (Flathead), Tsitsistas/Suhtai (Cheyenne), and Ihanktonwan (Yankton Dakota) communities. As was the case at Carlisle, the children at Fort Shaw slept in dormitories converted from old military barracks.[7]

Like other Indian boarding schools of the day, the children's days were split between classroom education and manual training. Faculty divided students along gender lines dictated by Euro-American ideas of work. Native girls at Fort Shaw learned Western methods of sewing, making clothes, doing laundry, and performing general household duties. Boys, on the other hand, received instruction in Western farming, animal husbandry, and other trades, including carpentry, shoemaking, tailoring, and blacksmithing. The latter was a skill Duvall learned during his Indian boarding school days, and one he continued to practice after returning home to the Blackfeet Reservation.[8]

Employment at Fort Shaw and in Browning

While it is unclear if Duvall attended the Fort Shaw Indian Boarding School, he was employed there in 1895. The school superintendent's annual report for that year lists eighteen-year-old Duvall as a school employee, assigned the vague title of "Indian Assistant." His exact duties in this position are unknown, but his pay was meager, at $5 per month. Although not a student at this time, Duvall nevertheless experienced much of what the rest of the student body did. By 1895 there were approximately 250 students representing a diverse commingling of Native American communities attending Fort Shaw. Regardless of these differences, all were compelled to assimilate to the same Euro-American citizenship model.[9]

Based on his later work, Duvall most likely took on blacksmith or apprentice blacksmith duties while employed at Fort Shaw. Newspapers describing the school at the time reported blacksmiths shoeing the school's horses as well as repairing wagons and other farm implements. Just as Richard Henry Pratt did at Carlisle, the Fort Shaw authorities regularly shone a spotlight on the good works created by Native students. They even held exhibits to display the "improvements" the children made in their steps toward assimilation. A Great Falls, Montana, newspaper reported on the handiwork of Fort Shaw's pupils, particularly their industrial education. Chains, bolts, and other products of the school's blacksmith shop were exhibited, as were items made in related trade departments. Reviewers argued products from the Fort Shaw Indian Boarding School were the equal of if not superior to those produced at any other industrial school, Native or non-Native, throughout the country.[10]

By 1899 Duvall had left his job at Fort Shaw and returned the one hundred miles west to his home in Browning on the Blackfeet Reservation. There he worked for the Indian Agency as an assistant mechanic, making $20 per month, a full four times what he had made at Fort Shaw. What Duvall's exact duties were is uncertain, but no doubt they drew on his earlier blacksmithing work. Indeed, two years later the Montana *Dupuyer Acantha* newspaper applauded the twenty-four-year-old for the work he did in his leather apron at the Browning smithy.[11]

A few years later Duvall took advantage of a business opportunity presented to him. He purchased John Merchant's blacksmith shop in Browning, including all the man's associated blacksmithing tools. Without the available funds to buy this blacksmith business outright, Duvall sold his existing ranch and associated lands a few miles outside of Browning. Despite his hopes for success, though, his business venture never took off, and after a few more years he sold his blacksmith shop.

Like many returned Indian boarding school students, Duvall found much of the knowledge, skills, and trades he received at school largely irrelevant on his Indian reservation. Boarding schools such as Carlisle and Fort Shaw impressed upon Native youths that they must erase their heritage and embrace Euro-American Christian society to succeed in the world. And many students did embrace this new culture and all it promised. Others, disillusioned by the lack of opportunities after finishing their boarding school education, instead chose to celebrate their own Native cultures. These students turned the power against an unjust society methodically working to assimilate or destroy them. Despite the racist indoctrination they had received at school, many of these former students created a niche for themselves as mediators between their own Native communities and non-Native anthropologists. It was through this new field of anthropology that twenty-six-year-old Duvall found a means to fight back against federally mandated assimilation and the forced erasure of his culture.[12]

Clark Wissler, the AMNH, and Anthropological Fieldwork

A few years after returning from the Fort Shaw Indian Boarding School, Duvall first met Clark Wissler in the summer of 1903. Wissler was conducting ethnological fieldwork among several Indigenous nations of the northern plains for New York's American Museum of Natural History, and the two men immediately hit it off. Impressed by Duvall's English abilities and clear passion for preserving everything about the Pikuni Blackfeet past, Wissler hired Duvall to collect information. The pay was scant, but in addition to supplementing what he made from his blacksmith shop, Duvall was happy to play a part in documenting his people's culture.[13]

Wissler received his PhD in psychology at Columbia University, but by 1902 he had abandoned his former studies to commence anthropological work with Franz Boas at the AMNH. He moved quickly up the ladder, becoming the museum's curator of anthropology in 1907, a position he held for the next thirty-five years. Although Wissler's professional fieldwork was limited, he contributed to the AMNH and the anthropological profession in a major way through his administrative and theoretical labors. Under his direction the AMNH initiated a number of field projects among several northern plains communities, making that region arguably the best-known ethnographic area in North America at the time.

Even more important was Wissler's development of the culture area concept, one of the organizing principles of modern anthropology. This concept applied the term "culture area" to a group of Native nations with similar cultures occupying an area where ecological conditions were generally uniform. In essence, Wissler's theoretical contribution altered the focus of study from individual, isolated Native communities to a cross-cultural perspective highlighting cultural influence and diffusion.[14]

Under the leadership of Frederic Ward Putnam, Franz Boas, and later Wissler, the AMNH instituted a broad collecting policy, sending expeditions throughout North America and beyond. Around 1900 the museum also initiated fieldwork among several Indigenous Plains communities, including the A'aninin (Gros Ventre), Apsáalooke, Dakota, Inunaina, Minitari (Hidatsa), Numakiki (Mandan), Pikuni Blackfeet, and Tsitsistas/Suhtai. According to Wissler, during this time practically every major Plains nation was visited, with the end goal of supplying the museum with a comprehensive collection of Indigenous materials for its holdings. That same year the scholarly journal *Science* reported on AMNH museum staff working in California and Oregon, where a number of allegedly unknown Native peoples were believed to be on the verge of extinction. The AMNH also sent expeditions to the U.S. Southwest, always an area of interest to the public with its paradoxical allure of beauty and austerity. There museum staff collected among the Apache, A:shiwi (Zuni), and Hopi peoples just as Tichkematse and Frank Hamilton Cushing had for the Smithsonian Institution decades earlier.[15]

The AMNH represented Native American cultures to the public through a variety of formats, including exhibitions, lectures, and publications. Its exhibits at the turn of the twentieth century were immense, covering Indigenous communities from Alaska in the north to Tierra del Fuego in the south. Wissler wrote that to make exhibits both effective and authentic, it was necessary to send duly qualified men to visit the out-of-the-way places of the earth. These men, and occasionally women, were specially trained, one magazine editor noted. They closely observed cultural phenomena and recorded everything they saw and heard in the field. After compiling their observations, the museum later published these reports as scholarly papers, providing descriptions of American Indian lifeways invaluable to students. Missing in this description of anthropological work, of course, is any mention of the English-speaking Native collaborators who worked alongside these non-Native anthropologists, providing them entrée into their communities.[16]

Wissler's fieldwork consisted mainly of three years spent among Indigenous Plains communities soon after joining the staff of the AMNH. There on the Blackfeet Reservation in Browning, Wissler and Duvall first met. The two men went on to collaborate in their studies of the Pikuni Blackfeet people for the next eight years. Soon after their initial encounter, Wissler engaged Duvall first as an interpreter and later as a collaborator and collector, gathering narratives and statements from elders on the Blackfeet Reservation.[17]

Duvall's methodology consisted of interviewing elders in their homes and speaking in the Pikuni Blackfeet language. A lifelong resident of Browning later described Duvall as ever-curious, asking questions about the old ways and carrying a notebook with him to jot down all he was told. After each interview Duvall reviewed his notes, translated them to English, and mailed them to Wissler. Wissler sent back questions or edits, which Duvall brought to community elders for clarification. This rather tedious back-and-forth process was common at the time between non-Native anthropologists and Native collaborators in the field, such as the other collaborators featured in this book. It was a process that Franz Boas practiced and taught Wissler during their time at AMNH.[18]

Pikuni Blackfeet community members willing to provide information to Duvall were mostly older men, though some women did as well. Wissler encouraged Duvall to interview first those with memories of pre-reservation life. Many of these individuals were residents of Duvall's mother's community, Heart Butte, or lived in the southwest area of the Blackfeet Reservation. As was the case with many Native collaborators, Duvall's primary sources of information were often his own family members, including grandparents, parents, and even spouses.[19]

In his correspondence with Wissler we can see the balancing act Duvall managed between his blacksmithing work, taking on odd jobs around the agency, and anthropological collecting. He submitted to the AMNH anthropologist detailed lists delineating the hours and even days he spent with various "old timers," gathering all the stories he could. Duvall noted in one letter how his speakers would be offended if he interrupted them, so he scribbled down everything he could in quick notes. Later he went over this information, adding from memory to make them more understandable before sending them to Wissler for his own review. An elder woman who provided information to Duvall repeatedly spoke of her reluctance to supply the requested information, fearing divine retribution. Eventually Duvall prevailed upon her to speak of some of the ceremonies, but he received only partial information before she abruptly ended the interview. Incidents like these raise questions about the influence Native collaborators held over those informing them, as well as the reliability of the information collaborators such as Duvall received.[20]

Based on his published anthropological accounts, Wissler attended at least two in-person Sun Dance ceremonies on the Blackfeet Reservation with Duvall. In addition to these, Duvall provided Wissler with extensive notes on the Horse Dance, the Black and Yellow Buffalo Lodge, the Black Tail Deer Dance, a Wolf Song, and a Grass Dance. Duvall considered these papers his most important contribution in preserving his people's culture. He later coauthored with Wissler collections of these narratives and ceremonies in published form. Among the collected narratives were stories titled The Buffalo's Adopted Child, The Split Feather, The Man Cut in Two Below the Waist, and Seven Heads. Such collected tales were sought out by anthropologists and collaborators at the time. Many of these anthropologists, Wissler and Duvall included, then made comparative studies between Native communities, seeking common origins for the collected stories.[21]

Despite his years of work with Wissler collecting narratives, songs, and ceremonies, only one compilation was published during Duvall's lifetime. This was the 1908 *Mythology of the Blackfoot Indians*, released as part of the AMNH Anthropological Papers. Notable for its time, this publication listed Duvall's name alongside that of Wissler's as a coauthor rather than simply attributing the collecting work to a nameless Native individual. In the authors' words, this work made available for an English-reading public the tales, narratives, and "myths" of the Niitsitapii or people of the Blackfoot Confederacy. The bulk of the information Duvall collected from among his family members and community elders near Browning.[22]

Clark Wissler went on to publish five other major works on the Pikuni Blackfeet that relied heavily on Duvall's collecting work. These included *Material Culture of the Blackfoot Indians* (1910), *The Social Life of the Blackfoot Indians* (1911), *Ceremonial Bundles of the Blackfoot Indians* (1912), *Societies and Dance Associations of the Blackfoot Indians* (1913), and *The Sun Dance of the Blackfoot Indians* (1918). Recent scholars have noted that the collaborative fieldwork done by Wissler and Duvall during the first decade of the twentieth century continues to constitute the most extensive collection of ethnographic materials ever produced on the Pikuni Blackfeet people. Importantly, it is debatable how much of this information would exist without the determination of Duvall in his race against the supposed disappearance of his own community.[23]

Collecting Material Culture Objects

In addition to documenting and recording the songs, customs, ceremonies, and religious beliefs of his Native community, Duvall also collected their material culture objects. Oftentimes these items were created on request to supply museum needs, and some were even fabricated by Duvall's own family members. This process was not that unusual. As in the case of Sac and Fox anthropologist William Jones's collecting work in the United States and the Philippines, many anthropologists at the turn of the twentieth century requested objects to be made when none of an older age were available.

Less than a year after Duvall and Wissler started working together, Wissler placed orders with Duvall for objects he wanted the younger man to find. In their correspondence Duvall updated the AMNH anthropologist on the status of these items. Throughout the fall of 1904, for instance, Duvall apprised Wissler about a bow and arrows, a rattle, a robe, a baby board, and a turnip bonnet, all of which were in production by Pikuni Blackfeet community members. All these objects were intended for exhibition, many of them accompanying mannequins dressed in Pikuni Blackfeet clothing in the AMNH anthropology displays. A collection of particular interest to later museum visitors were children's toys and games, including bison rib bones that Native children used as sleds in the winter. All these items were collected by Duvall and placed on exhibit by Wissler.[24]

As noted, many of the people fabricating these items for museums were individuals close to Duvall, including his own family. A power dynamic of this nature raises a host of questions. How did Duvall's role as an anthropological collaborator and collector change his status within the community? Was he sought out as a potential revenue source, or did people avoid him because he collaborated with colonizer anthropologists? Further, in his personal dealings with community members, did Duvall favor certain people while ignoring others? Finally, to what extent were Duvall's and Wissler's interactions exploitative in which they took advantage of Pikuni Blackfeet people?

There are no easy answers to these complicated questions. Certainly Duvall gained some amount of power and status because of his work with Wissler. Absent from the anthropological record are the perspectives of those who refused to supply Duvall with stories or objects, regardless of the amount he was willing to pay. Related to the exploitative nature of anthropology on Indian reservations more generally, Pikuni Blackfeet scholar Rosalyn LaPier has raised the issue of reciprocal exploitation. Although she agrees that anthropologists and Native collaborators offered much needed cash in poverty-stricken communities, that doesn't mean those who sold their stories or belongings were helpless victims. Rather, she posits, the historical record shows that Pikuni Blackfeet community members quickly adapted to the new value outsiders placed on their cultural heritage, recognizing the potential for a source of income free from Bureau of Indian Affairs interference. Indeed, despite the federal government's relentless policing of Indigenous peoples, the Pikuni Blackfeet never lost control of their ability to sell the things they were willing to part with. Many of them even successfully negotiated for higher prices than anthropologists initially offered.[25]

Not surprisingly, some of the items Duvall acquired were of a sensitive or sacred nature. In March 1911, for instance, he wrote Wissler about the opportunity to purchase a medicine bundle—a collection of sacred objects that provided the owner with spiritual power. Duvall noted that the Native seller was hesitant to turn the bundle over to him, fearing human or divine retribution. People were afraid to sell sacred bundles, Duvall informed Wissler, adding that they wouldn't even talk about selling such powerful objects "to a white man." The solution agreed upon was to transfer the medicine bundle from the owner to Duvall in a special ceremony, thus avoiding the wrath of community members or divine powers. A transfer of this type, common among salvage anthropologists in their race to collect everything valuable in American Indian cultures, points to the important role Duvall and other Native collaborators played as go-betweens. Due to his Native ancestry Duvall could receive objects otherwise prohibited to be sold or given to non-Native individuals. In this way he provided entrée to anthropologists unfamiliar with the language and customs of the Pikuni Blackfeet Nation.[26]

Work with Other Anthropologists

Unlike many of the Native anthropologists and collaborators in this book, Duvall's anthropology career never took him far from home. He didn't work in museums in distant cities, as did Tichkematse, James R. Murie, or Florence and Louis Shotridge. Nor did he exhibit himself in world's fairs or Wild West shows like Richard Davis or Cleaver Warden. The anthropologists with whom he collaborated were never many in number, whereas John V. Satterlee worked closely with nearly a dozen anthropologists throughout his long life. Duvall, instead, really only worked with a handful of outside scholars, men such as Clark Wissler from the AMNH, Truman Michelson from the BAE, the naturalist George Bird Grinnell, and Walter McClintock, an amateur anthropologist and photographer affiliated with the U.S. Forest Service.

Two of these non-Native scholars who visited the Blackfeet Reservation were George Bird Grinnell and C. C. Uhlenbeck. Grinnell was a nineteenth-century naturalist and editor of the magazine *Forest and Stream*. In addition to observing and writing about wildlife, Grinnell was fascinated by the Indigenous peoples of North America. He made a career out of visiting western reservations and then writing about his travels among the Chaticks si Chaticks (Pawnee), Tsitsistas/Suhtai, and the Pikuni Blackfeet. His work *Blackfoot Lodge Tales*, published in 1892, remains popular today. C. C. Uhlenbeck was a Dutch linguist and scholar. He and his wife visited Browning, Montana, at least twice between 1910 and 1911, recording all they could about the culture and daily lives of the Pikuni Blackfeet people. Although neither Grinnell nor Uhlenbeck worked extensively with Duvall on the Blackfeet Reservation, they were aware of his anthropological collecting and interpretation work for others.[27]

An anthropologist with whom Duvall had a brief but much closer relationship was Truman Michelson. A linguistic expert who joined the staff of the Smithsonian's Bureau of American Ethnology in 1910, Michelson received his PhD from Harvard University in 1904. After Harvard, he then went on to study anthropological linguistics with Franz Boas in New

York before accepting a federal position with the BAE in Washington DC. There Michelson remained for the rest of his life, collecting grammars and vocabularies from Indigenous nations across the United States. In addition to his linguistic work with Duvall in Montana, Michelson worked with Menominee collaborator John V. Satterlee in Wisconsin and Southern Inunaina collaborator Cleaver Warden in Oklahoma, and he edited Sac and Fox anthropologist William Jones's Algonquian fieldnotes after the latter's death in 1909.[28]

During the summer of 1910 Duvall and Michelson first met and began working together as Native collaborator and non-Native anthropologist. Michelson stayed in Browning for a month, taking photographs, recording linguistic information, and taking notes on songs, narratives, and everything he could get his hands on. Not conversant in the Pikuni Blackfeet language, Michelson engaged Duvall as his interpreter and collector. The two men interviewed prominent community elders willing to supply stories and provide insight into their shared past. Michelson later published a series of articles in the *Journal of American Folklore* with the information collected by Duvall.[29]

With the exception of Wissler, the other main outsider with whom Duvall collaborated was Walter McClintock. Beginning in 1896 and continuing for numerous summers thereafter, McClintock traveled from his home in Philadelphia to Montana, living for weeks at a time on the Blackfeet Reservation. Initially traveling west under the aegis of the U.S. Forest Service, McClintock worked to identify forest preserve locations for this federal agency. After being so impressed by the Pikuni Blackfeet people, however, McClintock ended up staying in western Montana, taking photographs, recording songs, and writing down his observations. Like Truman Michelson, McClintock could not speak the language of his hosts, so he paid Duvall to interpret for him. Duvall's work with McClintock also influenced the 1910 publication *The Old North Trail: Life, Legends and Religion of the Blackfeet Indians*, a largely autobiographical account of McClintock's experiences living among this community at the end of the nineteenth century.[30]

McClintock's name occurs repeatedly in Duvall's correspondence over the years, most notably in letters between Duvall and Wissler in early 1911. Apparently McClintock wanted Duvall to work with him, but before agreeing to do so, Duvall wrote Wissler, asking the older man's advice. Wissler encouraged his Pikuni Blackfeet collaborator to take on the work as a supplemental source of income, but he cautioned Duvall not to provide McClintock with any information on the sacred ceremonies, songs, and ceremonial bundle information on which the two of them had been working for AMNH. According to Wissler, the notes Duvall had already provided on these points were the first time such information had been written down. And as Wissler and Duvall intended to write up this material for their forthcoming publication, Wissler asked Duvall not to give McClintock or anyone else any information that could possibly beat them to the punch. In reading through more of Duvall's fieldnotes and correspondence, however, Wissler had little to worry about when it came to McClintock. Duvall did not like the man and said as much to both Wissler and Michelson on several occasions. According to Duvall, McClintock not only was demanding, but he also was limited with his expenses, unwilling to pay Duvall the fees he deserved for his anthropological work.[31]

Despite Duvall's work with several non-Native anthropologists, it was Wissler with whom he worked most closely and struck up a lasting friendship. Having first met in 1903, the two men maintained a regular correspondence over the next eight years, providing advice and support to each other from across the country. They also planned future fieldwork together, including traveling to Canada to collect objects and conduct interviews with First Nation communities of the Blackfoot Confederacy there. During this long period Duvall and Wissler's relationship grew from that of colleagues to friends. It was that closeness that made Duvall's sudden death in 1911 all the harder for Wissler to bear.

Duvall's Death

On July 10, 1911, D. C. Duvall took his own life. The Dutch linguist C. C. Uhlenbeck and his wife, Wilhelmina, were visiting the Blackfeet Reservation at the time, and Wilhelmina's diary provides a firsthand account of this tragic event. As the Uhlenbecks enjoyed a meal in the Browning inn on the afternoon of Monday, July 10, they heard a most horrible screaming. Numerous individuals gathered in the street, where the Uhlenbecks learned that Duvall, the well-known interpreter, had shot himself. That Monday was the day Duvall's second wife, Cecile Trombley, was to appear in court to request a divorce from Duvall. Set against this, yet unsure how to prevent it, Duvall in a fit chose to end his life.[32]

Wilhelmina Uhlenbeck wrote that the screaming, sobbing, and lamenting of Duvall's female relatives sounded eerie to her Dutch ears. Duvall's mother, Yellow Bird, sat in the doorway of the inn, venting her frustration over the loss of her eldest son. The Uhlenbecks, unsure of their place during this outpouring of sorrow, retreated to their room in the inn. Despite their attempts to escape the mourning going on outside their room, the sounds of crying reached them there as well, pervading the whole of Browning for the remainder of the day. Later that afternoon Wilhemina witnessed a sight that remained with her for many years—in front of the inn lay a stretcher with a cloth spread out on it. Underneath the cloth were the remains of Duvall, with only his shoes visible at the end of the cloth. The Dutch woman wrote in her diary that she could only take in the scene briefly before fleeing back to her room and away from the sadness on the street.[33]

Duvall was thirty-three years old when he died on July 10, 1911. At the time he and his Pikuni Blackfeet wife of less than half a year, Cecile Trombley, were separated. The two married in January 1911 in a Methodist ceremony performed by the local minister, T. A. Riggin. Notably, Duvall's former marriage to a Pikuni Blackfeet woman named Gretchen occurred in 1900 and was officiated by a priest from the Holy Family Catholic Mission. After nearly a decade together, D.C. and Gretchen divorced in 1909. There were no children from either of these marriages. Though purely conjecture, perhaps Duvall's willingness to have his marriages performed by a Catholic priest and later a Methodist minister shows a change occurred after he became an anthropological collaborator. As time passed, maybe Duvall felt freer to break away from the enforced Catholic teachings of his early Indian boarding school days, if not from Christianity altogether.[34]

Many then and now have suggested different reasons that Duvall took his own life. His nephew, James Eagle Child, believed Duvall's suicide was due to his recent separation from his second wife, Cecile. A modern historian has posited, without much reliable information, that Duvall had always been unhappy. Wissler struck a similar note when speaking of Duvall. In a semi-fictionalized account written a quarter century later, Wissler suggested Duvall's struggle to reconcile his Native and non-Native identities led to his ultimate demise. Romanticized for his audience, Wissler's book

Indian Cavalcade, or Life on the Old-Time Indian Reservations portrayed the younger Pikuni Blackfeet man as melancholy. "You are a white man," Duvall's character says to Wissler in this 1938 novel. "You have a place among your people, you count for something. Around us here are Indians, they revere their past, they have the respect of their fellows." "Here I am," Duvall is depicted as saying, "neither an Indian nor a white man—just nothing." Wissler thus primes his audience to believe Duvall's inability to fit in among his community was the motivating factor for taking his own life.[35]

As Duvall left no explanation for his suicide, conjecture on the part of Wissler and other historians is largely moot. Nevertheless, having complicated understandings of one's own identity was a recurrent issue for many turn-of-the-twentieth-century Native anthropologists and collaborators and is worth brief mention here. As readers know, Sac and Fox anthropologist William Jones struggled with his identity as a Native man, often preferring to consider himself more Euro-American than anything else. Throughout his life he wrestled with these two parts of himself, seeking to fit into a non-Native assimilationist world but never wanting to fully abandon his Native culture. Other Native anthropologists and collaborators abound who faced similar challenges based on their ancestry. Perhaps that is the reason J. N. B. Hewitt, George Hunt, James R. Murie, John V. Satterlee, and other Native individuals first entered the field of anthropology—to feel a deeper connection to Native nations in which they felt they only partly belonged.

Although in his writings Duvall never explicitly detailed any inner conflict over his identity, it is possible that such concerns were there. The most prominent example of this was in a letter in which he called himself a "breed" or "half-breed," and not a full-blood member of the Pikuni Blackfeet community. This statement, combined with Wissler's depiction of a melancholy man who did not fit in to his community and had marital problems, could be the reason he took his own life that July day in 1911.

Having noted this, however, there is also the possibility that questions of identity did not factor into Duvall's death at all. Not too many years ago, for instance, people in the Pikuni Blackfeet community still spoke of Duvall's death as the result of divine punishment for meddling in anthropology in the first place. Those who subscribed to this opinion noted that his bad fortune and eventual suicide were rooted in his recording details of holy ceremonies never meant to be written down or made public. Notably, Duvall's nephew James Eagle Child, who no doubt knew him better than Wissler, McClintock, or other non-Native outsiders, simply attributed Duvall's suicide to trouble over his second wife, Cecile. Perhaps that is where we should leave our line of questioning—allowing Duvall and his memory to rest in peace.[36]

D. C. Duvall and Anthropology Today

Regardless of why it came about, Duvall's death was a major loss for his community and family, as well as for the young field of anthropology. Wissler was understandably shocked and saddened when he learned the news. Informing his AMNH supervisor of Duvall's death, Wissler wrote of the younger man's talents and the contributions he had made to the field, mentioning that in 1911 alone Duvall generated more than 750 pages of unpublished manuscript material on the Pikuni Blackfeet people. Wissler also included an "In Memoriam" page at the beginning of his 1912 publication in which Duvall had played such a major role. Therein Wissler wrote of Duvall's investigative mind, linguistic ability, and passion for the work he undertook.[37]

Although Duvall's death was undeniably tragic, his life and his work within the field of anthropology were not terribly unique for Native peoples at the turn of the twentieth century. Native youths educated in Indian boarding schools and willing to collaborate with non-Native anthropologists became a prime commodity. As culture brokers, they provided outsiders with priceless information about their societies and their beliefs. In the process these collaborators became rare and valuable themselves. In the years before discovering anthropology, Duvall worked odd jobs that financially sustained him but did not fulfill him. After he began collaborating with Wissler and Michelson, he became passionate about his work and his community. He associated with important men who lived in distant cities and who cared about what he thought. Finally, Duvall became the leading chronicler of his people, translating their lives and histories into a language understood by a mass audience.

Duvall's experiences in anthropology mirrored those of the other Indigenous collaborators featured in this book. These Native anthropologists and collaborators worked to counteract the racist and assimilationist doctrines forced on them in the Indian boarding schools of their youth. They turned the power by using their English-language abilities to record the richness and beauty of their cultures rather than abandoning their Indigenous pasts. Like Duvall, many of them found a form of celebrity through their collecting work. Several of these Native women and men, Duvall included, even discovered their shared connections to each other. For instance, while Duvall was largely isolated from the work of his fellow Native anthropologists and collaborators, he nevertheless was familiar with their work. Duvall and Wissler's published anthropological account, for example, compared Pikuni Blackfeet stories with those documented by William Jones among the Sac and Fox, Richard Davis among the Tsitsis-tas/Suhtai, James R. Murie among the Chaticks si Chaticks, and Cleaver Warden among the Inunaina. All this illustrates that Duvall was conversant with broader happenings in the field, including being knowledgeable about his contemporaries' collecting work.[38]

Sadly, Duvall never had the opportunity to meet these other Indigenous women and men whose lives mirrored his own in so many ways. If he had met Native collaborators and anthropologists such as Murie, Jones, the Shotridges, or Satterlee, maybe his life would have ended differently. Perhaps he would have found commonality in a shared passion for documenting their cultures, preserving their histories, and collecting everything there was to be got.

5

We Can Get Fine Work Out—Better Than
Any That's Been Out on Indians

James R. Murie (Pawnee, Oklahoma, 1911)

James R. Murie tried to control his excitement as he sat down to pen his response, but it was proving difficult. After many decades of struggling to make a living that combined his English fluency with his passion for preserving his Chaticks si Chaticks (Pawnee) culture, it looked like he now had the best opportunity to do so. More than that, he was in demand. Several anthropologists almost overnight realized Murie had value, with skills that were important to them. Responding to a January 1911 letter from Frederick Webb Hodge, director of the Smithsonian's Bureau of American Ethnology, Murie agreed to commence anthropological work for the Smithsonian. Distancing himself from thoughts that he was taking on the work simply for financial return, Murie informed Hodge that since a young age he wanted to document and save the ceremonies of his people.[1]

Like all the Native anthropologists and collaborators in this book, Murie truly believed he was saving his culture through his anthropological collecting. By the age of forty-nine, he had witnessed rapid change within the Chaticks si Chaticks community. He feared that if he didn't save some of it from federally sanctioned assimilation and enforced acculturation, his culture would eventually disappear, maybe even within his own lifetime.

Worried his culture would soon vanish, Murie used a variety of formats and new technologies to aid him in collecting all he could. Using a Smithsonian-loaned phonograph machine and camera, Murie recorded ceremonial songs and photographed sacred dances. Importantly, as a Chaticks si Chaticks man raised among his people, he possessed a level of access non-Native anthropologists would never have.[2]

Murie responded to Hodge at the BAE a few weeks later. He said he knew many non-Native anthropologists who had closely observed Native ceremonies, falsely believing that such observations made them experts. But they never got to the bottom of the ceremonies, Murie pointed out. These non-Native anthropologists never really understood the sacred information expressed in these ceremonies foundational to Indigenous ways of life. But Murie did. And he wanted to collect, document, photograph, and record everything he could in order to save his culture.[3]

The man who wrote Murie that January day in 1911 was no newcomer to the field of anthropology. Frederick Webb Hodge had already made his name working in this discipline for more than a quarter century and would continue to be a major presence for another several decades. Hodge was born in England in 1864 but immigrated to the United States with his family in his youth. He attended school at Columbian College, now George Washington University, in Washington DC and got his first taste of fieldwork under the direction of Smithsonian anthropologist Frank Hamilton Cushing in 1886. Accompanying Cushing on the Hemenway Southwestern Archaeological Expedition, Hodge worked in the New Mexico and Arizona Territories for three years, returning to Washington DC in 1889. Recognizing the young man's talents, BAE director John Wesley Powell hired him as part of their anthropological staff. Hodge worked for both the BAE and the Smithsonian's National Museum, becoming BAE director in 1910. It was around this time that Hodge first reached out to James R. Murie in Oklahoma, seeking to acquire more information about the Plains Indigenous nations of that region.[4]

Illustrative of the close-knit nature of the anthropological field at the time, Hodge not only worked alongside Cushing but even became a member of his extended family. In 1891 he married Margaret Magill, the sister of Cushing's wife, Emily. Outside of his personal relationships, Hodge's professional life also showed the relatively insular state of the field. After working with the BAE and Smithsonian for twenty-five years, in 1918 the then fifty-four-year-old Hodge accepted a position from George Gustav Heye at the recently created Museum of the American Indian, Heye Foundation (MAI) in New York. Hired for his editorial skills, Hodge increased the MAI's publishing output, remaining there until the economic downturn of the Great Depression. Although he was sixty-eight, in 1932 Hodge accepted an offer from the Southwest Museum in Los Angeles. There he stayed for another quarter century as director, working alongside his former MAI colleague M. R. Harrington and retiring in 1956.[5]

Nor was Hodge the first anthropologist to tap into Murie's extensive knowledge of Native American cultures. Murie's life, more than any of the other Native collaborators in this book, illustrated the interconnected nature of U.S. anthropology at the turn of the twentieth century. Over a thirty-year period he worked for four different museums across the country, collaborated with a handful of prominent non-Native anthropologists, and produced more information on American Indian ethnography than many of his peers combined. Simply put, by early 1911 when Murie responded to Hodge's request to collaborate, he was already well traveled in the anthropological terrain.

Youth and Reservation Schools

In the eighteenth century the Chaticks si Chaticks people were one of the largest and most powerful Indigenous nations living on the Great Plains. Their territory covered present-day Nebraska and Kansas, with a population numbering approximately ten thousand. This massive community included four distinct bands: the Chaui, Kitkehahki, Pitahawirata, and Skidi. While linguistically and culturally related, the four bands lived apart and were politically independent of each other. This changed in the early nineteenth century when leaders of the Chaticks si Chaticks bands signed a treaty with the U.S. government, ceding large portions of their territory in exchange for money and goods. Another treaty and further land loss followed in 1857, only five years before James R. Murie's birth. Born in Grand Island, Nebraska Territory, in 1862, Murie was the son of a non-Native soldier named James Murie and a Chaticks si Chaticks woman named Anna Murie. Like his mother, Murie was a Skidi Chaticks si Chaticks, or member of the Skidi band.[6]

In 1867, when Murie was five years old, Nebraska became part of the Union. Nebraska's state government immediately stripped the Chaticks si Chaticks people of their rights and territory, dismantling the reservation to sell to eastern settler colonizers hungry for land. The federal government failed to prevent this infringement of its peoples' rights and instead sought lands for Murie's Chaticks si Chaticks community in the Indian Territory of present-day Oklahoma. Federal removal of Murie and his people from their ancestral lands in Nebraska followed between 1872 and 1874, with Murie and his mother among the last group to arrive in their new home four hundred miles to the south.[7]

Before leaving Nebraska, Murie's mother desired her son receive a Western-style education. Acceding to her wishes, he attended the Pawnee Day School at Genoa in Nebraska for approximately four months. After moving to the Indian Territory, Murie continued his schooling, this time at the new Pawnee Agency Indian Day School and later at the Pawnee Indian Boarding School that opened in 1878. At these schools Murie learned English quickly, even working for the reservation agent as an unofficial interpreter. The young man excelled at his studies so much that the following year he was invited to attend Virginia's Hampton Normal and Agricultural Institute. Hampton had only begun admitting Native students in 1878, with Southern Tsitsistas/Suhtai future anthropological collaborator Tichkematse among the first class. Murie jumped at the opportunity to continue his schooling and see the East Coast.[8]

Hampton Institute

Sixteen years old in October 1879, Murie left his home on the Pawnee Reservation and traveled east to Virginia. While we lack Murie's account of his early travels, we do have the recollections of another Hampton student—Thomas Wildcat Alford, a young Shawnee man who made this journey at nearly the same time as Murie. Alford later recalled his train racing through beautiful country with well-cultivated fields and large homes occasionally interrupted by bustling cities and small towns. For Alford this changing scenery was strange, accustomed as he was to western prairies and lowlands. Although no record exists of the two meeting, it is notable that Murie entered Hampton only six months after fellow future Native collaborator Tichkematse's departure from this school. Coincidentally, Murie left Hampton in 1883, only a few years before another Native anthropologist, William Jones, also became a Hampton student.[9]

As we have seen with the experiences of Tichkematse and William Jones at Hampton, the school was semi-military in nature, as was Carlisle. School authorities prided themselves on strict rules and regulations requiring promptness in their execution. Like other Indian boarding schools, the Hampton school day was divided in two—one half dedicated to classroom education and the other spent in manual training and industrial pursuits. For Murie during his first year, this meant working on the school's farm.[10]

By his second year at Hampton, Murie transitioned from farm work to the Hampton Institute's student printing office. He had a desire to learn the printer's trade and went on to work two days a week setting type for the student-run newspaper, the *Southern Workman*, a trade he greatly enjoyed. As recent scholars have noted, Indian boarding school newspapers were complex sites of negotiation. Indigenous students found ways to highlight their Native pasts and celebrate their cultures in their writing, creating networks among their fellow pupils that lasted for decades. This, despite the strict editorial control school authorities exerted over the newspapers. Murie was not alone among future Native collaborators drawn to the printing trade. Carlisle student Richard Davis, Hampton student William Jones, and Haskell student Amos Oneroad all followed the same path in boarding school.[11]

A notable Hampton teacher who encouraged Murie in the printing trade was educator and Hampton alumnus Booker T. Washington. When the Virginia school was founded to educate Black youths, Washington left his teaching post in West Virginia for a new position at Hampton in September 1880. Although he taught at the school for less than a year before becoming head of Alabama's Tuskegee Institute, Washington had a large impact on the Black and Native students at the Virginia school, including Murie. As noted in Tichkematse and William Jones's experiences there, Hampton's multiracial student body of Black and Native students was a rarity in the late nineteenth-century southern United States. School authorities believed this association benefited the students, asserting that Black pupils and teachers would help usher Native Americans into so-called civilization and Christianity.[12]

A Sahnish (Arikara) woman who attended Hampton in its early years later wrote of this mingling between Native and Black youths. According to her, although contact between the two groups was heavily monitored by school officials, she felt the Native students still learned a great deal from their Black counterparts. Particularly, she noted Indigenous young men at Hampton learned from their fellow students the "civilized way of treating women with respect," so unlike what she had seen growing up on a western reservation.[13]

Unsurprisingly, Murie was heavily influenced by the assimilationist doctrine taught at Hampton. During his few short years there he became a member of the local Episcopal church and even wrote to the commissioner of Indian affairs requesting more of his Chaticks si Chaticks fellows be allowed to enter Hampton. In 1881 Murie even met President James Garfield while the latter paid a short visit to Hampton. There the U.S. president addressed the student body, encouraging the young women and men in attendance to accept assimilation and become good Americans.[14]

Just as Richard Henry Pratt at Carlisle capitalized on his students' "progress" to build support for his assimilation projects, so too did Hampton's founder and superintendent General Samuel C. Armstrong. Accordingly, in 1882 Armstrong toured several East Coast cities, seeking financial help to expand his school. He visited Philadelphia, New York, and Boston and brought along a few of his more promising students, including James R. Murie and Thomas Wildcat Alford. While on these fundraising tours Murie and Alford frequently spoke to wealthy individuals, praising Armstrong's work in assimilating Native American youths. The fundraising venture was a wild success, with Armstrong and his Indigenous proteges raising nearly $60,000 during this one tour alone.

Speeches and meeting with wealthy donors were not the only activities, either. Alford recalled how he and Murie once lost their way while sightseeing in New York City and had to spend hours retracing their steps. While no doubt a scary experience, Alford remembered it as being quite enjoyable as well. In many ways it was a liberating trip for two Native teenagers to explore the streets of the country's largest city. For Alford the speaking tour was delightful. It provided an opportunity for him and Murie to finally see many things they had only read about but couldn't fully comprehend until witnessing them in person. According to both young men, this trip through major East Coast cities enlarged their vision of the world.[15]

Despite several sources reporting that Murie graduated and received his diploma from the Hampton Institute in 1883, questions about the truth of this remain. Based on correspondence at the time, Murie most likely plagiarized another student's work and was ejected from the school only days before the term was up. Whether true or not, Murie departed Hampton in the spring of 1883 and returned west to the Pawnee Reservation, the first member of his community to attend an East Coast Indian boarding school. Soon after returning home Murie encouraged those around him, including his younger brother Alfred, to attend Indian boarding schools. At least in the case of Alfred he was successful. His young brother took Murie's advice, arriving at Hampton in October 1886. There Alfred remained for three years, returning to the Pawnee Reservation to rejoin his brother in the Indian Territory in 1889.[16]

A Teacher at Pawnee and a Disciplinarian at Haskell

Much had changed on the Pawnee Reservation during the four years James R. Murie was at Hampton. When he left in 1879 few Chaticks si Chaticks people worked on farms. Instead, they lived in small villages as they had in Nebraska years before. Returning in 1883, though, Murie saw farms on both sides of the road, owned and worked by members of his community. Many now lived in log houses rather than mud lodges, and several people raised cattle and even worked for the federal government at the Pawnee Agency. All these changes illustrated marked progress as far as Murie was concerned. Paralleling Richard Davis's experience at Carlisle, Murie became an advocate of the assimilationist doctrine that had been drilled into him at Hampton. During his time in the East he began to dress in the "white man's style" and accepted Christianity as his religion. Once back in Pawnee, he wanted to become a teacher to share the benefits of Euro-American civilization as he saw them.[17]

Unfortunately for Murie, no teaching positions were available in 1883, so he became a clerk in a local store in the town of Pawnee. There he worked as a bookkeeper, making use of his newfound English and math skills. His pay was high, at $45 per month. That fall the Pawnee Agency Boarding School opened, and Murie jumped at the opportunity to teach, despite the pay cut he received. Only two teachers were employed to instruct eighty students, with Murie aiding them in their work as an assistant teacher. He primarily taught six- and seven-year-olds who knew little English. Instructing them in the colonizer's language, he first identified objects, then words, and eventually sentences to help his pupils along. In addition to his teaching duties, Murie oversaw the boys' dormitory. Hearkening back to his Hampton days, he even set up a printshop with himself as editor of the school's monthly publication, the *New Era*.[18]

At the same time Murie returned from Hampton in the spring of 1883, the citizens and local legislature of Lawrence, Kansas, agreed to establish an Indian boarding school in their town, and donated three hundred acres of land to the federal government for the Haskell Institute, officially opening on September 17, 1884. Anticipating the new school's opening, Murie resigned his teaching position at the Pawnee Indian School in early September to lend his skills where needed at Haskell. Traveling the 250 miles north, Murie brought with him twenty-one students from the Pawnee school, hoping to further their education in Lawrence. He and his charges arrived at Haskell on September 18, 1884, one day after the school's official opening.[19]

Dr. James Marvin was Haskell's first superintendent. A deeply religious man, Marvin brought with him his zeal for spreading the Christian gospel. He introduced compulsory church services for all students on Sunday mornings, with Bible school classes following in the afternoon. An advocate of Native assimilation, in his opening address Marvin told the gathered faculty and students Haskell was not a school for the teachers "to learn Indian." Rather, he declared, it was an institute for Native pupils to learn to speak, write, and think in English. Gone would be Indigenous ways of knowledge, Marvin hoped, replaced by the blessings of an enlightened and civilized Christian people.[20]

When Murie arrived in Lawrence that September day in 1884, Superintendent Marvin correctly identified the twenty-two-year-old Chaticks si Chaticks man as the ideal recruit to help mold the student body. Murie was not only a pronounced Christian and an Indigenous proponent of assimilation but also one of the first class of Native students at the Hampton Institute and a sterling example of everything that it represented. Despite Marvin snatching Murie up on the latter's arrival, he received no compensation for his employment other than room and board. It wasn't until January 1885 that Murie was finally placed on the staff payroll. Employed as the school's assistant disciplinarian and drillmaster, he received the paltry sum of $15 a month more than three months after his first day on the job. His duties included serving as a mentor to the young students, while simultaneously doling out punishments for school infractions such as speaking in their Native languages.[21]

Murie's first winter at Haskell in 1884–85 was a harsh one for students and faculty alike. With 61 girls and 219 boys, the total student population of 280 was the highest enrollment the school reached for several years. An inoperative boiler house left countless students without heat during the unusually cold fall of 1884, causing respiratory infections including diphtheria and pneumonia. Illness was so rampant that Superintendent Marvin was forced to hire on a full-time nurse to care for the sick. Enrollment the following spring and summer of 1885 dropped precipitously, and the resulting uproar from students and parents was so great that Marvin eventually resigned in July, less than a year after his position began. His replacement, Colonel Arthur Grabowskii, proved to be an even worse selection to oversee the students' welfare.[22]

Murie continued to work as an assistant disciplinarian at Haskell during this transitional period. In June 1885, just before resigning, Superintendent Marvin sent Murie to the Pawnee Agency to recruit more Chaticks si Chaticks students. Like William Jones, Murie delighted in this recruiting work, certain in the correctness of guiding Native youths along the assimilationist path. Returning to Lawrence with recruits in tow that July, Murie met his new boss—Superintendent Grabowskii.[23]

Like Marvin before him, Grabowskii believed deeply in the need to Christianize and assimilate the Indigenous pupils in his care. Grabowskii went a step further, though, pushing for stricter discipline and introducing a rigid system of organizing the students into cadet battalions. Modeling Haskell on Richard Henry Pratt's military structure at Fort Marion and Carlisle, this method not only enforced discipline—it also intentionally subverted efforts among the students to group themselves by Native nation or culture. Grabowskii's innovations included the introduction of harsher punishments and even a school prison. Not surprisingly, student desertion increased dramatically after the new superintendent's changes. Many students wrote home complaining of their treatment and requesting to return to their reservations. Enrollment fell, with only forty-three new students joining the student body by the end of 1886.[24]

Despite Grabowskii's authoritarian attitude at Haskell, Murie continued in his role as assistant disciplinarian, helping the new superintendent mete out punishments for any perceived infractions. While not a student during

Murie's time at Haskell, a pupil later recalled the harsh nature of gruff, short-tempered disciplinarians policing student actions at the school. Whether Murie actually fit this image is difficult to determine. By 1886, though, he had had enough of Haskell. Murie resigned his position that spring and returned home to the Pawnee Reservation in the Oklahoma Territory.[25]

Assimilation, Allotment, and Resistance in Pawnee

Back in Pawnee, Murie picked up where he left off two years earlier. He continued teaching at the Pawnee Indian Boarding School in his former position, earning double and eventually triple the pay received at Haskell. It was also during this time that Murie decided to settle down, marry, and raise a family. At age twenty-five in 1887, he married Mary Esau, a member of the Chaticks si Chaticks community. Like Murie, Mary was forced from her home in Nebraska as a child and similarly made the trek to the Indian Territory.[26]

Some scholars have argued that due to his Hampton Institute boarding school education, Murie was at best a marginal member of the Chaticks si Chaticks community. They contend that because of his assimilationist mindset gained at the school, he was largely divorced from those who refused to abandon their ceremonial and religious traditions. This does seem to be the case at least in his immediate post-Hampton days. In the late 1880s and early 1890s, for instance, Murie followed the progressive, anti-traditional element of the Chaticks si Chaticks community in Pawnee. His correspondence to former Hampton teachers highlights his embrace of Euro-American ways of life. In an 1890 letter, for example, Murie shared with his former instructors the news of his recent marriage and the birth of the couple's first child. He noted that his son's name was Fred Wallace Murie, "not *Le-coots, Tah-Kah*," or any other Native name. "I want my little boy to grow up with white man's ideas," Murie declared to his pro-assimilationist audience. He could envision no future in which adhering to the traditions of their Indigenous ancestors would benefit his children.[27]

While Murie's words are disheartening for many modern-day readers, it is important to point out he may have been exaggerating his own views to please those at Hampton. This is a practice Ho-Chunk (Winnebago) anthropologist Renya K. Ramirez describes as "doubling." In these situations Indigenous peoples took on either Native or non-Native traits or perspectives to fit in, depending on their audiences. Although it is unclear if Murie applied this strategy at the time, it was something he later embraced as a Native collaborator working with non-Native anthropologists. Nor was he alone in doing so. Doubling was a strategy many Indigenous peoples used to retain their cultures, their languages, and their beliefs. To pass or be accepted in a non-Native society, these same individuals often resorted to masking their Native identities and dismissed or denigrated their cultures without ever truly abandoning them.[28]

In 1892 Murie left his position at the Pawnee Indian Boarding School. With his younger brother Alfred he worked as a private with the Pawnee Agency Indian Police, for which they each received $20 a month. Around this time Murie also became more involved in Pawnee Agency matters. He subsequently served as an interpreter, recorded census information, and, most calamitously for his community, pushed for allotment. Convinced this was the proper step forward toward U.S. citizenship, he frequently advocated for allotment, encouraging young men to take up farming. In November 1892 Murie, his brother Alfred, and 156 Chaticks si Chaticks men signed an agreement with U.S. commissioners, dismantling their collective landholdings. By signing this agreement, the Chaticks si Chaticks people surrendered all title, claim, and interest of the Pawnee Reservation lands to the federal government. From that day forward they became recipients of federal allotment and citizenship. Gone was communal ownership of land, replaced by individual plots for farming. The Pawnee Reservation was hardly alone, either. U.S. commissioners traveled from one reservation to another during these years, "encouraging" allotment and the sale of Native lands. Their goal was clear—opening these territories to Euro-American settlement.[29]

According to Murie, what resulted was nothing but bitter experiences for him and his people. Initially believing allotment was a panacea for the ills confronting Native peoples, Murie later viewed these actions by the U.S. government as an attempt to exterminate the country's American Indian nations. Prior to the 1892 signing of this agreement, the Chaticks si Chaticks were farmers largely free from the intrusion of settler colonizers on their lands. With the dismantling of communal landholdings, though, non-Native settlers from the East flocked to the area. Persecution of Native landholders quickly followed, as Chaticks si Chaticks women and men were threatened and cheated out of their allotments. Murie saw large numbers of his own people pushed onto lands either too poor or unhealthy for the new settler colonizers to want.

The effects of allotment on his community changed Murie. He soon after traveled to Washington DC to protest the government's actions and advocate for Native resistance against further allotment efforts. This was the point when Murie began to turn the power, using his English skills to be a voice against federal assimilation and allotment, rather than in favor of them. Nor was it just coincidence that this change occurred at the same time he took on his first real anthropological work, documenting and preserving his culture for future generations.[30]

Anthropological Fieldwork with Fletcher

Alice C. Fletcher and Murie met in the early 1880s while he was still a student at Hampton. However, it wasn't until fifteen years later that the two began collaborating. Indeed, it was Fletcher who first launched Murie along the anthropological path to which he devoted the rest of his life. The most well-known female anthropologist of her day, Fletcher worked as an ethnological assistant at Harvard's Peabody Museum of American Archaeology and Ethnology under the direction of Frederic Ward Putnam. She became interested in anthropology in 1879 after attending a speech by Susette and Francis La Flesche on Omaha land rights. Then and there Fletcher decided to undertake anthropological fieldwork, despite the fact that a non-Native woman working alone among American Indian nations was virtually unheard of.[31]

Never one to be told what she could not do, Fletcher traveled westward making a name for herself studying the lives of Native women among the Upper Missouri River communities. Returning from fieldwork in 1881, Fletcher relentlessly lobbied Congress on behalf of Native land rights, eventually helping pass the Omaha Act in 1882 and the Dawes Act in 1887. Despite her initial advocacy of allotment policies, the resulting legislation failed to accomplish what Fletcher hoped. Rather than transform American Indians into farmers on their own plots of land, many Native peoples instead became objects of greed for settler colonizers eager for land. As with the 1892 allotment of Pawnee Reservation lands, such federal actions wrought untold devastation on Native communities across the United States.[32]

Following in Fletcher's footsteps a half century later, anthropologist Margaret Mead reported on the outcome of her predecessor's allotment work on the Omaha Reservation. According to Mead, this was a culture so shrunk from its earlier style that there was very little out of the past that was recognizable and still less in the present that was aesthetically satisfying. Recognizing the failure of allotment, Mead wrote that she had the unrewarding task of discussing the long history of mistakes in U.S. policy toward North America's Indigenous peoples and of prophesying a still more disastrous fate for them in the future.[33]

In addition to her advocacy of federal allotment policies, Fletcher received condemnation from more recent generations for the close relationship she maintained with Carlisle Indian Industrial School founder Richard Henry Pratt. Believing the best schooling for Native Americans was to mix with Euro-American populations, she eagerly supported Pratt's Indian boarding school policy of assimilation through education. As early as 1882 Fletcher worked for Pratt, recruiting Native children to attend Carlisle. Troubled by her continued anthropological endeavors, Pratt attempted to tip the scales in his favor, suggesting her Christian reform work would reach farther into eternity than her work as an anthropologist. Frederic Ward Putnam at Harvard also competed for Fletcher's allegiance, urging that she must give up her allotment work altogether and devote herself completely to anthropological writing and study. In hindsight, it is difficult to label which of the two approaches was ultimately worse for Native Americans—forced removal and loss of culture at Indian boarding schools or loss of culture through the salvage anthropology ethos of museums.[34]

Native contemporaries of Fletcher also had mixed opinions on her life and work. Francis La Flesche, Fletcher's Omaha teacher, student, collaborator, and erstwhile companion from 1879 until her death in 1923, unsurprisingly wrote of her in glowing terms. To La Flesche, Fletcher was a woman with a courageous heart, full of true sympathy for humankind, and a "great friend of the Indians." Carlisle publications by Native students reveal many children supportive of assimilation who also praised the work of Fletcher. The *Indian Helper* of April 1, 1887, for example, noted her excellent advice to American Indian youths. Three years later a different article in the school newspaper highlighted a visit in which she interpreted and explained to pupils the importance of the Dawes Bill and allotment acts for their future.[35]

Other Native peoples, including the parents of Carlisle students, viewed Fletcher differently. The parents of Alice Springer are one example. Springer was a fourteen-year-old Omaha girl whom Fletcher recruited and who subsequently died of illness while attending Carlisle in 1883. Mourning their daughter's loss, her parents voiced their complaints to Richard Henry Pratt. They requested their two other children at Carlisle be immediately sent home. They also expressed their confusion over the necessity of sending their children so far away to be educated, when they had good schools closer to home. At these schools, too, Alice's mother continued, parents could at least attend to their children when sick, rather than lose them to disease and death hundreds of miles away. Alice Springer's mother, in particular, wrote that she did not see why the government put so much power and confidence in Fletcher, as she could not be trusted. According to her, Alice Fletcher did "no good to the Omahas, but much harm."[36]

Despite some Native peoples' mixed feelings about her, Fletcher was an up-and-coming name in the anthropological field. Thus, it was no surprise James R. Murie agreed to work with her. Though they had met years earlier, it wasn't until 1896 that Murie and Fletcher were reintroduced by their mutual friend Francis La Flesche. Soon afterward Fletcher pursued fieldwork among the Chaticks si Chaticks community, and in 1898 the two started working together under the auspices of Harvard's Peabody Museum and the Smithsonian's BAE.[37]

Fletcher recruited Murie as an interpreter and collaborator, a working relationship they maintained for the next four years. Although Murie provided brief ethnographic information to George Bird Grinnell in the 1880s, his work with Fletcher was the first time he truly entered the field as an anthropological collaborator. Murie and Fletcher were interested in documenting the histories of ceremonies and dances, and their correspondence teems with ethnographic descriptions of the Calumet ritual or Hako ceremony, the Buffalo Head ceremony, and many others. Fletcher traveled to the Oklahoma Territory on a number of occasions, and Murie, likewise, worked in person with Fletcher when he traveled to Washington DC. Murie recorded, transcribed, and translated songs, and in 1898 and again in 1900 Murie even brought Chaticks si Chaticks elders with him to work with Fletcher in DC.

One Chaticks si Chaticks elder in particular came to be a source of great information to Fletcher and Murie. Murie convinced this Keeper of Sacred Objects to work with Fletcher so his cultural knowledge would live on after him. He had never traveled east of the Mississippi River, but he and Murie traveled to Washington DC in 1898. There they accompanied Fletcher on a tour of the U.S. Capitol Building and the Library of Congress. Acknowledging the beauty of these structures, the Chaticks si Chaticks elder nevertheless remarked that such buildings were not a fit home to contain the sacred symbols of his ancestors. Instead, he informed Murie and Fletcher, the objects in his care needed to reside in an earth lodge, among their people. Alongside his concerns about a proper home for Chaticks si Chaticks culture, the elder also repeated to Murie that while he agreed that this ceremonial information should be preserved, he did not want it made public where non-Chaticks si Chaticks people could read it and possibly mock it or use it for nefarious purposes. Despite the elder's admonitions, Fletcher published English translations of these sacred songs in 1904, making them available for public consumption.[38]

Soon after returning from his trip to the nation's capital, the Chaticks si Chaticks Keeper of Sacred Objects regretted his collaborative work with Murie and Fletcher. By 1901 the elder's wife and grandchild died, actions that community members blamed on him for providing sacred information to outsiders. Mourning the loss of his loved ones, the elder told Murie he believed Fletcher had done him wrong. After she got the information she desired, he told Murie, she had no further use for him and did not even write him. More trouble soon followed. Some community members claimed Murie and Fletcher duped the elder into giving away secret information. Rumors circulated in the town of Pawnee that Murie kept the money owed to the elder, seeking to line his own pockets. When Murie approached the elder again in late 1901, the latter flatly refused to collaborate any further with anthropologists.[39]

Anthropological Fieldwork with Dorsey

By the early 1900s the Chicago Field Museum's curator of anthropology, George A. Dorsey, had also taken an interest in the Indigenous peoples of the Great Plains. Acquiring material culture objects and information from these communities was a priority for him. Visiting the Oklahoma Territory in 1901 and 1902, Dorsey displayed his accustomed tenacity in getting what he wanted. And what he wanted was Murie as a Native collaborator. In June and August 1901 the Field Museum curator made repeated overtures of employment to Murie, even visiting him at his home unannounced. By early the following year Dorsey's continued promise of higher wages and paid travel to and from the Chicago museum started to sway the Chaticks si Chaticks man.

Murie was conflicted over competing loyalties to individual anthropologists, to their museums, and to Dorsey's offer of better pay. This is clear in his correspondence with Fletcher, whom he wrote numerous times asking advice over what to do about Dorsey. Finally, in April 1902 Dorsey offered Murie $100 per month and a contract of four years, and Murie accepted. He wrote another letter to Fletcher, apologizing for terminating their collaborative relationship so suddenly. On account of his financial situation, he felt he could not refuse Dorsey's offer.[40]

This example illustrates better than most the important level Native American collaborators attained during the height of the U.S. salvage anthropology movement. Access to a Native person who could speak, read, and write English, and who, more importantly, was willing to collaborate with non-Native anthropologists and provide them with sacred objects and sensitive cultural information—this was what all anthropologists hoped for. In many ways, then, James R. Murie was an anthropologist's dream.

Beginning in 1902 and continuing for the next five years, Murie and Dorsey collected Chaticks si Chaticks and Sahnish objects and recorded ceremonies and ritual songs throughout the Oklahoma Territory and North Dakota. As most Native collaborators were the ones doing the actual anthropological collecting in the field, Murie twice traveled to the Fort Berthold Indian Reservation in North Dakota by himself. There he spent the summers of 1903 and 1905 among the Sahnish people, collecting information on their ceremonies and recording narratives. According to

Dorsey, Murie was fluent in the Sahnish language, having learned it from other young boys during his Indian boarding school days.[41]

Murie and Dorsey's process was for Murie to write out ethnographic data and then send it to Dorsey for use in publications and exhibitions. Murie did this for collected material on both Chaticks si Chaticks and Sahnish communities. Unusual, however, was that the Field Museum's board of directors repeatedly paid for Murie to travel to Chicago to consult on exhibit design, construction, and interpretation of the museum's Native displays. For extended periods between 1902 and 1906, Murie and his family relocated to Chicago for weeks and even months at a time. There Murie worked on-site with Dorsey preparing their anthropological publications.[42]

As Murie had done with Fletcher in Washington DC, the Chaticks si Chaticks collaborator also brought community elders to Chicago to provide sacred and ceremonial information to Dorsey. In 1904, for instance, Murie and a Skidi Chaticks si Chaticks priest traveled to the Field Museum to record narratives on wax cylinders. Their visit lasted several weeks, resulting in hours of recordings of Chaticks si Chaticks belief systems, rituals, narratives, and reminiscences of daily life. Murie wrote transcripts of the recordings in the Skidi dialect and translated them into English. A few years later Murie and Dorsey even cobbled together funding to travel to New York City to work alongside anthropologist Franz Boas. There the three men refined the Chaticks si Chaticks transcriptions with Boas's linguistic guidance. Busy with other projects, however, Dorsey never published the results of this collaborative work. This information remains today in museum archives.[43]

Murie was hardly the only Native collaborator within Dorsey's orbit. During these same years Richard Davis and William Jones also worked with Dorsey at the Field Museum. In following chapters readers will meet yet another former Carlisle Indian Industrial School student and Native collaborator who worked with Dorsey—Cleaver Warden. Each of these men informed non-Native outsiders about their cultures. They collaborated with anthropologists to collect objects and information from their communities. At times they even requested to exhibit themselves in anthropological displays at world's fairs.

Promoters at world's fairs constructed human zoos, known as ethnographic or Indian villages, for the entertainment of fairgoers. Popular at expositions in Chicago in 1893, Omaha in 1898, and St. Louis in 1904, these enclosed areas housed Indigenous peoples from North America and around the globe. Native people on display illustrated to overwhelmingly non-Native audiences the latest scientific theories on humankind's supposed linear progress from savagery and barbarism to enlightenment. Fairgoers witnessed a variety of the world's peoples exhibited from allegedly lower to higher humanity. Viewing these exhibits, Euro-American fairgoers gained not so much an appreciation for the diversity of humankind as they did the reassurance that they were the pinnacle of human development.

Despite their explicitly racist and pseudo-scientific messaging, these Indian villages did provide something to the Native Americans who participated in them. If nothing else, they offered a temporary escape from reservation life that was a form of imprisonment itself. As shown by Richard Davis's experience at the St. Louis World's Fair, participation in Indian villages offered some financial opportunities, paltry as they were. Those living in the villages went about their daily lives, creating crafts and practicing "Aboriginal arts" as non-Native audiences looked on. Fair promoters intended for them to construct dwellings, weave blankets, and make clothes out of animal skins, all the while educating and entertaining the visiting public. Additionally, those on exhibit sold blankets, baskets, and other items to earn a profit. Some used their business savvy in other ingenious ways, such as when Chiricahua Apache chief Goyathlay, known more popularly as Geronimo, charged St. Louis fair visitors ten cents apiece for his signature, which they kept as souvenirs.[44]

In 1904 Murie decided he could earn some additional income by participating in one of these world's fairs. That spring he, his wife Mary, and their four children moved to the St. Louis fairgrounds, where they literally put themselves on display. Like Richard Davis, Murie recruited Native community members to participate in the St. Louis World's Fair. Notably, while James, Mary, and three of their children lived in the Indian village, their eldest daughter Caroline took a break from her studies as a student at the Haskell Institute and participated in the Bureau of Indian Affairs' model Indian boarding school exhibit.[45]

Directing this exhibit was Samuel McCowan, a longtime Bureau of Indian Affairs employee. Wanting to distance himself from anthropologist WJ McGee's Indian village and its focus on the past, McCowan contrasted the two exhibits by describing the Indian village as representative of "the old Indian," while the school represented the path of the young, modern, assimilated American Indian. The model school was fully operational with 150 Native American students in a classroom environment that fairgoers observed on the fairgrounds. For McCowan, the BIA model school exhibit and the St. Louis World's Fair symbolized the wisdom of federal policies geared toward assimilating American Indians. The old ways of Native American life were rapidly disappearing, McCowan believed, and he for one was happy to see them go.[46]

Anthropological Fieldwork with Hodge

By 1907 Dorsey and the Field Museum began transitioning away from exhibits about the Indigenous peoples of North America. In its place they sought greater information on the more "exotic" cultures of Africa, Asia, and Oceania. As noted previously, it was due to the Field Museum's change in geographical focus that Sac and Fox anthropologist William Jones conducted fieldwork in the Philippines and there lost his life. Relatedly, a few years before Jones's death Dorsey made a similar offer to Murie, asking if he would be interested in an expedition to Borneo. Foreshadowing Jones's demise soon after, Murie declined the offer, joking that he did not wish to lose his head to headhunters. Work between Murie and Dorsey continued sporadically for a few more years. Due to the Field Museum's changing global focus, though, their collaborations grew less frequent and eventually trailed off completely by 1909.[47]

After four years of work with Fletcher followed by seven with Dorsey, by 1909 Murie found himself out of the anthropological profession. Fortunately, he had never relied on anthropological work as his only income. In addition to collecting work, he served as an interpreter in federal delegation meetings between his Native nation and members of the U.S. government and, more prosaically, worked as a clerk and teller at the Pawnee National Bank in town.[48]

Although Murie took on various jobs over the years, his true passion was documenting, preserving, and, in his words, "saving" his culture. In

January 1911, less than two years after ending his employment with Dorsey and the Field Museum, he was back at it. This time Frederick Webb Hodge at the Smithsonian's BAE sought him out. Knowing of Murie's talents, interests, and access to information, Hodge requested Murie document Chaticks si Chaticks ceremonies, specifically the New Fire and Morning Star sacred bundle ceremonies. Hodge additionally asked Murie to write up biographical information on celebrated "chiefs and warriors of the Pawnee tribes" for inclusion in Hodge's magnum opus at the Smithsonian, *The Handbook of American Indians North of Mexico*. Murie readily accepted the task.[49]

In demand and accustomed to a higher monthly wage under Dorsey at the Field Museum, Murie told Hodge the sum the BAE paid him for his collecting work was too small. To better equip Murie materially if not financially, Hodge then supplied the Chaticks si Chaticks collaborator with a graphophone, records, a typewriter, a camera, and two tents for his fieldwork. Over the following years Murie observed and documented ceremonies, collected songs never before recorded, and procured sacred objects to augment the Smithsonian's collections.[50]

Murie's correspondence during this time highlights the challenges he faced getting community members to provide information. This was particularly difficult when locating volunteers to sing songs into his Smithsonian graphophone machine. Some songs proved easier to collect, of course. Murie told Hodge he had recorded many songs on butterflies, grasshoppers, turtles, and birds, as well as others addressing the sun, moon, and meteorites. Chaticks si Chaticks songs about medicine and ceremonies, however, were a different story. Murie wrote that even when offered ample money, many community members refused to share this knowledge. In another letter to Hodge, Murie observed that his people were wary of outsiders learning this sacred information. It's their religion, Murie wrote, so they are very careful about the individuals to whom they impart these things. As for himself, Murie told Hodge he was happy to record and preserve these sacred songs, but he did not intend for "outside people" to learn them. One of Murie's concerns was that his English translations of these sacred songs might leave out the nuances of the singers and knowledge keepers. Despite Murie claiming he did not want outsiders to learn these

sacred songs, the Chaticks si Chaticks collaborator still provided translations to Hodge, knowing the Smithsonian would publish this material.[51]

Six months after Murie started working with Hodge, he told the BAE
curator about the death of a Chaticks si Chaticks elder. The recently
deceased was Keeper of the Elk Dance. As such, tradition dictated he be
buried with sacred objects fitting his station. Murie, however, encouraged
community members to ignore the normal burial procedures, hoping to
acquire these items for the Smithsonian's collections. Hodge, too, wanted
the sacred objects but told Murie that it would depend on the museum's
available funding. No further correspondence exists on this subject matter,
and Murie made no other references to potential grave robbing.[52]

Examples like this raise a fundamental question about the work of Native
American collaborators—what were their intentions? Murie, for instance,
explicitly stated on several occasions that he wanted to save Chaticks
si Chaticks culture. He believed Native cultures were vanishing, due in
large part to enforced assimilation policies of which he himself was a part.
Perhaps Murie thought it better to save at least some of his community's
tangible culture in a museum rather than bury it in the ground. That way
his supposedly vanishing culture might still continue on.

Maybe this was Murie's thought process, but we don't know for sure. All
his correspondence leads in that direction. Nevertheless, the fact remains
that by placing these community objects in the hands of outsiders, Murie
gave away his culture. Even more egregiously, Murie didn't simply give it
away. He sold his community's culture and kept the profits. Nor was he
alone in doing so. As we see again and again, all the Native collaborators
in this book willingly provided information and material culture objects
to non-Native anthropologists to keep in museums. Whether their actions
were good, bad, or somewhere in between depends on one's perception
of anthropology's race to preserve Indigenous cultures. That legacy is
something many Native and non-Native people continue to debate today.

By 1912 Murie was more confident with his place in the field of anthropology. He had grown as a person since beginning this work with Fletcher
fifteen years earlier. At this point he better recognized the value of his
work, as well as the power he wielded as a liaison between different cultures. And it didn't hurt that his accomplishments had made the rounds

of the anthropological circles. Subsequently more and more members of the profession were eager to work with him. With this newfound status Murie demanded better pay for his ethnographic work. He also realized he could take on more than one collaborative project at a time, in effect working for multiple anthropologists and multiple museums simultaneously. Thus, after only one year of working with Hodge at the BAE, Murie also began collaborating with Clark Wissler, head curator of anthropology at the AMNH in New York. While his relationship with Hodge ended in 1918 when the latter left for the Museum of the American Indian, Heye Foundation, Murie's relationship with Wissler at the AMNH continued until the end of his life.

Anthropological Fieldwork with Wissler

As had been the case with Hodge in 1911 and Dorsey and Fletcher before that, museum anthropologists were the ones who sought out Murie. This pattern repeated itself in September 1912 when Clark Wissler first wrote to Murie. Just prior to this Wissler had been concentrating much of his research on Indigenous nations of the upper Great Plains. Specifically, he had collaborated with D. C. Duvall on studies of the Pikuni Blackfeet (Piegan) people in northwestern Montana when Duvall ended his life in July 1911. After Duvall's death Wissler largely abandoned his work in Montana. The tragedy was too much for him. Instead, Wissler chose to focus on the Chaticks si Chaticks community in Oklahoma.[53]

From the start, Murie and Wissler had a rapport unlike that of many of their colleagues. The formality in their letters in which they addressed each other as Mr. Murie and Dr. Wissler belied a warmth and a personal friendship between the two. They corresponded over great distances but also met in person in Oklahoma and New York when they could. As time went on, they spent extended weeklong sessions together in Wissler's summer home in Indiana, compiling ethnographic fieldnotes for publication and use in museum exhibitions. Emblematic of the friendship between their two families was the naming of Murie's daughter born in 1916. Writing Wissler to share the happy news, Murie noted that despite his daughter's small size, he and his wife had given her a big name—Viola Gebhart Wissler Murie, named after Clark Wissler's wife, Viola Gebhart Wissler.[54]

The anthropological work Murie and Wissler undertook together was similar to that of other Native collaborators and non-Native anthropologists. As in his work with Fletcher, Dorsey, and Hodge, Murie provided Wissler with information related to Chaticks si Chaticks songs, ceremonies, and men's societies. Notably, though, Murie told Wissler he was providing the latter with a lot of information kept back from the other anthropologists with whom he had previously worked.[55]

When it came to objects, Wissler was particularly interested in medicine bundles and other sacred items entrusted to secret society members. Acquiring these objects involved a series of delicate maneuverings and negotiations for Murie. He told Wissler that he had to go slowly when it came to medicine bundles because their keepers were often afraid to sell them for fear of reprisal, human or divine. One case in 1915 well illustrates the competitive nature of museums in the race to acquire these sacred objects before their competitors could. Murie told Wissler about a Chaticks si Chaticks woman in possession of several medicine bundles who was willing to sell them. Murie advised speed, though, as the woman needed money and might sell to other museums or collectors. Learning of this opportunity, Wissler appealed to his superiors at the AMNH to immediately make available the funds to acquire these objects before Dorsey at the Field Museum or Heye at the MAI could get their hands on them. From the catalog record at the AMNH, it does not appear that Murie and Wissler succeeding in acquiring these items.

While these specific medicine bundles were not acquired by the AMNH, many other sacred objects eventually were. Once described and cataloged, museums displayed these items to the world, regardless of the wishes of community members. For Wissler and Murie, such collections made for a great exhibit. It is doubtful that many Chaticks si Chaticks people would have agreed.[56]

Between 1912 and 1921 much happened in Murie's and Wissler's lives that challenged their ability to procure objects and information. Murie ended his marriage of thirty years with his first wife, Mary Esau, in 1915. Around this same time he also quit his job at the Pawnee bank where he had been employed for more than two decades. Writing Wissler soon after, Murie said he was more interested in anthropological work than anything else.

He wanted to devote all his free time to it, he continued, and was willing to work every day for Wissler and the AMNH. Despite his enthusiasm, throughout 1917 and 1918 Murie's work was compromised by a debilitating rheumatism in his elbows and hands, largely preventing him from working on his translations and manuscripts. As anthropological work was both his passion and primary source of income, he had few choices but to continue writing. Wissler, for his part, suffered continual ill-health during these years. His condition required long periods of recuperation away from the office and thus away from his anthropological responsibilities.[57]

Obstacles also arose on national and international levels, limiting the amount of time both men could spend collaborating. Only days after the United States formally declared war on Germany in April 1917, Murie told Wissler his youngest son, Peter, wanted to join the military to fight for his country against German aggression. Perhaps facetiously, Murie also wrote Wissler that he hoped the Germans would not blow up New York City while the AMNH anthropologist and his family were there. Due to internal anxieties in their personal lives and socioeconomic pressures in their professional lives, it wasn't until two years later in January 1919 that Murie and Wissler once again took up their collaborative work. With the war now over, Wissler pushed the two men to focus on their publications.

Despite a so-called return to normalcy, locating proper funding for their work proved to be its own challenge as cultural heritage businesses tried to stay afloat in the aftermath of the war. Consequently, anthropological fieldwork and collecting were often interrupted and even completely abandoned when more pressing national and international events occurred. And when there was a lack of funding for fieldwork, there was a consequent lack of income for Native collaborators such as Murie, Davis, Warden, and others. These examples illustrate the unreliable nature of anthropological work faced by Native collaborators and their families, dependent as they were on availability of museum funding.[58]

James R. Murie and Anthropology Today

For more than a quarter century James R. Murie worked in practice, if not in name, as an anthropologist in the field. He collected tangible and intangible cultural information from his own Chaticks si Chaticks community and from the Sahnish people of North Dakota. As a writer, collaborator, interpreter, and intermediary, Murie compiled the largest amount of information on the Chaticks si Chaticks people in existence. He worked with nearly every major anthropologist interested in the Indigenous nations of the Great Plains, from Alice C. Fletcher in the 1890s to Frances Densmore after the end of the First World War. Although the good or ill effects of his collecting work can be debated, his desire to save what he saw as his vanishing culture was still laudable. As scholars have noted, if not for Murie's anthropological work, much of the written information about the Chaticks si Chaticks people, including their songs, ceremonies, and material culture, might no longer exist. Despite this, by the time of his death in 1921 Murie had only one major publication to his name—*Pawnee Indian Societies*.[59]

Although not often mentioned in the media of his day, Murie did receive some attention for his anthropological writing. The April–June 1915 issue of the *Quarterly Journal of the Society of American Indians* honored Murie for his *Pawnee Indian Societies*, coauthored with Wissler. The journal's editor, Seneca archaeologist Arthur C. Parker, described Murie as an Indigenous man who had done a great amount of work for students, writers, and others interested in Chaticks si Chaticks culture. While not a common name in anthropology today, Murie was the major source of information on his community in the early decades of the twentieth century. His influential writings shaped the public's understanding of Chaticks si Chaticks history and culture that continues to the present day.[60]

In many ways, this is exactly what Murie hoped to accomplish. As he often noted, he was more interested in accurately portraying his Native community to non-Native outsiders than anything else. In a 1920 letter to Wissler, Murie employed an informal tone when he urged, "Now Doc, I want you and me to do good work on Pawnee stuff so we can get fine work out—better than any that's been out on Indians." Murie spent decades doing just that—correcting inaccurate and racist depictions of Chaticks si Chaticks and other American Indian nations in the anthropological literature. He continued this type of outreach and education right up until the day he died. He suffered a fatal heart attack in November 1921, only a few days before he was to travel to New York to present anthropological films with Wissler to AMNH audiences. Murie died at age fifty-nine and was buried among friends and family in Pawnee, Oklahoma.[61]

Murie's friend and colleague Clark Wissler outlived him by more than a quarter century, dying in New York in 1947 at the age of seventy-six. A few years after Murie's death, Wissler wrote a short piece in AMNH's *Natural History* magazine intended for a general audience. In describing the work of anthropologists, Wissler wrote that he and other non-Native anthropologists regularly lived "for brief intervals with the Indians." While living with these communities, he continued, anthropologists made observations and often received instruction from community elders about Native philosophies on life. Wissler added, no doubt thinking of his friend James R. Murie, "Sometimes life friendships have sprung up in this way."[62]

Fig. 1. Percy Zadoka and Cleaver Warden at Carlisle Indian Industrial School, c. 1884. Cumberland County Historical Society, PA-CH1-065c.

Fig. 2. Cleaver Warden, 1898. National Anthropological Archives, Smithsonian Institution, INV.02910901

Fig. 3. Francis La Flesche, c. 1880. National Museum of the American Indian, Smithsonian Institution, P09175.

Fig. 4. Tichkematse (*third row, fourth from left*) with fellow prisoners and Richard Henry
Pratt (*second row, far left*) at Fort Marion, Florida, 1878. National Anthropological Archives,
Smithsonian Institution, OPPS NEG.54546.

Fig. 5. Tichkematse, c. 1880. National Anthropological Archives, Smithsonian Institution, INV.00439500.

Fig. 6. Young Bull Bear with his sons Oscar Bull Bear and Richard Davis at Carlisle Indian Industrial School, 1879. National Anthropological Archives, Smithsonian Institution, INV.06826600.

Fig. 7. Richard Davis worked in this print shop at Carlisle Indian Industrial School, 1880. National Anthropological Archives, Smithsonian Institution, INV.06802700.

Fig. 8. James R. Murie, c. 1900. National Anthropological Archives, Smithsonian Institution, INV.06247400.

Fig. 9. John V. Satterlee, c. 1920. National Museum of the American Indian, Smithsonian Institution, P23487.

Fig. 10. Alanson Skinner and Amos Oneroad, c. 1920. National Museum of the American Indian, Smithsonian Institution, P27199.

Fig. 11. Louis and Florence Shotridge dressed in Plains Indian clothing, c. 1913. National Museum of the American Indian, Smithsonian Institution, P28181.

Fig. 12. Florence Shotridge dressed in Plains Indian clothing, c. 1913. National Museum of the American Indian, Smithsonian Institution, P26788.

Fig. 13. Louis Shotridge, c. 1913. National Museum of the American Indian, Smithsonian Institution, P13314.

6

Making a Great Collection of Relics for My People

John V. Satterlee (Keshena, Wisconsin, 1911)

Even though he had already read the letter from his nephew several times, John V. Satterlee needed to read it once more. Of course, Alanson Skinner wasn't technically his nephew by blood or even by marriage. But as the younger man had been ceremonially adopted as a member of the Menominee Nation, Satterlee honored and respected their familial relationship. Nevertheless, the request in his nephew's latest letter required a bit more thought before he could respond with a simple yes or no.

The twenty-five-year-old Skinner was an assistant curator of anthropology at the American Museum of Natural History in New York. Only one year earlier in 1910 Skinner conducted fieldwork with Satterlee's Menominee community in Keshena, Wisconsin. That was when the two men met and instantly hit it off. At nearly sixty, Satterlee had worked with several prominent anthropologists before meeting Skinner. He enjoyed anthropological work—documenting and preserving his people's history and culture—and he took a great deal of pride in it. However, Skinner's letter of September 23, 1911, asked for something a bit more.

In the letter Skinner asked his adoptive uncle if he would join the Midewiwin, a secret Menominee Medicine Lodge ceremony, to gather sacred information for future publication. "It would be better for you to join," Skinner wrote to Satterlee, "as there would be less opposition to telling you anything than there would be to telling me—a white man." If Satterlee did so, Skinner continued, the AMNH would furnish him with any money and backing necessary—provided that Satterlee supply the museum with full information on the subject. In closing, Skinner offered his collaborator, friend, and uncle a way out, reminding the older man he was not obligated to take on this work. Although Skinner and the AMNH wanted this information, the young anthropologist wrote, they did not want Satterlee doing anything that would put him in a dangerous or uncomfortable position.[1]

After reading the letter once again, Satterlee remained unsure which direction to take. He knew his culture, his history, and his community were under attack. The colonizing force of the U.S. federal government wanted Native peoples to abandon their distinct ways of dress, their beliefs, their languages—in short, everything that made them unique. With every Menominee elder's death, Satterlee's community lost another irreplaceable piece of their shared knowledge. Based on those factors alone, he knew he should join the Medicine Lodge ceremony and gather all the information he could. Satterlee reasoned that if he could find a way to preserve this history, to document those disappearing differences that made his people unique, then he should do so. That way there would be a permanent, written record of his community's beliefs and practices for future generations.

On the other hand, the Medicine Lodge ceremony was a sacred event attended only by those inducted into its secret society. The anthropologist in him wanted to observe and document the ceremony. But as a member of the Menominee Nation, Satterlee knew this information was sacred. He also knew if he provided this information to Skinner and the AMNH, they would publish it. If he did so, private Menominee information would be available to a non-Native public never meant to know such things. John V. Satterlee was conflicted . . . but probably not for that long.

Like other Native collaborators, Satterlee was motivated by a desire to preserve the history and culture of his people. He told Skinner this when they agreed to write the history of his community and make a great collection of Menominee cultural objects for Satterlee's people. Like D. C. Duvall, James R. Murie, and Louis Shotridge, Satterlee took a great deal of pride in his role as the foremost collaborator, chronicler, and linguist for his community. When outsiders wanted to gather material about the Menominee, Satterlee was the first person they came to.[2]

Preserving the history of his community and serving as a liaison to anthropologists were not the only reasons Satterlee took on these roles. Simply put, he was also motivated by money. Being a collaborator may have been a passion, but it was also a profession. And if money could be made preserving his culture, even if that meant sometimes providing sacred or secret information to outsiders, Satterlee reasoned, then why shouldn't he do it.[3]

From their later correspondence, we know Satterlee eventually refused Skinner's request, primarily due to the older Menominee man's adherence to Christianity. He told Skinner he was unable to join the Midewiwin, noting that turning from his Catholic faith was something he could not do. Nevertheless, Satterlee and Skinner moved forward on this project and continued to collect information and objects relating to the Midewiwin. It ended up being another Menominee man who provided Skinner with the information he coveted about the Medicine Lodge ceremony. This man was John Saint Baptist Perrote, an elder and an Indian court judge for the Menominee Nation. It was these two men—Satterlee and Perrote—who collaborated with Skinner for several more years, creating large collections of Menominee culture.[4]

In later years Skinner published the scholarly results of his Medicine Lodge research, titled *Medicine Ceremony of the Menomini, Iowa, and Wahpeton Dakota.* This publication compared what Skinner had learned of the Menominee ceremony with those of other Indigenous nations of the Great Plains and the Great Lakes he had studied. Referencing the Menominee Midewiwin member who supplied the information, Skinner noted in this publication's introduction that the identity of the narrator would never be revealed. If such a breach were known and made public, Skinner continued, it would result in the unnamed member's attempted murder by others in the Medicine Lodge society, either through physical violence or by magic. Even if we grant that Skinner was embellishing just a bit for his readers, repercussions of such magnitude certainly warranted the three men remaining quiet on the parts Perrote and Satterlee played in gathering and publishing such sacred information. Despite Skinner's earlier warnings against revealing his sources of secret information, though, the young anthropologist did just that, publishing an article naming Perrote as his source in the years immediately following the latter's death.[5]

Youth, Schooling, and Work

Six decades before Skinner's request, John V. Satterlee was born in the fur-trading settlement of Marinette in northern Wisconsin. In addition to large segments of Illinois and Michigan, much of what is now Wisconsin had been the territory of the Menominee people for countless generations. Unlike many Native peoples forcibly removed from their lands, at the time of Satterlee's birth the Menominee still retained a fraction of their former territory in Wisconsin. It was here, among friends and relatives on the Menominee Reservation, that John grew up. His father, Valentine Satterlee, was a non-Native army doctor who died while John was still a child, and his mother a Menominee woman named Kishigkokiu or Sky Woman.[6]

Sources differ as to the length of time Satterlee attended formal schooling, but he acquired at least the basics of English while still in his youth. His own writings indicate that he spent the years 1863 to 1865 in the local Keshena Indian Boarding School under the tutelage of Rosalie Dousman and her two daughters, who were also teachers. The Dousmans were devout Catholics who lived and worked on the reservation for decades. According to Satterlee, throughout their combined years they converted many Menominee children and adults to Christianity. Although he recalled all three women fondly, it was Rosalie who held a special place in Satterlee's heart. She was the one, Satterlee later wrote, who not only taught him how to read and write in English, but also instructed him in good morals.[7]

Beginning in his adolescence Satterlee worked several odd jobs on the Menominee Reservation, including as a logger and farmer and as an assistant teacher in the West Branch Indian Day School. He began this latter position in 1882, when he was approximately thirty years old, no doubt influenced by his own memories of Rosalie Dousman's teachings from two decades earlier. There he taught students in both Menominee and English. The U.S. Indian agent for the Green Bay Agency in Keshena, E. Stephens, told the commissioner of Indian affairs that Satterlee was an ideal teacher. Despite Satterlee's passion for instructing Menominee youths, however, he did not continue this position for long.[8]

A devoted family man, Satterlee married twice throughout his long life, both times to Menominee women. He first married Elizabeth Red Cloud in 1873, with whom he raised several children. After her passing in 1890, Satterlee married again, this time to Mary Gauthier in 1892. John and Mary remained together for several decades, with her also passing before John's death.[9]

Agency Interpreter and Indian Police Captain

Because of his fluency in English and Menominee, Satterlee became the official government interpreter for the Menominee Agency in 1899. In this role he worked with outsiders interested in conducting business with or learning about his people. His predecessor in this position was Joseph Gauthier Sr., who had held the position for over four decades. Although Satterlee would not meet that record, he nevertheless filled a very important role as a liaison between the reservation agent, the Menominee people, and any outsiders. Indeed, he continued in a non-official capacity as interpreter for the rest of his life. Satterlee's beginning annual salary was $200 in 1899, though due to nationwide changes in federal pay for American Indian interpreters at the time, this amount decreased over the following years. By 1904, Satterlee's final year as the official agency interpreter, his annual income had been cut nearly in half, to $120, or $10 per month.[10]

Perhaps due to resentment over his decreased pay, in July 1904 Satterlee quit his position as agency interpreter and instead became a member of the Menominee Reservation Indian Police. His personal decisions for this change are unknown, but if he hoped to receive better pay, he was no doubt disappointed. Reservation police at the time received $10 per month, the same pay he had ended on as an interpreter. Starting this new position, Satterlee wrote in his diary a description of what the job duties entailed. While they primarily consisted of policing and protecting the interests of the reservation agent, Satterlee's more mundane office duties also included sweeping the agency office and keeping fires lit during the cold winter months in Wisconsin. Supplemental benefits also accrued to his position as a member of the Indian Police, for which he received a suit of clothes annually, as well as monthly rations of pork, flour, coffee, and sugar for him and his family.[11]

It was in this latter role that Satterlee rose to the rank of captain or chief of police. Importantly, in his role as government interpreter and later as chief of police, Satterlee put himself at odds with community power structures that had been in place for generations. There is little doubt that Satterlee sought these positions for his financial well-being and to gain power and influence among the Menominee. Ironically, it was these very choices that earned him the antipathy of some of his community members, particularly in his job duties related to recruiting for Indian boarding schools.[12]

Satterlee often referenced the educational system that existed on the Menominee Reservation in his diary entries. In 1904, for example, he wrote that there were two schools in Keshena, Wisconsin, for Menominee children to attend—the agency boarding school and the Catholic boarding school. Both were sustained by federal tax dollars, and both enrolled nearly two hundred students each. Despite the difference in their names, both Keshena boarding schools also pushed adherence to Christianity and an abandonment of Menominee religious beliefs, language, and culture. Additionally, many Menominee youths also attended or were compelled to attend off-reservation Indian boarding schools built upon the model of the Hampton Institute in Virginia and Carlisle in Pennsylvania.

Satterlee viewed Indian boarding schools in general as a benefit to society. He believed Native children enrolled in these institutions received a good education, learned all manner of trades and farming, and, most importantly, were taught good morals. What Satterlee viewed as the beneficial parts of Indian boarding school education were little more than the same racist assimilation policies pursued by the federal government since Richard Henry Pratt began recruiting Indigenous children at Carlisle twenty-five years earlier.[13]

Less than a month after starting his job with the Menominee Agency police in July 1904, Satterlee began his own recruitment work. With backing from the reservation agent, Satterlee used his police position to travel throughout the local area in August and September of 1904 recruiting children for the two Indian boarding schools in Keshena. Accompanied by one of the non-Native schoolteachers and the non-Native agency physician, Satterlee assisted with interpreting to convince parents to part with their children, some as young as six and others up to eighteen years of age. Though he wrote little about the interactions that usually occurred, Satterlee's entry on September 1, 1904, noted some of the difficulties he experienced. On that day he wrote that many of the Menominee mothers were stubborn about letting their children attend these schools. For Satterlee, these schools provided a better life for Menominee youth. Left unwritten in Satterlee's diary were the punishments, harassment, and retaliation parents experienced for not compelling their children to attend Indian boarding schools.[14]

In the years 1905 and 1907 Satterlee again aided in the recruitment of Menominee youths. Non-Native teachers, primarily women, traveled to the Wisconsin reservation in annual cycles for their recruitment work. In his diary Satterlee recorded teachers coming from as close as the Tomah Indian Boarding School and as far away as Carlisle in Pennsylvania. Also among these recruiters were non-Native teachers from the Haskell Institute in Kansas and the Flandreau Indian Boarding School in South Dakota. Although he made only a passing mention of it in his diary, Satterlee recruited his own niece to attend the Tomah school in August 1907. He wholeheartedly believed he was helping her.

Not just Menominee youths, but children from numerous Native communities throughout Wisconsin were forcibly removed during these recruitment drives. Equally indiscriminate in their collecting work, recruiters sought children from among Stockbridge, Oneida, and Potawatomi families. According to Satterlee, the annual recruitment periods were ordered by the Bureau of Indian Affairs. They had occurred regularly on the Menominee Reservation since 1890.[15]

While Satterlee's personal feelings about his recruitment work for Indian boarding schools rarely made their way into his diary entries, he was generally in favor of such schools. As noted, he believed these schools promoted not only education but also good morals, referring to many of them as fine schools. One of the few claims he made against off-reservation Indian boarding schools was that after finishing their education and returning home, few Native youths ever actually did anything with the skills and education they had received. As far as Satterlee was concerned, the problem was with the children, not the schools. According to him, the returned students were lazy, squandering their time and money.[16]

While written histories of many Menominee youths' experiences at Indian boarding schools are difficult to locate, we know some Indigenous youths resisted government-sponsored assimilation in interesting ways. One form of resistance that appeared again and again in the historical record was arson. Angered by the racist policies of an unjust colonial government, students occasionally reacted by burning down the Indian boarding school buildings, thus ridding themselves temporarily of the problem. Recent scholars have noted that fires were a regular occurrence and concern of boarding school staff. While many of these incidents were blamed on poor construction, carelessness, and other factors, at least a handful were definitively linked to arson on the part of the students.[17]

As with cases of arson at Indian boarding schools in California and Michigan, the agency boarding school in Keshena experienced an incident of arson—though of a slightly different nature. In January 1905 a young Menominee woman determined she did not want to attend the school in Keshena. She then persuaded another young female student to aid her in burning down the school. While she succeeded in destroying the building, she was soon caught and sent to a reformatory. Unlike cases of arson at other Indian boarding schools, this young woman's actions were not aimed at boarding schools in general, but against the Keshena school in particular. In a voluntary statement she admitted starting the fire because she wanted to attend a larger school with more students. As her parents had refused her requests and wanted her to stay close to home, she felt she had no alternative but to take matters into her own hands. Her goal had been to burn down the local Keshena school to be sent to a larger school further away. Although not a typical case of arson by an Indian boarding school student, this incident illustrates another side to Native resistance, if for slightly different reasons.[18]

Beginnings of Anthropological Fieldwork

By the end of the first decade of the twentieth century Satterlee transitioned from his role as an unofficial interpreter to more in-depth collaborative work with visiting anthropologists. In 1908 he worked with Smithsonian physical anthropologist Aleš Hrdlička to study the spread of tuberculosis on the Menominee Reservation. Born in 1869 in what is now part of the Czech Republic, Hrdlička became the most influential name in the field of physical anthropology in the early decades of the twentieth century.[19]

Hrdlička immigrated to the United States as a teenager and attended the New York Eclectic Medical College. He began his first anthropological work in 1898, working for the AMNH on a collecting expedition to Mexico. He joined the staff of the Smithsonian Institution's National Museum in

1902 and remained there for the next four decades. Although no records exist of Satterlee and Hrdlička's 1908 collaboration, stories continue to circulate in anthropological circles over Hrdlička's poor relationships with American Indian peoples in the field. His fieldwork consisted of little more than taking physical measurements and photographs of his "subjects" and then moving on with his data to another Indigenous community to repeat the process over again. Hrdlička was emblematic of the period in which he lived, and his colonialist, racist, and sexist views were at the fore in his anthropological work. A Smithsonian colleague later said of the man that his prejudices were so much a part of him that he did not realize he had any.[20]

A few years after Hrdlička worked with Satterlee on the Menominee Reservation, the planners of the 1915 San Diego World's Fair invited Hrdlička to contribute his expertise for the anthropological displays. Agreeing to do so, Hrdlička created a physical anthropology exhibit more comprehensive than any previously attempted at a world's fair. He collected human skeletal remains, took photographs, and created busts and life masks of what he called "the most primitive" peoples living in different parts of the world. With this information he created a chart of humankind's historical and evolutionary progress, as he saw it. Not surprisingly, Hrdlička's displays were laden with statements about race and evolutionary potential, advancing the belief in Euro-American biological superiority over all other peoples. Readers may recall WJ McGee espousing similar statements for his anthropological displays at the 1904 St. Louis World's Fair. Through these San Diego physical anthropology displays, Hrdlička indoctrinated the public with ideas of evolutionary-based racism presented in the guise of scientific objectivity. Illustrative of broader social movements of the time, Hrdlička's work also reflected many of the teachings of the eugenics movement then taking center stage in the nation's cultural discourse.[21]

Regardless of his own personal feelings about the man, soon after collaborating with Hrdlička on his 1908 tuberculosis study, Satterlee became enamored with the field of anthropology. From then on he devoted more of his time and energy to anthropological work. He collected material culture objects, observed ceremonies, and recorded songs across the Menominee Reservation. But he didn't limit himself to only gathering Menominee cultural heritage, either. Working with the young AMNH anthropologist Alanson Skinner, Satterlee also visited neighboring Indigenous nations throughout Wisconsin. In Forest County, for instance, he studied the manners and customs of the Potawatomi people, later collecting objects ranging from clothing to baskets to jewelry. As we have seen, the salvage anthropology ethos popular in Satterlee's time predicated itself on the belief that Native peoples were either quickly dying off or becoming assimilated. Thus, it was the accepted responsibility of Native and non-Native anthropologists and collaborators to preserve all they could of Indigenous cultures in this race against time. In a letter Satterlee sent Skinner years later, the older Menominee man wrote about the large amount of money that had passed through their hands as they purchased Native-made objects from across Wisconsin. He wryly noted that the two of them had nearly wiped out all sacred objects found on the Menominee Reservation. In that same vein, their collecting records show that Satterlee and Skinner eagerly sought sacred medicine bundles from the Menominee and Potawatomi Nations. Many of these items still reside in the collections of the AMNH in New York and the National Museum of the American Indian (NMAI) in Washington DC rather than with their people.[22]

Perhaps most notoriously, Satterlee participated in several excavations of Native burial grounds. Although not taking a direct hand in excavation work until 1919, Satterlee nevertheless expressed his interest in excavating Native mounds as early as 1903. In that year he wrote in his diary of several Menominee men who accidentally uncovered a mass grave while hauling large amounts of gravel across the reservation. Directly after learning of the incident, Satterlee investigated as a private community member, later writing up his findings in his diary. His notes included detailed descriptions of the deterioration of the skulls, jaws, and teeth of the human individuals uncovered. Satterlee's words display a predilection toward science and history, reflecting his first real interest in anthropology. At the same time, Satterlee's actions display a surprising disregard for the sacred nature of a human resting place, specifically for Indigenous ancestors.[23]

It was not until many years later in June 1919 that Satterlee participated in his first hands-on excavation work of Native remains. That summer the Museum of the American Indian, Heye Foundation (MAI, which later became the NMAI, the National Museum of the American Indian), represented by Alanson Skinner, and the Milwaukee Public Museum, represented by Samuel A. Barrett, excavated several large mounds in the vicinity of Lake Shawano, a few miles southeast of the Menominee Reservation. Skinner and Barrett both wrote in their findings that they uncovered numerous human skeletons, many representing previous occupations by Menominee people centuries earlier. Skinner and Barrett were indebted to Satterlee, they wrote, because he guided them to several unknown mounds. Satterlee himself located five human burials that summer. Eager to publish the results of their excavations, Satterlee queried Skinner on how quickly they could get their findings into print and available to the larger world. He enjoyed the work to such an extent that years later, in 1927, the then seventy-five-year-old Menominee man continued his excavation work in these same mounds. He located additional ancestral remains and several large clay pots. Simply put, Satterlee's work in this arena can be described as anthropologically curious, but ethically problematic.[24]

Satterlee justified disturbing the resting place of ancient Indigenous communities through his devotion to science. Not surprisingly, Satterlee's excavation of Native peoples' tombs increased the ill will some community members felt toward this anthropological collaborator. According to an account recorded many years later, some among the Menominee community believed Satterlee was a witch. His work in digging up Native remains, collecting and selling medicine bundles, and the subsequent deaths of numerous family members seemed to confirm these suspicions.[25]

How Satterlee felt about removing his community's cultural heritage is difficult to answer. Clearly, he believed what he was doing was for the good of humanity in general. He felt he was participating in the race to preserve Indigenous cultures before they vanished. Satterlee sought to write the history of the Menominee, at least symbolically, through the collection and distribution of this material in museums. And this he surely did. Throughout his more than three decades of anthropological collecting, Satterlee personally collected objects that now live on only in a diasporic existence in museums in Oshkosh, Milwaukee, Chicago, New York, Washington DC, and other cities.

Anthropological Fieldwork with Densmore

As the self-designated chronicler of his people, Satterlee collaborated with more than a dozen non-Native individuals in documenting Menominee culture over a thirty-year period. Though not as prolific as Chaticks si Chaticks (Pawnee) collaborator James R. Murie in his output, Satterlee nevertheless surpassed many other collaborators by the sheer number of anthropologists with whom he worked. In addition to Skinner and Hrdlička, these individuals included Samuel A. Barrett and the ethnobotanist Huron H. Smith at the Milwaukee Public Museum, Arthur Kannenberg at the Oshkosh Public Museum, the linguist Leonard Bloomfield at the University of Illinois at Urbana-Champaign, and both Truman Michelson and Frances Densmore at the Smithsonian's Bureau of American Ethnology. Densmore, unique among early twentieth-century anthropologists for her work as an ethnomusicologist and for being a woman, deserves a brief mention.[26]

Born in eastern Minnesota in 1867, Densmore and fellow women anthropologists Matilda Coxe Stevenson, Erminnie Smith, and Alice C. Fletcher represented a diversity and inclusivity prevalent in the early days of U.S. anthropology. Exhibiting a passion for music at a young age, Densmore attended the Oberlin Conservatory of Music, where she studied piano, organ, and harmony. Like her role model Alice C. Fletcher, Densmore chose not to marry. Beyond her fieldwork, lectures, and publications, she joined several scholarly organizations including the Anthropological Society of Washington, the Women's Anthropological Society, and the Society for Ethnomusicology, the latter of which she was a founding member and an officer.[27]

In 1893 Densmore attended the Chicago World's Fair, where she was mesmerized by the anthropological displays of Native people dancing and singing. She wrote in a letter decades later that this experience first got her started on North American Indian music. It was also around this time that Densmore wrote to Fletcher about her interest in the field. If Fletcher had been less gracious in her response, Densmore recalled, it is probable that she would not have taken up the study of American Indian music. Fortunately Fletcher encouraged the younger woman in her pursuit. By 1900 Densmore was conducting fieldwork at her own expense among the Native communities of Minnesota and Wisconsin.[28]

Often accompanied by her sister Margaret, Densmore visited several Indigenous nations in the upper Midwest, including the Minnesota Chippewa peoples living on the Grand Portage and White Earth Reservations. There she witnessed ceremonies, photographed dances, and recorded songs with a borrowed phonograph. Impressed with her documenting abilities, the BAE provided her with a new Columbia graphophone in 1908. Her work over the following years spanned the development of mechanical recording equipment from wax cylinders to audio tape and took her throughout North and Central America, visiting dozens of different Native communities. During these visits she regularly hired Native collaborators to interpret for her. She noted that she preferred interpreters educated at one of the many Indian boarding schools such as the Hampton Institute or the Carlisle Indian Industrial School.[29]

Although she was never a permanent, full-time staff member of the BAE, Densmore's collaborative work with the bureau and with the Smithsonian Institution lasted decades. In addition to her work with the BAE, she collected material culture objects while in the field. These she sold to cultural heritage repositories including the MAI and the Minnesota Historical Society. Densmore relied on other part-time work throughout her life to pay her bills and continue her ethnographic passion. Her constantly changing job titles from music teacher to "writer of Indian music" to freelance writer for scientific publications listed in federal census records testify to this fact.[30]

Anthropological Fieldwork with Skinner

While Satterlee's collaborative work with Frances Densmore was unique in their collection of Menominee songs, his closest and longest-lasting relationship with an anthropologist was between him and his adopted nephew, Alanson Skinner. A passionate anthropologist whose career was cut short by his sudden death in 1925, Skinner was Satterlee's junior by nearly three decades. He was born in New York State in 1885 and attended both Columbia and Harvard Universities, where he studied under prominent men in the field including Franz Boas and Frederic Ward Putnam.[31]

Beginning in 1904 and continuing for more than two decades, Skinner conducted anthropological fieldwork throughout many parts of the United States and Canada. When just nineteen he got his first taste for the discipline by accompanying M. R. Harrington into the field on a Peabody Museum–funded expedition to the Seneca people on the Cattaraugus Reservation in western New York. Skinner was hooked from the start. In later years he also worked among Indigenous nations of the Great Plains and Great Lakes, including the Baxoje (Iowa), Oto, Potawatomi, Sauk, Sisseton Wahpeton Oyate (Sisseton-Wahpeton Sioux), and, most notably, Menominee.[32]

Although familiar with the work and staff of the AMNH since his high school years, Skinner did not become a paid assistant in the Anthropology Department there until 1907. Despite being employed by the AMNH, Skinner was ever eager to explore his professional options. In 1912, for example, he wrote Frederick Webb Hodge at the BAE, seeking employment in the nation's capital. Four years later Skinner abruptly resigned from the AMNH, giving only two days' notice before his departure. In his letter of resignation to the chair of the AMNH Anthropology Department, Clark Wissler, Skinner wrote that he believed his services for some time past had not been adequately compensated. He added that as his advancement at AMNH seemed to have reached its peak, it was time for him to leave.[33]

So it was that in 1916 Skinner joined the staff of the MAI, traveling only a short four miles to the newly opened museum in upper Manhattan. There he again worked alongside his good friend and fellow anthropologist M. R. Harrington, whom he had known from early days at the AMNH and the Peabody Museum in Cambridge. Skinner remained with the MAI until 1920, when he accepted a position as assistant curator, and later curator, in the Anthropology Department at the Milwaukee Public Museum (MPM). Although he stayed in Milwaukee only a few years, Skinner enjoyed the work immensely and declared his supervisor, Samuel A. Barrett, the best museum director in the United States. During his short time at the Wisconsin museum, Skinner and his fellow MPM anthropologist Amos Oneroad took advantage of their proximity to the Menominee Reservation to conduct fieldwork with their friend and adopted uncle, John V. Satterlee. Despite Skinner's closeness to Satterlee and his affections for his MPM supervisor Barrett, in June 1924 he left the job after the sudden death of his wife, Esther Florence Allen, in childbirth. Skinner returned to New York and to the MAI, in whose employ he spent the rest of his career. At each of these institutions Skinner also maintained his personal and professional relationship with Satterlee. After first meeting in 1910, the two men continued to document and collect Menominee culture together for another fifteen years.[34]

Unlike some of the more typical working relationships between Native collaborators and non-Native anthropologists, the friendship between Satterlee and Skinner was close from the beginning, growing more intimate as their work progressed. Satterlee not only taught Skinner how to hunt, fish, and cook as a member of the Menominee Nation but also provided information, support, and encouragement to his younger friend. After the publication of Skinner's 1921 work, *Material Culture of the Menomini*, for instance, Satterlee applauded the anthropologist for his "true, straight history." According to Satterlee, no one had yet been able to do such a fine job describing the lifeways of his Menominee ancestors. Satterlee added that he doubted anyone could best Skinner in the future in this regard, either.[35]

Along with applauding Skinner's role in documenting his Menominee culture, Satterlee supported his young friend and nephew during life's challenges and setbacks. Overjoyed at Skinner's mention of moving to Wisconsin to work at the MPM in 1920, for example, Satterlee was distraught when Skinner returned to New York four years later after his wife's death. Satterlee was nevertheless there to play the role of the surrogate "Uncle John" to Skinner's young daughter, Esther Mary Skinner, named for her late mother. In his frequent letters to Skinner, Satterlee never forgot to ask after his dear niece. He regularly sent her gifts of necklaces, moccasins, and even simple songs he wrote to cheer her up when she might be feeling down.[36]

In addition to their relationship of uncle and nephew, Satterlee and Skinner also developed a relationship of Native collaborator and non-Native anthropologist. Like Richard Davis and George Dorsey studying the Southern Tsitsistas/Suhtai (Cheyenne) in the Oklahoma Territory, or D. C. Duvall and Clark Wissler studying the Pikuni Blackfeet (Piegan) in Montana, Native collaborators were the ones in the field doing the actual anthropological collecting work. Non-Native anthropologists also did fieldwork, but they more often remained in museums and relied on Native collaborators to collect materials. Non-Native anthropologists regularly requested Native collaborators to acquire knowledge ranging from origin stories to narratives to sacred ceremonial songs or rituals.

Native collaborators wrote detailed descriptive notes on the intangible information they gathered and then sent it to anthropologists for edits, review, and follow-up questions.

The collaborative relationship between Satterlee and Skinner followed this same pattern. In 1911 and 1912, for instance, Satterlee mailed Skinner an extensive series of stories and linguistic information about the Menominee people. The following year Skinner asked Satterlee to travel to the neighboring Potawatomi Nation to study the manners and customs of the local community. Skinner additionally provided Satterlee with a lengthy questionnaire on which to base his initial inquiries, reminding the Menominee man that interviewing elders was of primary importance.[37]

Just as Satterlee and Skinner modeled their collaborative relationship on this standard back-and-forth process, so too did their relationship illustrate the competitive nature of museums during the height of salvage anthropology. Many anthropologists at the time, and more than a few still today, felt an ownership over the Indigenous communities they studied. Anthropologists guarded the knowledge they acquired against the prying eyes of their peers, at least until their exhibitions opened and their scholarly articles went to press.

An example of Skinner's territoriality is seen in his correspondence from 1913. In that year Satterlee wrote to let the AMNH anthropologist know that other anthropologists were entering the field in northern Wisconsin. Skinner responded by recommending that if Satterlee was propositioned by the newcomers, he should let them know he was very busy working for the AMNH and unable to do anything for them. If they persisted, Skinner suggested another Menominee man who could escort the anthropologists around, instead of Satterlee. Importantly, Skinner continued, he didn't want the new anthropologists getting anything good or sacred that the AMNH should have. After learning of a proposed visit to the Menominee Reservation by a different anthropologist several months later, Skinner sent another letter to Satterlee, echoing his previous concerns. Even if Satterlee agreed to work for these new anthropologists, Skinner wrote, the AMNH anthropologist did not want them getting anything too good. Rather, Skinner emphatically wrote, the AMNH needed it instead.[38]

Skinner wrote extensively about his experiences developing relationships with Native collaborators throughout North America. His words reveal anthropologists' often questionable fieldwork methodologies during the height of salvage anthropology. Skinner wrote that it was his business to ferret out "non-progressive" or "pagan Indians" living on reservations, establish mutual confidence with them, and obtain their sacred medicine bundles and other religious objects. After winning the trust of Menominee elders, Skinner and Satterlee collected hundreds of objects along with thousands of pages of ethnographic information documenting the community's history and culture. Esther Florence Allen, a woman of Wyandot ancestry and Skinner's second wife, also aided Skinner and Satterlee in their collecting work among the Menominee people. In 1921 she gathered information and objects from women that the two men did not have access to.[39]

Typical of salvage anthropologists, Satterlee and Skinner collected all manner of objects from the people they studied. Foremost among these were medicine bundles. Satterlee cautioned Skinner in 1911 to move slowly when approaching Native people about such sacred items. Despite the older man's call for patience, the two men still collected a surprisingly large number of medicine bundles. These they often purchased from family members of the former owner after the latter's death. Satterlee and Skinner purchased so many, in fact, that during an outbreak of illness in the winter of 1911–12, they were accused of prolonging this sickness due to their greed. A Menominee elder blamed them for buying too many of these sacred objects, thus depriving community members of an antidote to prevent further illness. Satterlee eventually shared one of the bundles to alleviate the outbreak.[40]

Although Satterlee professed a strict adherence to Christianity, the Menominee collaborator nevertheless displayed a surprising concern for the medicine bundles and other sacred items he collected. Throughout 1911 and 1912 Satterlee repeatedly wrote Skinner about how to properly care for the medicine bundles they had collected, despite their new location in museums. In January 1911 Satterlee reminded Skinner that sacrifices of tobacco were required at least two to three times a year so the spirits would not be offended. The following year Satterlee again wrote Skinner about the need to make these offerings. He even suggested traveling to New York to instruct the AMNH museum staff in properly carrying out the necessary sacrifices. More surprisingly, in at least one instance in 1914 Skinner wrote Satterlee that tobacco had been placed on all the sacred bundles at the New York museum according to Satterlee's instructions. While it is unclear how often these actions were taken by staff, this may be the first case in which museum employees made an effort to steward items according to the wishes of members of Native community members.[41]

Satterlee's insistence on the continuation of sacrifices raises the issue of his professed adherence to Christianity alone. We know during his younger years he enjoyed working as an interpreter with Catholic priests visiting the reservation. On occasion he even assisted at mass alongside them. Also, as we saw when Skinner and Wissler asked Satterlee to join the Menominee Midewiwin, the latter refused, arguing his Catholic faith prevented him from doing so. Despite his refusal, Satterlee's writings and actions show a deep interest in the beliefs of his non-Christian community members. As early as 1903 Satterlee wrote of attending "pagan" or non-Christian funerals and weddings on the Menominee Reservation. Highlighting the intolerance of his Christian education, though, he nevertheless pushed for the cessation of these activities, labeling them as "evils" that needed to be stopped.[42]

Throughout his long life Satterlee allowed Christian and non-Christian principles, beliefs, and practices to guide him. While in his younger years he strove to be "a good Catholic," he deviated from this path as an anthropologist. In the latter role he documented and preserved those aspects of his society frowned upon by his Christian contemporaries and teachers. Nor was this transition unique for Satterlee. As readers have seen, each of the Native collaborators in this book was indoctrinated into accepting the assimilationist doctrine during their adolescence in Indian boarding schools. All of them to varying degrees emerged from these schools espousing the supposed benefits Euro-American society offered Native peoples. It was later through their work with anthropology that these Native collaborators turned the power, using their English language skills to document and preserve the histories of their Indigenous nations rather than abandon them.[43]

Relationships with the Menominee and with Outsiders

As noted, Satterlee was not the only Menominee man who aided Skinner in documenting his culture. John Saint Baptist Perrote, a Menominee elder and Indian court judge, also collaborated with Satterlee and Skinner in their early collecting work. According to Skinner, it was Perrote and not Satterlee who first adopted the AMNH anthropologist and made him a member of the Menominee community. As with other collaborator-anthropologist relationships, both parties found creative ways to sidestep community taboos against transferring sacred objects and information to noncommunity members. Perrote's adoption of Skinner is one example.

Skinner wrote that Perrote was always interested in learning which sacred items the young AMNH anthropologist collected. When Skinner told him he lacked thorough information on the Menominee Midewiwin, the Indian court judge happily obliged . . . for a fee. Perrote told Skinner he could not simply reveal such powerful teachings to an outsider. Doing so would expose him to the potential wrath of community members and divine forces, thus endangering his own life. To solve this dilemma, Perrote adopted Skinner as his nephew. The older man then invoked the sacred powers by name, arguing that as the young anthropologist was now a member of the Menominee Nation, any potential hurdles caused by teaching "these sacred things to a white man" were erased. Importantly, this exchange was not as one-sided as it sounds. As an adoptive act, it allowed Perrote to transfer sacred teachings forbidden to outsiders, thus supplying Skinner with information he desired for his anthropological career. As a financial transaction, though, Perrote demanded from Skinner $75 in clothing, food, tobacco, and other trade goods. This example illustrates what Pikuni Blackfeet scholar Rosalyn LaPier has termed "reciprocal exploitation." In these scenarios Native peoples and non-Native anthropologists used or "exploited" each other for their own ends. Acknowledging reciprocal exploitation recognizes Native agency and challenges the common belief that Indigenous community members were victims in these exchanges.[44]

We know from anthropological fieldnotes and correspondence contemporary to the time that transactional relationships like the one between Skinner and Perrote were not unique. Many non-Native anthropologists shared the privilege of being adopted into the Menominee community with John V. Satterlee as their "uncle." Arthur Kannenberg, curator of archaeology at the Oshkosh Public Museum, and Charles E. Brown, curator and director of the Wisconsin Historical Society Museum, number among these men. Satterlee did not limit himself to museum professionals either. He also regularly worked with private collectors interested in "Indian curios" to whom he sold Menominee cultural heritage items. He identified with this line of work to such an extent that in the 1920 federal census he named himself a "Curio Collector" first and foremost.[45]

At over eighty years of age in 1933, Satterlee continued documenting his community's history. In that year he worked with a Wisconsin publishing company to supply narratives and, in Satterlee's words, Menominee "legends." Satterlee's enjoyment in teaching outsiders about Menominee culture had not ebbed at all in later life. Indeed, it is clear that a motivating factor of his anthropological work was the attention he received from those outside his community. This was hardly unique to Satterlee. Many Native collaborators understandably took pleasure in being sought out for their knowledge and expertise. Although Satterlee did not write about this, one of his contemporaries and a fellow Native collaborator wrote of his own relationship with anthropologists. He recalled fondly that such interactions made him feel important. Like Satterlee, this Native collaborator also created strong familial relationships with anthropologists. He served as an uncle to his nephews and enjoyed teaching those unfamiliar with his culture and history.[46]

John V. Satterlee and Anthropology Today

John V. Satterlee fought to preserve his culture right up until the day he died in 1940 at the age of eighty-eight. He worked with more than a dozen anthropologists over a thirty-year period and gained a level of celebrity through his collaborations with non-Native outsiders. His longtime partner and friend, Alanson Skinner, wrote that Satterlee labored incessantly to complete the annals of his people. A more recent anthropologist argued Satterlee was responsible for much of what we now know about Menominee culture.[47]

Throughout his long life Satterlee did more than just work with anthropologists to "save" Menominee culture. Like other former Indian boarding school students, Satterlee also used his English language skills to become a voice for his people. He turned the power against a federal government determined to assimilate his community. In 1928, for example, Satterlee spoke out to journalists investigating conditions on the Menominee Reservation. Not often openly critical of the federal government, in this instance Satterlee voiced bitterness against what he called the unjust attitude taken by the American people against his Native community. The Menominee people have money, Satterlee argued, but it was all kept in Washington DC. It was maintained in trust by the federal government, but this money's absence from the people who needed it kept the Menominee community in poverty. Worried his words might bring a reprisal, Satterlee closed by saying he still believed it was a good government. The problem, he figured, was that the people running it simply didn't understand how much the Menominee needed this money to survive.[48]

Satterlee and his legacy continue to be controversial on and off the Menominee Reservation today. During the height of salvage anthropology he directly aided in the removal of untold numbers of material culture items from the Menominee people. These he delivered into the hands of non-Native museum anthropologists and private collectors. Like other Native anthropologists and collaborators, Satterlee personally profited from these many exchanges. Finding himself in a position of power during anthropology's race to collect Native American cultural heritage, Satterlee gathered objects and information with the ostensible goal of making a "great collection of relics" for the benefit of Menominee people. As most of these items now reside in museums hundreds of miles distant from the homeland of the Menominee, it is difficult to argue Menominee people personally benefited from Satterlee's work. Not surprisingly, the results of his massive collecting project and his own character continue to be polarizing. For some, Satterlee is remembered as an idealist who devoted decades of his life to teaching the outside world about his culture and history. For others, he was in many ways an outsider himself who made a career out of selling Menominee culture to the highest bidder. And maybe, like many Native anthropologists and collaborators at the turn of the twentieth century, he was a bit of both, equal parts hero and villain.[49]

7

A True Indian Is Someone Who Helps Their Race

Cleaver Warden (Washington DC, 1918)

"I have made a careful study of my people in every way," Cleaver Warden told the all-male congressional subcommittee members of the Committee on Indian Affairs who sat before him on the raised platform. The fifty-one-year-old Southern Inunaina (Arapaho) man testified that day in the U.S. Capitol Building in Washington DC. He informed the subcommittee that he had spent three decades in the employ of several of the most prominent museums in the country. These included the Field Museum in Chicago, the American Museum of Natural History in New York, and the Smithsonian Institution in Washington DC. While working for these institutions, Warden documented the customs, rituals, and material culture of his Southern Inunaina community, along with numerous other Indigenous nations throughout Indian Country. Based on the combination of his Native heritage and his anthropological work, Warden considered himself an expert. Frankly, he thought the three men who made up the congressional subcommittee should recognize him as such. Due to his experience alone he believed himself better qualified than the other so-called experts gathered that day in the nation's capital, Native or non-Native.[1]

On that March morning in 1918 Warden wasn't simply an anthropological observer. Rather, he was an advocate for his people. After several hours of testimony presented by missionaries, physicians, anthropologists, and current and former Bureau of Indian Affairs personnel, the subcommittee chairman asked if there were any others who wished to speak before the hearings concluded. One of the last to make his voice heard, Warden spoke for his community's freedom to practice their religious beliefs as they saw fit. He provided several examples of the good lives that Native peoples led because of their religious worship. This, he argued, despite the fact that their forms of belief differed from those of others across the country.

Warden advocated for his culture's freedom before an elected representative body of U.S. citizens for which most Native Americans could not even vote. It would be another six years before the Indian Citizenship Act passed, and even then thousands of Indigenous peoples were barred from exercising their voting rights. The collective body Warden addressed that day included U.S. representatives William W. Hastings, Homer P. Snyder, and John N. Tillman, who together made up a subcommittee of the larger federal government. These men and their fellows in the U.S. House of Representatives and in the U.S. Senate had the final say on how hundreds of thousands of Native American "wards" of the United States worshipped. What made these Subcommittee hearings so important was that they were set to decide the legality of Peyote in religious practices. Many non-Native and even a few Native people viewed Peyote as an evil, sinful, and dangerous substance. Rather than permit its continued use in religious ceremonies, they sought to criminalize it altogether. For Warden and other Peyote advocates pushing for religious freedom, it was an uphill battle.[2]

Youth and Schooling

March 23, 1918, was not the first time Cleaver Warden spoke for his people in defense of their culture. Testifying before representatives of the colonizing body that occupied his ancestral land, Warden thought about what had led him there that day. Raised in what is now the state of Oklahoma, he came from an influential Southern Inunaina family, the son of Heap of Bears and nephew to Chief Powder Face.

As discussed in the early life of Richard Davis, the histories of the Tsitsistas/Suhtai (Cheyenne) and Inunaina Nations were interconnected. Like Davis's Southern Tsitsistas/Suhtai, the Southern Inunaina also signed the Medicine Lodge Treaty in 1867, the same year Cleaver Warden was born. As stipulated in this treaty, several Indigenous nations sold their landholdings in the Colorado and Wyoming Territories. The exchange promised new land, food, and supplies in the Indian Territory of present-day western Oklahoma. Although many Southern Inunaina people remained in the Denver area until the early 1870s, they eventually agreed to resettle in the Indian Territory. Their relatives among the Northern Inunaina, on the other hand, remained in the Wyoming Territory. This was one of the places Warden conducted anthropological fieldwork in later decades.[3]

Growing up on the Cheyenne and Arapaho Reservation, Warden was encouraged by his family to learn the ways of Euro-American society. Today we lack the exact words his family members said to him, but we can speculate that it was similar to the words spoken by another American Indian father to his son, insisting the latter attend Western schooling. This father told his son that to live with the white people, he and his sisters and brothers had to attend Indian boarding schools to learn all they could about Euro-American ways. A similar conversation occurred between nine-year-old Cleaver and his relatives when the Arapaho Manual Labor and Boarding School opened in early 1876.[4]

Of the more than one hundred students attending the agency boarding school that January, Warden was one of seventy-eight Southern Inunaina youths. The remainder consisted of Southern Tsitsistas/Suhtai and a few Apache girls and boys. As noted, future anthropology collaborator Richard Davis was also among this group encouraged by their families to attend Western schooling. According to school records, in addition to learning the basics of English, geography, and mathematics, many of the female students received instruction in domestic arts. The boys cut and hauled wood, assisted in butchering, and were responsible for raising corn, potatoes, melons, and beans on the agency school's many acres.[5]

Around this time Richard Henry Pratt transitioned in his role from jailor of Tichkematse and the Fort Marion prisoners to Indian boarding school founder. In 1879 he received permission from his superiors to host his assimilation project in the old U.S. Army barracks in Carlisle, Pennsylvania. By that autumn Pratt began visiting western reservations to recruit students to fill his school. Surprisingly to readers today, there was no shortage of eager Native students. Importantly, though, neither the children nor their parents understood what truly awaited them out east. Certainly none of them realized the extent to which Pratt's educational system aimed at the wholesale erasure of Indigenous cultures.

In October 1879 Pratt left the Cheyenne and Arapaho Reservation with more than fifty Native American youths in tow, Richard Davis among them. The reservation agent, John D. Miles, was barraged by Tsitsistas/Suhtai and Inunaina parents who demanded their children also attend Pratt's school. Miles wrote that not a day passed without someone asking for their child to be included in the next group of Carlisle students. In August 1880

Miles himself escorted the second group of Native students who left the reservation for Pratt's school. Consisting of twenty-two Tsitsistas/Suhtai, eleven Inunaina, and eight Niuam (Comanche) children, they arrived at Carlisle on September 6, 1880. Half of the Carlisle newcomers had already received some form of limited instruction at their agency boarding schools. Notably, this group included thirteen-year-old Cleaver Warden.[6]

As a member of only the second class to enter Carlisle, Warden lived under the daily racist pronouncements and military-style rigor required by the school's founder and superintendent, Pratt. As he did with all students under his charge, Pratt demanded Warden speak only in English to cast off his supposedly savage past. Only by doing so would the young man assimilate, compete, and succeed in U.S. society, Pratt believed. Although we lack Warden's thoughts about Pratt, we know other former students recalled the Carlisle founder as a many-sided individual—demanding, self-righteous, but not without a sense of fairness and humor. Many Carlisle students wrote that they viewed Pratt at the time as a sort of substitute father, harsh and exacting, but at times loving toward the children in his charge. For Warden, as for lots of other Native students, breaking away from Pratt's racist and assimilationist teachings was a challenge few could confront until years after leaving the school.[7]

During his earliest days at Carlisle, Warden befriended fellow students suffering through the same hardships. Although they had known each other from the Cheyenne and Arapaho Reservation, it was at Carlisle that Warden developed a lasting friendship with Richard Davis—the Southern Tsitsistas/Suhtai boy of his own age whose career in anthropology would so closely mirror Warden's. Like Davis, Warden also requested to take part in Pratt's outing system. This was the assimilation project started in 1881 that literally took children "out" of the school to live and work with non-Native families in the Carlisle countryside. Warden embraced the outing system and participated in three separate programs in 1882, 1884, and 1885. Unlike Davis, who stayed at Carlisle as Pratt's student and employee for nearly fifteen years, after seven years Warden decided it was time to depart.[8]

In Carlisle's early days, students were expected to remain at the school for a minimum term of at least three years. This time commitment was believed necessary to indoctrinate them as fully as possible into Euro-American Christian society. Either the students themselves or, more often, their parents agreed to these three-year term limits with Pratt and his staff. By 1883, then, Warden and those who left the Indian Territory back in 1880 were able to return home. A small contingent of these pupils decided instead to remain at Carlisle to continue their education, however, and Warden was among them. Warden signed on for another two-year term, and when that period expired in 1885, he extended one more time. Finally, in the spring of 1887 Warden departed the Carlisle Indian Industrial School and returned to his home on the Cheyenne and Arapaho Reservation.[9]

Return to the Indian Territory

After being away for the better part of a decade, Warden was happy to reunite with the people he had left behind. Though we lack a direct record of his homecoming, we know the experiences of another Southern Inunaina young man who returned from Carlisle at about the same time. This young man said it was a welcome feeling to return to his family in the Indian Territory, to hear his Native language spoken again, to take part in Inunaina ceremonies once more, and, not surprisingly, to eat the foods he had grown up with.[10]

Within six months of returning home Warden enlisted as an Indian scout at a nearby U.S. Army fort in the Indian Territory. Like fellow Native collaborator Tichkematse before him, Warden recognized that his ability to speak, read, and write in English was in demand. And Fort Reno was one of the few places able to provide steady employment for individuals like him. Though no longer at Fort Reno when Warden arrived, Tichkematse had also enlisted there three years earlier. In fact, by the time Warden signed up at Fort Reno in 1888, Tichkematse had reenlisted as a sergeant at Fort Supply, only a hundred miles to the northwest. What interactions these two Native anthropological collaborators had together are sadly lost to the historical record.[11]

After six months as an Indian scout at Fort Reno, Warden did not reenlist. Rather, he wanted to settle down. One month later he married a Southern Inunaina woman, Bertha Yellowman, the sister of a Carlisle classmate. With a young wife at home, Warden searched for other forms of employment. Discouraged by the few opportunities available to him, he nevertheless found a job in the fall of 1889 as a clerk for the Cheyenne and Arapaho Agency. He, along with many returned Indian boarding school students, gravitated to this work, as it made use of his English abilities and record-keeping skills. Warden served as an agency clerk for three years before taking on similar work at an Indian trader's store on the reservation.[12]

Anthropological Fieldwork with Mooney

While clerking in the Cheyenne and Arapaho Agency office in 1891, Warden met James Mooney, a Bureau of American Ethnology anthropologist with whom he maintained a lifelong collaborative relationship. It was also through Mooney's influence that Warden advocated for his community's constitutional freedoms. One of the most sympathetic of the non-Native anthropologists of his era, Mooney was born in Indiana in 1861 to Irish Catholic immigrant parents. From a young age he displayed an intense interest in American Indian nations. As early as 1882, at the age of twenty-one, he wrote to Director John Wesley Powell of the BAE asking for a place on his staff. Receiving negative responses, Mooney wrote again in 1883, and yet again in 1884. Finally, after visiting Powell personally in Washington DC in 1885, the director recognized the young man's intelligence and tenacity and hired him as an ethnologist. Mooney retained this position for the next thirty-six years.[13]

As a BAE employee, Mooney worked on his "Indian Synonymy," a complex list of Native and non-Native naming conventions for Indigenous nations throughout North America. This project was the foundation of what became the BAE's landmark two-volume publication *The Handbook of American Indians North of Mexico*, edited by Frederick Webb Hodge and published in 1907 and 1910. Mooney was more well-known for his anthropological fieldwork, however, which he undertook primarily among Southeast and Great Plains communities.[14]

In 1887, the same year Warden departed Carlisle for the Indian Territory, Mooney lived with the Eastern Band of Cherokee in North Carolina. There he worked day and night collecting ethnographic information. He wrote Powell that he had invited his collaborators to live in the same room with him to continue their work late into the night. Three years later, on his way to conduct anthropological fieldwork in the Oklahoma Territory, Mooney learned of trouble brewing with the rise of the Ghost Dance. Recognizing that many Euro-American fears of this ceremony stemmed from racism and misunderstanding, Mooney sought to investigate and report what he believed to be the truth. After receiving permission from Powell to do so, Mooney arrived on the Cheyenne and Arapaho Reservation in early 1891.[15]

Originating from the teachings of a Northern Paiute (Paviotso) prophet named Wovoka, the Ghost Dance movement spread quickly through the Great Plains. Many Southern Inunaina embraced it in 1890, shortly before Mooney arrived in the area. This religious movement promised a return to peaceful days, with plentiful buffalo, free of Euro-American society. Variations of the prophet Wovoka's message emphasized Native peoples as members of one family, one culture, or one chosen people. While this was not explicitly a call to arms, many non-Native outsiders saw the Ghost Dance movement as a source of potential violence against Euro-American settler colonizers in Indian Country.[16]

When Mooney arrived in January 1891, many Southern Tsitsistas/Suhtai and Inunaina youths were aware of newspaper stories and U.S. Army reports claiming "Indian mischief" connected with the Ghost Dance. This nineteenth-century version of fake news further stoked the racial anxieties of Euro-Americans, and more than a few Native youths understandably feared the outcome of such stories. Thus, a handful of young men, several of whom had been educated in Indian boarding schools like Warden, welcomed Mooney's arrival. Once there, they used him as an outlet to explain their belief system and the reason so many of their people were taking part in this ritual.

Mooney interviewed young men like Warden who had recently returned from eastern Indian boarding schools, and he also relied on their interpretive abilities to interview participants in the Ghost Dance. With his Smithsonian-issued tripod camera and an additional Kodak, Mooney photographed the dance and recorded some of the sacred songs with a graphophone machine. Mooney's respect for the beliefs of the Southern Inunaina and members of other Indigenous nations who practiced the Ghost Dance was something truly unique among non-Native peoples. Unlike many anthropologists at the time, he asked permission to observe and document sacred ceremonies and dances. According to another young Southern Inunaina man who worked with Mooney, it was hard for their community to accept that someone employed by the U.S. government believed that their art, history, and religion had value. Rather than trying to eradicate everything Native about them, as Richard Henry Pratt and other assimilationists advocated, Mooney and a few like-minded anthropologists sought to understand, collect, and record all they could of Indigenous cultures. For this Native young man, Mooney's passion for all things Native instilled in many Southern Inunaina people a redoubled pride for the beliefs of their own people.[17]

Warden and the other young men with him were happy for the Smithsonian employee's interest and explained to him in detail the Ghost Dance doctrine, its vision, and its songs. They repeatedly stressed to Mooney that they wanted other non-Native people to understand what they were doing, why they were doing it, and that they had no intentions of hurting anyone or causing fear. Mooney did just that in his popular 1893 publication, *The Ghost Dance Religion and the Sioux Outbreak of 1890*. To his credit and unlike many anthropologists of his day, Mooney identified and thanked Warden and his young Southern Inunaina friends by name for their contributions to this monumental work.[18]

Warden and Mooney's relationship, like that between many Native collaborators and non-Native anthropologists, was mutually beneficial. Without Warden, Mooney would have been unable to make inroads into the Southern Inunaina community or several other Native nations in the Oklahoma Territory. Warden provided both entrée and access to vast amounts of Indigenous peoples' tangible possessions and intangible cultural information. Mooney, on his side, acted as a mouthpiece or link between Native communities and a non-Native public ever-ready to believe the worst about Indigenous peoples.

Despite the scores of missionaries, educators, and BIA staff employed supposedly for the benefit of Native peoples, virtually the only means that American Indians had at their disposal to influence Washington policy-makers was through cooperation with sympathetic non-Native men and women like Mooney, George A. Dorsey, Harriet Maxwell Converse, and a handful of other well-meaning anthropologists. In fact, decades later Mooney testified alongside Warden during the congressional subcommittee hearings on Peyote use in 1918. Thirty years after collaborating to correct racist misinformation about the Ghost Dance, these two men worked together again and fought for Native American religious freedoms.

Anthropological Fieldwork with Kroeber and Dorsey

Ten years after entering the anthropological field with Mooney in 1891, Warden supplied important ethnographic information to another up-and-coming leader of early U.S. anthropology—Alfred L. Kroeber. Kroeber was a PhD student at Columbia University under Franz Boas and wanted to conduct his graduate fieldwork with the Northern and Southern Inunaina Nations. Typical of salvage anthropology, Boas instructed Kroeber to get "old things"—those believed more authentic or traditional—rather than newly made items. In June 1899 Boas made an introduction between Kroeber and the reservation agent at the Cheyenne and Arapaho Agency. With those formalities taken care of, Kroeber sought Warden's aid in interpreting Inunaina art in the Oklahoma Territory.[19]

The following year the Columbia PhD student traveled west to conduct fieldwork among Warden's Northern Inunaina relatives in Wyoming. Warden aided Kroeber again by interpreting for him, introducing him to important people in the community, and collecting tangible and intangible cultural information Kroeber deposited in the collections of the AMNH in New York. As James Mooney had done, Kroeber relied heavily on Warden for interpretation, translation, and research between 1899 and 1900. In subsequent years Kroeber published several academic works on decorative symbolism and beadwork of the Inunaina. Sadly, he neglected to mention his debt to Warden, without whom none of this work would have been possible.[20]

Around this time Warden became acquainted with another figure already familiar to readers—George A. Dorsey of Chicago's Field Museum. With a doctorate in anthropology from Harvard and his recent promotion to the Field Museum's head anthropology curator position, Dorsey sought to fill gaps in the Field Museum's collections, particularly its Plains Indian materials. During these years Dorsey was interested in the social organization of the Chaticks si Chaticks (Pawnee), Southern Inunaina, and Southern Tsitsistas/Suhtai Nations in the Oklahoma Territory. He undertook fieldwork, gathering information on these communities' intangible aspects—their society, religion, and language—as well as their material culture items for display in the museum's exhibitions. What this meant in reality was hiring on Native American collaborators from these communities who had the knowledge and ability to collect this type of information and, more importantly, the willingness to sell it to Dorsey.[21]

Having learned of Warden's abilities and anthropological acumen from his colleagues in the field, in early 1901 Dorsey offered to employ the thirty-five-year-old Southern Inunaina man on a temporary basis at $40 per month. In January of that year Dorsey asked Warden to collect and write down everything relating to the Inunaina Dance Societies he could locate. Specifically, Dorsey said he was interested in the origin stories of these societies and, more generally, in their associated clothing, dances, and songs. In response, Warden eagerly set to work collecting information and objects from his community in the Oklahoma Territory.

In 1901, the same year Warden started working as an anthropological collaborator with Dorsey, several individuals on the Cheyenne and Arapaho Agency requested that the new reservation agent, George W. H. Stouch, allow them to hold a Sun Dance ceremony. Stouch agreed, and Dorsey traveled to the Oklahoma Territory, eager to document all he could. With Warden once again as his interpreter and collaborator, Dorsey observed the public and private portions of the ceremony, having been granted permission by those in charge. In fact, in the aftermath of the 1901 Sun Dance, Warden and one of the leading Southern Inunaina priests traveled back to Dorsey's office in the Field Museum in Chicago. There Dorsey provided room and board for a period of two weeks while the three men discussed the origins and details of the ceremony, with Dorsey taking copious notes all the while. The following year Dorsey was once again invited to witness the 1902 Sun Dance ceremony, with Warden again interpreting, observing, and recording information for the Field Museum anthropologist.[22]

Dorsey and Warden's fieldnotes of these events were academic in nature. As such, they completely leave out the feeling of community and togetherness that accompanied these ceremonies. A young Southern Inunaina man summarized these engagements as so much more than a dance or religious ceremony. For him they were a communal undertaking, a time to visit with friends and family. His description paints a picture of people coming together from all directions, singing as they came. Everywhere was movement, with tipis raised in a great circle, their doorways to the east, their poles skyward. Everyone wore their finest clothes, too, rode their best horses, and brought great quantities of food for feasting. It was nothing short of a festival atmosphere where people celebrated their shared culture, history, and beliefs. The young Southern Inunaina observer who left this description said that when the time came for Sun Dance ceremonies to finally close, there was always a feeling of happiness and good will toward each other along with a hopeful energy that things would be better in the coming year.[23]

Fieldwork, Sacred Items, and Peyote in Wyoming

After witnessing two Southern Inunaina Sun Dance ceremonies, Dorsey published the results of his research conducted with Warden—a two-volume set titled *The Arapaho Sun Dance*. That same year he and Alfred L. Kroeber published an additional work—*Traditions of the Arapaho*. In 1902, just before his publications came out, Dorsey asked Warden to conduct fieldwork a little farther from home. Like Kroeber a few years earlier, Dorsey wanted to learn more about the Northern Inunaina people living on the Wind River Reservation. He asked Warden to travel to Wyoming to collect objects and information. Warden readily agreed, though as a shock to Dorsey, he requested that his new wife, Eva, accompany him and aid him in his collecting work.[24]

When Warden first began collaborating with Dorsey in 1901, the former was still married to Bertha Yellowman, and they were raising their two-year-old son, Robert. Although it is unclear if Bertha passed away or if she and Warden divorced, in September 1902 Warden married Eva Rogers at the Congregational Indian Mission in Darlington in the Oklahoma Territory. Eva, like her husband, was a Southern Inunaina community member and a former Carlisle Indian Industrial School student. According to Carlisle student records, Eva arrived at the school in 1889, shortly after Warden returned to the Cheyenne and Arapaho Reservation. Like anthropological collaborators Richard Davis and Warden before her, Eva requested multiple placements with non-Native families in Pratt's outing system. Every summer between 1894 and 1902 Eva lived and worked as a domestic servant doing housework for non-Native families in Pennsylvania, Maryland, and New Jersey. After completing her final outing assignment in June 1902, Eva left Carlisle—her home for thirteen years—and returned to the Oklahoma Territory. Less than two months later she married Cleaver Warden.[25]

Over her thirteen years at Carlisle Eva undoubtedly accepted at least some of Pratt's assimilation agenda. Nevertheless, she still aided her new husband in recording the richness and variety of their shared Indigenous heritage and culture, rather than throwing it all away. Despite the long years of Euro-American Christian indoctrination at Carlisle, completely abandoning her cultural identity was something Eva would never do. Thus, in October 1902 Warden wrote Dorsey from Casper, Wyoming, letting the Field Museum anthropologist know he and Eva were on their way to the Wind River Reservation where the Northern Inunaina lived. Once there, he hoped Eva would be able to collect material on women's societies, quillwork, and other secret information inaccessible to Cleaver.[26]

Despite their optimism for the anthropological work ahead of them, Eva and Cleaver's visit to Wyoming was short-lived. Upon arriving at Fort Washakie on the Wind River Reservation they presented reservation agent Colonel H. G. Nickerson with a letter of introduction from Dorsey explaining the work they would be conducting. After reading the letter Nickerson heaped verbal abuse on Dorsey, the Field Museum, anthropology in general, and on Cleaver and Eva in particular for being Native people engaged in such work. With no further explanation, he demanded they depart the reservation at once.

After learning of the debacle in Wyoming, Dorsey wrote the commissioner of Indian affairs that Nickerson harbored a personal grudge against him from years earlier and was obstructing his work. Dorsey had previously encouraged the Northern Inunaina community to hold religious ceremonies, even though Nickerson as their reservation agent banned the events and denied any requests to allow them. In subsequent years Dorsey also encouraged Indigenous peoples on other reservations to ignore the directives of BIA agents about practicing their religious beliefs. As far as Dorsey was concerned, American Indians needn't ask agents' permission to hold their own religious ceremonies. Nickerson, like many BIA agents and Christian missionaries, did not care for Dorsey and his anthropologist ilk. For Nickerson and his fellow assimilation advocates, anthropologists such as Dorsey were the enemy. They encouraged "old Indian customs and ways" and stymied Native American progress and assimilation to Euro-American Christian society.[27]

Although the Wardens' first anthropological fieldwork as a married couple was cut short through Nickerson's actions, they returned to Wyoming in future years to collect information and objects from Northern and Southern Inunaina Nations. Warden's correspondence with Dorsey from this period sheds light on power dynamics between Indigenous communities and salvage anthropologists. As recent scholars have noted, salvaging American Indian cultures meant gathering the profane as well as the sacred. Native collaborators and non-Native anthropologists collected everything they could get their hands on, from spiritual items to everyday, mundane objects. These they deposited in museums for study and exhibition, separating them from the objects' creators and users. Warden's correspondence from these days also illuminates the unprecedented state Native communities found themselves in with so much of their material culture heritage taken from them.[28]

Writing from the Oklahoma Territory in September 1906, Warden told Dorsey that members of the Southern Inunaina Nation would hold the Lime Crazy Lodge ceremony in coming weeks. The priests invited Dorsey to come and observe. Unusual in this invitation, however, was the request that Dorsey loan them their own Lime Crazy sacred objects. These items had been acquired by Warden and Dorsey years earlier in their limitless collection gathering and now resided in the Field Museum. Without Dorsey to facilitate this loan, Warden wrote, the ceremony could not take place. In their request to Dorsey, Warden and the community members wrote that after using the objects, they would repolish them for better appearance and return them to the museum. It remains unclear if the Field Museum actually approved this loan request. Nevertheless, its occurrence depicts the stark colonial relationship in which sovereign Indigenous nations found themselves at the whim of anthropologists simply to worship as their ancestors had for countless generations.[29]

Warden sent a similar letter to Dorsey one year earlier, also concerning ceremonial objects and their relationship to museum collections. Writing in January 1905, Warden told his colleague a Sun Dance ceremony was soon to occur. Several people involved in the ceremony were interested in selling related items after the ceremony's completion, Warden wrote. While these objects held a priceless value for those involved, community members also acknowledged the monetary value these items held among museum staff. Selling them, therefore, would bring some much-needed cash—a rare source of income for poverty-stricken individuals confined to the reservation. As noted with the anthropological collecting work of D. C. Duvall and Clark Wissler among the Pikuni Blackfeet (Piegan) in Montana, this is another example of the role salvage anthropology played in the lives of Native communities. By commodifying and fetishizing Indigenous material culture, museum anthropologists gave rise to an unintended economy that supplemented Native peoples' meager reservation rations—though one that simultaneously also robbed communities of their histories and cultures.[30]

In addition to collecting sacred items, Warden studied under community religious leaders while observing the ceremonies of his Northern Inunaina relatives in Wyoming. His time there helped spread new ideas and beliefs across hundreds of miles. Scholars believe Warden's personal work between the two reservations led to the dissemination of the Peyote faith from the U.S. southern plains and the Oklahoma Territory into Wyoming in the first decade of the twentieth century. Indeed, if the Field Museum had not employed Warden to conduct fieldwork at this time, the development and dispersal of Peyotism may not have come to the Northern Inunaina until significantly later. By 1905 Warden's Peyote use was so well known to Dorsey that he recommended Warden temporarily give up his "Mescal ceremonies" while in Wyoming. Dorsey reminded him he was an official representative of the Field Museum, and that the Peyote faith was prohibited on the Wind River Reservation. Thus, Dorsey continued, it would be best if Warden delayed personally practicing his religious beliefs until he returned to the Oklahoma Territory.[31]

Fifteen years earlier, just about the time the Ghost Dance and Peyotism were spreading across western reservations, the commissioner of Indian affairs ordered his BIA agents to seize all Peyote and punish anyone found guilty of selling or using this substance. Labeling Peyote an intoxicant and a narcotic, the BIA initiated a campaign of eradication. Despite their efforts, however, Peyotism continued to spread. Surprisingly, one of the primary reasons for the increase of Peyotists and dissemination of the Peyote faith throughout Indian Country was due to Indian boarding schools. Many early Peyotists attended Indian boarding schools, knew each other from their time in these institutions, and, due to their fluency in English, were able to communicate cross-culturally with other Indigenous peoples. Information sharing and a nascent pan-Native identity, then, were two of the most important unintended consequences of the Indian boarding school system. Rather than eliminating Native American cultural identities, the forced grouping together of Indigenous youths led to broader notions of what it meant to be Native, including the later dissemination of Peyotism beliefs and practices.[32]

Warden, like the other Native anthropologists and collaborators in this book, used his fluency in English to document and preserve his Inunaina culture via anthropology. In this way he turned the power against the intentions of his racist and assimilationist former teachers. Similarly, Christian missionaries and proponents of conversion were foiled by these same former Indian boarding school students who embraced Peyotism and its syncretization with tenets of Christianity. In time this latter group of Indian boarding school survivors used the knowledge learned at school to form the Native American Church as a safeguard against further federal encroachment on their religious freedoms.[33]

Participation in Fairs and Indian Villages

Throughout these years Warden was adept enough to know the fickle power balance he held in the anthropological field. Because of this, he did not rely solely on ethnological fieldwork to pay the bills. To supplement his earnings, he also sought out opportunities to participate in regional and world's fairs. The earliest record of Warden's participation in an event of this nature is from the Topeka Fairgrounds in Topeka, Kansas, in the fall of 1897. Accompanying him was his good friend Robert Burns, a Southern Tsitsistas/Suhtai man who had grown up with Warden on the Cheyenne and Arapaho Reservation. Throughout much of their lives, these two men followed similar paths—both attended Carlisle Indian Industrial School under Pratt's tutelage, clerked together in the Cheyenne and Arapaho Agency office, collaborated with James Mooney about the Ghost Dance, and later traveled to Washington DC as interpreters for their communities in several important delegations.

The English language skills Warden and Burns learned during their Indian boarding school days provided them the means to work as liaisons between their communities and non-Native fair organizers. Thus, at the 1897 Topeka Fair Warden and Burns supervised the parties assembled from their respective Indigenous nations. In their roles they selected which individuals went to the fair, chaperoned them while off the reservation, and advised on issues ranging from where to set up camp, what dances to perform for the crowds, and even what clothing to wear to meet the public's demand to see "real Indians."[34]

Like fellow Native collaborators Richard Davis and James R. Murie, Warden later reprised his role at the Topeka Fair by taking part in Indian villages at larger expositions, including at the 1904 World's Fair in St. Louis, Missouri. In addition to recruiting friends and relatives for the St. Louis fair's Indian village, Warden's wife Eva and their son George also accompanied him. There, as he had done in Kansas, Warden and his family made a small sum of money posing in photographs and selling crafts to fairgoers. Unlike in Topeka, though, Warden's role as a supervisor and recruiter for the Inunaina "Show Indians" at the St. Louis fair did not last long. He began recruiting and transporting community members from the reservation to the St. Louis fairgrounds in February 1904. Four months later he was back home in the Oklahoma Territory, having been expelled from the fair.

In June 1904 Warden wrote a friend that he was happy to be out of the constant rain and mud at the St. Louis fair's Indian village. Writing from the comfort of his home, Warden claimed there was no refinement or culture to be found under the management of the anthropology exhibits at the fair. As far as he was concerned, the blame for his abrupt departure lay completely at the feet of former BAE anthropologist WJ McGee and BIA agent Samuel McCowan. Both men also worked in passing with Richard Davis and James R. Murie when the latter participated in the 1904 St. Louis fair.

As noted previously, McGee's views on racial progress and social evolution mirrored those of the fair's organizers. Reflecting the nineteenth-century teachings of his forebears Lewis Henry Morgan and John Wesley Powell, McGee believed the world's peoples illustrated concrete steps in the development of humankind's intelligence. Through his anthropological exhibits he sought to show an identifiable course of progress from lower to higher humanity, with the different stages of progress marked by various physical and cultural types. The result of this scientific exhibit, McGee believed, would benefit fairgoers by informing "our half of the world how the other half lives," as well as benefit Indigenous persons, like Warden, on exhibit. According to McGee, the less advanced profited by association with the more advanced, eventually adopting aspects of so-called civilization absent in their own societies.[35]

McGee envisioned the Indian village and the larger anthropological exhibits at the 1904 St. Louis fair as the most elaborate ever made, with representatives of every country on display. There they would illustrate McGee's view of social evolution and human progress from the darkness of its earliest ages to its highest enlightenment. Not surprisingly, within McGee's racist and Social Darwinist model Native Americans occupied the lower end of human progress while Euro-Americans existed at the other extreme—the pinnacle of humanity so far reached.

It is clear that McGee was distracted by his own lack of experience in managing the fair's Indian village. He left himself little to no time to monitor daily events. According to gossip then circulating among other anthropologists, McGee made a mess of the fair's anthropology displays, figuratively digging himself a hole from which he was unable to get out. What resulted were a myriad of problems with the management of the Indian village. With McGee otherwise occupied and the anthropology exhibits in shambles, many of the decisions for the day-to-day operations fell to BIA agent Samuel McCowan.[36]

McCowan was a veteran BIA employee, ardent assimilation advocate, and director of the BIA's model Indian boarding school exhibit at the fair. Unlike McGee, McCowan took an instant dislike to Warden and the Southern Inunaina with him in the Indian village. In May 1904 McCowan called Warden into his office and castigated him for rumors of heavy drinking among the Inunaina participants. As "Show Indians" temporarily granted leave from their reservation, they were prohibited by the fair organizers from alcohol use. According to McCowan, Warden, as their supervisor and chaperone, should have been on watch for any of this illicit behavior. Believing the rumors true, McCowan labeled Warden and the Southern Inunaina performers drunkards. He said their actions did not reflect well on how assimilated Native Americans should conduct themselves. McCowan then informed Warden that his services were no longer needed. Immediately following this, he instructed Warden and the Southern Inunaina to break camp and return to their reservation at once.[37]

Dorsey was irate when he learned of McCowan's actions. He wrote Warden that he was shocked on finding one of the "finest group[s] of Indians ever assembled" gone from the fairgrounds with only mud to mark where they had been. Aggrieved at the situation, Dorsey told his friend he was sorry enough to weep over the disgrace Warden had suffered. He requested Warden report everything in detail that led to his departure and asked if he would return if they could convince BAE anthropologist James Mooney to lead the Indian village in place of McGee and McCowan. Warden refused. Two weeks later Dorsey reported continued discontent from those Native performers who stayed on in the Indian village under McGee and McCowan's management.[38]

Despite the debacle at the 1904 St. Louis World's Fair, Warden and Dorsey maintained their friendship and collaborative partnership. Repeatedly over the next two years Warden conducted fieldwork in Wyoming and the Oklahoma Territory under the auspices of the Field Museum. He also spent long stretches of time in Chicago collaborating with Dorsey over their findings. Notwithstanding their continued work, steady, long-term employment in the anthropological field was a rarity for Warden. He and many Native collaborators were reliant on the availability of funds from non-Native museum anthropologists and dependent on seasonal ceremonial calendars of the year. Latter determinations such as when the Sun Dance took place were the purview of individual Native pledgers and at the discretion of reservation agents. To make ends meet, Warden and other collaborators had to cobble together varying anthropological assignments. Warden's correspondence with Dorsey from the time reflects this. In 1904, for instance, he wrote the Field Museum anthropologist that it was embarrassing for him to be idle. He hoped Dorsey could help him in securing seasonal fieldwork with museums in California, New York, or Washington DC. This not only illustrates Warden's passion for documenting and preserving Indigenous cultures but also demonstrates how broad and fluid anthropological work was for Native collaborators at the turn of the twentieth century.[39]

With few openings in the anthropological field, Warden took on odd jobs around the reservation. In late 1904, for example, he performed road work near Darlington in the Oklahoma Territory. This temporary position lasted two months and paid $2.50 per day. He told Dorsey he was glad to do anything that would keep his family fed. By 1906 Dorsey and Warden's joint ethnographic labors tapered off due to changes in the Field Museum's collecting policies. As noted, Dorsey also ended his collaborative endeavors with Warden's fellow Native collaborators, Richard Davis and James R. Murie, around this same time.[40]

Delegation Work and Advocacy for His People

While securing steady employment proved difficult, Warden was never truly idle. Alongside his anthropological fieldwork, participation at regional and world's fairs, and cobbling together odd jobs around the reservation, he worked tirelessly as an advocate for his people. At least four times between 1895 and 1909 he traveled to Washington DC as an official interpreter for Cheyenne and Arapaho Agency delegations.

By the late nineteenth century Native delegations in the nation's capital were a common sight. They were also something government policymakers encouraged. Hoping to impress and intimidate Native American delegates with the federal government's power, U.S. officials funded travel and lodging for visiting delegations. When the BAE was established as part of the Smithsonian Institution in 1879, it too took on an important role with Native delegations—photographing Native American "types" thought to be vanishing. Warden himself appeared in several of these photos taken by BAE staff over the years. One image shows Warden and fellow delegation members standing in front of the Beveridge family boardinghouse near the Capitol Building during their 1899 delegation visit.[41]

Warden's first official delegation in which he served as the Southern Inunaina interpreter was in 1895. Along with Robert Burns, who interpreted for the Southern Tsitsistas/Suhtai delegates, Warden accompanied several community leaders including Row of Lodges and Chief Left Hand or Nawat. These men traveled 1,300 miles to discuss with the secretary of the interior and the commissioner of Indian affairs the ill effects allotment policies had had on their people. Four years later, in 1899, Warden, Burns, and several other delegates including Young Bull Bear, the older brother of anthropological collaborator Richard Davis, traveled again to DC to petition the federal government. During this visit they presented claims of theft and avarice leveled against the agent of the Cheyenne and Arapaho Reservation, A. E. Woodson. The delegates not only succeeded in having Woodson replaced but also managed to get the following year's federal appropriation for their communities increased by $10,000.[42]

Warden visited the nation's capital as an official Southern Inunaina delegate again in 1906, in 1909, and, as indicated at the beginning of the chapter, a final time in 1918 when he testified before members of Congress on behalf of Native American religious freedoms. A newspaper article reporting on Warden's 1909 delegation visit quoted him as saying that the Southern Inunaina Nation had not received the money due them from the government's sale of their surplus lands. Thus, Warden visited the commissioner of Indian affairs to convince him to allow the community to employ competent attorneys to aid them in their case against the federal government. Five years later Warden again sought legal aid in prosecuting land claims denied to his people. Warden's continued advocacy during these years illustrates how he turned the power against the assimilationist goals of the Indian boarding school system. Like the other Native anthropologists and collaborators in this book, Warden endured the boarding school experience and emerged with the necessary English skills to challenge racist federal policies aimed at eradicating his culture and stealing Native land.[43]

Membership in the Society of American Indians

In addition to his ethnographic and interpretive work, Warden also sought to preserve and promote his culture in other ways. In his later years, for instance, he was elected vice-president of the General Counsel of the Cheyenne and Arapaho Tribes. In this role he weighed in on important matters affecting his community. For at least a few years, too, he was a member of the Society of American Indians (SAI). Founded in 1911, SAI was the first national Native American advocacy organization in the United States. The naming of the organization was quite intentional—marking it unmistakably as an American Indian movement. Importantly, SAI disassociated itself from Progressive Era Christian reform societies that promised aid to Native peoples but adhered to the agendas set forth by their non-Native membership base. SAI's leaders lauded their new organization as one in which "all Indians" could discuss the rights of their people. As it turned out, certain Indigenous voices were more welcome than others.[44]

Membership in SAI was robust in its early years. It included several Native anthropologists and collaborators such as J. N. B. Hewitt, Francis La Flesche, Arthur C. Parker, and Amos Oneroad. Rapidly, however, leading SAI voices advocated assimilation and an abandonment of "the old ways." Native members who lived in urban areas and embraced Euro-American Christian society outnumbered those such as Cleaver Warden, Richard Davis, and James R. Murie, who remained on reservations and celebrated their communities' pasts. BAE anthropologist and Tuscarora Nation member J. N. B. Hewitt voiced his concern over what he saw as the SAI leadership's unwillingness to take the latter group into its confidence. Writing to SAI member Arthur C. Parker in 1915, Hewitt argued that American Indians who dwelt on reservations or on restricted allotments were surrounded by forces of greed and graft. They were the ones who most needed wise counsel and efficient legal services from SAI, Hewitt contended, yet they rarely if ever received it. Hewitt viewed the society's leadership as out of touch with actual American Indian matters, and he, like several others, became less of a presence in the organization in following years.[45]

Representing a growing factionalism that tore the organization apart in 1923, SAI included several Native Americans emphatically opposed to anthropological work. These included Gertrude Simmons Bonnin, Chauncey Yellow Robe, Charles Eastman, and Rosa Bourassa, the latter the third wife of Francis La Flesche. Arthur C. Parker in particular, though himself a Native anthropologist, used his editorship of SAI's magazine to voice his personal grievances. He railed against Wild West shows as "injurious fakery" and labeled Peyote a harmful narcotic that impeded Native peoples' "progress" in fully assimilating into Euro-American society. Although Warden attended the 1915 annual conference in Lawrence, Kansas, with James R. Murie, he eventually left the organization due to differences over Peyote use in religious ceremonies. Warden favored such use, while SAI's pro-assimilationist leadership under Bonnin and Parker opposed it.[46]

Peyote Congressional Subcommittee Hearings

And that brings us back to the congressional Peyote hearings in early 1918 in Washington DC. These hearings were held to determine whether the use and possession of Peyote should be criminalized throughout the country and on Indian reservations in particular. A slew of missionaries, physicians, anthropologists, BIA staff, and Peyotists attended and testified on each side, determined that their voices be heard.

Among those testifiers opposed to criminalization were several Native leaders including Fred Lookout, principal chief of the Osage Nation, Little Hand of the Southern Tsitsistas/Suhtai, and Wilbur Peawa of the Niuam (Comanche). Peawa was a former Carlisle Indian Industrial School student like Cleaver Warden. Other Native leaders unable to travel the long distance from their homes in the west sent testimonials to be read at the hearings. Southern Inunaina member Jack Bull Bear, for instance, requested in his written testimonial that Congress not prohibit Peyote use. He argued that the U.S. Constitution guaranteed him and his people freedom of religious worship. Aware of the government's case against Peyote, Bull Bear also said that the charges against this "Indian religion" were untrue. Like Bull Bear, several other Native leaders testified that missionaries' stories about Peyote use leading to sin and depravity were falsehoods and nothing more. Such misinformation existed, they claimed, so missionaries could control Native religious beliefs and ceremonies, rather than allow American Indian peoples to practice how they saw fit.

Alongside Indigenous leaders testifying in favor of Peyote use were a handful of Native and non-Native anthropologists opposed to criminalization. The well-known Omaha anthropologist Francis La Flesche provided his support during these hearings. Like his BAE colleague James Mooney, La Flesche testified before the subcommittee that Peyote use should not be criminalized. Statements like these earned La Flesche the enmity of missionaries, politicians, and leading SAI members. Not surprisingly, these same individuals harbored ill feelings toward Mooney, believing his influence detrimental to Native American progress. Mooney first studied Peyote use in 1891, fascinated by its syncretic nature of combining Native religious beliefs and practices with elements of Christianity. Over the succeeding decades the dogged anthropologist championed Peyote as a

Native reconciliation with the past, not hesitating to argue with missionaries and BIA agents who labeled its use demoralizing and evil.[47]

Gertrude Simmons Bonnin, also known as Zitkála-Šá, was one of those individuals who could not abide Mooney, Warden, or the work they did as anthropologists. Bonnin, as previously mentioned, attended the Quaker-run White's Manual Labor Institute in Wabash, Indiana, alongside future Sac and Fox anthropologist William Jones. She later worked as an employee of Richard Henry Pratt's at Carlisle. Bonnin was both a member of the Ihanktonwan (Yankton Dakota) community and a leader in SAI. The way she saw it, Mooney's defense of Peyote among Native "traditionalists" on reservations was self-serving. She testified he took advantage of his anthropological fieldwork as a government employee to encourage Peyote consumption among American Indian communities. In so doing, Bonnin continued, Mooney won over Peyotists and gained privileged information for his books.[48]

Carlisle founder Richard Henry Pratt, never far from any discussion on the topic of Native American "progress," echoed Bonnin's criticisms of Mooney in his own congressional testimony. Pratt went further, though, extending such criticisms to La Flesche, Native collaborators, and the field of anthropology in general. Cleaver Warden and Richard Davis, as two of Pratt's former Carlisle students working in the field of anthropology, were a particular embarrassment to him. Government anthropologists gathered curious and peculiar facts about Native peoples, Pratt argued, and portrayed them in their immense illustrated books. By such actions, he believed, anthropologists misinformed the public, highlighted and romanticized antiquated belief systems, and impeded the progress of American Indian education across the country.

On the morning of February 25, 1918, Pratt testified that the BAE staff at the Smithsonian had never been helpful to American Indians in any respect. Instead of civilizing Native peoples or ushering them toward citizenship, he continued, anthropologists always led their minds back into the past. In a final thrust at Warden, Mooney, and other anthropologists, Pratt stated it was a well-established fact that men like Mooney were the promoters if not the originators of the Ghost Dance movement of the 1890s. This "peyote craze," he concluded, was simply more of the same. Caustic and false statements like these from Pratt, BIA officials, and numerous missionaries typified the congressional hearings. They are just one more example in a centuries-long history of the U.S. government and its colonial representatives trying to exert control over Native American lives.[49]

Closing of the Peyote Hearings and the Beginning of the Native American Church

After more than twelve hours of testimony debating Peyote use, subcommittee chairman Tillman tried, ineffectively, to conclude the hearings. However, Cleaver Warden rose to speak one more time before the subcommittee members made their decision. Warden previously submitted a statement on behalf of the Southern Tsitsistas/Suhtai and Southern Inunaina Nations, arguing they wanted only a fair and impartial trial by "reasonable white people." He fumed against the words of people such as Gertrude Simmons Bonnin, SAI secretary. In emphatic language Warden singled her out, accusing Bonnin of not knowing her Native ancestors or her kindred. Although not explicitly saying so in his congressional statement, in other documents Warden wrote that he considered Bonnin an "urban Indian" and an assimilationist. As far as he was concerned, she represented a body of American Indians who knew little of reservation life and sought to distance themselves from their Native nations' histories and cultures. For him, a "true Indian" was someone who helped their race, not someone like Bonnin who obstructed Native peoples' efforts to worship how they wished.[50]

In the last few minutes of the last day's hearings, Warden addressed the three subcommittee members. Before these men rendered a decision affecting hundreds of thousands of his fellow people, Warden asked them to remember the words and speeches of the Native individuals who testified throughout the hearings. Several of them had traveled more than a thousand miles to speak on behalf of their communities, he argued. They represented their peoples' voices in demanding a freedom guaranteed in the Constitution and granted to all other U.S. citizens. Warden reflected on the many years he had spent studying Native communities in Indian Country. In everything but name he was an anthropologist. He knew his people, their rituals, their ceremonies, and their beliefs. Again and again he had fought to document and preserve their diverse cultures. Now all he asked of the subcommittee members was to simply be just in their decision.

Moments after Warden delivered his final plea, Chairman Tillman declared the hearings closed. Despite the testimonies of those in favor of keeping Peyote legal for religious observance, the following year the U.S. House of Representatives voted to criminalize its use and possession. Although this legislation ultimately stalled in the U.S. Senate, defenders of Peyote knew which way the wind was blowing. Even though Congress did not criminalize Peyote use in 1918, Warden and Mooney reasoned that the concerted efforts of missionaries, BIA officials, and Native SAI members would eventually push such legislation through.

Soon after the Peyote hearings concluded, a handful of Native American leaders and Peyotists came up with a solution. With James Mooney's encouragement and advice, in October 1918 these men founded the Native American Church of Oklahoma. Lawyers for this organization successfully argued that Peyote use in religious ceremonies represented a constitutional right to religious freedom that could not be infringed upon. From its founding until the 1940s, the Native American Church existed at local and state levels only. But in 1944 Peyotists chartered the Native American Church of the United States, which became the Native American Church of North America ten years later. In 1978, a full six decades after the founding of the Native American Church, the U.S. Congress passed the American Indian Religious Freedom Act guaranteeing such worship.[51]

It should come as no surprise that Gertrude Simmons Bonnin, Richard Henry Pratt, and a host of other detractors were loath to allow Peyote use to continue as a constitutionally protected religious right. As far as they were concerned, Peyote was just another symptom of Native American backsliding into primitive habits. Bonnin and Pratt hounded Warden and Mooney following the outcome of the Peyote hearings because of their public support of Peyote. Writing Pratt in early 1919, Bonnin suggested prompt action be taken to "disarm" Mooney of his government position. In this she and Pratt were partially successful, as Mooney's supervisor bowed to political pressure and recalled Mooney to Washington DC permanently. Although he kept his job as a federal anthropologist, Mooney was barred from conducting fieldwork in Oklahoma. Notably, this was the state where he and Warden first collaborated three decades earlier, advocating for Native religious beliefs as a constitutional right. Warden's longtime friend Mooney died less than two years later, in 1921.[52]

Cleaver Warden and Anthropology Today

Despite the opposition arrayed against him, Warden encouraged Peyote as a religious sacrament among Native peoples for the rest of his life. First instructed in the Peyote faith by Southern Inunaina leader Left Hand or Nawat, Warden passed along these teachings to his extended relatives in Oklahoma and Wyoming over many years. Numerous Native people from his own community and from other Indigenous nations viewed Warden as a teacher and sought him out for his knowledge.[53]

In contrast to his Peyote advocacy and his work in the anthropological field, Warden still encouraged his son and other Native children to attend Indian boarding schools. In this he was like all the Native anthropologists and collaborators in this book. They each shared similar complicated feelings toward Indian boarding schools as institutions of racism and cultural erasure. While these individuals fought against assimilation and turned the power against the federal government's attempts to eradicate their cultures, they also encouraged their children and family members to attend Indian boarding schools. Despite the racism and abuse Warden suffered during his Carlisle days, for instance, he nevertheless sent his eldest son, Robert, to the Chilocco Indian Boarding School. Robert graduated from Chilocco in 1920 and, with his father's blessing, attended the American Indian Institute in Wichita, Kansas. One of the first Native-run high schools in the country, the American Indian Institute, or Roe Indian Institute, was established by Ho-Chunk (Winnebago) educator and intellectual Henry Roe Cloud only five years earlier. After graduating from the American Indian Institute in 1922, Robert returned to Oklahoma, where he started a family and lived near his father. Robert died unexpectedly a few years later in 1926.[54]

The question remains why someone like Cleaver Warden, after enduring the hardships of Carlisle and going on to fight against its racist teachings, would encourage his own child to receive a similar education. Clearly Warden and his fellow Native anthropologists and collaborators saw something to be gained through these educational facilities. In spite of the attempts made by school staff to convert Native students, to abandon their cultures, and to assimilate into Euro-American Christian society, Warden and other future Native anthropologists and collaborators endured. They emerged from these schools with English fluency that equipped them to battle against those who sought to change them. In a colonial world that prided itself on only speaking English, these products of Indian boarding schools now spoke in English for their mothers, fathers, and community members whose voices went unrecognized in the United States. Perhaps these thoughts motivated Warden and other Native collaborators to send their children to Indian boarding schools—to instill future generations of Native youth with the will and the language skills to fight their oppressors.

Warden used the knowledge gained in his early education to preserve his Inunaina culture and history rather than abandon it as assimilationists demanded. This he did by studying his community through an anthropologist's eyes, while collaborating with non-Native anthropologists. Despite his life's work, though, Warden's role in anthropology is largely overlooked today. Although his name is sometimes mentioned in relation to the fieldwork of James Mooney, Alfred L. Kroeber, or George A. Dorsey, it is often just as an "informant" or supplier of information. But his actual impact was much greater. Warden produced much of the substantive information on Inunaina art, religion, and culture in the early twentieth century. As recent scholars have noted, Mooney's, Kroeber's, and Dorsey's publications on the Northern and Southern Inunaina Nations relied on Warden's interpretation and information gathering. It was these publications that became the foundational knowledge for non-Native peoples on Inunaina culture for much of the twentieth century.[55]

Warden's anthropological career did not end when his collaborative work with Dorsey concluded in 1906. Over two decades later, in 1928, a younger generation of anthropologists still sought him out. In that year BAE ethnologist Truman Michelson traveled to Oklahoma to compile linguistic information with Warden for preservation at the Smithsonian Institution. Throughout all these years, Warden fought to retain his culture and history against constant pressure to abandon his community's lifeways. Warden died in 1935 in Oklahoma. He was surrounded by family, friends, and the community he protected and defended for so many years.

8

Both an Experienced Field Man and a Missionary among His People

Amos Oneroad (Tokio, North Dakota, 1925)

As the rain finally began to let up on August 17, 1925, Amos Oneroad continued to sit by his friend's lifeless body. The two men, Oneroad and Alanson Skinner, were anthropologists at the Museum of the American Indian, Heye Foundation (MAI), in New York. They were conducting fieldwork near what is now Spirit Lake Reservation in North Dakota when the accident happened. Heavy rains turned the steep road into a mud slick. Without chains on their tires, there was little Oneroad could do as the driver when their car stalled near the top of the hill and began to slide backwards. Within seconds their Ford rolled over the embankment, propelling Oneroad free from the crash but pinning Skinner face down in the mud. His upper body was trapped under the car's immense weight. Despite frantic attempts to move the upturned vehicle, Oneroad couldn't budge it by himself. It ultimately wouldn't have mattered. Skinner died instantly.

Oneroad sat on that muddy, desolate road for hours before another person passed. With the help of three other men, Oneroad was eventually able to move the car and free Skinner's body. The local coroner ruled Skinner's death an accident, and the anthropologist's remains were sent home to New York. Rather than accompany Skinner's lifeless body on its eastward journey, Oneroad instead returned to the embrace of his family and Sisseton Wahpeton Oyate (Sisseton-Wahpeton Sioux) community in South Dakota.

That August day marked the end of Oneroad's anthropology career. It was almost fitting, in a morbid sort of way. Just as Skinner brought Oneroad into the field of anthropology a decade before, his death served as an ending for Oneroad's anthropological work. Over the following months

Oneroad had frequent nightmares in which he relived the horror of that day. In letters to his former museum colleagues in New York, he noted only minor physical damage and bruises from the crash, but he wrote of the emotional aftereffects and mental shock he continued to experience. He suffered a form of survivor's guilt, questioning again and again why he was spared and Skinner died. Oneroad took stock of his life and soon transitioned to a missionary calling wholly separate from his anthropological work. Despite trying not to think about it, another question kept coming to his mind—would he ever have another friendship like the one he had with Alanson Skinner?[1]

Youth and Schooling

Over four decades earlier Amos Oneroad was born on the Lake Traverse Reservation in the Dakota Territory. For generations this land had been the home of the Sisseton Wahpeton Oyate, an Eastern Dakota community living along the Minnesota and Mississippi Rivers area. Over time, non-Native settler colonizers from the East encroached more and more on their lands. By the mid-nineteenth century the federal government forced the Eastern Dakota people to relinquish much of their former landholdings. In 1867 these land dealings were formalized with the creation of the Lake Traverse Reservation. The U.S. Congress stipulated that this territory was the permanent home of the Sisseton Wahpeton Oyate community.[2]

Less than five years after the Lake Traverse Reservation was created, Presbyterian missionaries flocked to the area. They went to convert the Native inhabitants and assimilate them into Euro-American Christian society. In 1869 the Goodwill Presbyterian Church was built, and the following year an accompanying mission school was constructed to educate Native youths in supposed Christian virtue. According to Sisseton Wahpeton Oyate community members at the time, missionary control across the reservation was very strong in the 1870s and 1880s. Extending beyond the church and school, Presbyterian missionaries and Bureau of Indian Affairs agents searched the homes of residents on the reservation. Any objects they deemed non-Christian were seized, burned, or otherwise destroyed. As a result, large numbers of Native residents converted to Christianity or continued to practice their beliefs in private, away from the prying eyes of non-Natives in their midst.[3]

In 1891 the federal government mandated allotment on the Lake Traverse Reservation. Communal ownership of land was replaced by individual allotments intended for small family farming. The U.S. government lost little time selling all "surplus lands" at $2.50 per acre. By presidential proclamation, in April 1892 land-hungry settler colonizers rushed to enter former Sisseton Wahpeton Oyate territory, eager to stake their claims on these supposedly vacant lands.[4]

This is the world Amos Oneroad was born into in 1884. His father, Cankuwanzidan or Peter Oneroad, was a member of the Ihanktonwan (Yankton Dakota) community but married into and resided among the Sisseton Wahpeton Oyate family of Wamnonhna Koyakewin or Nancy Shepherd, Amos's mother. Young Amos grew up with his many brothers and sisters along the west side of a lake and in a township now bearing their anglicized surname, Oneroad.[5]

At age seven, Amos's parents enrolled him and his siblings into the nearby Goodwill Presbyterian Mission School. As was the case with other Native collaborators, Amos's parents encouraged him to attend and learn all he could in these Euro-American institutions. They hoped that by doing so, Amos would speak on behalf of his community and better compete in the new society. At the Goodwill Mission School the children received English fundamentals and Christianity, the latter something Amos embraced for the rest of his life. The Goodwill Mission School was built in 1870, and four years later the federal government constructed the Sisseton Indian Boarding School alongside it. After initial schooling at the Goodwill Mission School, in 1895 Amos transferred to the government's Sisseton School on the Lake Traverse Reservation.[6]

Like many Indian boarding schools that cropped up across the country at the end of the nineteenth century, the Sisseton School was founded as a manual training institution. The government's goal was to educate Native youths and assimilate them into Euro-American society. But an additional hope was to introduce Indigenous children to trades and agricultural skills that would lead to them become productive, self-sufficient laborers in a capitalist nation. With children ranging in age from seven to eighteen, half the day was devoted to classroom education, with the remainder spent in industrial, farming, or domestic work on the school grounds. Girls received training in domestic responsibilities, including working in the kitchen, dining room, sewing room, and laundry. Boys, on the other hand, milked cows, took care of the horses, chopped wood, and worked outside in the fields and gardens. Although students' parents and families lived in close proximity, the children were confined to the school grounds during the school year from September until June.[7]

Amos entered the Sisseton School in 1895, one of approximately 120 boarding pupils that made up the student body. The school grounds included a dozen buildings consisting of dormitories, classrooms, and shops where students learned trades. The superintendent oversaw the school's management and was aided by a staff of between fifteen and twenty teachers. According to one teacher, it was a special honor when the teachers selected "English names" for the young students in their care. In addition to being forced to abandon the names their parents gave them, students were prohibited from speaking their own languages in favor of English. Try as they might, though, Sisseton's teachers found it difficult to prevent children from doing so. Many students continued to speak in their Native languages when out of earshot of teachers and disciplinarians whose job it was to monitor them for such infractions.[8]

In 1905 Amos decided to follow his father's and grandfather's advice to continue his education. That November he traveled five hundred miles south and enrolled at the Haskell Institute in Lawrence, Kansas. Although preceding Oneroad by more than two decades, Chaticks si Chaticks (Pawnee) collaborator James R. Murie also traveled to Haskell, where he worked as a disciplinarian for a few years. Unlike Murie, who went seeking employment, Oneroad went to Haskell seeking education.

Modeled after Richard Henry Pratt's Carlisle Indian Industrial School, Haskell divided students' days between the classroom and either working in the trades, on the farm, or, in the case of female students, in different domestic capacities. Like other Indian boarding schools, the primary goal at Haskell was to assimilate Indigenous youths into Euro-American Christian society. Attending church services was compulsory, as was Bible study, which Oneroad greatly enjoyed. Sadly, Oneroad left few personal reflections from his Haskell schooldays. However, we know he excelled at his studies and graduated in June 1909 with a specialization in agricultural sciences.[9]

Another area in which Oneroad received praise in his youth was for his artistry. Multiple individuals at the time labeled him a very good or exceptional artist. He was even sought out to exhibit his artwork at the 1904 World's Fair in St. Louis. While still a student at the Sisseton School in South Dakota in 1903, one of the fair's planners learned of Oneroad's artistic talents. Samuel M. McCowan, director of the BIA model Indian boarding school at the fair, believed Oneroad's artwork showed "considerable native genius." Readers may recall McCowan as the same man who expelled Cleaver Warden and the Southern Inunaina (Arapaho) "Show Indians" from the fair in 1904. McCowan asked Oneroad if he would like to participate in the BIA's exhibit, where he could display his talents. Oneroad's travel, lodging, food, and even clothing while attending the fair would all be covered, McCowan promised. Oneroad felt he could not refuse such an offer.[10]

In the summer of 1904 twenty-year-old Oneroad found himself transported from South Dakota's Lake Traverse Reservation to the St. Louis World's Fair in Missouri. Along with a rotating cast of Native American youths, Oneroad exhibited his skills in McCowan's BIA-run model Indian boarding school. As coincidence would have it, one of Oneroad's fellow exhibitors in the model school was Caroline Murie, a twelve-year-old Haskell student and daughter of Chaticks si Chaticks collaborator James R. Murie. Murie, Richard Davis, Cleaver Warden, and their families were also on display at the fair that summer, as "Show Indians" in WJ McGee's mismanaged Indian village. How much interaction Oneroad had with any of these individuals is unknown. Notably, though, their collective attendance at the fair illustrates both the popularity of world's fairs at the time and the scarcity of employment opportunities for Native peoples.[11]

Just before embarking on his studies at Haskell, Oneroad again received praise for his artistic skill. The *Sisseton Weekly Standard* newspaper highlighted Oneroad's drawings of the Sisseton School's 1905 closing exercises, but the biggest recognition he received for his artwork was in 1909. During his final year at Haskell, Oneroad submitted several drawings to the *Denver Post* newspaper in Colorado. These cartoons were printed, and the newspaper offered him a position as their staff cartoonist. The combination of his artistic gift and sense of humor made him highly desirable, with the staff wanting to snap him up.

From all accounts, it appears Oneroad never accepted the *Denver Post's* offer. His name next turns up in the historical record in May 1910, when he was again living with his parents on the Lake Traverse Reservation. He also worked at the Goodwill Presbyterian Mission School in 1912, aiding missionaries assimilate Native children into Christianity. There he might well have remained, never to enter the field of anthropology, if not for a desire to further pursue his education. Whereas previously he traveled five hundred miles to Kansas, this time his New York City destination was three times this distance.[12]

Life in New York

Oneroad again followed the advice of his family to learn about Euro-American Christian society. So in the autumn of 1913 he moved to New York and enrolled in the Bible Teachers' Training School, later renamed the New York Theological Seminary. In the months preceding this move Oneroad took part in a Missionary Exposition held in Chicago. There he proudly represented himself as both a member of the Sisseton Wahpeton Oyate community and a devout Christian. The elation he felt attending this event further motivated him to continue on the path he believed his Christian faith set out for him.[13]

Soon after arriving in New York, Oneroad began frequenting the American Museum of Natural History. Whenever he had free time he toured the museum's ethnological halls, observing the exhibits and reading the often incorrect and racist descriptive labels. He wanted to see how his community and other Indigenous nations were represented in the country's largest metropolis. He soon developed a passion for anthropological work and started a close friendship with anthropologist Alanson Skinner. According to museum staff, Oneroad was an interesting and interested visitor. Because of his extensive knowledge of the Native peoples of the Dakotas, AMNH anthropologists Skinner and Robert Lowie spent long hours taking notes from his dictation. So impressed was the staff with Oneroad that the AMNH's *American Museum Journal* published a piece on him in March 1914, highlighting his community's social relations, war customs, and ceremonies.[14]

Around the same time AMNH featured Oneroad in its monthly journal, Alanson Skinner wrote to his friend, collaborator, and adopted Menominee uncle John V. Satterlee to share with him some good news. Skinner informed the older man that over the past few months he had been working with Oneroad, a "Sioux Indian" living in New York. As Satterlee and Skinner had recently gathered information on several Native American Medicine Lodge ceremonies, the young AMNH anthropologist knew his Menominee uncle would be happy to have Oneroad as another resource. Skinner wrote that his new acquaintance and already fast friend was happy to share any information he could about the Sisseton Wahpeton Oyate version of the Medicine Lodge ceremony, which he called the "Wakan watchoopi." Further, Skinner continued, Oneroad promised to provide even more details about other religious practices and ceremonies of his people. The collaborative friendship between Oneroad and Skinner was already off to a good start.[15]

These initial meetings with Skinner in 1913 and 1914 touched off an anthropology career that consumed much of the next decade of Oneroad's life. They also led to his employment at three of the major anthropology museums in the country. Oneroad worked at the American Museum of Natural History from 1914 to 1916, the Museum of the American Indian, Heye Foundation, from 1918 to 1919 and again from 1924 to 1925, and the Milwaukee Public Museum from 1922 to 1924. While he was at the latter museum, Skinner sung his friend's praises to a local Milwaukee newspaper, proclaiming Oneroad both an excellent field man and a missionary among his own people in South Dakota. Thus, Skinner continued, the Milwaukee Public Museum was very fortunate to have the Sisseton Wahpeton Oyate man's experience.[16]

Museum Work

Like many museums at the time, the Milwaukee Public Museum (MPM) was emblematic of the Golden Age of American Anthropology. Scholars viewed these institutions as the last great encyclopedic project of the late nineteenth century. Like its predecessors in New York, Philadelphia, and Washington DC, and those that followed in Chicago and San Francisco, the MPM contained large Native American collections. Henry L. Ward was named the museum's director in 1902, and he subsequently hired

Samuel A. Barrett as the curator of anthropology. It was largely Barrett who shaped the direction of anthropology at the MPM for much of the early twentieth century.[17]

A student of Alfred L. Kroeber's at the University of California, Berkeley, Barrett received his PhD in anthropology there in 1908, the first person to do so. Following this, he worked briefly as an anthropologist for George Gustav Heye, collecting ethnological and linguistic material in Ecuador, before accepting a curatorial position at the MPM. Barrett exponentially increased the museum's anthropological holdings soon after starting at the Midwest institution. Delighting in his research among the Pomo, Me-Wuk (Miwok), and Maidu Nations while under Kroeber's tutelage in California, he continued this type of fieldwork in the Great Lakes after moving to Milwaukee. Foremost among these communities were the Menominee of Wisconsin. There he befriended and collaborated with John V. Satterlee, the same man with whom Oneroad later worked.

Barrett remained curator at the MPM from 1909 until 1920. After Henry L. Ward's departure, he became director, a position he retained until retiring in 1940. Under his directorship and at Alanson Skinner's recommendation, Barrett brought Amos Oneroad onto the museum staff in 1922. Oneroad and Skinner enjoyed working together at the MPM. They went out into the field on regular collecting trips and shared an office when in the city. Despite this, Oneroad's time at MPM was short-lived. By 1924 he and Skinner returned to New York and their former employment at the MAI.[18]

Oneroad worked at three prestigious museums throughout his life—the AMNH, the MPM, and the MAI. But it was the latter where he spent the bulk of his time in the anthropological profession. The Museum of the American Indian, Heye Foundation, was conceived, founded, and directed by a wealthy New Yorker named George Gustav Heye from its establishment until his death in 1957. Born in New York City in 1874 to a family of German background, Heye attended Columbia University and received his bachelor's degree from the School of Mines, the predecessor to today's Earth and Environmental Engineering Department. Heye married three times throughout his life. He married Blanche Agnes Williams in Wellesley, Massachusetts, in 1904, and the two divorced nine years later. In 1915 he married again, this time to Thea Kowne Page, a woman fourteen years his junior. Their marriage was a happy one, with both sharing a passion for ethnology and archaeology. For their honeymoon they rejected overseas travel in favor of participating in a Native American mound excavation in Georgia. Later writers even described Thea as George's "anthropologophilic," or anthropology-loving, wife. After Thea died in 1935, Heye married for a third and final time to Jessica Peebles Standing in New York in 1936. The two divorced not long after in 1940.[19]

Heye had neither academic training nor any particular interest in anthropology during his early life. He got his start while working in the Arizona Territory in 1897. There he purchased a deerskin shirt from a local Diné (Navajo) woman. As Heye later recalled, once he had a shirt, he immediately wanted a rattle and moccasins. "And then the collecting bug seized me, and I was lost." The foundation of the MAI began with that first shirt. By the time of Heye's death sixty years later, the museum included more than seven hundred thousand material culture objects plus photographs and archival items representing Indigenous cultures across the Western Hemisphere.[20]

In 1904 Heye made inroads into the scholarly anthropological world, meeting leading figures such as Frederic Ward Putnam at the Peabody Museum of American Archaeology and Ethnology in Cambridge, Massachusetts, and Franz Boas at New York's AMNH. During this time Heye also made the acquaintance of Marshall Saville, professor of American archaeology at Columbia University, and George H. Pepper, assistant curator of archaeology at the AMNH. These two men taught Heye the importance of systematic collecting, scientific recording, and preservation of anthropological items.[21]

As his Native American collections grew, Heye considered creating an independent anthropological museum separate from those in New York, Philadelphia, and Washington DC. On May 10, 1916, he did just that, officially founding the Museum of the American Indian, Heye Foundation, in New York City. According to its first Annual Report, the MAI was to be a museum for the collection, preservation, study, and exhibition of all things connected with the anthropology of the aboriginal peoples of North, Central, and South America, specifically containing objects of artistic, historic, literary, and scientific interest.[22]

Although the MAI did not officially open to the public until 1922, Heye employed anthropologists to collect materials in the field from the earliest years of the twentieth century. One of the most notable of Heye's anthropologists, well-known for his collecting prowess, was M. R. Harrington. A former pupil of Boas's at Columbia, Harrington traveled extensively for Heye. Between the years 1908 and 1928 he collected ethnological and archaeological material from Canada in the north to Cuba in the south, and from New York in the east to California in the west. Other MAI staff included Donald Cadzow, who worked among the Plains Cree (Prairie Cree) of Saskatchewan and the Apatohsipipiikani (Northern Piegan) of Alberta, Canada; William Wildschut, who worked among the Apsáalooke (Crow/Absaroke) of Montana; Skinner, who worked with Native collaborator John V. Satterlee among the Menominee of Wisconsin; and of course, Amos Oneroad, who worked with his own community members in North and South Dakota.[23]

Oneroad's role in the anthropological profession differed markedly from that of fellow Native collaborators Richard Davis, D. C. Duvall, John V. Satterlee, and Cleaver Warden. Oneroad did not work solely in the field as a paid temporary contractor or collector of material as these men did. Rather, he worked from within the museum system as a Native American anthropologist who also collected in the field. While this appears to be a minor distinction, it reflected a difference in status between him and other collaborators. The work Oneroad performed during these years mirrored that of Tichkematse at the Smithsonian, William Jones at the Field Museum, and Florence and Louis Shotridge at Philadelphia's University Museum. These men, and occasional women, collaborated with Native peoples and non-Native anthropologists in the field. But they also actively described, interpreted, and exhibited Native American cultural materials within museums. As such, they represented their own cultures in a manner unavailable to the majority of American Indian peoples.

Anthropological Fieldwork, Object Collecting, and Archaeological Excavations

In addition to doing anthropological work in museum settings, Oneroad participated in ethnographic and archaeological fieldwork. As early as the summer of 1914 Oneroad and Skinner collected stories and material culture items from Dakota communities in South Dakota. Skinner wrote AMNH staff that they were gathering information and having a bully time staying with Oneroad's family. The two men returned to collect from these Native nations again and again over the following years, including while working for the MAI in 1918 and for the MPM in 1922.[24]

Oneroad's membership in the Sisseton Wahpeton Oyate community granted him a level of access forbidden to outsiders. By extension, Skinner received this access, too. According to an interview Skinner gave the *New York Times* in October 1914, the two men succeeded in procuring information about secret ceremonies that community members had long been reticent to reveal. Skinner's account makes it clear that it would have been impossible for them to obtain this material without Oneroad's influence. Of course, not all the knowledge Oneroad gathered was of a secret or sacred nature. He and Skinner also collected a great many narratives, humorous tales, and trickster stories from the Sisseton Wahpeton Oyate community, including several told to them by Oneroad's own family members.[25]

Oneroad's methodology in the field was to seek out candidates to supply him with information. He then translated it into English for Skinner, who took copious notes during these interactions. The two men followed a similar process when they worked with anthropological collaborator John V. Satterlee in 1922. That autumn Oneroad, Skinner, and Satterlee conducted fieldwork, gathering information and items from members of Satterlee's Menominee Nation.[26]

Just as Oneroad and Skinner collected intangible cultural heritage in the form of songs, ceremonies, and stories from the communities they visited, so too did they collect tangible material culture objects. Their correspondence to each other often referenced the communities they planned to visit, noting promising regions where they hoped to make "a good haul." Oneroad wrote of the large number of sacred and profane items available for purchase on the Pine Ridge, Rosebud, and Standing Rock Reservations in South Dakota, as well as some among the First Nation communities near Portage la Prairie, Manitoba, Canada. As many Lakota and Dakota peoples lived in these areas, Oneroad's kinship provided entrée for him and Skinner to collect there.[27]

Like many collaborators, Oneroad relied on family and friends to supply him with information and objects. For instance, he collected a pair of important moccasins from his father and a calico shirt adorned with silver brooches from his grandmother. Alongside sentimental items were everyday objects ranging from wooden ladles to powder horns to woven baskets. These Oneroad acquired for the MPM in Wisconsin and the AMNH and MAI in New York. While his motive to preserve his community's belongings was laudable, keeping them confined in distant museums had the unintended consequence of separating generations of people from their cultural heritage.[28]

Like John V. Satterlee and Louis Shotridge, Oneroad also excavated Native human remains. In 1916 he traveled to southwestern Arkansas to undertake archaeological work alongside fellow MAI anthropologist M. R. Harrington. Near the small town of Ozan the men excavated several large earthen mounds, uncovering stone beads, bowls, pottery, and Indigenous human skeletons. Two years later Oneroad was at it again, this time accompanying Skinner on an archaeological excavation in New York City's Bronx borough. There the team uncovered village sites of early Indigenous inhabitants. As before, in addition to digging out shell heaps and stone pottery, Oneroad excavated human remains. What qualms, if any, he had about desecrating a Native resting place are unknown. As with Satterlee and Shotridge, though, members of Oneroad's Sisseton Wahpeton Oyate community attributed certain calamities to such archaeological work that he never should have performed in the first place.[29]

Skinner, Socializing, and the Santee School

Oneroad and Skinner were close from the very beginning. Their budding personal and professional relationship only grew stronger over the dozen years the two men worked side by side. Where Skinner went professionally, so too did Oneroad. Whether changing museums from AMNH to the MAI in New York City or moving across the country to work at the MPM in Wisconsin, the two were inseparable. Perhaps because he had no family or community upon arriving on the East Coast, Oneroad was drawn to Skinner. In May 1914 the two even informally adopted each other as brothers-in-law. From then on they used the Dakota word "tahan," or brother-in-law, when they referred to each other. Skinner's close friend and fellow anthropologist M. R. Harrington also considered Oneroad his brother-in-law, as is evidenced in the three men's frequent letters.[30]

The influence Oneroad and Skinner had on each other was clear in the organizations they joined and the lectures they gave, and it even extended to them enlisting in the same military company during World War I. Since his days at Haskell, Oneroad was a proud member of the Young Men's Christian Association (YMCA). During his school days this membership afforded him many opportunities. Through the YMCA he became a leader among fellow students, socialized in a manner Haskell staff approved of, and traveled to YMCA conferences as an attendee and presenter. One of his earliest engagements was as a delegate of the first Native American YMCA convention held at the Flandreau Indian Boarding School in South Dakota in 1912. Moving to New York the following year, Oneroad continued his responsibilities as the recently elected secretary of this young organization. Attending events at the Newark, New Jersey, chapter of the YMCA in late 1914, for example, he spoke about his culture and sang Indigenous songs for the gathered audience.[31]

Oneroad regularly lectured at other venues in New York, including the AMNH and the Staten Island Institute of Arts and Sciences. His friend and colleague Skinner often accompanied him on these outings as well. There the two men reported on the diverse cultures and histories of North America's Indigenous peoples. On several occasions Oneroad spoke to rapt audiences about topics ranging from Native ways of living to hunting, sports, love, and marriage. In addition to his spoken words, he also often dressed in Sisseton Wahpeton Oyate clothing to appeal to audiences eager to see a "real Indian." Unlike his Tlingit contemporary Florence Shotridge, who put on Plains Indian garb to become an "Indian princess" for her Philadelphia audiences, Oneroad had the benefit of wearing the clothing of his own community when he spoke before non-Native crowds.[32]

In 1913 Oneroad also became a member of the Society of American Indians. While non-Native individuals served in supporting roles in this organization, only Indigenous members were elected to positions of power to make policy decisions. Oneroad regularly corresponded with Native anthropologist and SAI member Arthur C. Parker during the organization's early years. He also attended two of the 1914 conventions, one in Philadelphia and another in Washington DC. Playing to Oneroad's strong Presbyterian faith, Parker commended the Sisseton Wahpeton Oyate man for his attendance at the latter convention. Parker told Oneroad that the presence of Native Christian men at such events lent a certain strength that would have otherwise been lacking. Despite its early days of success, the Society of American Indians unraveled little more than a decade after its founding. Divisive issues including Native participation in Wild West–type shows and Peyote use splintered the group into factions. Oneroad ceased being a member by the time the organization dissolved in 1923.[33]

The organization that played a decisive role during Oneroad's anthropology days was the Freemasons. Many of Oneroad's fellow anthropologists belonged to Masonic lodges, including Skinner, Harrington, Barrett, and Parker. Influenced by these men, Oneroad also joined. Skinner even presented his friend for membership in the New York lodge where he and Harrington were members. Despite his acceptance in New York, racist policies prevented Oneroad from joining a South Dakota lodge in 1922. Furious over the news, Skinner threatened to publicize the bigoted actions of the South Dakota lodge members in the Masonic newsletter *The Builder* if the situation was not remedied. Although unclear how this situation resolved itself, by the end of that year Oneroad was living in Milwaukee and attending Masonic meetings alongside his fellow Milwaukee Public Museum anthropologists Skinner and Barrett. This organization not only provided him with a sense of belonging while away from home and family but also aided him professionally as so many of his colleagues were already members.[34]

Oneroad joined organizations such as the YMCA, SAI, and Freemasons because they reflected elements of what he thought his life as a Native American Christian man should be. In much the same way, he believed he could better lead future generations of Native youths by working within the educational system then available to them—through mission schools and Indian boarding schools. As with other Native anthropologists and collaborators, Oneroad's feelings about Indian boarding schools were complicated and at times contradictory. His anthropological work shows he did not believe in the wholesale abandonment of Indigenous languages, histories, and cultures. Nevertheless, he subscribed to at least partial assimilation for Native youths to Euro-American society. This was especially true when it came to conversion to Christianity.

Oneroad's desire to assimilate Indigenous peoples can be traced to the Western schooling of his adolescence. By the time he was twenty-five he had already spent seventeen years of his life in government-sponsored mission and Indian boarding schools. Like Richard Davis and other Native collaborators before him, Oneroad largely accepted and even advocated for assimilation policies espoused by Christian missionaries, BIA agents, and Indian boarding school staff. Unlike Davis, Murie, Warden, and others, though, Oneroad had more difficulty breaking away from the indoctrination he received in his youth. Because of this, it is not surprising he followed a path that led him back toward Indian boarding schools.

As noted, Oneroad worked at the Goodwill Presbyterian Mission School on the Lake Traverse Reservation in 1912 before departing for New York. One decade later he accepted a joint teaching position at the Santee Normal Training School and pastorship in the Pilgrim Congregational Church in Santee, Nebraska. The job included a cottage on the schoolgrounds plus living expenses and a monthly salary of $75 for a one-year contract. After visiting the school and meeting the student body, Oneroad wrote Skinner about this exciting new opportunity. He continued that he had an instant rapport with the schoolchildren, noting this was his chance to instruct Native girls and boys in "useful lives of service" through Christianity.[35]

While employed as a teacher and translator at the Santee Normal Training School, Oneroad simultaneously kept up his anthropological fieldwork with Skinner. Throughout this entire period he continued collecting objects and information from his own community in South Dakota. He also served as a source of information to non-Native anthropologists George Bird Grinnell and Melvin Gilmore when they visited him in Santee. Although Gilmore was a respected ethnobotanist working for the MAI in New York, Oneroad found him a difficult man with whom to collaborate, and their work together did not last long.[36]

By the end of his second year of teaching at Santee, Oneroad grew restless. He loved the small children and generally enjoyed the schoolwork itself, but he found the constant squabbles between the school's hierarchy and the local church members intolerable. Writing Skinner in May 1924, Oneroad spoke of wanting to be back with his anthropological friends on an archaeological dig finding "some good relics." He finally resigned his position at Santee in April 1925 because of his mother's failing health. Although he returned to the Lake Traverse Reservation to care for her, he lost little time planning for upcoming fieldwork with Skinner.[37]

Lacking any civil or legal recognition of their ties to one another, Oneroad and Skinner nevertheless truly viewed themselves as family.

Skinner knew Oneroad's first wife, Etta Ortley, whom the latter married in April 1919. Oneroad likewise was close with Skinner's wives—Gladys Macrae, Esther Florence Allen, and Dorothy Preston—as well as Skinner's young daughter, Esther Mary Skinner, who always requested another visit from her dear "Uncle Ames." Sadly, Skinner and Oneroad both knew repeated tragedy in their lives. Skinner's first two wives died in childbirth—Gladys in 1918 and Esther Florence in 1921. Oneroad also lost his first wife, Etta, in May 1922, only three years after their marriage. He married again in 1926 to Emma Wantawa, who eventually outlived him. To some extent their shared personal loss brought these two men even closer together over the years.[38]

Throughout all his anthropological work, the project most important to Oneroad was the manuscript he and Skinner wrote together on Eastern Dakota beliefs and ethnology. This work represented in a very literal way Oneroad's family, as it included the stories and traditions of his friends, relatives, and other community members interviewed over many years. Although the two men began collecting information for this manuscript in 1914, it wasn't until nearly a decade later that they determined what their end goal was. In February 1922 Skinner penned a letter to Oneroad, suggesting they combine the information already gathered into a new study of the Eastern Dakota peoples. This mirrored what Skinner and John V. Satterlee earlier wrote on the Menominee of Wisconsin. Skinner cautioned his friend that the work would not be easy and would take them a long time. But, he continued, with Oneroad's knowledge of the communities, it would no doubt be a success. Skinner added that this was their chance to document Oneroad's people as had never been done before—in a friendly attitude and with sympathy and understanding. Sounding the salvage anthropologist's call to arms, Skinner also pointed out that it was their duty to the world at large to record all they could of the Eastern Dakota communities. They had to do so, Skinner argued, before the cultures of the "best, bravest, and most generous of Indian people" were forever lost to assimilation. For his part, Oneroad didn't need any encouragement to pursue such a task.[39]

What Oneroad and Skinner produced was a two-hundred-page manuscript. It contained sections titled "Eastern Dakota Ethnology" and "Traditions of the Wahpeton Dakota Indians" and included subsections on narratives and trickster stories. Their manuscript notations indicate where they intended to add to the text at a future date. Of course, this was all cut short by Skinner's sudden death in 1925. As a result, their joint work was left unpublished. It was not until seven decades later that a researcher came across this manuscript in California and recognized its significance. Acknowledging the importance of this material, the scholar published the unfinished work under the title *Being Dakota: Tales and Traditions of the Sisseton and Wahpeton*. Over a half century after being set aside, the results of Oneroad and Skinner's collaborative efforts were finally available to the world.[40]

A Missionary among His People

It goes without saying that the intimate familial relationship these two men shared only made Skinner's sudden death in 1925 that much harder for Oneroad to bear. With his friend's death on August 17 of that year, Oneroad's anthropology career also effectively died. Importantly, this tragic event finally motivated him to devote himself completely to another path. Since starting in anthropology in 1913, Oneroad's true passion had always been Christian ministry and missionary work. With Skinner gone, he decided to follow that path alone.

While enrolled at the Bible Teachers' Training School in New York, Oneroad maintained close relations with his family and church back in South Dakota. In 1914 he accepted the office of vice president of the Dakota Missionary Society. Following his graduation from the seminary three years later, he became an ordained and licensed Presbyterian minister. During these same years Oneroad made it a point of pride to evangelize and celebrate his Christian faith as an Indigenous man. On at least two occasions during 1914 and 1915 he visited the Carlisle Indian Industrial School and spoke to the student body there, hoping to encourage others to follow in his footsteps.[41]

Between his work for the MAI in 1919 and the MPM in 1922, Oneroad also accepted a position with the Office of Evangelism of the Dakota Presbytery. In this role he preached during his travels through Montana, Nebraska, South Dakota, and Utah. During this time he and his wife Etta made a happy home for themselves in Wolf Point, Montana. There he worked as a missionary and teacher in the local Presbyterian mission school. The

Wolf Point Herald newspaper regularly mentioned his name, reporting on his participation in missionary conferences and his directorship of church programs such as the 1919 Christmas service at the mission school. Sadly, the Oneroads' happiness did not last long. Their first child, born in April 1920, died young. So too did their second child, who passed away little more than two years later. An additional loss, Etta herself died that spring due to complications from childbirth.[42]

Following Skinner's death in 1925, Oneroad returned home to Sisseton, South Dakota. There he mourned the loss of his friend and decided to start over. Less than six months later, in January 1926, Amos married for a second time to a Sisseton Wahpeton Oyate woman named Emma Wantawa. Leaving anthropology behind him to focus on his ministry, he and Emma soon after traveled to Canada to begin missionary work. Based out of Uno, Manitoba, Oneroad ministered to exile Dakota communities whose members had fled the U.S. government's punitive actions in the aftermath of the 1862 Dakota War. His salary was $1,800 per year, and he and Emma were delighted with the beauty of their new home on the bluffs of the Assiniboine River. Still struggling with the death of his friend, Oneroad wrote to Skinner's widow, Dorothy, shortly after arriving in Canada. He addressed her as "sister," as he had similarly called Skinner "tahan" or brother-in-law. He wrote of his ministering in the neighboring towns of Portage la Prairie and Pipestone. Oneroad reminded Dorothy that these were two of the Indigenous communities he and Alanson planned to visit before tragedy struck. He was still wracked with guilt over his friend's death and his own role in the fatal accident.[43]

After more than two years of missionary work in Canada, Amos and Emma returned to South Dakota in 1928. His ministry took them around the state, working with congregations in Rapid City and Flandreau before he accepted an appointment at the Yankton Agency Presbyterian Church in Greenwood, South Dakota. There he and Emma made a new home for themselves and started a small family. For the rest of his days Oneroad shepherded his flock until he died at age fifty-three in 1937. His congregation buried him among friends and family in a small church cemetery in Greenwood.[44]

Oneroad's Anthropology and His Christianity

Seemingly contradictory, Oneroad believed his anthropological work and his Christian ministry complemented each other. For a dozen overlapping years he worked as both a museum anthropologist and a Presbyterian minister. Though these two vocations were not wholly incompatible, few other Christian ministers were as determined as Oneroad to document the non-Christian cultures of American Indian nations. Similarly, while many early twentieth-century anthropologists were at least nominally Christian, Oneroad was certainly in the minority of those who also preached the gospel and led their own congregation.[45]

As an Indian boarding school survivor and ordained Presbyterian minister, Oneroad was well familiar with the U.S. government's policies of Christianization and so-called civilization of American Indians. He was intimately aware of the federal government's establishment of the Courts of Indian Offenses in 1882. These courts banned the possession of Native religious objects on reservations and the performance of dances and ceremonies considered "savage." Richard Davis, Cleaver Warden, and other Native collaborators openly defied these very same racist and unconstitutional laws in pursuit of their anthropological work. Although some reservation agents were more lax than others about these "offenses," the official ban remained during Oneroad's adolescence on the Lake Traverse Reservation.[46]

Oneroad was not that different from a great many Native Americans at the turn of the twentieth century. He never wholly abandoned his own history, culture, or language; nor did he completely adopt the trappings of Euro-American Christian society. He did not view this as an either-or situation. Instead, he retained those aspects from both cultures that appealed to him most. While he sincerely strived to propagate the Christian faith taught him in his youth, other factors may have motivated him to dress in a non-Native manner and speak in English. As previously discussed, large numbers of Indigenous peoples at the turn of the century practiced what Ho-Chunk (Winnebago) anthropologist Renya K. Ramirez has labeled "doubling." Many camouflaged or masked themselves when in the presence of other non-Indigenous groups. Depending on their audiences, people such as Oneroad adopted either a Native or non-Native persona to meet the expectations of those around them. Importantly, though, few wholly abandoned their cultures and Native identities. In this light Oneroad's "doubling" acts were attempts to be treated as an equal in anthropology and the Christian ministry—professions overwhelmingly dominated by Euro-American men.[47]

When faced with the option of destroying sacred objects or transferring these belongings to Native anthropologists, many American Indians chose the latter course. Examples of Native anthropologists who worked within their own communities add another layer to the salvage anthropology movement. In these cases, Indigenous peoples sometimes gave their cultural history away rather than see it destroyed. Indeed, some of them saw Native anthropologists such as Oneroad as guardians of their collective heritage in museums.

Oneroad's status as a member of the Sisseton Wahpeton Oyate community and a Native anthropologist were crucial in convincing Eastern Dakota peoples to part with their cultural heritage. Some of these objects even included Oneroad's grandfather's sacred religious items, which were deposited in museum collections in New York and Wisconsin. Whether Oneroad's actions saved his people's history or hastened some of its loss is the crux at the heart of this book. Ultimately, his descendants believe he created a balance in his work between the oppositional poles of cultural anthropology and the Christian ministry. Instead of replacing his community's lifeways, he preserved them.[48]

Amos Oneroad and Anthropology Today

Amos Oneroad is largely remembered today for his evangelizing work as a Presbyterian missionary and minister. Little is known about the role he played in anthropology. Few know that he worked in three of the leading anthropology museums of the early twentieth century, or that he spent a dozen years documenting and preserving his and other American Indian cultures. Like other Native anthropologists and collaborators, Oneroad used his English knowledge to turn the power and be a voice for his community. In 1906, for instance, he worked as an interpreter in the South Dakota court system, where he spoke on behalf of his non-English speaking fellows. Additionally, twice in the early 1920s Oneroad's community selected him to travel to Washington DC as a representative for the people. His purpose was to inquire into land claims that the federal government had repeatedly disregarded.[49]

Oneroad continued to turn the power and rail against injustice through his work as a small-town Presbyterian minister in South Dakota. In 1933, for example, he wrote the new commissioner of Indian affairs, John Collier, arguing that his Sisseton Wahpeton Oyate community should govern its own affairs as a sovereign American Indian nation and not be subject to federal interference. Two years later he wrote a South Dakota senator requesting money to build hospitals on the Yankton, Crow Creek, and Lake Traverse Reservations. The federal government had made it illegal for Native people to practice their generations-old healing practices, Oneroad declared. Yet at the same time the government refused to provide medical facilities for these communities. The result, Oneroad concluded, was widespread illness and death. Again and again Oneroad used the education he received in mission and Indian boarding schools to turn the power and fight back against a government openly hostile to his people's welfare. Although his anthropology days were long behind him, Oneroad continued to fight for his community and preserve his culture until the day he died.[50]

Civilized Indians Exploring the Wilds of Alaska

Florence and Louis Shotridge (Sitka, Alaska Territory, 1929)

The elderly Tlingit women wouldn't stop crying, and it was all his fault. By 1929 these women were the last remaining guardians of the Kaagwaan-taan shark helmet—formerly the most sacred object and still a powerful symbol of the Tlingit Kaagwaantaan clan of Southeastern Alaska. And he was taking it away from them.

It wasn't that Louis Shotridge didn't feel a certain amount of regret at his actions. He did. As a Tlingit man, he felt he was betraying his culture and his identity, a traitor to both his family and their long history. But he also felt excitement. As an anthropologist and assistant curator at Phila-delphia's University Museum, he was overjoyed at his success in obtain-ing this ethnological specimen for the museum's collections. Justifying his actions, Shotridge wrote he was actually saving this object and other "abandoned" pieces like it that were quickly disappearing. He reasoned that if anything, he was prolonging their life by placing these sacred items in a museum where they served as evidence of the diversity and creativity of Indigenous cultures.[1]

Family Background

Over seventy-five years before Louis Shotridge "acquired" the Kaagwaan-taan shark helmet, his grandfather, Shatrich, faced a different challenge from settler colonizers trying to change his community. Shatrich was the powerful and undisputed leader of the Chilkat Tlingit Nation for much of the second half of the nineteenth century. Incensed by the Hudson's Bay Company's construction of Fort Selkirk on the Yukon River, Sha-trich devised a way to cast out the interlopers. In 1852 he led an attack on Fort Selkirk and destroyed the buildings. Wanting to avoid bloodshed, he released the Hudson's Bay Company employees, warning them never to return. Notably, Shatrich's attack on Fort Selkirk was designed to keep out European invaders but, more importantly, to also control the preexisting and lucrative Tlingit trading systems into the interior of Canada. Although a minor skirmish, Shatrich's victory illustrated that the Tlingit people could handle their own against outside forces. But outside forces continued to come.[2]

The U.S. Congress formally accepted the purchase of Alaska from Russia fifteen years after the Chilkat Tlingit destruction of Fort Selkirk. This act ignored the wishes of the Indigenous peoples who had inhabited these lands for untold generations, and Alaska and its people became yet another part of the expanding U.S. empire in 1867. Despite Alaska becoming a U.S. territory soon after the Civil War, it took nearly a century for this resource-rich land to be admitted into the union as a state with guaranteed voting rights and full citizenship for its residents. The glacial pace at which this occurred was due to racist fears in the rest of the country of placing a largely Native state on an equal footing with majority non-Native states.[3]

Along with U.S. territorial recognition of Alaska came missionaries—those uncompromising Christians eager to spread what they believed was the one true faith. One of the first of these missionaries to visit the Klukwan village of the Chilkat Tlingit people was the Presbyterian Reverend S. Hall Young in 1879. Along with the famous naturalist and explorer John Muir, Young traveled throughout the Alaska Territory in the 1870s and 1880s. While Muir wished to visit Glacier Bay, Young wanted to meet, and hopefully convert, the Chilkat people living in Klukwan. In 1880 Young got his wish. That year he met Shatrich, the Chilkat Tlingit leader still in power nearly three decades after his ousting of the Hudson's Bay Company men.[4]

Described by his contemporaries as a tall, intelligent, imposing figure, Shatrich held power in Southeast Alaska for more than four decades. According to the missionary Young, Shatrich had a great reputation for wealth and power, but also for pride and cruelty. Both Shatrich and the influential Tlingit healer Scundoo escorted Young through their territory and around the village of Klukwan. After much back and forth, Shatrich and Scundoo eventually permitted Young's request to send missionaries and teachers to the Tlingit people. What these Tlingit men thought of Young is unknown, but Young was not quiet about his thoughts on Shatrich and Scundoo. He believed Shatrich a cruel and arrogant tyrant, but most of his enmity was for the healer Scundoo. Young viewed the world in terms of white and black, good and bad, Christian and pagan. Because of this the Presbyterian missionary looked down on the Tlingit healer. He referred to Scundoo as a heathen of heathens and claimed he cheated his own people out of material possessions with his witchcraft. Despite this animosity, these three men compromised on what they believed best for the future of the Tlingit people.[5]

Much changed in Klukwan within a few years of Young's first visit. By 1883 a Presbyterian mission station was created in Haines, a small village twenty miles southeast of Klukwan. Shatrich died, and his power fell to his son George Shotridge, the latter's surname an anglicization of Shatrich. By the time of Shatrich's death, young Louis Shotridge, George's son and Shatrich's grandson, was one year old. Born in 1882 into the Kaagwaantaan clan of the Chilkat Tlingit people, Louis never got to know his grandfather Shatrich. He did, however, have a close relationship with his mother, Kudeit.saakw, and his father, Yeilgooxu or George.[6]

Louis's father George was described by those around him as a splendid, thoughtful man, though given to drink. Some resources indicate he spent his youth at the Forest Grove Indian Boarding School in Oregon, but there is scant documentation to confirm this. Regardless of where George Shotridge received his schooling, he used his linguistic abilities and position of influence to speak on behalf of his community. In 1900, for instance, George sent a letter to U.S. president William McKinley and Canadian prime minister Wilfrid Laurier protesting the provisional boundary line drawn between these settler colonial nations. For the Chilkat Tlingit people, George argued, this boundary and the taxes associated with crossing it created an undue burden on the people who had hunted, fished, and traversed this region from time immemorial. Due to their collective dependence on hunting and fishing in this disputed land, George requested that the settler colonial governments respect the rights and privileges of the Tlingit peoples to use their land as they saw fit. Although no response to George Shotridge's letter is available in the historical record, this example still illustrates the important role the Shotridges played in their community.[7]

Youth and Schooling for Florence and Louis

Life radically changed for the Chilkat Tlingit community after Shatrich and Scundoo permitted Presbyterian missionaries to settle near Klukwan. An early Christian visitor to the area described Klukwan as a rich and substantially built community, with three of the largest and most elegant houses belonging to Shatrich. One of these buildings the Tlingit leader gave to the Presbyterian Mission, and it soon became a temporary Indian boarding school. By 1885, with the construction of the Presbyterian Mission in Haines, a more permanent school was founded.[8]

Due to a lack of formal school records, there is little documentation of Louis Shotridge's time at the Presbyterian-run Indian mission school in Haines. Sources note that the young man attended school there off and on for approximately eighteen months. According to the Presbyterian missionary S. Hall Young, this school was a place where Tlingit children could learn "the white man's ways and Christian habits." Designed to root out Indigenous languages and beliefs, this school was mirrored after other Indian boarding schools across the country. All sought to force Native children to abandon their cultures and assimilate to Euro-American Christian society.[9]

Despite the racism and abuse Louis faced at the Haines mission school, the highlight of his schooldays was that his future wife, Florence Scundoo, was there alongside him. Florence, like Louis, was born in approximately 1882 or 1883 in Chilkoot, in the Alaska Territory. She was the daughter of the powerful and respected Tlingit healer Scundoo, the same man who allowed Presbyterian missionaries to settle near Klukwan. Unlike Louis, Florence attended the Haines mission school for four years. Like other survivors of mission and Indian boarding schools, her schooling was full of racist declarations about the backwardness of her culture. Fortunately for her, Florence also had the good fortune to receive instruction in beadwork, basket weaving, and Chilkat blanket weaving from female relatives.[10]

In 1902 Florence and Louis married and began their life together as a young Tlingit couple. The following year Richard Henry Pratt, founder of the Carlisle Indian Industrial School, visited the village of Haines on one of his many recruiting trips across the country. Although no record exists of their interaction, Pratt and the Shotridges most likely met during his visit to the area. Florence and Louis possessed many qualities Pratt sought in Native youth: intelligence, adaptability, fluency in English, and a willingness to assimilate to Euro-American society. This interaction with Pratt no doubt motivated the young couple to begin looking at the wider world beyond the confines of Klukwan and Haines.[11]

By a happy coincidence, Alaska's territorial governor visited the Klukwan area soon after Pratt's 1903 recruiting trip. The governor personally selected twenty-year-old Florence to travel to Portland, Oregon, and demonstrate her weaving skills at the upcoming 1905 Lewis and Clark Centennial Exposition. Florence jumped at the opportunity. Louis accompanied her to Portland, where the two exhibited not only her weaving but also their Tlingit culture to throngs of curious onlookers. While this was Florence's first experience representing her people before an audience, it was not the last time she became a general representative for the Indigenous peoples of North America.[12]

At the 1905 Portland Exposition

Eager to reap the financial rewards previous exposition host cities had in Philadelphia in 1876, Chicago in 1893, Omaha in 1898, and St. Louis in 1904, Portland's residents decided to host their own fair. It was saddled with the lengthy title of the Lewis and Clark Centennial and American Pacific Exposition and Oriental Fair, but most fairgoers simply called it the Lewis and Clark Centennial. Commemorating the Lewis and Clark Expedition of a century earlier, the Portland Exposition ran from June to October 1905. Like its world's fair predecessors, it aimed to increase regional trade, showcase local industry, and reinforce messages of Euro-American racial superiority among the populace.

Highlighting U.S. colonial expansion around the world, fair organizers wanted exhibits that showcased Euro-American dominance over supposedly primitive peoples. As at previous fairs, an Indian village was constructed. It was anticipated to display representatives of various American Indian nations from across the United States, but the bulk of Native peoples willing to exhibit themselves in the Indian village were about two dozen members of the Nimi'ipuu (Nez Perce) community from Idaho. Mirroring the actions of past successful world's fairs, the Lewis and Clark

Centennial recruited representatives of more far-flung locales, creating an Indian village, a Japanese village, and an Igorot village, which received great acclaim for its display of Igorot peoples from the Philippines in their artificially constructed Native dwellings. There the "pagan" inhabitants reportedly had a proclivity for slaughtering and eating dogs, much to the revulsion and excitement of the crowds.[13]

As in past expositions, the Smithsonian Institution and its Bureau of American Ethnology maintained exhibits at the Portland fair. The BAE showcased models of Kiowa tipis and shields by James Mooney previously displayed at the 1898 Omaha World's Fair. While the Smithsonian exhibits did not include an Indian village or any "living exhibitions" of Native peoples, some individual state and territorial displays did. It was common practice for states, territories, and even foreign governments to request exhibition space to display their region's trade goods, agricultural products, and other unique materials. The Territory of Alaska did just that, exhibiting cases of cereals, grains, and animal furs representative of the flora and fauna of the area. Also included were totem poles, baskets, "curios" of Native manufacture, and two Alaska Natives—Florence and Louis Shotridge.[14]

The Shotridges' attendance at the 1905 Portland Exposition started the young married couple on a lifelong path centered around museum anthropology. The ever-savvy Louis, for example, early on recognized the public's desire for Native-made objects. Because of this, he brought with him to the fair several dozen items of Tlingit manufacture for sale. One of his customers was George Byron Gordon of the Philadelphia Free Museum of Science and Art, later Philadelphia's University Museum, who played a major role in the anthropology careers of Florence and Louis in subsequent years. It was at the 1905 Portland Exposition that the two also met Antonio Apache. Like Gordon in Philadelphia, Apache in Los Angeles played an oversized role in the early careers of this Tlingit couple.

Florence and Louis returned home to the Alaska Territory after the Portland Exposition closed in October 1905. Though happy to reunite with their families and friends, they did not remain long in Haines. Like other Native collaborators, the Shotridges depended on any available work as a source of income. In 1906, for example, Louis found a job helping build the Fort William Seward army barracks in Haines. While the money was welcome, the Shotridges still wished for something more.[15]

Florence and Louis maintained their newfound friendship with George Byron Gordon in the months immediately after returning from Portland. As early as October 1905 Gordon asked them to come to the Philadelphia museum to catalog and describe Northwest Coast collections there. He also encouraged the young couple to acquire more items from their Tlingit community before departing Alaska. Florence and Louis told him they would be happy to leave for Philadelphia as soon as Gordon would have them. After their time in Portland, they added, Haines had become altogether too lonesome. Not hearing anything definite from Gordon for several months, Florence and Louis eventually accepted an offer from Antonio Apache to work at his newly opened Indian Crafts Exposition in Los Angeles. Like their contemporary Richard Davis and his work with world's fairs, Wild West shows, films, and American Indian theater troupes, the Shotridges gravitated toward the few career opportunities open to Native peoples outside of Indian Country. Further, after their first taste of life outside of Alaska at the 1905 Portland Exposition, Florence and Louis caught a traveling bug that remained with them for the rest of their lives.[16]

Antonio Apache and His Indian Crafts Exposition

In the fall of 1906 the Shotridges departed their home in Alaska for a warmer climate with Antonio Apache at his Los Angeles–based Indian Crafts Exposition. Antonio Apache is one of the most intriguing figures in turn-of-the-twentieth-century U.S. anthropology, and his life remains mostly shrouded in lies of his own making. Little verifiable documentation exists regarding his date and place of birth, education, employment, marriage, and, most importantly, his alleged Native ancestry. The documentation that does exist to piece together Apache's life consists almost entirely of early twentieth-century newspaper articles, a smattering of correspondence, and a few federal records.[17]

In the first decade of the twentieth century many of Apache's Native and non-Native contemporaries branded him an impostor. They claimed he was really Tony Simpson, a Black man posing as a member of the White Mountain Apache community for financial gain. Several historians have also recently labeled Apache a fraud. He used his appropriated cultural identity for fiscal and professional advantage, they contend, while excluding qualified Indigenous peoples from anthropological opportunities. Despite such accusations, Apache argued until his dying breath that he was the Native man he claimed to be.[18]

In an 1892 newspaper interview, Apache originally said he was born in the White Mountains of Arizona in 1870. Five years later, however, he claimed in the *San Francisco Call* newspaper that 1873 was his birth year. Several times in the early twentieth century he documented his birth as 1878. By the time he died he modified his birth year yet again—this time to 1884. A similar pattern emerged with Apache's "capture" by U.S. military personnel in Arizona and with the dates and locations of his education.[19]

In newspaper interviews Apache claimed U.S. Army soldiers captured him while still a child in Arizona in 1872. This date consistently switched over the years to 1879, 1880, or 1881. As with his changing birth year, the date of Apache's supposed capture changed depending on the year he was interviewed to better match his current age. Apache variously claimed either to have been captured by men under General Oliver Otis Howard in the 1870s or later by men under General George R. Crook in the 1880s. In some tellings Apache reported he was raised by a well-to-do family in Massachusetts, and in other versions it was either a wealthy family in New York City or, more vaguely, a "wealthy lady" from the East Coast.[20]

Apache told journalists he received his primary education at the Hampton Institute beginning in 1877. Conversely, he also claimed he attended the Carlisle Indian Industrial School beginning in 1880. Likewise, one of his major claims to educational excellence was his professed attendance at Harvard University. Contradicting this, the *Albuquerque Morning Journal* reported his alma mater as Cornell. While Apache often referred to having graduated with honors from Harvard University, Hampton, Carlisle, Cornell, and Harvard maintain no records of an Antonio Apache or a Tony Simpson during these years. Indeed, the only instance of actual educational instruction on record was in 1896 at New Hampshire's Phillips Exeter Academy. According to school records, though, Apache did not continue class work after his first year due to poor academic performance.[21]

Antonio Apache married at least once that we know of. In 1919 he wed Mary Cota Weed in Los Angeles. Just one year later Weed sought an annulment on the grounds of fraud. She charged that Apache falsely represented himself as "a member and spokesman for the Apache Indians."[22]

Apache's employment history straddled many careers, with Carlisle Indian Industrial School recruiter and publicity agent numbering among them. The bulk of his professional work, however, gravitated around the field of anthropology. In the years immediately following the celebrated Chicago World's Fair of 1893, for instance, Apache secured employment with the recently founded Field Museum. There he worked in the Anthropology Department from 1894 until 1896. The following year he continued his collecting work on behalf of the New England Sportsmen's Association. He acquired material culture objects of the Indigenous peoples of Maine and eastern Canada and exhibited these items in Boston soon after. Through the influence of Field Museum anthropologist George A. Dorsey, Apache also worked for the Fred Harvey Company's Indian Department in Albuquerque, New Mexico, before moving west to California.[23]

In late 1905 railroad magnate Henry E. Huntington loaned Apache the sum of $50,000 to construct an Indian Crafts Exposition at Eastlake Park, now Lincoln Park, in Los Angeles. The site just happened to be conveniently located on Huntington's privately owned Pacific Electric Railway, increasing business for both men. The *Albuquerque Morning Journal* called the exposition "an Indian settlement and curio collection," with Native cultures from Alaska and "all points west." The newspaper told readers that Apache's anticipated Indian village would be one of the most interesting and expensive ethnological displays in the country, rivaling anthropology museums in the Midwest and East Coast.[24]

Apache's Indian village entertained the Los Angeles public for approximately six years. From its opening in 1906 until its closure in 1912, it represented Indigenous communities across North America. The Shotridges ended up working there for the bulk of the exposition's existence. To create the Indian village, Apache built upon his experiences as an employee at the Chicago World's Fair and the Fred Harvey Company. Over the years he had also keenly observed anthropological displays at the 1901, 1904, and 1905 world's fairs, the latter where he met the Shotridges in Portland. At each of these venues, Apache learned how anthropologists exhibited Indigenous cultures, how the public consumed these representations, and how he could do likewise to earn a profit. Not only did he emphasize the display of "authentic" dwellings constructed at the Indian village, but like his anthropological contemporaries at many world's fairs, Apache sought Native artists and craftspeople to live and work there. Non-Native visitors to the LA Exposition watched Indigenous people make their wares and could purchase the finished products for a small fee. These transactions generated income for the Native artists and for Apache as the Indian Crafts Exposition's manager.[25]

Apache successfully gathered Native basket makers, blanket weavers, silversmiths, and canoe builders into a self-supporting anthropological village during the exposition's half-decade existence. By 1907, however, questions about Apache's identity surfaced in newspapers across the country. Media attention quickly shifted from highlighting the anthropological attractions of the Indian village to focusing on Apache himself.

In July 1907 U.S. newspapers big and small published stories attacking Antonio Apache's supposed Native ancestry. One East Coast paper labeled Apache "the most fantastic faker that ever fooled New York." Within days the *Washington Times, New York Times*, and *San Francisco Examiner* reported that Apache was in fact a Louisiana-born Black man by the name of Tony Simpson who tinted his skin with bronze paint and wore a wig of straight black hair.[26]

When approached for a response to the accusations against him, Apache replied that there was not a drop of Black blood in his veins. He further stated that the story was news to him, and he could not understand the motive behind it. Despite Apache's claim that this was a new story, however, questions surrounding his identity had been in circulation since at least 1900. Richard Henry Pratt, for example, had briefly employed Apache as a recruiter for the Carlisle Indian Industrial School. In February 1900, soon after Apache left his employ, Pratt wrote a Native friend that he believed Apache was an impostor. The following year Carlisle's newspaper, the *Red Man and Helper*, ran a piece titled "An Impostor." The anonymous author told the paper's readers that he was credibly informed that Antonio Apache was "not an Indian." Further, he continued, "the Apache Indians where he claims origin" disclaim all knowledge of him. The author concluded that Apache was a fraud but noted that he was willing to admit a mistake if evidence proved otherwise. No evidence supporting Apache's claim to Native ancestry ever surfaced.[27]

Lurid newspaper articles trailed Apache for the rest of his days branding him a faker, fraud, and impostor. Despite their regularity, these headlines had surprisingly little adverse impact on his professional career. Apache continued as manager of the Indian Crafts Exposition for several more years, eventually closing the ethnological village in 1912. For the next quarter century he worked various jobs in the Los Angeles area, including as a miner and as a real estate and oil development promoter. First and foremost, though, he always considered himself an anthropologist. Apache died at the Rancho Los Amigos medical facility, formerly the Los Angeles County Poor Farm, in 1938. With his dying breath he clung to the lie that he was Antonio Apache—born to Apache parents in the White Mountains of Arizona.[28]

Apache was a charismatic individual adept at charming journalists and the public. He regularly gave newspaper interviews lauding the exposition and its supposedly all-Indigenous staff. In addition to three dozen participants who lived in Native dwellings on the grounds, Apache was the designated manager, Louis Shotridge the exposition's salesman, and Pikuni Blackfeet (Piegan) artist Lone Wolf or Hart Merriam Schultz their official clerk. Louis and Florence performed and entertained audiences, educating people about their Tlingit culture. The young couple made their home among this unique Native collective for several years before trying their luck on the vaudeville circuit.[29]

Although no evidence exists to suggest the Shotridges knew Apache's true identity, their ignorance on the subject would have been surprising. Rumors had circulated about Apache for many years. Newspapers across the nation labeled him a fraud less than a year after the Shotridges joined the Indian Crafts Exposition. As mentioned, Florence and Louis first met Apache at the 1905 Portland Exposition. At his urging they joined him in managing the Los Angeles–based Indian Crafts Exposition. While their complicity in his deception remains unverified, there is little doubt that they knew him long enough to see who he really was.[30]

Mademoiselle Toona's Indian Grand Opera Company

Soon after departing Antonio Apache's Indian Crafts Exposition in 1911, the Shotridges joined the cast of a popular Native theater company. This company was managed by Mademoiselle Toona, also known as Mathilde

A. Coutts-Johnstone. As discussed previously, Southern Tsitsistas/Suhtai (Cheyenne) anthropology collaborator Richard Davis also worked for Mademoiselle Toona and the Toona Indian Grand Opera Company. Davis began working with Toona as a Native performer, singer, and actor in early 1913, at nearly the same time as the Shotridges.[31]

Toona's specialty as a manager was in selecting and training Native entertainers to sing grand opera in the original French, German, and Italian. This she combined with popular Native American dances and songs for the audience's enjoyment. Native performers had to wear Plains Indian clothing, meeting expectations of how a "real Indian" should look. During their years with Apache and later with Toona, the Shotridges studied music and took English lessons with private tutors. As a result, Florence's skill at the piano and Louis's rich singing voice made them a welcome addition traveling the vaudeville circuit across the United States.[32]

Florence and Louis kept in touch with George Byron Gordon at Philadelphia's University Museum during their years with Apache's Indian Crafts Exposition and Toona's Indian Grand Opera Company. Ever since first meeting at the Portland Exposition in 1905, all three instantly recognized the market potential they had together. As an English-speaking Tlingit couple, the Shotridges provided Gordon entrée to Northwest Coast material culture items otherwise inaccessible to non-Native museum anthropologists. Gordon sought to nurture this relationship for the advantages it posed for him and his museum. For Florence and Louis, this reciprocal relationship offered steady employment in the field of museum anthropology, something they had circled for years.[33]

Gordon rose quickly through the museum's ranks in the years since they first met—and this fact benefited all of them. Like George A. Dorsey at Chicago's Field Museum, Gordon had studied under Frederic Ward Putnam at Harvard, receiving his PhD in anthropology in 1903. He started at Philadelphia's University Museum soon after, and seven years later museum officials appointed him director. With his new position secure, Gordon invited the Shotridges to join him in Philadelphia in late 1911. There they entered a new chapter of their lives as the museum's first Indigenous wife and husband employees.[34]

Philadelphia's University Museum

Like many anthropology and natural history museums at the dawn of the twentieth century, Philadelphia's University Museum was a new creation. It was not yet twenty-five years old when Florence and Louis started working there. Founded by University of Pennsylvania provost William Pepper, the "museum" was little more than a small exhibit space when it opened in 1890. Four years later Pepper acquired land from the city for his institution, which he renamed the Free Museum of Science and Art. Although the new name accurately reflected the institution's mission and its welcoming nature, the title did not stick, with most people simply calling it the University Museum. By 1913 museum authorities even officially adopted the latter title. More recently it changed its name to the University of Pennsylvania Museum of Archaeology and Anthropology—or the Penn Museum for short.[35]

Gordon started at the museum in 1903 and remained there for nearly a quarter century. Under his leadership museum staff conducted research around the globe—in Africa, Asia, and Oceania and throughout the Americas. Gordon himself led collecting expeditions to Alaska in 1905 and 1907. A *Philadelphia Inquirer* article reported on these successful museum ventures. Gordon spent the summer of 1905 covering over two thousand miles in the Alaskan interior and along the coast of the Bering Sea, the newspaper noted. He reportedly visited "primitive" villages where he observed Native customs and collected anthropological items for the university. These collections, the anonymous reporter opined, formed one of the most interesting exhibitions in the museum.[36]

From the start Gordon sought to change the existing relationship between the Philadelphia museum and the university. He drew inspiration from Putnam's work at Harvard with the Peabody Museum of American Archaeology and Ethnology and Franz Boas at Columbia University with the American Museum of Natural History. Gordon encouraged university officials to institute course offerings including instruction in archaeology, ethnology, linguistics, and physical anthropology. Four years later the university created an official Department of Anthropology under the chairmanship of Frank G. Speck, a recent student of Boas's at Columbia.

Due to personality conflicts between Gordon and Speck, a sustained educational and training program did not take hold between the university and museum until years later, despite the opportunities such cooperation promised.[37]

Under Gordon's tenure from 1910 to 1927, museum visitorship increased dramatically. This was due in part to greater numbers of schoolchildren attending educational tours and lectures. Curators, museum staff, and visiting scholars including BAE anthropologist WJ McGee lectured and presented their research for free during these public programs. Particularly popular were lectures geared toward children and led by Native museum employees. Museum anthropologist J. Alden Mason later wrote that American Indian staff members dressed in Plains Indian clothing greatly appealed to school classes. The museum's administration lost no time in utilizing this appeal to the institution's benefit. Mason further noted that at various times and for short periods the museum employed several Native staff at once. Tlingit wife and husband Florence and Louis Shotridge were among this number.[38]

Philadelphia's University Museum was not unique in its practice of hiring Native staff to appeal to the masses. Just like the "Indian princesses" who entertained audiences at New York's AMNH, many anthropology and natural history museums introduced similar programs to pull in greater numbers of the public. Native women and men, often labeled princesses and chiefs and dressed in Plains Indian attire, regularly addressed young museum audiences. There they danced, sang songs, and spoke about Indigenous cultures and lifeways.

In 1912 Director George Byron Gordon wrote an encouraging letter to one of his field-workers, reminding him of the museum's goal. "We are trying to make this institution an instrument for the preservation of truthful records of the aboriginal people of America," Gordon wrote. Like many museum colleagues across the country, Gordon viewed anthropology as an objective science. He believed the University Museum's representations of Native peoples were truthful and accurate. Although the University Museum did not advocate on behalf of American Indian nations, it did employ Indigenous staff, incorporating their voices into museum exhibitions, lectures, and publications. Throughout much of its early existence, the University Museum struggled to balance accurate portrayals of Native cultures and stereotyped images of "real Indians" the public had come to expect. Florence and Louis, too, struggled with this balance in their anthropological work for the museum.[39]

Museum Work as a Couple

Florence and Louis took on several roles when they started at Philadelphia's University Museum, including interpreting, arranging, describing Northwest Coast items in the collections, and even creating miniature models of Tlingit villages for exhibition. The museum conferred upon Louis the title of curatorial assistant. As a woman, and an Alaska Native woman at that, Florence's museum-sanctioned title was slightly different. Rather than a curatorial assistant, she became an "Indian princess." Although she possessed the same qualifications as her husband, Gordon assigned Florence the role of costumed storyteller, primarily there to entertain children.[40]

Before each performance, Florence entered a small, temporarily vacant room in the museum to transform herself. She regularly shed the garments of many urban women of her day and replaced them with a buckskin Plains Indian–style dress. To this she added moccasins, bracelets, and a necklace. Finally, she placed a headband with a single feather atop her head, complimenting her long, straight dark hair. When she was done, there was no sign of Florence's life in 1912 Philadelphia. She transformed herself into something reminiscent of picturesque 1880s Lakota (Sioux) culture. With her costume complete, Florence greeted her audience of schoolchildren eager to learn about Native American histories and cultures.

Marketed by the museum as an "Indian princess," Florence embraced this persona with its accompanying stereotypes of Native American life. She personified what many museumgoers imagined Indigenous life to be. In appearance she became a horse-riding, feather headdress–wearing, tipi-inhabiting woman of the Great Plains. In this she mirrored the many "Show Indians" who performed in Buffalo Bill's Wild West.[41]

Although none of the schoolchildren in Philadelphia's University Museum would have noticed, the glass beads Florence habitually wore around her neck belied her supposed Plains Indian heritage. This necklace was of Russian manufacture and an heirloom passed down to Florence from her Tlingit grandmother. Rather than being a "modern Minnehaha" or an "Indian princess" of the American Great Plains, as the newspapers reported, Florence in reality came from much further west than many in her audience ever imagined.[42]

While we do not know Florence's thoughts about this type of work, we know she wowed museum audiences. Building on earlier performances with Antonio Apache's Indian village and Toona's Indian Grand Opera Company, Florence embraced her fictional persona at the Philadelphia museum. Dressed in Plains Indian clothing, she ironically appeared as a Plains Indian princess despite being a Tlingit woman from Southeastern Alaska. Not surprisingly, her depiction met rave reviews. A journalist from the *Philadelphia Inquirer*, for example, described the twenty-nine-year-old Florence as "a real Indian, clad in buckskin and beads."[43]

Nor was Florence alone in being pigeonholed into the role of an Indian princess. Numerous other Native women in the early twentieth century found employment on stage and in museums depicting caricatures of Native American life. Three of Florence's contemporaries worked at New York's AMNH during these years: Princess Watahwaso or Lucy Nicolar, a Penobscot woman; Princess Chinquilla or Mary C. Newell, a Tsitsis-tas/Suhtai woman; and Princess Te Ata or Mary Frances Thompson, a Chickasaw woman. Despite their varied cultural backgrounds, each of them dressed in Plains Indian clothing, performed songs and dances for audiences, and adopted the title of Indian princess.[44]

These women all shared something else in common. They each used their celebrity status to speak out about injustice in Indian Country. Lucy Nicolar advocated for Native American sovereignty, campaigning for Penobscot voting rights in her home state of Maine. Mary C. Newell, a former Carlisle Indian Industrial School student who toured with Buffalo Bill's Wild West before moving to New York City, also worked for Indigenous rights. While she was Princess Chinquilla to AMNH audiences, outside of the museum Newell organized the American Indian Association, a Native-led aid society for American Indians living in the city. Finally, Mary Frances Thompson or Princess Te Ata did not confine herself to speaking to museum audiences but toured the world. As an artist, performer, and storyteller, she championed Native American cultures on a global scale.

Jobs for Native women in the field of anthropology were often few, far between, and socially constrained by gender. Importantly, Indigenous women nevertheless supplied invaluable information about their communities to anthropologists. Oftentimes, though, it was their husbands or other male relatives who took the credit and reaped the financial benefits for these collaborative endeavors. Native women in urban areas had more opportunities than their contemporaries on reservations, but within the anthropological profession they were relegated to being Indian princesses in museums or performers in traveling shows. A handful of Native women, however, successfully fought to escape these confining roles. Women such as Ella Cara Deloria, Gladys Tantaquidgeon, and Florence Shotridge broke down the barriers before them and created new spaces as anthropologists in their own right.[45]

Mixing in Anthropological Circles

In addition to their professional work at Philadelphia's University Museum, the Shotridges maintained a robust social life in the city. Soon after moving to Philadelphia they immersed themselves in anthropological circles and struck up a friendship with the chair of the University of Pennsylvania's Anthropology Department, Frank G. Speck. At his insistence they even temporarily moved in with him while they looked for other quarters in the city.[46]

Speck matriculated at Columbia University in 1899. Like many emerging anthropologists of his day, he pursued studies under Franz Boas. He received his bachelor's and master's degrees there, the latter in 1905. Although Speck continued his doctoral studies at Columbia, he eventually received his PhD in anthropology from the University of Pennsylvania in 1908, the first student to do so. He commenced his professional career in 1907 after accepting a fellowship in anthropology at the Free Museum of Science and Art at the University of Pennsylvania. Alfred L. Kroeber and Frederic Ward Putnam at the University of California, Berkeley were so impressed with Speck's qualifications that they tried to snatch him away to work on the West Coast, offering to increase his salary from $1,200 to $1,400 per year. Speck ultimately refused, telling them he wished to remain in Philadelphia. Although he severed his relationship with the University Museum in 1911, he stayed on at the University of Pennsylvania for several more decades. He largely built the Anthropology Department there as he advanced from instructor to assistant professor to full professor. In this way Speck, along with Frank Boas, Alfred L. Kroeber, and others, represented anthropology's changing nature in its transition from museums to academia in the early twentieth century.[47]

Soon after arriving in Philadelphia, Florence and Louis developed close friendships with not only Gordon and Speck, but also with anthropologists M. R. Harrington and Alanson Skinner. Fulfilling a virtual rite of passage for young anthropologists at the time, Louis even attended a few classes at Columbia University under the tutelage of Franz Boas. In this he followed in the footsteps of William Jones and preceded aspiring Native anthropologists Ella Cara Deloria and Archie Phinney. Between November 1914 and January 1915, Louis studied with Boas in New York, taking up temporary quarters on West 121st Street near Columbia University. There the two men worked together every morning on Tlingit linguistics. They later published a Tlingit grammar based on this collaborative work. Florence's involvement in this linguistic project remains unclear, but we know she joined Louis in New York that December. The two of them then returned to their home in Philadelphia in early 1915.[48]

Unlike Native collaborators Richard Davis or D. C. Duvall, who primarily collected objects and information on Native reservations, Florence and Louis's anthropological responsibilities also lay within the Philadelphia museum. Like Native museum anthropologists James R. Murie and Amos Oneroad, the Shotridges constructed exhibits, interpreted objects, and represented their Tlingit community to the public through lectures and presentations. Juggling a full schedule of exhibition work and public talks, they were frequently in the limelight. They educated non-Indigenous listeners about Alaskan Native cultures and regularly recited Tlingit stories and songs. In 1915, for example, Louis spoke before a sixty-member audience of the Lancaster, Pennsylvania, Travel Club before then lecturing to one of his most popular audiences—the Boy Scouts. Before a group of several hundred adolescent boys eager to romanticize Indigenous cultures and "play Indian," Louis spoke of "what Indian boys must endure to become first-class woodsmen." Like his wife, Louis frequently wore Plains Indian clothing in front of his audiences. He left unsaid any misgivings he felt wearing the dress of other Native nations instead of his own.[49]

Enamored by his intelligence, charm, and unprecedented role as a Tlingit museum employee, newspapers described Louis in glowing terms. The *Phil-*

adelphia Inquirer called him a brilliant young man who brought unknown facts about Native cultures to light. Seneca archaeologist and Society of American Indians (SAI) member Arthur C. Parker likewise commended Louis's expertise in judging the antiquities and artifacts of the Northwest Coast. These qualities, Parker continued, made him an invaluable member of the anthropological staff at Philadelphia's University Museum.[50]

Louis's intelligence and photogenic nature endeared him to newspaper editors eager to report on his life and work. But no less captivating were these same attributes in Florence. A Philadelphia paper described her as Louis's pretty young wife and a woman of excellent birth. As a couple, the two received constant media attention. The *Philadelphia Sun* labeled them talented and educated. And the *Philadelphia Inquirer* lauded their English skills, indicative, the paper continued, of every evidence of refinement and breeding. Presenting himself as a mouthpiece for assimilationist-leaning American Indians, Arthur C. Parker wrote of Florence and Louis's sincere love of their people and the proud manner in which they upheld the dignity of their race.[51]

The media's descriptions of the Shotridges reveal much about the criteria Native peoples had to possess to be accepted in Euro-American society. Due to their celebrated high birth and education, Florence and Louis became social darlings. They defined what Tlingit culture was and how their audiences understood the Northwest Coast region. As we will see, though, possessing such power later earned Louis the enmity of Tlingit community members back home in the Alaska Territory.

Anthropological Fieldwork as a Couple

In addition to their work with museum presentations and exhibitions and even publishing scholarly articles, Florence and Louis also conducted ethnographic fieldwork. In June 1915 they led an anthropological collecting expedition to the Northwest Coast communities of Alaska. On the way the Shotridges stopped over in San Francisco and visited the recently opened Panama-Pacific International Exposition, better known as the 1915 San Francisco World's Fair. Examining the Northwest Coast collections on exhibit, they wrote George Byron Gordon that they were unimpressed with the materials on display. According to Louis, the bulk of the Northwest Coast items were newly made, created for tourists and curio collectors. After their brief stop in California, the two continued on to the Alaska Territory to begin their fieldwork.[52]

The Shotridges were the first Native-led wife and husband anthropological expedition, so their work was wholly unprecedented. Newspaper reporters across the nation scrambled to write of the Shotridges—"Civilized Indians" who explored the "wilds" of Alaska. From their homebase in the village of Haines, the two attended potlatches, wrote observations, and used a phonograph to record Tlingit songs on wax cylinders. Florence and Louis worked with community members to gather the stories of elders brought up according to "the old traditions." During their two years of fieldwork they collected the stories, songs, and beliefs of their people, along with countless Northwest Coast material culture items destined for the Philadelphia museum.[53]

Florence and Louis's collaborative fieldwork ended abruptly in June 1917. Louis sent a letter to Gordon in Philadelphia, telling him Florence had been exhibiting signs of illness, probably tuberculosis, since the previous summer. Things had gotten progressively worse in the interim, he said. Illustrative of their bond of friendship, Gordon sent a heartfelt response, recommending Florence return to Philadelphia, where the climate was better for her health. With no signs of improvement, Gordon wrote again the following month, telling Louis to put his collecting work on hold. Florence should receive his attention first, he continued, and the museum second. Regardless of Louis's ministrations, Florence passed away on June 12, 1917, at age thirty-five. She spent her last moments surrounded by friends and family in her Native land. Three days later Florence was buried in a cemetery along Chilkoot Lake, not far from where she and Louis first attended school together.[54]

Louis was heartbroken at her death. Gone was his wife, his anthropological partner, and his best friend. For twelve years the two had crisscrossed the country, performing as entertainers and working as anthropologists. Now he found himself alone. He wrote Gordon a month later, noting that he was having trouble focusing on his work, with his mind frequently a total blank. Gordon recommended Louis take a break from anthropology. "You are burdened by a great sorrow," Gordon wrote, "and your mind and body need time to rest and refresh."[55]

Louis Shotridge's Continued Anthropological Fieldwork

Given time to grieve Florence's death, Louis Shotridge slowly returned to his love of anthropology. He felt he needed to continue the work the two of them started years earlier. Shotridge spent the next decade and a half traveling on behalf of the museum between Philadelphia, Haines, and Sitka. Two years after Florence's death, Shotridge remarried. His second wife, Elizabeth Cooke, was also a member of the Tlingit community. Like Florence, Elizabeth joined Louis in conducting anthropological fieldwork throughout Southeastern Alaska. The two collected all manner of objects and information, racing to preserve aspects of these communities they believed in need of immediate salvage.[56]

Like many Native collaborators, Shotridge used the latest forms of technology in his collecting work. In addition to a camera and a phonograph machine, he ordered a custom-built typewriter with a keyboard to type in a Tlingit linguistic script. In 1922 he purchased a boat, granting him access to more distant communities throughout the year. He named it *Penn* in honor of the museum where he worked, and he traveled along the coasts of Alaska and British Columbia, seeking out rare and sacred items.[57]

While collecting anthropological information in the form of traditions, beliefs, and songs, Shotridge also sought out ceremonial and sacred objects for the Philadelphia museum's Northwest Coast Hall. In 1922, for instance, he addressed the men of his Klukwan community and tried to convince them their way of life was ending. He argued that their sacred belongings should be preserved in a museum rather than returned to the earth where they would be forgotten. Foremost among the items Shotridge sought were the four elaborately carved interior house posts, rain dance screen, and fourteen-foot feast dish that made up the Klukwan Whale House collection.

Shotridge ended his speech to the male gathering by volunteering to be a go-between for the parties involved—the Chilkat Tlingit on one side and the Philadelphia University Museum on the other. He added that if the community elders agreed to sell these items, he promised large sums of money for the construction of a new Whale House. His entreaty did not fall entirely on deaf ears. Several of the older men saw reason, and some saw potential profit, in the younger man's plan. The majority, however, would not consider selling their heritage at any price. The community was at loggerheads from the start, and the situation became more fraught over the following years.

So determined was Shotridge to acquire these objects that in the spring of 1924 he schemed to remove them while the villagers were away from home. Suspicious of Louis, his uncle placed a guard to watch over the Whale House collection, preventing such an action. Finally, in August 1924 Shotridge acknowledged defeat. He wrote a letter to the Philadelphia museum staff that the Tlingit community members would allow him to remove these objects "only over their dead bodies." Louis and his uncle even reconciled the following year, agreeing the Whale House collection would stay within the community.[58]

The example of the Tlingit Whale House collection shows that Louis Shotridge was not always successful in his collecting endeavors. A few years before this, for instance, he was gathering materials among the Tsimshian First Nation peoples in British Columbia. Writing Gordon in Philadelphia, Shotridge said he was at a disadvantage by not being fluent in the region's other languages. Nevertheless, he continued, he would do his best to acquire materials for the museum. Traveling along the Naas and Skeena Rivers in 1918, Shotridge visited fourteen different villages, taking over one hundred photographs, and collecting nearly fifty objects.[59]

During his 1918 trip, Shotridge met Ksgoogmdziiws (Gago-gam-dzi-wust), chief of the village of Kitsumkalum (Gitsumkelum). He soon learned that this man was in possession of a sacred stone eagle carving passed down through his family for generations. Despite Shotridge's repeated attempts to convince the older man to part with the carving, Chief Ksgoogmdziiws refused all offers. "This is the only thing I have left from all the fine things my family used to have," the Tsimshian chief told the Tlingit anthropologist. "I feel as if I might die first before this piece of rock leaves this last place," he stated with finality, putting an end to any talk of selling it. As with the Klukwan Whale House Collection, Shotridge was unable to acquire this rare and sacred Northwest Coast object. As we know, though, with his 1929 acquisition of the Kaagwaantaan shark helmet, he did eventually get his hands on one of the prizes he sought.[60]

Neither Shotridge nor any of his fellow Native collaborators operated in a vacuum. They regularly worked at the mercy of factors beyond their control. In 1927, for instance, two years before Shotridge "acquired" the Kaagwaantaan shark helmet, his collecting work hit a roadblock. While doing fieldwork near Sitka that February, Shotridge received word his friend George Byron Gordon had died suddenly from a fall. The news was a severe blow to Shotridge. He was in shock for days, writing that he had lost a true friend. As we have seen, Amos Oneroad experienced similar devastation after Alanson Skinner's death in 1925. Time for Shotridge's grief was something the Philadelphia museum could not afford, however. With Gordon's death the museum lost one of its most knowledgeable staff on American Indians. Museum management urgently requested that Shotridge come to curate the ever-growing collection there. He agreed, and by November 1927 he was back in Philadelphia.[61]

The following January Shotridge took on another unprecedented role—directing the installation of the museum's new Northwest Coast Hall and its Tlingit gallery. It was a momentous step for an Indigenous anthropologist. While Native collaborators regularly supplied objects and information for museum exhibits, only a handful such as James R. Murie, John V. Satterlee, and Amos Oneroad provided input on exhibit design and layout. Even fewer filled Tichkematse's role of personally interpreting items to the public. But this was the first time an Indigenous person had major control over the creation and implementation of a Native-themed museum exhibit specifically about their own culture. Completed in 1928, Shotridge's exhibit remained open for three years, until a reinstallation occurred in 1931.[62]

In the aftermath of his installation, Shotridge decided that he and his eldest son, Louis Jr., deserved a vacation. That summer of 1930, he and ten-year-old "Junior" drove across the country from Philadelphia to Seattle. This was a quarter century before the interstate highway system, and their trip lasted twenty days. Shotridge later noted that the actual driving only took about five days or 130 hours. The rest of the time they spent camping and sightseeing. Though he enjoyed the trip greatly, Shotridge expressed regret that the Native peoples he met along the way were too modernized for his taste, knowing little about the "aboriginal life." By that July Shotridge and his son were back home in Sitka. After this much-needed respite, he was ready to collect again.[63]

Collecting Human Remains

As noted in several chapters, many Native collaborators found ways to justify removing their community's sacred belongings. D. C. Duvall obtained Pikuni Blackfeet (Piegan) medicine bundles for the AMNH, John V. Satterlee dug up burial mounds in Wisconsin, and Amos Oneroad did likewise in Arkansas and New York. Louis Shotridge was no different. Like Satterlee and Oneroad, he also collected ancestral remains—a practice universally decried as abhorrent. The notable difference between the actions of Shotridge and these other men was that he occasionally voiced his misgivings, making them more prevalent in the anthropological literature.[64]

A year after Shotridge's cross-country drive, he learned about the body of a revered Tlingit healer, or what he called a shaman, being held in the Sheldon Jackson Indian Boarding School in Sitka. Louis tried to acquire these ancestral remains for Philadelphia's University Museum, but they ended up going to a higher bidder at New York's AMNH. Six months later in January 1932 Louis wrote the Philadelphia museum's new director, Horace Jayne, about "one of the luckiest finds" he had yet come across— the remains of another Tlingit healer. Shotridge located a sacred area, he confided to Jayne, where Tlingit healers' bodies had been laid to rest for years. Under cover of darkness and with the aid of a few paid laborers, Shotridge took the ancestral remains from their resting place to Sitka and then sent them along to Philadelphia. He knew his ghastly acts would stoke community anger. He removed the ancestral remains at night to avoid suspicion and potential trouble from Tlingit people in the area. This was not an isolated event for Shotridge, either. A few months later he wrote Jayne about another opportunity to acquire Tlingit ancestral remains for the Philadelphia museum. Though interested, Jayne refused because of a lack of funds.[65]

Life for Louis after Philadelphia's University Museum

By 1932 the United States was suffering through the Great Depression. Like other businesses across the country, museums experienced financial loss and cut staff to make ends meet. That May Philadelphia's University Museum fired nearly all members of the American Section staff, including Louis Shotridge. Director Horace Jayne expressed regret at letting Louis go. He wrote that it was with intense dislike that he had to acknowledge the necessity of decreasing his staff. Louis was distraught and worried how to support his three children born to his second wife, Elizabeth. He had worked for the museum for two decades, but the position that had provided him with power and purpose no longer existed. Shotridge was nevertheless graceful in his response to the museum's decision, writing that he had done the best job he could while employed there. In a closing note, he added that he hoped the Tlingit objects he worked so hard to acquire remained on exhibit to represent their Tlingit creators.[66]

In addition to losing his long-held position at the University Museum, Shotridge suffered the loss of his wife Elizabeth in 1928. Like Florence, Elizabeth succumbed to tuberculosis. Left to raise their young children, Shotridge married for a third and final time to a Tlingit woman named Mary Kasakan.[67]

Beginning in 1924, Shotridge became involved with the Alaska Native Brotherhood (ANB). This group was a pan-Alaska Native organization that fought for civil rights and opposed racism in the Alaska Territory. Shotridge's fellow ANB members were so impressed by him that they elected him "Grand President" in 1930. Keen to continue his anthropological observations, Shotridge wrote Jayne that his membership in the ANB gave him the means to learn more about his own people. Additionally, he confided to Jayne, his role as ANB president benefited the Philadelphia museum. Alaska Native peoples previously suspicious of his anthropological collecting work began to place more trust in him, he wrote, even offering him items for sale.[68]

Despite his success within the Alaska Native Brotherhood, by 1932 Louis was adrift personally and professionally. He buried two wives in little more than a decade and lost the assistant curator position that meant so much to him. He continued to write his former museum colleagues about potential objects he could acquire for them, but there was simply no money left for such expenses. He never returned to the anthropology career he loved and the preservation work he deemed all-important. After a lifetime of collecting and representing Native cultures, Louis Shotridge died in 1937 from the result of a fall. He was buried in a cemetery in Sitka, Alaska.[69]

The Shotridges and Anthropology Today

Florence had just started her most rewarding work when she died in 1917. As she saw it, she was saving her people's history and culture—ensuring they would live on after her. She was also making great strides for Indigenous women within the anthropological profession—not just as overlooked collaborators on reservations or as "Indian princesses" in museums, but as actual anthropologists who led field expeditions to study and preserve their peoples' cultures.

We don't know what else Florence may have accomplished had she not died so young. No doubt she would have created a more permanent place for herself and for other Native women within museum anthropology. Inevitably, Florence would have continued to educate people about the diversity, beauty, and rich histories of the Indigenous nations of North America. Finally, if she had lived longer, perhaps she also would have tempered her husband's questionable collecting practices that later earned him the antipathy of his people.

Florence and Louis set out to save Tlingit history and culture. They believed they were battling wholesale culture loss resulting from a toxic mixture of non-Native theft and Native indifference. In some ways they were correct. They were also successful to a certain extent in stopping it. The tangible and intangible items they gathered over a century ago exist today because of their efforts. These materials continue to reside in the archives and object collections of what is now the Penn Museum in Philadelphia.

While the Shotridges initially hoped to "save" their culture, what they ended up doing was something quite different. Despite their best intentions, Florence and Louis separated their community from vast amounts of its history, depositing these items in a museum over three thousand miles away. In this way they were like many of their fellow Native collaborators and anthropologists during the height of salvage anthropology. The irreparable harm and identity loss these actions caused continue to plague Indigenous communities today.

Louis's anthropological collecting work after Florence's death became more complicated. Without his wife's guidance Louis took more ethically questionable steps in acquiring Northwest Coast objects. Despite being well received by audiences and anthropological circles on the East Coast, back home in Alaska it was a different story. By the end of his life he had earned the mistrust and antipathy of many fellow community members.[70]

To say that Tlingit community members were ambivalent about Louis's anthropological collecting is putting it mildly. He repeatedly attempted to purchase or otherwise acquire sacred and ceremonial objects that belonged to the community as a whole, not to individual members. In some cases, such as with the Klukwan Whale House collections, he was rebuffed. In others, such as his acquisition of the Kaagwaantaan shark helmet, he was successful—at least from his point of view. He was opportunistic, as can be seen in his correspondence with museum director Horace Jayne in 1933. In that year Louis wrote Jayne about the large number of Tlingit families desperate for money. The country was already two years into the Great Depression, with no end in sight. The Depression had hit the people of Alaska hard, Shotridge said, compelling many Tlingit families to dispose of their old collections. Callous to the needs of those around him, Louis wrote Jayne that he wished to take advantage of this situation.[71]

Despite the passage of time, Shotridge's words and deeds have not been forgotten in southeastern Alaska. In a *Juneau Newspaper* article from 1976, ill will against him continued to run high, four decades after his death. According to this piece, Shotridge was ostracized by his community in his last years. Because of his removal of Tlingit cultural heritage from Alaska, he was held in contempt by his fellows even beyond death.[72]

Louis Shotridge, like many Native anthropologists and collaborators, led a complicated and contradictory life. His desire to document Indigenous lifeways he believed were vanishing was laudable. It was the actions he took in trying to salvage these materials that were problematic. Although he died nearly a century ago, Shotridge's legacy continues to be a divisive issue today. So too does the museum retention of many Northwest Coast objects he spent decades collecting.

Conclusion

What Happened After (Hoonah, Alaska, 2017)

The Sealaska Heritage Institute in Juneau, Alaska, was full of music, dancing, and joy in early October 2017. After a century of separation, the sacred
Snail House collection belonging to the Tlingit T'akdeintaan clan returned
home to Hoonah. On its way the repatriated collection received a Welcome Home Celebration in the state capital of Juneau before going home.
Three days later the Snail House collection completed the final leg of its
journey, returning to Hoonah, where Tlingit community members held a
ceremony of sovereignty and healing. This homecoming was accompanied
by feasting, giving of numerous gifts, and an outpouring of emotion over
the long-anticipated reunion.[1]

Ninety-three years earlier Tlingit anthropologist and Philadelphia
museum employee Louis Shotridge visited Hoonah. There in 1924 he
purchased four dozen items that collectively make up the Hoonah T'akdeintaan clan's Snail House collection. Ever the savvy anthropologist,
Shotridge was enthused with his good luck in securing such a rich collection for Philadelphia's University Museum. He believed the museum a
more appropriate home for these items where they would be appreciated
by a much larger audience. Shotridge was not only happy at securing this
collection for the museum but also that he got it for a steal. He bragged
to his friend and supervisor George Byron Gordon that the $500 he paid
for it was less than half what the Tlingit seller requested.[2]

According to Hoonah Tlingit residents, the man who sold the Snail
House collection to Shotridge never had the authority to do so. The items
comprising the T'akdeintaan Snail House collection represented communal, rather than individual, heritage. Rumors and questions persist over
the methods Shotridge used in convincing the seller to part with these
items. Some suggest the seller was tricked into doing so. In January 1925

Shotridge sent this collection via ship to Seattle and then by railroad car to Philadelphia, where it remained in Philadelphia's University Museum, now the Penn Museum, for the next century.[3]

It wasn't until seven decades later, in 1995, that a strong enough legal infrastructure was in place for the Tlingit residents of Hoonah to demand the Penn Museum return their heritage. A complex legal back-and-forth followed for the next twenty years, with both parties claiming ownership. After much wrangling, in 2011 eight sacred items were repatriated to Hoonah, with three more returned in the Welcome Home Celebration of 2017. The rest of the Snail House items Shotridge collected remain in limbo. They are not with their community of origin in Hoonah, nor in the Penn Museum's holdings in Philadelphia, but instead in the Alaska State Museum in Juneau. The interested parties agreed to "resituate" these materials there in 2017 in a shared stewardship agreement. Though technically not repatriated, relocating the Snail House collection closer to Hoonah has increased community access to their cultural heritage from which they were so long separated.[4]

Though it received less media attention than the Snail House repatriation, in 2019 the Penn Museum returned other materials collected by Shotridge. In that year staff at the Penn Museum solemnly transferred the ancestral remains of a Tlingit healer Shotridge secreted out of Sitka in late 1931. As discussed, in addition to sacred objects, the Tlingit anthropologist was not opposed to collecting the remains of his community's ancestors for study. According to Shotridge, securing this individual and his associated funerary belongings for the museum's collections was a "splendid opportunity." For three quarters of a century the ancestral remains of this revered Tlingit healer lay in storage in the Penn Museum, three thousand miles from his home and people. Between 1998 and 2017 Northwest Coast Tlingit community representatives and Penn Museum staff worked cooperatively to determine this individual's culture and identity. Two years later, in 2019, this Tlingit healer, like many of the sacred items in the Snail House collection, finally returned home.[5]

Museums and Indian Boarding Schools as Continuing Colonial Institutions

Although returning ancestral remains and sacred items to Alaska were cause for celebration, such acts were highly unusual in the history of U.S. museums. Anthropology museums by their nature are institutions of colonial power. They literally put on display the cultural heritage of people they have colonized, or at least those they have found curious and worthy of exhibition. It has traditionally been the job of anthropology museum staff to acquire tangible and intangible materials. These personal belongings of other cultures today fill shelves, rooms, wings, and entire buildings. Historically museums, and the people who work in them, have not made a habit of returning items they spent years and much money to acquire.

So what changed in the past hundred years for repatriations such as those between the Penn Museum and Alaska Native communities to occur? And how did these changes impact relationships between Indigenous nations, museums, and the "ownership" of cultural items? Not surprisingly, change came from Indigenous peoples themselves rather than non-Native museum employees. While many American Indians distrusted anthropologists from the start, in the mid-twentieth century they became more vocal opponents of anthropological representations and appropriations of their cultures. Native American intellectual Vine Deloria Jr., for example, argued in his 1969 book that anthropologists' attempts to "capture real Indians in a network of theories" contributed substantially to the invisibility of present-day American Indian peoples. Advocating change in the current power structure, Deloria in *Custer Died for Your Sins: An Indian Manifesto* called for anthropologists "to get down from their thrones of authority . . . [to] begin helping Indian tribes instead of preying on them."[6]

Resulting from the work of Deloria and others, a host of laws and policies protecting Native rights were passed at the turn of the twenty-first century. They called for the physical return or repatriation of Indigenous cultural heritage materials held in non-Native repositories such as museums and universities. These laws did not emerge overnight, to be sure. As noted, they were due to the advocacy of Native peoples from the outside instead of a demand for change within museums. This legislation included the 1978 American Indian Religious Freedom Act, the 1989 National Museum of the American Indian (NMAI) Act, the 1990 Native American Graves Protection and Repatriation (NAGPRA) Act, the 2007 United Nations Declaration on the Rights of Indigenous People, and, more recently, the Society of American Archivists' 2018 endorsement of the

Protocols for Native American Archival Materials. A trend in museums toward ethical returns and shared stewardship over the past few years shows a willingness on the part of some cultural heritage institutions to cultivate better relationships with communities whose materials they steward. Smithsonian secretary Lonnie Bunch III, for instance, in April 2023 acknowledged the unethical nature of previous collecting policies at that federal institution. In a public statement, Bunch voiced that what was once standard in the museum field is no longer acceptable today. He further apologized for the pain and historical trauma salvage anthropology practices caused countless individuals, families, and communities in the United States and around the globe. Formal recognition of culpability on the part of the Smithsonian Institution, while only a small step, is still a step in the right direction.[7]

Anthropology museums were hardly the only colonial institutions that inflicted irrevocable harm and culture loss on the Indigenous peoples of North America. Indian boarding schools, too, faced changes in the twentieth century, though not in the way many Native peoples hoped. Instead of recognition that they were racist and abusive assimilation factories, their numbers steadily increased in the early decades of the twentieth century. Whereas Native attendance in Indian boarding schools in the year 1900 numbered twenty thousand children, by 1925 that number had tripled, to over sixty thousand Indigenous youths confined in more than 350 schools across the country.[8]

While Indian boarding schools were on the rise in the first half of the twentieth century, other national and international developments likewise impacted the lives of Native Americans. Congress's passage of the 1924 Indian Citizenship Act, for instance, long overdue and not wholly implemented in some states and territories, nominally granted citizenship to many Indigenous people in the United States. Sadly, this act did not significantly alter the public's conception of Native Americans or change how anthropologists acquired Native cultural heritage items for museums. Four years later, in 1928, the Meriam Report was released, making public the horrendous state of U.S. Indian boarding schools. The federal government received particular condemnation in this report—appropriately titled *The Problem of Indian Administration*. Citing neglect by federal representatives to address poverty, disease, and poor living conditions on reservations and in Indian boarding schools, the Meriam Report echoed the same complaints voiced by Native students and their families for decades. Richard Henry Pratt's outing system at the Carlisle Indian Industrial School likewise came under fire. The report's authors charged that students were used as a source of free labor, rarely if ever receiving any real vocational training. By the time the Meriam Report came out in 1928, Pratt and many original proponents of the Indian boarding school system were either dead or retired. But the report nevertheless shed light on the rampant abuse and racism on which these schools were founded.[9]

Despite the Meriam Report's alarming revelations, attendance numbers in Indian boarding schools did not see a serious decline until the second half of the twentieth century. It was only in the 1970s with the Indian Education Act and the Indian Self-Determination and Education Assistance Act that Native peoples wrested enough power from the federal government to mandate how their children should be educated. According to the National Native American Boarding School Healing Coalition, as of 2020 seventy-three Indian boarding schools remain open in seventeen states across the country.[10]

Despite encountering daily racism and abuse at Indian boarding schools, the Native anthropologists and collaborators portrayed in this book documented, collected, and preserved their cultures. They accomplished this in the face of massive federal opposition and at the mercy of limited museum funding. Each of these individuals embraced their communities and Indigenous heritage, often to a greater extent than before attending such schools. It is surprising to learn, then, that these Native anthropologists and collaborators encouraged their children, grandchildren, and other relatives to go to the very same Indian boarding schools they themselves had. Their reasons for doing so were many. No doubt these decisions were due in part to reservation agents and other federal officials continuing to enforce compulsory education for children on reservations. Lacking alternatives to Western-style education, parents often reluctantly complied with this enforced schooling. Wanting to pass along their cultural knowledge to the next generation, many Native parents nevertheless taught their children the old ways in secret, under the government's radar.

Reexamining the Lives of Native Anthropologists and Collaborators

The Penn Museum's repatriation of sacred objects to Alaska Native communities, though commendable, is the exception rather than the rule. Due to federal constraints, the time it takes museums to repatriate materials to Indigenous nations is staggeringly slow. Additionally, despite the passage of repatriation laws more than thirty years ago, millions of Native American heritage items remain in museum collections. Given this sad state of affairs, how should we view the Native anthropologists and collaborators who first put this heritage behind museum doors?

Many Indigenous people today mention being conflicted about the problematic nature of museums and Native participation in salvage anthropology. Some argue that if not for individuals such as Florence Shotridge, D. C. Duvall, and Tichkematse, a host of cultural items and information would be gone, lost to us forever. At the same time, others point out that the majority of the tangible and intangible cultural heritage collected by people such as Cleaver Warden, Amos Oneroad, and John V. Satterlee are in museums hundreds or thousands of miles from their creators. Federal repatriation policies make it possible for some items to be returned to their communities, yet millions upon millions of items of Native manufacture remain inaccessible to most Native peoples. While significant changes have taken place in the past century, and even in the past decade, greater change is needed to begin to repair the damage inflicted by museums on Indigenous nations.[11]

After reading about the lives of these Native anthropologists and collaborators, how should we view them and their work in the anthropological field? There is no satisfying moral as at the end of one of Aesop's fables. Real life is not that simple. Instead, we are left with complexity—with individuals' contradictory and problematic natures, where they were often confronted by greed and power. Some readers will see these Native anthropologists and collaborators as heroes from an earlier era—saviors struggling against a settler colonial government to preserve their cultures from assimilation and outright annihilation. Other readers will see these same women and men as traitors to their Indigenous nations—thieves who sold their histories for a few dollars and a bit of fame. Maybe to a certain degree they were both—a little bit hero and a little bit villain. Though perhaps it is more accurate to label these Indigenous anthropologists and collaborators as tragic heroes. In this way we see them as active agents in the removal of their own cultural heritage, though unaware what the consequences would be.

D. C. Duvall, James R. Murie, and Amos Oneroad, among others, compiled an enormous amount of information collected over many years. Some of their fieldnotes have since been made accessible by non-Native scholars, but much of this priceless information remains unpublished. It survives in manuscript form in archives, seen by the occasional researcher instead of how these men intended—to carry on the thoughts and beliefs of their Native predecessors. To a considerable extent, too, these Native anthropologists and collaborators shaped the careers of their non-Native colleagues. They propelled people such as George A. Dorsey, Alice C. Fletcher, and Clark Wissler into celebrity while their own names were forgotten.

Labeling these Native anthropologists and collaborators as simply good or bad would be too easy. It would reduce them to less than the sum of their parts. Rather, we need to recognize them as three-dimensional characters who led complicated and at times contradictory lives. The differences between them were many, representing diverse cultures from across the country. But they all shared similar challenges battling racism and defending their cultures. Several of them even overlapped in their work, competing for access to people and collections. Finally, all of them have also become our avatars or guides into a period of history removed from us by more than a century. By retelling their stories, we experience what they did, even if just for a few moments and from a comfortable distance. In a real and lasting way, too, these individuals continue their work as interpreters and cultural liaisons more than a century later—providing entrée to communities we know only in passing, if at all.

The life stories of these Native anthropologists and collaborators teach us about resilience in the face of systemic racism, oppression, and settler colonialism. Through their collective experiences in mission schools and Indian boarding schools they provide firsthand victims' accounts of culture loss—forced to abandon their languages, clothing, and identities. But through such devastating experiences, they also learned to speak, read, and write in English, making them ideal candidates to work in the new anthropological profession.

Ironically, the racist instruction forced on these individuals in the Indian boarding schools of their youth did not weaken their appreciation for the richness of their communities. It increased it. Despite Richard Henry Pratt's efforts to eradicate Indigenous cultures, as adults these boarding school survivors turned the power, highlighting the beauty in their communities. Rather than abandoning their histories, they collectively spent decades documenting and preserving them. Although some of their actions had unanticipated negative outcomes, their intentions were often noble. They celebrated their cultures, traditions, and beliefs during a time when the rest of the country demanded they assimilate to Euro-American Christian society and abandon the very things that made them unique.

Power, Resistance, and Not-So-Silent Voices

The one woman and nine men portrayed in this book were active players in salvage anthropology at the turn of the twentieth century. Like their non-Native museum colleagues, these ten individuals raced across the country to preserve Indigenous cultures. Each of them feared their own Indigenous nation's lifeways were disappearing, and they used a variety of methods to salvage what they could. From photographing ceremonies to recording songs on wax cylinders, and from documenting stories to drawing color illustrations of battles, these ten Native anthropologists and collaborators amassed an enormous amount of cultural heritage information. They didn't limit themselves to only collecting, either. Several of them exhibited their cultural heritage in museums, published about it in scholarly journals, and spoke about it to groups of interested schoolchildren and adults.

Through their collecting, their exhibiting, and their presentations, these Native anthropologists and collaborators earned a living. But much more importantly, they worked in a profession where they represented the complexity and the beauty of their diverse cultures. Responding to a global demand that commodified Native material culture, these individuals also succeeded in saving it—or at least saving the parts they thought mattered. They documented what they believed was important, sometimes even excluding other Native voices within their own communities.

Deciding whose voices should be preserved in the anthropological literature relates to another component of their collecting work. From Tichkematse to Amos Oneroad, and from D. C. Duvall to Florence Shotridge, these anthropologists and collaborators represented their communities how they saw fit. They became de facto arbiters of how their cultures were seen and understood by the public, at least to a certain extent. Incidentally, many of them also happened to come from powerful families. As the children of community leaders, they were born with a certain amount of status in their respective Indigenous nations. This power imbalance between them and their community members increased as they developed professional ties with non-Native anthropologists and with the financial support of museums.

Native anthropologists and collaborators chose what to collect, who to buy objects from, and who to interview when working among their families, their friends, and sometimes their enemies. While they passionately worked to preserve their cultures, they also exercised an incredible amount of power over how their communities were represented to the world. As a result, many voices remain conspicuously silent. The voices of women, the voices of marginalized families within each Native community, the voices of those who refused to dole out their collective heritage for a few dollars in payment—all of their stories are absent from the anthropological literature. Those voices most prevalent in the record today represent only individuals willing to speak or collaborate with anthropologists. Because of this, certain Indigenous families or individuals came to dominate the anthropological record, while others were often excluded by their own community members.[12]

In addition to Native collaborators and non-Native anthropologists who raced to salvage Indigenous cultures, another group of players also existed. They are the countless Native individuals who never appear in fieldnotes or scholarly journals. Despite their absence, these Indigenous people also worked to preserve their cultures against assimilation and Christianization. Like Native anthropologists and collaborators, they cared deeply about the beliefs of their forebears, but they chose to retain their sacred stories and songs by passing them down orally, rather than collaborate with non-Native outsiders. Many allowed their sacred items and their ancestors to return to the earth, ignoring the financial enticements of anthropologists and curio collectors.

A compelling incident from an early twentieth-century non-Native anthropologist's fieldwork helps illustrate how some Indigenous people refused to collaborate with representatives of a settler colonial government. In February 1909 anthropologist M. R. Harrington traveled to Pawhuska, Oklahoma, for collecting work. In the Osage Nation lands he faced this type of resistance, recording the experience in his fieldnotes. Sent to Oklahoma to collect objects and information for George Gustav Heye's growing collections in New York, Harrington met a different message of hostility than any he had previously confronted. There he encountered a man he labeled an "enemy" to salvage anthropology work.

"If we sell all our old things, we'll no longer be Indians!" an elderly Osage man shouted to anyone who approached Harrington. According to Harrington, the elder shadowed him throughout his days in Osage County, warning people not to sell anything to the New York anthropologist. Loss of identity, and with it the loss of a shared past, were very real fears for this Osage man. Significantly, the unidentified Osage man's words still ring true—the loss of Native cultural heritage materials in the past is directly tied to decreased cultural identity today. As noted, individuals such as Harrington and other Native and non-Native anthropologists and collaborators, whether well-intentioned or not, were the biggest culprits of this identity loss.[13]

Although the sale, and sometimes theft, of Native cultural possessions did not automatically lead to loss of a distinct identity as this Osage elder predicted, Indigenous peoples' lifeways were quite literally under attack at the turn of the twentieth century. From federally mandated Indian boarding schools that rallied behind the infamous slogan "Kill the Indian in him, and save the man," to BIA agents who outlawed ceremonies on sovereign Native lands; from U.S. congressional representatives who classified American Indians as "wards" instead of citizens, to museum anthropologists who raced to "salvage" Indigenous nations before they supposedly disappeared into the melting pot of American society—all of these factors threatened the existence of unique Native identities.[14]

But like the Osage man who challenged Harrington in 1909, there were people beyond just Native anthropologists and collaborators who worked to save their cultures. The unnamed Osage man who received only a passing mention strove just as passionately as all ten of these Native anthropologists and collaborators to preserve his culture. His story and the stories of thousands of other Indigenous people who fought for their identities against racism, assimilation, and settler colonialism still need to be told.

Notes

Abbreviations

AMNH	American Museum of Natural History
APS	American Philosophical Society
BAE	Bureau of American Ethnology
BIA	Bureau of Indian Affairs
MPM	Milwaukee Public Museum
NAA	National Anthropological Archives
NARA	National Archives and Records Administration
NMAI	National Museum of the American Indian Archives Center
PHS	Presbyterian Historical Society
SAI	Society of American Indians
SIA	Smithsonian Institution Archives

Introduction

1. La Flesche, *Middle Five*, xvii; Coleman, *American Indian Children*, 153.

2. Pratt, "Advantage of Mingling Indians," 260–61; Eastman, *Pratt*, 196; Coleman, *American Indian Children*, 95.

3. Liberty, "Francis La Flesche," 45–46; 1900 U.S. Federal Census, Washington DC; 1910 U.S. Federal Census, Washington DC; Mark, *Stranger in Her Native Land*, 325.

4. A. Fletcher to F. W. Putnam corr., June 7, 1884, MS 4558, NAA; Temkin, "Alice Cunningham Fletcher," 96; Fletcher and La Flesche, *Omaha Tribe*.

5. F. W. Hodge to F. La Flesche corr., August 10, 1910, BAE, NAA; F. W. Hodge to R. Rathbun corr., January 14, 1911, BAE, NAA; "Peyote Hearings," 117.

6. Mark, *Stranger in Her Native Land*, 165.

7. "Items," *School News* (Carlisle PA), May 1883.

8. Alexander, "Francis La Flesche," 328.

9. Conn, *Do Museums Still Need Objects?*, 20–22.

10. Dippie, *Vanishing American*; Ramirez, *Standing Up to Colonial Power*, 9.

11. "Pacific Christian Advocate," June 22, 1921, AC.228, NMAI; Coleman, *American Indian Children*, 44; D. W. Adams, *Education for Extinction*, xv; Trafzer, Keller, and Sisquoc, *Boarding School Blues*, 10.

12. Trafzer, Keller, and Sisquoc, *Boarding School Blues*, 15; D. W. Adams, *Education for Extinction*, 35–36; Hagan, "Private Property," 126.

13. Pratt, "Report of Training-School" (1890), 308; Child, *Boarding School Seasons*, 71–81.

14. Alford, *Civilization and the Story*, 73, 90.

15. D. W. Adams, *Education for Extinction*, 69; Coleman, *American Indian Children*, 45.

16. Child, *Boarding School Seasons*, 100.

17. Dippie, *Vanishing American*, xi–xii; Smithsonian Institution, 1875 Annual Report, 70.

18. Cole, *Captured Heritage*, xii; Redman, *Prophets and Ghosts*, 6, 62.

19. P. J. Deloria, *Playing Indian*, 90.

20. Trafzer, Keller, and Sisquoc, *Boarding School Blues*, 1; D. W. Adams, *Education for Extinction*, xi–xii; Ramirez, *Standing Up to Colonial Power*, 7, 31.

21. Bruchac, "My Sisters Will Not Speak," 151–71.

22. J. R. Murie to C. Wissler corr., March 3, 1916, Anthropology Archives, AMNH; J. R. Murie to C. Wissler corr., June 10, 1916, Anthropology Archives, AMNH.

1. A Great Favorite at the Smithsonian

1. Mann, *Cheyenne-Arapaho Education*, 8.

2. Oestreicher, "On the White Man's Road?," 38–39.

3. Oestreicher, "On the White Man's Road?," 43–45.

4. Oestreicher, "On the White Man's Road?," 45–46; Pratt, "Report of Training-School" (1891), 594.

5. Kalesnik, "Caged Tigers," 21; Pratt, "Report of Training-School" (1890), 308.

6. Haley, *Buffalo War*, 215–19; Kalesnik, "Caged Tigers," 22–25.

7. Pratt, "Report of Training-School" (1891), 594.

8. Pratt, "Report of Training-School" (1891), 594; Pratt, *Battlefield and Classroom*, 108–9; Bass, *Arapaho Way*, 6.

9. Petersen, *Plains Indian Art*, 195–98; Glancy, *Fort Marion Prisoners*, 13.

10. Pratt, "Advantage of Mingling Indians," 50; Pratt, *Battlefield and Classroom*, 118.

11. Petersen, *Plains Indian Art*, 193; Pratt, "Advantage of Mingling Indians," 50, 260; Pratt, "Report of Training-School" (1890), 308.

12. Pratt, *Battlefield and Classroom*, 175.

13. Pratt, "Report of Training-School" (1891), 595; Stowe, "Indians at St. Augustine," 345.

14. Kalesnik, "Caged Tigers," 54; Oestreicher, "On the White Man's Road?," 151.

15. Pratt, *Battlefield and Classroom*, 130.

16. Hagenbuch, "Richard Henry Pratt," 54; Oestreicher, "On the White Man's Road?," 61–62; Kalesnik, "Caged Tigers," 52; Glancy, *Fort Marion Prisoners*, 89; Emery, *Recovering Native American Writings*, 69.

17. Glancy, *Fort Marion Prisoners*, 78.

18. Petersen, *Plains Indian Art*, 64–70; Kalesnik, "Caged Tigers," 49–50.

19. Pratt, *Battlefield and Classroom*, 183.

20. S. Baird to R. H. Pratt corr., May 21, 1877, MS S-1174, Beinecke Library; "Scientific Intelligence," *Harper's Weekly*, August 18, 1877.

21. Pratt, "Catalogue of Casts," 201.

22. Pratt, *Battlefield and Classroom*, 136–39.

23. S. Baird to R. H. Pratt corr., August 18, 1879, MS S-1174, Beinecke Library.

24. Hagenbuch, "Richard Henry Pratt," 58; Kalesnik, "Caged Tigers," 45.

25. Pratt, "Report of Training-School" (1890), 308.

26. Lindsey, *Indians at Hampton Institute*; Pratt, *Battlefield and Classroom*, 191–92.

27. Ludlow, *Ten Years' Work*, 6, 13; Ramirez, *Standing Up to Colonial Power*, 31.

28. Ludlow, *Ten Years' Work*, 31.

29. Ludlow, *Ten Years' Work*, 25.

30. Oestreicher, "On the White Man's Road?," 197; Ludlow, *Ten Years' Work*, 14.

31. Mann, *Cheyenne-Arapaho Education*, 47–48; Oestreicher, "On the White Man's Road?," 196.

32. Pratt, "Advantage of Mingling Indians," 50; Petersen, *Plains Indian Art*, 193–94.

33. Burleigh, *Stranger and the Statesman*, 2.

34. Smithsonian Institution, 1847 Board of Regents Report, 11; Fitzhugh, "Origins of Museum Anthropology," 180.

35. Smithsonian Institution, 1857 Annual Report, 36; Smithsonian Institution, 1858 Annual Report, 513.

36. Petersen, *Plains Indian Art*, 194; *Cheyenne Transporter* (Darlington, Indian Territory), February 25, 1881; Smithsonian Institution, 1881 Annual Report, 40.

37. Petersen, *Plains Indian Art*, 194–95.

38. Pratt, *Battlefield and Classroom*, 205.

39. *Yorkville (SC) Enquirer*, October 2, 1879; Pratt, *Battlefield and Classroom*, 212.

40. Mark, *Four Anthropologists*, 97; Smithsonian Institution, 1875 Annual Report, 58, 70; Trennert, "Grand Failure," 118–20.

41. Smithsonian Institution, 1875 Annual Report, 67; Trennert, "Grand Failure," 122–23.

42. Smithsonian Institution, 1875 Annual Report, 69.

43. Braun, "North American Indian Exhibits," 41; Jacknis, *Storage Box of Tradition*, 80; Smithsonian Institution, 1875 Annual Report, 68; Trennert, "Grand Failure," 129.

44. McGee et al., "In Memoriam," 361; Gleach, "Cushing at Cornell," 110–11.

45. Petersen, *Plains Indian Art*, 195–98.

46. J. W. Powell to S. Baird corr., April 8, 1880, BAE, NAA.

47. McGee et al., "In Memoriam," 363–64; Cushing, "My Adventures in Zuni," 191; S. Baird to F. H. Cushing corr., January 24, 1882, Record Unit 7002, SIA.

48. F. H. Cushing to S. Baird corr., September 18, 1880, November 28, 1880, December 19, 1880, RU 7002, SIA.

49. Petersen, *Plains Indian Art*, 199.

50. *Cheyenne Transporter* (Darlington, Indian Territory), February 25, 1881.

51. According to Benjamin Kracht, Cushing's main residence was in Halona. Otherwise, he and Tichkematse would have camped in sheep encampments at Ojo Caliente or Nutria.

52. Cushing, "Nation of the Willows," 362; F. H. Cushing to S. Baird corr., June 24, 1881, RU 7002, SIA; Cushing, "Nation of the Willows II," 541–59.

53. Petersen, *Plains Indian Art*, 200; Green, *Cushing at Zuni*, 163–73.

54. *Cheyenne Transporter* (Darlington, Indian Territory), January 10, 1882; Petersen, *Plains Indian Art*, 204.

55. Petersen, *Plains Indian Art*, 201; John D. Miles, *Eadle Keatah Toh* (Carlisle PA), October 1881.

56. Green, *Cushing at Zuni*, 190–200; Kalesnik, "Caged Tigers," 75.

57. *Cheyenne Transporter* (Darlington, Indian Territory), January 10, 1882.

58. Pratt, "Advantage of Mingling Indians," 260–61; Eastman, *Pratt*, 196.

59. "Report of Indian School Superintendent" (1885), cxxxiii; Petersen, *Plains Indian Art*, 202.

60. Petersen, *Plains Indian Art*, 202; Oestreicher, "On the White Man's Road?," 101.

61. Tichkematse book of drawings, MS 7500, NAA.

62. Petersen, *Plains Indian Art*, 202; W. H. Stickler, "A Night with American Horse and a Ghost Dance on Duck Creek," *Globe-Republican* (Dodge City KS), December 24, 1891.

63. Petersen, *Plains Indian Art*, 203; J. Squint Eyes to T. J. Morgan corr., May 9, 1896, BIA, RG 75, NARA; W. H. Winslow to T. J. Morgan corr., May 30, 1896, BIA, RG 75, NARA.

64. D. W. Adams, *Education for Extinction*, 69; Child, *Boarding School Seasons*, 27.

65. 1906 Cheyenne and Arapaho Reservation Census List.

66. 1901–4 Cheyenne and Arapaho Reservation Agency Employees List; 1906 Cheyenne and Arapaho Reservation Census List.

67. Grinnell, "Buffalo Sweatlodge," 361; Petersen, *Plains Indian Art*, 203–4.

68. Petersen, *Plains Indian Art*, 203–5.

69. Montana, Death Index, 1907–2015, Ancestry.com; Oestreicher, "On the White Man's Road?," 208.

70. Petersen, *Plains Indian Art*, 204.

2. One Who Clearly Understands

1. Hinsley, "Museum Origins," 134–39.
2. Rideout, *William Jones*, 51; "William Jones Murdered," *Prague (OK) News*, April 8, 1909; W. Jones to F. Boas corr., March 30, 1900, Anthropology Archives, AMNH; Boas, "William Jones," 137.
3. Hagan, *Sac and Fox Indians*, 242–43.
4. Almazan and Coleman, "George A. Dorsey," 94; Rideout, *William Jones*, 7–10.
5. Zemanek, "Indiana School Days," 69, 72–73, 83.
6. Rideout, *William Jones*, 17–18; Eastman, *Pratt*.
7. Zemanek, "Indiana School Days," 85; Zitkala-Sa, "School Days," 185–87.
8. Rideout, *William Jones*, 17–18; Zemanek, "Indiana School Days," 88.
9. Zitkala-Sa, "School Days," 188.
10. Rideout, *William Jones*, 19–23.
11. Rideout, *William Jones*, 24.
12. Alford, *Absentee Shawnees*, 99–100.
13. Rideout, *William Jones*, 27; Alford, *Civilization and the Story*, 109.
14. *Kansas Star*, May 2, 1901; Alford, *Civilization and the Story*, 153.
15. Rideout, *William Jones*, 36–38.
16. Zitkala-Sa, "Indian Teacher," 382.
17. Freed, *Anthropology Unmasked*, 1:112–14.
18. Hinsley, "Museum Origins," 134; Harvard, 1902–1903 Annual Report, 281.
19. Boas, "Frederic Ward Putnam," 331.
20. Rideout, *William Jones*, 70–71.
21. Cole, *Franz Boas*, 16, 63–64, 105.
22. Cole, *Franz Boas*, 107; Stocking, *Franz Boas Reader*, 58; Hinsley and Holm, "Cannibal in the National Museum," 310–11.
23. Freed, *Anthropology Unmasked*, 1:446, 1:112; Cole, *Franz Boas*, 212–14.
24. Cole, *Franz Boas*, 276; Herskovits, *Franz Boas*, 100.
25. Cole, *Franz Boas*, 204, 278; P. J. Deloria, *Playing Indian*, 93–94.
26. Boas, "William Jones," 138; Harvard University, 1902–1903 Annual Report, 281.
27. "Hampton School Record," *Southern Workman*, April 1892, 56.
28. Rideout, *William Jones*, 27, 32.
29. W. Jones to J. W. Powell corr., February 13, 1895, BAE, NAA.
30. W. Jones to J. W. Powell corr., February 13, 1895, April 16, 1896, BAE, NAA.
31. Rideout, *William Jones*, 45–47.
32. Fisher, Preface, viii–ix.
33. Vigil, "Death of William Jones," 214; Boas, "William Jones," 138; Rideout, *William Jones*, 72–73; F. Boas to E. D. Perry corr., June 18, 1902, Anthropology Archives, AMNH.

34. W. Jones to G. A. Dorsey corr., April 5, 1907, Field Museum.

35. Rideout, *William Jones*, 92–93.

36. *Red Man and Helper* (Carlisle PA), March 6, 1903.

37. F. Boas to Butler corr., March 19, 1901, Anthropology Archives, AMNH; F. Boas to C. D. Walcott corr., December 7, 1903, MS B.B.61, APS; C. Wissler to Bumpus corr., July 12, 1906, Anthropology Archives, AMNH.

38. Lindsey, *Indians at Hampton Institute*, 90–91, 165; Rideout, *William Jones*, 125.

39. W. Jones to F. Boas corr., August 1, 1905, September 25, 1905, Anthropology Archives, AMNH.

40. Vigil, "Death of William Jones," 214–15.

41. Tooker and Graymont, "J. N. B. Hewitt," 75–76; F. W. Hodge to F. La Flesche corr., August 10, 1910, BAE, NAA; Milburn, "Louis Shotridge," 63; NMAI, 1918–1919 Annual Report, 4.

42. Almazan and Coleman, "George A. Dorsey," 94.

43. F. Boas to W. Jones corr., September 18, 1906, MS B.B.61, APS; W. Jones to F. Boas corr., September 21, 1906, MS B.B.61, APS; Rideout, *William Jones*, 127.

44. G. A. Dorsey to W. Jones corr., July 19, 1907, Field Museum.

45. G. A. Dorsey to W. Jones corr., July 19, 1907, Field Museum.

46. G. A. Dorsey to W. Jones corr., August 16, 1907, Field Museum; Stoner, "Why Was William Jones Killed?," 10.

47. W. Jones to G. A. Dorsey corr., August 24, 1907, September 15, 1907, Field Museum; W. Jones to S. Simms corr., September 15, 1907, Field Museum.

48. Immerwahr, *How to Hide an Empire*, 69–74.

49. W. Jones Diary, October 28–29, 1907, Field Museum.

50. W. Jones Diary, October 6, 1907, Field Museum.

51. W. Jones Diary, April 5, 1908, April 16, 1908, Field Museum.

52. W. Jones Diary, April 16, 1908, Field Museum; Rideout, *William Jones*, 198; Rosaldo, *Ilongot Headhunting*, 2.

53. W. Jones Diary, January 4, 1909, April 17, 1908, Field Museum.

54. W. Jones Diary, May 18, 1908, Field Museum.

55. W. Jones to G. A. Dorsey corr., January 8, 1909, Field Museum; W. Jones to S. Simms corr., February 1, 1909, Field Museum; W. Jones to G. A. Dorsey corr., March 19, 1909, Field Museum; Stoner, "Why Was William Jones Killed?," 10.

56. Rosaldo, *Ilongot Headhunting*, 2.

57. Stoner, "Why Was William Jones Killed?," 13; Vigil, "Death of William Jones," 210; Davis, "Headhunting William Jones," 133–34; Philippines Official Court Hearings Report, April 1909, Field Museum.

58. "Tribesmen Kill Noted Scientist in Philippines," *New York World*, March 31, 1909; E. F. Jones to G. A. Dorsey corr., March 31, 1909, April 6, 1909, April 8, 1909, Field Museum; G. A. Dorsey to L. Jones corr., April 1, 1909, Field Museum.

59. G. A. Dorsey to F. Jones corr., April 12, 1909, Field Museum; H. Jones to G. A. Dorsey corr., April 15, 1909, Field Museum; Davis, "Headhunting William Jones," 128, 137.

60. F. Boas to G. A. Dorsey corr., April 19, 1909, MS B.B.61, APS; Stoner, "Why Was William Jones Killed?," 13; Canilao, "Ruination and the William Jones Affair," 13.

61. Davis, *Headhunting William Jones*; G. A. Dorsey to H. Jones corr., April 7, 1909, Field Museum; Rosaldo, *Ilongot Headhunting*, 259–63.

62. Philippines Official Court Hearings Report, April 1909, Field Museum; Davis, "Headhunting William Jones," 139.

63. Davis, "Headhunting William Jones," 126, 138, 142–43.

64. Rideout, *William Jones*, 30–31.

65. Alford, *Civilization and the Story*, 109.

3. We as a Race Cannot Be Wiped Out

1. Prucha, *Americanizing the American Indians*, 295.

2. R. Davis to G. A. Dorsey corr., May 8, 1905, Field Museum.

3. G. A. Dorsey to F. Leupp corr., July 13, 1907, Field Museum; G. A. Dorsey to F. White Antelope corr., November 11, 1906, Field Museum.

4. Mann, *Cheyenne-Arapaho Education*, 8; Berthrong, *Cheyenne and Arapaho Ordeal*, 78–79.

5. Oestreicher, "On the White Man's Road?," 45–46; Pratt, "Report of Training-School" (1891), 594; Miles, "Report of the Cheyenne and Arapaho Agency" (1875), 268–69.

6. Miles, "Report of the Cheyenne and Arapaho Agency" (1876), 48; Krupat, *Boarding School Voices*, 198–99, 203; Berthrong, *Cheyenne and Arapaho Ordeal*, 78–79.

7. Bass, *Arapaho Way*, 57; Berthrong, *Cheyenne and Arapaho Ordeal*, 78–79.

8. Pratt, "Report of Training-School" (1880), 178–79; Trafzer, Keller, and Sisquoc, *Boarding School Blues*, 2.

9. Campbell to E. A. Hayt corr., October 10, 1879, BIA, RG 75, NARA; Pratt, *Battlefield and Classroom*, 231.

10. Standing Bear, *My People the Sioux*, 127.

11. Pratt, "Report of Training-School" (1880), 178–79; Standing Bear, *My People the Sioux*, 139, 145–46.

12. Thunderbird, "Two Boys," 68.

13. Krupat, *Boarding School Voices*, 199–200.

14. *Morning Star* (Carlisle PA), December 1885.

15. "Indian School Examination," *Carlisle (PA) Weekly Herald*, May 7, 1885.

16. Adams, *Education for Extinction*, 174.

17. Pratt, *Battlefield and Classroom*, 312; Adams, *Education for Extinction*, 176.

18. Pratt, "Report of Training-School" (1881), 187; *Morning Star* (Carlisle PA), December 1885.

19. *Morning Star* (Carlisle PA), December 1885; "Employees in Indian School Service" (1888), 385; R. Davis to J. H. Oberly corr., December 25, 1885, BIA, RG 75, NARA.

20. *Indian Helper* (Carlisle PA), March 23, 1888; R. Davis to J. H. Oberly corr., December 25, 1885, BIA, RG 75, NARA.

21. R. Davis to J. H. Oberly corr., December 25, 1885, BIA, RG 75, NARA.

22. R. Davis to R. H. Pratt corr., December 6, 1890, MS S-1174, Beinecke Library.

23. Pratt, "Savagery Is a Habit," 170; *Morning Star* (Carlisle PA), September 1886.

24. R. Davis to J. H. Oberly corr., December 25, 1885, BIA, RG 75, NARA; "The Indians' Day," *Pittsburgh Dispatch*, July 17, 1892.

25. Ramirez, *Standing Up to Colonial Power*, 97.

26. R. Davis to R. H. Pratt corr., May 1, 1891, MS S-1174, Beinecke Library.

27. "Employees in Indian School Service" (1892), 865, (1894), 516; Pratt, "Report of School at Carlisle" (1893), 449.

28. Pratt, "Report of School at Carlisle" (1893), 452–53; *New York Recorder*, October 11, 1892; Pratt, *Battlefield and Classroom*, 294–95.

29. "Pokagon the Poet," *Chicago Tribune*, October 4, 1893; Peyer, *American Indian Nonfiction*, 241; Pokagon, *Red Man's Rebuke*, 1.

30. Pokagon, *Red Man's Rebuke*, 1–2.

31. "Chief Pokagon Wants an Even $2,000," *Chicago Tribune*, October 15, 1893.

32. *Indian Helper* (Carlisle PA), July 21, 1893; Suzan Shown Harjo, "Carlisle Indian School's History Must Be Preserved So Those Who Suffered Aren't Forgotten," ICT News, September 13, 2018, https://ictnews.org/archive/carlisle-indian -schools-history-must-be-preserved-so-those-who-suffered-arent-forgotten; "Brief History of the CIS Cemetery," Carlisle Indian School, accessed November 8, 2022, https://carlisleindian.dickinson.edu/cemetery-information/resources.

33. Oestreicher, "On the White Man's Road?," 110–12.

34. *Indian Helper* (Carlisle PA), March 23, 1888; "Employees of Indian Service" (1895), 543; Berthrong, *Cheyenne and Arapaho Ordeal*, 251.

35. R. Davis to R. H. Pratt corr., January 22, 1895, MS S-1174, Beinecke Library.

36. R. Davis to R. H. Pratt corr., November 25, 1895, MS S-1174, Beinecke Library.

37. "Employees in Indian School Service" (1902), 701; "Oklahoma Outlines," *Wichita (KS) Daily Eagle*, July 13, 1900; R. Davis to R. H. Pratt corr., January 3, 1897, MS S-1174, Beinecke Library.

38. Moses, *Wild West Shows*, 7; *Indian Helper* (Carlisle PA), September 30, 1898; *Indian Helper* (Carlisle PA), October 28, 1898.

39. Coleman, *American Indian Children*, 182–83.

40. Mooney, *In Sun's Likeness and Power*, 185–88.

41. Mooney, *In Sun's Likeness and Power*, 189; Dorsey, *The Cheyenne*, 1:5.

42. Hinsley, *Savages and Scientists*, 231; WJ McGee to R. H. Pratt corr., August 25, 1902, MS S-1174, Beinecke Library; "Ethnological Pique," *Red Man and Helper* (Carlisle PA), May 27, 1904; Parezo and Fowler, *Anthropology Goes to the Fair*, 35; A. N. McGee, "Women's Anthropological Society of America," 240; "Woman's Anthropological Society," 60–61; Lamb, "Story of the Anthropological Society of Washington," 577.

43. Parezo and Fowler, *Anthropology Goes to the Fair*, 115–16; R. Davis to WJ McGee corr., March 19, 1902, BAE, NAA; WJ McGee, "Anthropology at the Louisiana Purchase Exposition," 821.

44. R. Davis to WJ McGee corr., March 19, 1902, BAE, NAA.

45. Parezo and Fowler, *Anthropology Goes to the Fair*, 86–88, 405–7.

46. Thunder Bird, "Secret Rites and Ceremonies of the Ancient Cheyennes" (unpublished manuscript), 38, MS 641, Autry Museum.

47. R. Davis to G. A. Dorsey corr., August 3, 1905, Field Museum.

48. G. A. Dorsey to R. Davis corr., August 5, 1905, Field Museum.

49. Moses, *Wild West Shows*, 4, 22, 182; Beck, "Fair Representation?"

50. "How the Wild West Show Has Developed," *New York Times*, April 7, 1901; White, "Frederick Jackson Turner and Buffalo Bill," 34–35; Moses, *Wild West Shows*, 144; Advertisement, *New York Times*, April 11, 1863; Betts, "P. T. Barnum," 359–60; B. Adams, "Stupendous Mirror," 35–36.

51. Fields, "Circuits of Spectacle," 443–51.

52. Moses, *Wild West Shows*, 182–83.

53. Standing Bear, *My People*, 263.

54. Pratt, *Indian Industrial School*, 40–41; "Our Duty," *Jamestown (NY) Evening Journal*, August 25, 1904.

55. "There Can Be But One Good Reason," *Red Man and Helper* (Carlisle PA), July 4, 1902; WJ McGee to R. H. Pratt corr., August 25, 1902, MS S-1174, Beinecke Library.

56. *Red Man and Helper* (Carlisle PA), February 12, 1904; "Ethnological Pique," *Red Man and Helper* (Carlisle PA), May 27, 1904.

57. Hertzberg, *American Indian Identity*, 51–58; Allen, "Locating the Society of American Indians," 3–4; Moses, *Wild West Shows*, 5–8; Hoxie, *Talking Back to Civilization*, 16–17.

58. Yellow Robe, "Indian and the Wild West Show," 39; Yellow Robe, "Menace of the Wild West Show," 224–25.

59. "Fairyland Theater," *Long Beach (CA) Telegram*, July 1, 1913; *Pittsburgh Press*, December 13, 1914.

60. Rosenthal, *Reimagining Indian Country*, 33, 47.

61. P. J. Deloria, *Indians in Unexpected Places*, 13, 55–56.

62. 1920 U.S. Federal Census, Washington DC; 1930 U.S. Federal Census, Washington DC.

63. Fields, "Circuits of Spectacle," 458–59; Rosenthal, *Reimagining Indian Country*, 37.

64. Rosenthal, *Reimagining Indian Country*, 33.

65. "Indians in Organizations," *Los Angeles Times*, May 17, 1931; Rosenthal, *Reimagining Indian Country*, 40–46; Thunder Bird, "Secret Rites and Ceremonies," MS 641, Autry Museum.

66. "Plan Entertainment at Switzer's Resort," *Pasadena (CA) Post*, November 22, 1927; "Chief Tells History of 'Lost' Tribe," *Pasadena (CA) Post*, March 4, 1928; L. M. Oak to R. Davis corr., March 21, 1931, MS 641, Autry Museum.

67. R. Davis to M. Stirling corr., April 8, 1929, April 26, 1929, BAE, NAA; Thunderbird, "Two Boys," 68; Thunder Bird, "Secret Rites and Ceremonies," MS 641, Autry Museum.

68. M. Davis to R. Davis corr., May 20, 1942, MS 641, Autry Museum; R. Davis to R. Davis corr., May 24, 1942, MS 641, Autry Museum; "Chief Thunderbird, 80, Son of Massacre Leader, Dies," *Pasadena (CA) Star-News*, April 6, 1946; Rosenthal, *Reimagining Indian Country*, 31.

4. All the Information There Is to Be Got

1. D. C. Duvall to C. Wissler corr., October 3, 1910, Anthropology Archives, AMNH.

2. LaPier, *Invisible Reality*, xvii.

3. LaPier, *Invisible Reality*, 49–88.

4. Eggermont-Molenaar, *Montana 1911*, 3; Wissler and Duvall, *Mythology of the Blackfoot Indians*, vi; DeMarce, *Blackfeet Heritage*, 93; "A Wanderer," *Anaconda (MT) Standard*, February 28, 1898.

5. Although Rosalyn LaPier records Duvall as having attended Carlisle, no record of his time there appears to exist. Similarly, Clark Wissler noted in Duvall's 1911 obituary that he had attended Fort Hall Indian School during his boyhood years, but there, too, Duvall's name appears absent. LaPier, "Piegan View of the Natural World," 108; LaPier, *Invisible Reality*, 110; Wissler and Duvall, *Mythology of the Blackfoot Indians*, vi–vii; Palladino, *Indian and White in the Northwest*, 226.

6. John T. Greer provides this information, despite Clark Wissler reporting that Duvall attended the Fort Hall Indian Boarding School in Idaho. Greer, "Brief History," 2–4.

7. Greer, "Brief History of Indian Education," 6, 39.

8. Greer, "Brief History of Indian Education," 45.

9. "Employees in Indian School Service" (1895), 520.

10. *Helena (MT) Weekly Herald*, May 28, 1896; *Great Falls (MT) Weekly Tribune*, October 4, 1894; *Great Falls (MT) Daily Tribune*, October 6, 1897, May 20, 1900.

11. "Employees of Indian Service" (1899), 598; *Dupuyer (MT) Acantha*, July 25, 1901; *Redman and Helper* (Carlisle PA), September 20, 1901.

12. J. Z. Dare to Commissioner of Indian Affairs corr., September 7, 1905, BIA, RG 75, NARA; D. C. Duvall to J. Hagen corr., August 8, 1905, BIA, RG 75, NARA; Coleman, *American Indian Children*, 182–83.

13. Wissler and Duvall, *Mythology of the Blackfoot Indians*, vii–viii.

14. Freed and Freed, "Clark Wissler," 804, 810; Herskovits, *Franz Boas*, 21; Freed, *Anthropology Unmasked*, 2:625–26; Wissler, *American Indian*, 242.

15. Cole, *Franz Boas*, 240; "Opening of the Anthropological Collections," 721–22; Freed, *Anthropology Unmasked*, 1:404–9; Wissler, "Man as a Museum Subject," 251.

16. "Work of Clark Wissler," 265; "Museum of Natural History," *New York Evening Post*, April 5, 1895; Wissler, "Man as a Museum Subject," 254.

17. Wissler and Duvall, *Mythology of the Blackfoot Indians*, v–vi; Freed and Freed, "Clark Wissler," 810.

18. Wissler and Duvall, *Mythology of the Blackfoot Indians*, viii–x.

19. Wissler and Duvall, *Mythology of the Blackfoot Indians*, xxiv; Wissler, Kehoe, and Miller, *Amskapi Pikuni*, 229, 241–42.

20. D. C. Duvall to C. Wissler corr., November 18, 1910, November 28, 1910, January 28, 1911, Anthropology Archives, AMNH; LaPier, *Invisible Reality*, 68.

21. Wissler, "Sun Dance of the Blackfoot Indians"; C. Wissler to D. C. Duvall corr., February 9, 1911, February 1, 1911, Anthropology Archives, AMNH; Wissler, "Ceremonial Bundles," 70; Wissler and Duvall, *Mythology of the Blackfoot Indians*, 5.

22. Wissler and Duvall, *Mythology of the Blackfoot Indians*.

23. LaPier, *Invisible Reality*, 111–12.

24. D. C. Duvall to C. Wissler corr., January 30, 1904, October 12, 1904, September 16, 1904, Anthropology Archives, AMNH; LaPier, *Invisible Reality*, 59–60, 111.

25. LaPier, *Invisible Reality*, 101–2.

26. D. C. Duvall to C. Wissler corr., March 23, 1911, Anthropology Archives, AMNH; LaPier, *Invisible Reality*, 66.

27. Wissler and Duvall, *Mythology of the Blackfoot Indians*, xx–xxi; Eggermont-Molenaar, *Montana 1911*, 1.

28. Cooper, "Truman Michelson," 281–82; LaPier, *Invisible Reality*, 112.

29. LaPier, *Invisible Reality*, 5, 112–13, 133; Michelson, "Piegan Tale," 408–9.

30. Wissler and Duvall, *Mythology of the Blackfoot Indians*, xx–xxi; LaPier, *Invisible Reality*, 108; McClintock, *Old North Trail*.

31. C. Wissler to D. C. Duvall corr., April 13, 1911, Anthropology Archives, AMNH; D. C. Duvall to C. Wissler corr., May 5, 1911, June 19, 1911, Anthropology Archives, AMNH; LaPier, *Invisible Reality*, 109.

32. Eggermont-Molenaar, *Montana 1911*, 95.

33. Eggermont-Molenaar, *Montana 1911*, 95–96.

34. DeMarce, *Blackfeet Heritage*, 93; Indian Agent to C. Wissler corr., July 29, 1911, Anthropology Archives, AMNH.

35. J. Eagle Child to C. Wissler corr., July 18, 1911, Anthropology Archives, AMNH; Freed, *Anthropology Unmasked*, 2:634; Wissler, *Indian Cavalcade*, 236.

36. D. C. Duvall to C. Wissler corr., March 23, 1911, Anthropology Archives, AMNH; Wissler, Kehoe, and Miller, *Amskapi Pikuni*, 139.

37. Wissler, "Social Organization and Ritualistic Ceremonies," 70.

38. Wissler and Duvall, *Mythology of the Blackfoot Indians*, 148.

5. We Can Get Fine Work Out

1. J. R. Murie to F. W. Hodge corr., February 20, 1911, BAE, NAA.

2. J. R. Murie to F. W. Hodge corr., January 23, 1911, May 31, 1912, BAE, NAA.

3. J. R. Murie to F. W. Hodge corr., February 20, 1911, BAE, NAA.

4. Judd, "Frederick Webb Hodge," 401–2.

5. Hinsley, "Anthropology's Organization Man," 3–9.

6. Murie, *Ceremonies of the Pawnee*, 4–5, 18; Parks, "James R. Murie," 75–76.

7. Dorsey, *Pawnee Mythology*, xi–xii; Murie, "Pawnee Marriage Customs," 299.

8. Murie, *Ceremonies of the Pawnee*, 21.

9. Parks, "James R. Murie," 76–77, 85; U.S. Indian Census Rolls, 1885–1940, Ancestry .com; Armstrong, "Report of Hampton School," 182; Alford, *Civilization and the Story*, 95.

10. Alford, *Civilization and the Story*, 99; Murie, *Ceremonies of the Pawnee*, 21–22.

11. *Southern Workman*, March 1881; Ludlow, *Twenty-Two Years' Work*, 197; Emery, *Recovering Native American Writings*, 2–5.

12. Lindsey, *Indians at Hampton Institute*, 95–97; Ludlow, *Ten Years' Work*, 15; D. W. Adams, *Education for Extinction*, 355.

13. Ludlow, *Ten Years' Work*, 58.

14. Murie, *Ceremonies of the Pawnee*, 22; J. R. Murie to Commissioner of Indian Affairs corr., May 29, 1881, BIA, RG 75, NARA; D. W. Adams, *Education for Extinction*, 166.

15. Alford, *Civilization and the Story*, 107–8.

16. J. Haworth to H. Price corr., September 7, 1883, BIA, RG 75, NARA; Ludlow, *Twenty-Two Years' Work*, 453.

17. *Southern Workman*, December 1883.

18. Murie, *Ceremonies of the Pawnee*, 22; "A Visit to the Indian Territory," *Morning Star* (Carlisle PA), July 1882; J. Haworth to H. Price corr., September 7, 1883, BIA,

RG 75, NARA; Armstrong, "Hampton Normal and Agricultural Institute, 1884," 192; "Report of Indian School Superintendent" (1885), clvi–clvii.

19. Marvin, "Report of Haskell Institute," 228–29; Ludlow, *Twenty-Two Years' Work*, 347.

20. Vuckovic, *Voices from Haskell*, 130.

21. Ludlow, *Twenty-Two Years' Work*, 347–48; "Report of Indian School Superintendent" (1885), cxc–cxci.

22. Vuckovic, *Voices from Haskell*, 21–22.

23. Ludlow, *Twenty-Two Years' Work*, 347–48; "Report of Indian School Superintendent" (1886), cxiii.

24. Vuckovic, *Voices from Haskell*, 22–23.

25. Winnie, *Sah-Gan-De-Oh*, 45–49, 58; Ludlow, *Twenty-Two Years' Work*, 347–48.

26. "Employees in Indian School Service" (1888), 400, (1890), 356; 1900 U.S. Federal Census, Washington DC.

27. Parks, "James R. Murie," 83; Ludlow, *Twenty-Two Years' Work*, 347–48.

28. Ramirez, *Standing Up to Colonial Power*, 31.

29. "Employees of Indian Service" (1893), 553; Murie, *Ceremonies of the Pawnee*, 23; Ludlow, *Twenty-Two Years' Work*, 347–48; "Agreement with Pawnees," 526–28.

30. "Indians Revolt," *Evening Star* (Washington DC), January 18, 1902.

31. Mark, *Four Anthropologists*, 69; La Flesche, "Alice C. Fletcher," 115.

32. A. C. Fletcher to J. W. Powell corr., August 10, 1881, BAE, NAA; Temkin, "Alice Cunningham Fletcher," 96–97.

33. Mead, *Blackberry Winter*, 190–91.

34. Fletcher, "Lands in Severalty to Indians," 663; Fletcher, *Life among the Indians*, 67; R. H. Pratt to A. C. Fletcher corr., May 23, 1882, MS 4558, NAA; F. W. Putnam to A. C. Fletcher corr., July 25, 1891, MS 4558, NAA.

35. La Flesche, "Alice C. Fletcher," 115; *Indian Helper* (Carlisle PA), April 1, 1887, March 28, 1890.

36. A. Springer to R. H. Pratt corr., November 20, 1883, MS 4558, NAA.

37. Fletcher, "The Hako," 14; J. R. Murie to A. C. Fletcher corr., February 12, 1900, MS 4558, NAA.

38. Fletcher, "The Hako," 14–15; J. R. Murie to A. C. Fletcher corr., October 25, 1901, MS 4558, NAA.

39. J. R. Murie to A. C. Fletcher corr., August 24, 1901, October 25, 1901, MS 4558, NAA.

40. J. R. Murie to A. C. Fletcher corr., April 29, 1902, May 28, 1902, MS 4558, NAA.

41. Parks, "James R. Murie," 83–84; Dorsey, *Traditions of the Arikara*, 5.

42. DeMallie and Parks, "George A. Dorsey," 68; Parks, "James R. Murie," 80–84; G. A. Dorsey to F. Skiff corr., April 2, 1905, Field Museum.

43. Murie, *Ceremonies of the Pawnee*, viii.

44. R. Davis to WJ McGee corr., March 19, 1902, BAE, NAA; Edmund Philibert Diary, A1212, Missouri Historical Society Archives.

45. Nellis to Lipps corr., April 24, 1904, BIA, RG 75, NARA; Parezo and Fowler, *Anthropology Goes to the Fair*, 413.

46. Parezo and Fowler, *Anthropology Goes to the Fair*, 86–88, 405–7.

47. Stoner, "Why Was William Jones Killed," 10; Parks, "James R. Murie," 81.

48. Parks, "James R. Murie," 81.

49. F. W. Hodge to J. R. Murie corr., January 18, 1911, BAE, NAA; J. R. Murie to F. W. Hodge corr., March 20, 1915, BAE, NAA; F. W. Hodge to J. R. Murie corr., March 7, 1911, BAE, NAA.

50. Parks, "James R. Murie," 81; F. W. Hodge to J. R. Murie corr., December 26, 1916, BAE, NAA; J. R. Murie to F. W. Hodge corr., January 23, 1911, BAE, NAA.

51. J. R. Murie to F. W. Hodge corr., June 7, 1911, February 20, 1911, June 9, 1913, July 5, 1913, BAE, NAA.

52. J. R. Murie to F. W. Hodge corr., July 8, 1911, BAE, NAA; F. W. Hodge to J. R. Murie corr., July 21, 1911, BAE, NAA.

53. C. Wissler to J. R. Murie corr., September 7, 1912, Anthropology Archives, AMNH.

54. J. R. Murie to C. Wissler corr., June 10, 1916, Anthropology Archives, AMNH; J. R. Murie to C. Wissler corr., October 24, 1916, Anthropology Archives, AMNH.

55. J. R. Murie to C. Wissler corr., November 5, 1913, Anthropology Archives, AMNH.

56. J. R. Murie to C. Wissler corr., October 11, 1915, Anthropology Archives, AMNH; C. Wissler to F. A. Lucas corr., June 30, 1915, Anthropology Archives, AMNH; C. Wissler to J. R. Murie corr., March 10, 1916, Anthropology Archives, AMNH.

57. J. R. Murie to C. Wissler corr., June 15, 1915, July 12, 1915, Anthropology Archives, AMNH; Freed and Freed, "Clark Wissler," 802.

58. J. R. Murie to C. Wissler corr., April 13, 1917, Anthropology Archives, AMNH; C. Wissler to J. R. Murie corr., January 17, 1919, Anthropology Archives, AMNH.

59. Murie, *Ceremonies of the Pawnee*, vii–viii; J. R. Murie to C. Wissler corr., May 2, 1919, Anthropology Archives, AMNH; C. Wissler to J. R. Murie corr., May 7, 1919, Anthropology Archives, AMNH.

60. Parker, "Book on Secret Societies," 134.

61. J. R. Murie to C. Wissler corr., July 12, 1915, December 22, 1920, Anthropology Archives, AMNH; Parks, "James R. Murie," 82.

62. Freed and Freed, "Clark Wissler," 802; Wissler, "Man as a Museum Subject," 251.

6. Making a Great Collection of Relics

1. A. Skinner to J. V. Satterlee corr., September 23, 1911, Anthropology Archives, AMNH; J. V. Satterlee to A. Skinner corr., September 30, 1911, Anthropology Archives, AMNH.

2. A. Skinner to J. V. Satterlee corr., January 25, 1913, Anthropology Archives, AMNH.

3. Hodge, "John Valentine Satterlee," 8.

4. Skinner, "Recollections of an Ethnologist," 47–48.

5. Skinner, *Medicine Ceremony*, 17–18; Skinner, "Recollections of an Ethnologist," 47.

6. Skinner, *Medicine Ceremony*, 210; Satterlee Police Diaries, 369, 435, 508, David R. M. Beck Private Collection.

7. Skinner, *Medicine Ceremony*, 210; Satterlee Police Diaries, 369, 435, 508, David R. M. Beck Private Collection.

8. E. Stephens to Commissioner of Indian Affairs corr., October 31, 1882, BIA, RG 75, NARA; "Report of Agents in Wisconsin," 172.

9. Hodge, "John Valentine Satterlee," 3; Skinner, "John Valentine Satterlee," 209–12.

10. Satterlee Police Diaries, 49; "Employees of Indian Service" (1899), 603, (1900), 685, (1901), 769, (1902), 714, (1904), 639.

11. "Employees of Indian Service" (1905), 526; Satterlee Police Diaries, 357.

12. Beck, "Collecting among the Menomini," 168–71; Hodge, "John Valentine Satterlee," 6.

13. Satterlee Police Diaries, 358–59.

14. Satterlee Police Diaries, 374–76.

15. Satterlee Police Diaries, 238, 502.

16. Satterlee Police Diaries, 248, 503.

17. D. W. Adams, *Education for Extinction*, 257; Coleman, *American Indian Children*, 166.

18. Satterlee Police Diaries, 248; Churchill Journal, AC.058, NMAI.

19. Hrdlička, *Tuberculosis among Certain Indian Tribes*.

20. Loring and Prokopec, "Most Peculiar Man," 27–30; John Lee Swanton, "Notes Regarding My Adventures in Anthropology and with Anthropologists," 36, MS 4651, NAA.

21. Prado, "History of the San Diego Museum of Man," 7; Loring and Prokopec, "Most Peculiar Man," 38; Hrdlička, *Descriptive Catalog*, 5; Parezo and Fowler, *Anthropology Goes to the Fair*, 323; Rydell, *All the World's a Fair*, 223.

22. A. Skinner to J. V. Satterlee corr., April 2, 1913, Anthropology Archives, AMNH; J. V. Satterlee to A. Skinner corr., May 7, 1924, MS 201.4.8, Autry Museum.

23. Satterlee Police Diaries, 146.

24. Skinner, "Recent Mound Explorations," 105–6; Barrett and Skinner, "Certain Mounds and Village Sites," 411, 423–28; Satterlee Police Diaries, 512–14; J. V. Satterlee to A. Skinner corr., May 7, 1924, MS 201.4.8, Autry Museum.

25. Hodge, "John Valentine Satterlee," 6–9; Beck, "Collecting among the Menomini," 171.

26. Beck, "Collecting among the Menomini," 170; J. V. Satterlee to A. Skinner corr., October 10, 1921, September 12, 1920, MS 201.4.8, Autry Museum.

27. 1870 and 1880 United States Census, Red Wing, Goodhue County, Minnesota, Ancestry.com; Frisbie, "Frances Theresa Densmore," 51; Patterson, "She Always Said," 43–44.

28. Frisbie, "Frances Theresa Densmore," 51; Patterson, "She Always Said," 33, 40.

29. Lurie, "Women in Early American Anthropology," 70; Frisbie, "Frances Theresa Densmore," 52–55.

30. Jensen and Patterson, *Travels with Frances Densmore*, 1; 1900, 1930, and 1940 United States Census, Red Wing, Goodhue County, Minnesota, Ancestry.com.

31. Oneroad and Skinner, *Being Dakota*, 37; Harrington, "Alanson Skinner" (1925), 250–51.

32. A. Skinner to C. Wissler corr., June 21, 1923, Anthropology Archives, AMNH; Oneroad and Skinner, *Being Dakota*, 26; Harrington, "Alanson Skinner" (1925), 249–51.

33. Harrington, "Alanson Skinner" (1926), 275; A. Skinner to F. W. Hodge corr., June 12, 1912, BAE, NAA; A. Skinner to C. Wissler corr., January 13, 1916, Anthropology Archives, AMNH; Pope to A. Skinner corr., September 12, 1922, MPM.

34. Harrington, "Alanson Skinner" (1925), 251.

35. Skinner, "Material Culture of the Menomini"; J. V. Satterlee to A. Skinner corr., February 13, 1922, MS 201.4.8, Autry Museum.

36. J. V. Satterlee to A. Skinner corr., September 25, 1920, May 7, 1924, October 10, 1921, MS 201.4.8, Autry Museum; A. Skinner to J. V. Satterlee corr., October 25, 1924, MS 201.4.8, Autry Museum; J. V. Satterlee to A. Skinner corr., February 20, 1923, March 25, 1925, March 16, 1922, MS 201.4.8, Autry Museum.

37. A. Skinner to J. V. Satterlee corr., September 23, 1911, November 26, 1912, April 2, 1913, Anthropology Archives, AMNH.

38. A. Skinner to J. V. Satterlee corr., April 2, 1913, September 25, 1913, Anthropology Archives, AMNH.

39. Skinner, "Recollections of an Ethnologist," 53.

40. J. V. Satterlee to A. Skinner corr., January 26, 1911, Anthropology Archives, AMNH; Skinner, "Social Life and Ceremonial Bundles," 84.

41. J. V. Satterlee to A. Skinner corr., January 10, 1911, February 21, 1912, August 8, 1912, Anthropology Archives, AMNH; A. Skinner to J. V. Satterlee corr., December 9, 1914, Anthropology Archives, AMNH.

42. Satterlee Police Diaries, 151–52, 241–42, 278, 330; Hodge, "John Valentine Satterlee," 4–6.

43. Satterlee Police Diaries, 278.

44. Skinner, "Recollections of an Ethnologist," 47–48; LaPier, *Invisible Reality*, 101–2.

45. Skinner, "John Valentine Satterlee," 212; 1920 U.S. Federal Census, Ancestry
   .com; "John V. Satterlee," *Oshkosh (WI) Daily Northwestern*, February 23, 1940;
   J. V. Satterlee to A. Skinner corr., March 25, 1925, MS 201.4.8, Autry Museum.
46. J. V. Satterlee to E. S. Holman corr., February 28, 1933, University Archives, University of Wisconsin–Green Bay; Simmons, *Sun Chief*, 307.
47. Skinner, "Material Culture of the Menomini," 26; Hodge, "John Valentine Satterlee," 10.
48. Derus, "What Has the Indian Done," 4.
49. A. Skinner to J. V. Satterlee corr., January 25, 1913, Anthropology Archives, AMNH;
   Beck, "Collecting among the Menomini," 171.

7. A True Indian

1. "Peyote Hearings," 191.
2. Holm, *Great Confusion in Indian Affairs*, 182; Maroukis, *Peyote Road*. As per
   Maroukis's *Peyote Road*, Peyote is capitalized out of respect for Native American
   Church members.
3. Mann, *Cheyenne-Arapaho Education*, 8; Berthrong, *Cheyenne and Arapaho Ordeal*,
   78–79; Dorsey and Kroeber, *Traditions of the Arapaho*, viii–ix.
4. Standing Bear, *My People the Sioux*, 151–52.
5. Miles, "Report of the Cheyenne and Arapaho Agency" (1876), 48; "The Arap-
   ahoe Indian School," *The Democrat* (Wichita KS), March 20, 1897.
6. Almazan and Coleman, "George A. Dorsey," 96; Mann, *Cheyenne-Arapaho Education*, 52; Pratt, "Report of Training-School" (1880), 179.
7. Coleman, *American Indian Children*, 98.
8. Carlisle Indian Boarding School Student Files, Cleaver Warden, BIA, RG 75,
   NARA.
9. Berthrong, *Cheyenne and Arapaho Ordeal*, 89; "Indian Names," *Shippensburg
   (PA) Chronicle*, July 21, 1887.
10. Bol, "Collecting Symbolism among the Arapaho," 111–12; Bass, *Arapaho Way*, 66.
11. Indian Scout Enlistments Discharge, Cleaver Warden, 1888, BIA, RG 75, NARA;
    Petersen, *Plains Indian Art*, 202.
12. Bass, *Arapaho Way*, 40; *Indian Helper* (Carlisle PA), November 22, 1889, August
    22, 1890, January 16, 1891, August 11, 1893; "The Arapahoe Indian School," *The
    Democrat* (Wichita KS), March 20, 1897.
13. C. Warden to G. A. Dorsey corr., September 1, 1902, July 31, 1905, December 24,
    1906, Field Museum; "James Mooney," 209; J. Mooney to J. W. Powell corr., June
    9, 1882, February 14, 1883, BAE, NAA; J. Mooney to Peltney corr., December 14,
    1884, BAE, NAA.
14. Hinsley, *Savages and Scientists*, 157–58; "James Mooney," 209.

15. J. Mooney to J. W. Powell corr., October 29, 1887, BAE, NAA.

16. Moses, *Indian Man*, 52; Oestreicher, "On the White Man's Road?," 123.

17. Mooney, *In Sun's Likeness and Power*, 103; Bass, *Arapaho Way*, 62.

18. Mooney, "Indian Ghost Dance," 171–72.

19. Bol, "Collecting Symbolism among the Arapaho," 116; F. Boas to A. L. Kroeber corr., August 10, 1899, Anthropology Archives, AMNH; F. Boas to WJ McGee corr., June 22, 1899, Anthropology Archives, AMNH.

20. Bol, "Collecting Symbolism among the Arapaho," 111; Dorsey and Kroeber, *Traditions of the Arapaho*, v; Kroeber, "Symbolism of the Arapaho Indians," 69–87; Kroeber, "Decorative Symbolism of the Arapaho," 308–36; Kroeber, "The Arapaho," 1–150.

21. Almazan and Coleman, "George A. Dorsey," 88.

22. *Cheyenne (OK) Sunbeam*, December 20, 1901; Berthrong, *Cheyenne and Arapaho Ordeal*, 292–93; Dorsey, *Arapaho Sun Dance*, 3–4.

23. Bass, *Arapaho Way*, 74–75.

24. Dorsey and Kroeber, *Traditions of the Arapaho*; C. Warden to G. A. Dorsey corr., September 1, 1902, Field Museum.

25. Carlisle Indian Boarding School Student Files, Eva Rogers, BIA, RG 75, NARA.

26. G. A. Dorsey to C. Warden corr., January 27, 1901, Field Museum; C. Warden to G. A. Dorsey corr., October 10, 1902, Field Museum; Dorsey and Kroeber, *Traditions of the Arapaho*, 28–29.

27. G. A. Dorsey to W. A. Jones corr., October 29, 1902, BIA, RG 75, NARA; G. A. Dorsey to C. Warden corr., December 30, 1905, Field Museum; T. J. Davis to Kinney corr., November 18, 1918, MS S-1174, Beinecke Library.

28. Redman, *Prophets and Ghosts*, 46.

29. C. Warden to G. A. Dorsey corr., September 6, 1906, Field Museum.

30. C. Warden to G. A. Dorsey corr., January 15, 1905, Field Museum; LaPier, *Invisible Reality*, 101.

31. Bol, "Collecting Symbolism among the Arapaho," 113–14; Dorsey and Kroeber, *Traditions of the Arapaho*, xiv; Trenholm, *The Arapahoes*, 297.

32. Despite the rise in English fluency, many Indian boarding school students nevertheless communicated in rudimentary sign language cross-culturally.

33. Maroukis, *Peyote Road*, 31–36; D. W. Adams, *Education for Extinction*, 166.

34. "Author of Messiah Dance," *Topeka (KS) State Journal*, September 27, 1897.

35. Parezo and Fowler, *Anthropology Goes to the Fair*, 47–48; WJ McGee, "Anthropology at the Louisiana Purchase Exposition," 821–26.

36. G. Pepper to F. W. Putnam corr., June 29, 1904, AC.001, NMAI.

37. Parezo and Fowler, *Anthropology Goes to the Fair*, 86–88, 405–7; C. Warden to S. Simms corr., May 1904, Field Museum; C. Warden to G. A. Dorsey corr., June 16, 1904, Field Museum.

38. G. A. Dorsey to C. Warden corr., June 13, 1904, Field Museum; C. Warden to G. A. Dorsey corr., July 2, 1904, Field Museum.

39. G. A. Dorsey to C. Warden corr., August 4, 1904, Field Museum; C. Warden to G. A. Dorsey corr., October 10, 1904, April 22, 1905, Field Museum.

40. C. Warden to G. A. Dorsey corr., July 6, 1904, September 13, 1904, July 31, 1905, Field Museum; Almazan and Coleman, "George A. Dorsey," 96.

41. Viola, *Diplomats in Buckskins*, 26–28, 157, 184.

42. Trenholm, *The Arapahoes*, 273; "A Delegation of Indians Here," *Evening Star* (Washington DC), March 19, 1895; Fowler, *Tribal Sovereignty*, 39–40; "Our Visitors," *Haskell Indian Leader* (Lawrence KS), March 1, 1899.

43. C. Warden to G. A. Dorsey corr., January 9, 1906, Field Museum; "Indian Delegates Speak of Mission to Commissioner," *Wichita (KS) Eagle*, May 21, 1909; A. C. Parker to C. Warden corr., November 16, 1914, SAI; A. C. Parker to C. Warden corr., January 21, 1915, SAI; D. W. Adams, *Education for Extinction*, xi–xiii, 329.

44. Hertzberg, *Search for an American Indian Identity*, 71; Allen, "Locating the Society of American Indians," 3–4.

45. J. N. B. Hewitt to A. C. Parker corr., September 27, 1915, MSS 4271, NAA.

46. Parker, "Menace of the Fraudulent Wild West Show," 175–76; Parker, "Perils of the Peyote Poison," 12; Bol, "Collecting Symbolism among the Arapaho," 118; Maroukis, *Peyote Road*, 49.

47. "Peyote Hearings," 80–84, 120.

48. G. Bonnin to R. H. Pratt corr., January 29, 1919, MS S-1174, Beinecke Library.

49. "Peyote Hearings," 143–47.

50. "Peyote Hearings," 107.

51. Maroukis, "Peyote Controversy," 175; Maroukis, *Peyote Road*, 11–12, 56–58. Religious freedoms regarding Peyote use were strengthened by passage of the American Indian Religious Freedom Act Amendments of 1993.

52. G. Bonnin to R. H. Pratt corr., January 29, 1919, MS S-1174, Beinecke Library; John Lee Swanton, "Notes Regarding My Adventures in Anthropology and with Anthropologists," 44, MS 4651, NAA.

53. Trenholm, *The Arapahoes*, 273; Krupat, *Boarding School Voices*, 154–55.

54. *El Reno (OK) American*, June 12, 1917; "Death Claims Chilocco Alumnus," *Indian School Journal* (Chilocco OK), May 21, 1926; Ramirez, *Standing Up to Colonial Power*, 97.

55. Dorsey and Kroeber, *Traditions of the Arapaho*, xiv–xvii.

8. Field Man and a Missionary

1. A. Oneroad to F. Utley corr., September 18, 1925, AC.001, NMAI; A. Oneroad to G. G. Heye corr., November 7, 1925, AC.001, NMAI.

2. Oneroad and Skinner, *Being Dakota*, 3–9; Morris, *Historical Stories, Legends, and Traditions*, 118.

3. Oneroad and Skinner, *Being Dakota*, 12–13.

4. Oneroad and Skinner, *Being Dakota*, 10–11; Morris, *Historical Stories, Legends, and Traditions*, 118.

5. "Minutes of the Synod of South Dakota, 1937," 25, PHS; A. Skinner to G. B. Grinnell corr., November 7, 1923, MPM; Oneroad and Skinner, *Being Dakota*, 18–19; Morris, *Historical Stories, Legends, and Traditions*, 96.

6. "Minutes of the Synod of South Dakota, 1937," 25, PHS; Oneroad and Skinner, *Being Dakota*, 22; Morris, *Historical Stories, Legends, and Traditions*, 74.

7. Morris, *Historical Stories, Legends, and Traditions*, 33–34.

8. Morris, *Historical Stories, Legends, and Traditions*, 33–35, 77.

9. Vuckovic, *Voices from Haskell*, 171; Oneroad and Skinner, *Being Dakota*, 22.

10. "Minutes of the Synod of South Dakota, 1937," 25, PHS; S. M. McCowan to C. B. Jackson corr., December 24, 1903, BIA, RG 75, NARA.

11. C. B. Jackson to S. M. McCowan corr., December 30, 1903, February 11, 1904, BIA, RG 75, NARA; Parezo and Fowler, *Anthropology Goes to the Fair*, 413.

12. "Neighborhood News, Good Will Mission," *Sisseton (SD) Weekly Standard*, June 9, 1905; "Sioux Indian a Cartoonist," *Topeka (KS) State Journal*, July 14, 1909; 1910 U.S. Federal Census; "Good Will," *Sisseton (SD) Weekly Standard*, April 26, 1912.

13. Oneroad and Skinner, *Being Dakota*, 22–23; "Represents the Indian Race at Missionary Exposition," *Carlisle (PA) Arrow*, September 5, 1913.

14. AMNH, "Museum Notes," 119.

15. A. Skinner to J. V. Satterlee corr., March 24, 1914, Anthropology Archives, AMNH.

16. "Indian Gets Post at Milwaukee Museum," *Milwaukee Sentinel*, July 29, 1922; NMAI, 1918–1919 Annual Report; NMAI, 1919–1920 Annual Report.

17. Mead and Bunzel, *Golden Age of American Anthropology*; Conn, *Museums and American Intellectual Life*, 31; Peri and Wharton, "Samuel Alfred Barrett," 5–11.

18. Peri and Wharton, "Samuel Alfred Barrett," 3–11; A. Skinner to A. Oneroad corr., December 27, 1921, MPM; A. Oneroad to A. Skinner corr., January 7, 1922, MPM.

19. Massachusetts Marriage Records, 1904, Ancestry.com; New York Passenger Lists, Ancestry.com; Wallace, "Reporter at Large," 6; New York, Extracted Marriage Index, 1936, Ancestry.com; Mason, "George G. Heye," 27–28.

20. Mason, "George G. Heye," 11; McMullen and Galban, "Lost and Found," 230.

21. F. W. Putnam to G. Heye corr., July 2, 1904, October 20, 1904, AC.001, NMAI; Freed, *Anthropology Unmasked*, 2:656; Kidwell, "Every Last Dishcloth," 235–36; G. Pepper to F. W. Putnam corr., June 28, 1904, AC.001, NMAI.

22. NMAI, 1917 Annual Report; NMAI, Minutes and Annual Reports, vol. 1, 1916–1927, 3.

23. Wilcox, "Museum of the American Indian," 44; Kidwell, "Every Last Dishcloth," 252; "History of the Museum," 8–12; Harrington, "Reminiscences of an Archeologist: VI," 108.

24. Oneroad and Skinner, *Being Dakota*, 25; A. Skinner to B. Weitzner corr., August 6, 1914, Anthropology Archives, AMNH; A. Skinner to C. Wissler corr., November 2, 1918, June 21, 1923, Anthropology Archives, AMNH.

25. "Gets Rare Trophies of Vanishing Race," *New York Times*, October 8, 1914; Oneroad and Skinner, *Being Dakota*, 121; Skinner, "Medicine Ceremony," 262–63.

26. Pope to A. Skinner corr., September 12, 1922, MPM.

27. A. Oneroad to A. Skinner corr., January 28, 1922, MPM; A. Skinner to A. Oneroad corr., January 30, 1922, MPM.

28. Oneroad and Skinner, *Being Dakota*, 66, 103.

29. Harrington, *Certain Caddo Sites in Arkansas*, 13–14, 36; A. C. Parker to A. Oneroad corr., June 19, 1916, SAI; Skinner, "Exploration of Aboriginal Sites," 49–50; "Indian Gets Post at Milwaukee Museum," *Milwaukee Sentinel*, July 19, 1922; Oneroad and Skinner, *Being Dakota*, 33.

30. A. Oneroad to A. C. Parker corr., October 19, 1913, SAI; A. Skinner to J. V. Satterlee corr., May 14, 1914, Anthropology Archives, AMNH; Oneroad and Skinner, *Being Dakota*, 26; A. Skinner to M. R. Harrington corr., February 23, 1915, Anthropology Archives, AMNH.

31. Oneroad and Skinner, *Being Dakota*, 25, 44; "Goodwill News," *Sisseton (SD) Weekly Standard*, May 6, 1921; Vuckovic, *Voices from Haskell*, 130–31; "Indian Y.M.C.A.," *Reporter and Farmer* (Webster SD), June 20, 1912; "Y.M.C.A. Activities," *Newark (NJ) Evening Star*, December 22, 1914.

32. Oneroad and Skinner, *Being Dakota*, 24; "Indian Pageant in Madison," *Newark (NJ) Evening Star*, February 4, 1915.

33. A. Oneroad to A. C. Parker corr., October 19, 1913, SAI; A. C. Parker to A. Oneroad corr., December 16, 1914, SAI.

34. Oneroad and Skinner, *Being Dakota*, 25; A. Oneroad to A. Skinner corr., November 1, 1924, MS 201.4.7, Autry Museum; A. Skinner to M. R. Harrington corr., April 7, 1922, September 25, 1922, MPM; A. Skinner to A. Oneroad corr., November 18, 1922, MPM; A. Skinner to M. R. Harrington corr., October 11, 1923, October 17, 1923, MPM.

35. "Good Will," *Sisseton (SD) Weekly Standard*, April 26, 1912; Oneroad and Skinner, *Being Dakota*, 28; A. Oneroad to A. Skinner corr., October 14, 1922, November 27, 1922, MPM; A. Oneroad to A. Skinner corr., March 20, 1924, MS 201.4.7, Autry Museum.

36. "Minutes of the Synod of South Dakota, 1937," 25, PHS; *Word Carrier* (Greenwood SD), January 1, 1923; A. Oneroad to A. Skinner corr., November 27, 1922,

MPM; A. Skinner to G. B. Grinnell corr., November 7, 1923, MPM; A. Oneroad to A. Skinner corr., November 1, 1924, March 3, 1925, MS 201.4.7, Autry Museum.

37. A. Oneroad to A. Skinner corr., May 15, 1924, MS 201.4.7, Autry Museum; *Word Carrier* (Greenwood SD), May 1, 1925.

38. South Dakota, Marriage Records, 1905–2016, Ancestry.com; A. Oneroad to A. Skinner corr., July 11, 1924, MS 201.4.7, Autry Museum.

39. A. Skinner to A. Oneroad corr., February 27, 1922, MPM.

40. Oneroad and Skinner, *Being Dakota*, 3, 48–49; L. L. Anderson, "More Dakota Texts," 301–3.

41. Oneroad and Skinner, *Being Dakota*, 24–26; "General School News," *Carlisle (PA) Arrow*, October 2, 1914, March 19, 1915.

42. 1919 South Dakota Marriages, Ancestry.com; "Minutes of the Synod of South Dakota, 1937," 25, PHS; "Conference of Mission Workers," *Wolf Point (MT) Herald*, September 1, 1921; "Christmas at the Old Town Mission," *Wolf Point (MT) Herald*, January 1, 1920; "Births," *Wolf Point (MT) Herald*, April 8, 1920.

43. 1926 South Dakota Marriages, Ancestry.com; "Minutes of the Synod of South Dakota, 1937," 25, PHS; A. Oneroad to D. Skinner corr., August 27, 1926, MS 201.4.7, Autry Museum.

44. Oneroad and Skinner, *Being Dakota*, 35–37; "Minutes of the Synod of South Dakota, 1937," 25, PHS.

45. Oneroad and Skinner, *Being Dakota*, 33–34.

46. Prucha, *Americanizing the American Indians*, 295.

47. A. Skinner to A. Oneroad corr., October 29, 1924, MS 201.4.7, Autry Museum; Oneroad and Skinner, *Being Dakota*, 14; Ramirez, *Standing Up to Colonial Power*, 31.

48. Oneroad and Skinner, *Being Dakota*, 24–26, 33–37.

49. "Proceedings," *Reporter and Farmer* (Webster SD), July 19, 1906; A. Oneroad to A. Skinner corr., January 28, 1922, MPM; A. Oneroad to A. Skinner corr., July 28, 1924, MS 201.4.7, Autry Museum.

50. Oneroad and Skinner, *Being Dakota*, 36–37.

9. Civilized Indians Exploring the Wilds

1. Shotridge, "Kaguanton Shark Helmet," 339–43.

2. G. T. Emmons to J. A. Mason corr., April 1, 1942, PU-Mu 0047, Penn.

3. Immerwahr, *How to Hide an Empire*, 78–80.

4. Young, *Hall Young of Alaska*, 6–7.

5. Young, *Hall Young of Alaska*, 156, 209–13.

6. "Did Ju-Neau the Heritage of Klukwan," *Juneau (AK) Empire*, May 17, 1976; Auldridge, "Story of Haines House," 2; Dean, "Louis Shotridge," 202.

7. G. T. Emmons to J. A. Mason corr., April 1, 1942, PU-Mu 0047, Penn; Daniel Lee Henry, "New Indians," Haines Sheldon Museum, accessed October 2021, https://www.sheldonmuseum.org/?s=daniel+lee+henry; George Shotridge to W. McKinley corr., June 20, 1900, BIA, RG 75, NARA.

8. Auldridge, "Story of Haines House," 3–4; S. Jackson to J. W. Foster corr., September 14, 1898, BIA, RG 75, NARA.

9. Mason, "Louis Shotridge," 11; World War I Draft Registration Card, Ancestry .com; Young, *Hall Young of Alaska*, 210.

10. Preucel, "Shotridge in Philadelphia," 43–44; Milburn, "Weaving the 'Tina' Blanket," 552; Milburn, "Louis Shotridge," 60–62. Florence Scundoo Shotridge went by many names during her short life. She is elsewhere in the historical record referred to as Mary Dennis, Susy Scundoo, Florence Dennis, Katwachsnea, and Kaatkwaaxsnei.

11. Young, *Hall Young of Alaska*, 227.

12. Dauenhauer and Dauenhauer, "Louis Shotridge and Indigenous Tlingit Ethnography," 166; Milburn, "Louis Shotridge," 62.

13. Trafford, "Hitting the Trail," 168–75.

14. Hardt, *Official Catalogue of the Lewis & Clark Centennial*, 38–44.

15. Milburn, "Weaving the 'Tina' Blanket," 553; L. Shotridge to G. B. Gordon corr., July 27, 1906, PU-Mu 0047, Penn.

16. G. B. Gordon to L. Shotridge corr., October 17, 1905, January 9, 1906, July 27, 1906, August 28, 1906, PU-Mu 0047, Penn.

17. "Cultured Indians Make Home Here," *Philadelphia Inquirer*, February 11, 1912; "Alaskan Chief Here on Visit," *Philadelphia Sun*, February 10, 1912.

18. "An Impostor," *Red Man and Helper* (Carlisle PA), January 11, 1901; "Society's Pet Red-Man a Negro Painters Say," *San Francisco Examiner*, July 3, 1907; Beck, *Unfair Labor?*, 65.

19. "A. Apache, Esq.," *Arizona Republican* (Phoenix), October 6, 1892; "Grandson of Chief Cochise," *San Francisco Call*, September 17, 1897; Passenger Lists, January 11, 1906, Ancestry.com; 1910 U.S. Federal Census, Los Angeles; California Death Index, 1938, Ancestry.com.

20. "Society's Pet Red-Man a Negro Painters Say," *San Francisco Examiner*, July 3, 1907; "Antonio Apache," *Arizona Silver Belt* (Globe AZ), November 11, 1897; Apache, "Address," 38; "A Fine Indian Is Mr. Apache," *Buffalo (NY) Evening News*, May 1, 1900; "Is He Red or Black?" *Holbrook (AZ) Argus*, July 23, 1907; "An Educated Apache," *Coconino Weekly Sun* (Flagstaff AZ), December 22, 1892.

21. "A. Apache, Esq.," *Arizona Republican* (Phoenix), October 6, 1892; "Apache Indian Visits Fair," *St. Louis Republic*, March 9, 1904; Anna Cox Stephens, "An Apache Harvard Man," *San Francisco Examiner*, February 23, 1896; "Interesting Indian Visitors," *Red Man* (Carlisle PA), April 1897; "Antonio Apache Has Novel Project

in California," *Albuquerque Morning Journal*, December 6, 1905; A. Apache to F. Skiff corr., April 28, 1896, Field Museum; Browman and Williams, *Anthropology at Harvard*, 251.

22. California, County Birth and Marriage Records, 1849–1980, Ancestry.com; U.S. City Directories, Los Angeles, 1916, Ancestry.com; "Nurse Freed from Negro Who Posed as Apache Chief," *San Francisco Examiner*, February 16, 1921; Howard, "Creating an Enchanted Land," 184.

23. "Antonio Apache," *Arizona Silver Belt* (Globe AZ), November 11, 1897; Howard, "Creating an Enchanted Land," 177; U.S. City Directories, Los Angeles, 1920, Ancestry.com; "Apache Indian Visits Fair," *St. Louis Republic*, March 9, 1904; U.S. City Directories, Chicago, 1896, Ancestry.com; A. Apache to F. Skiff corr., April 28, 1896, Field Museum; "Grandson of Chief Cochise," *San Francisco Call*, September 17, 1897; Pardue, "Marketing Ethnography," 107.

24. Howard, "Creating an Enchanted Land," 160–61; "Antonio Apache Has Novel Project in California," *Albuquerque Morning Journal*, December 6, 1905.

25. "A Fine Indian Is Mr. Apache," *Buffalo (NY) Evening News*, May 1, 1900; "Apache Indian Visits Fair," *St. Louis Republic*, March 9, 1904; "Noted Indian Scientist Comes Here on a Mission," *San Francisco Call*, May 26, 1905; "An Educated Apache and His Wise Plan," *Minneapolis Journal*, November 19, 1905; "Redskins Show Peaceful Arts," *Los Angeles Herald*, December 7, 1906.

26. Howard, "Creating an Enchanted Land," 185; "Apache Flatly Denies Having Negro Blood," *Washington (DC) Times*, July 3, 1907; *New York Times*, July 4, 1907; "Society's Pet Red-Man a Negro Painters Say," *San Francisco Examiner*, July 3, 1907; "Antonio Apache a Negro," *Daily Arizona Silver Belt* (Globe AZ), July 10, 1907.

27. "Apache Flatly Denies Having Negro Blood," *Washington (DC) Times*, July 3, 1907; LaPier and Beck, *City Indian*, 58; "An Impostor," *Red Man and Helper* (Carlisle PA), January 11, 1901.

28. Browman and Williams, *Anthropology at Harvard*, 253; U.S. Passport Application, 1919, Ancestry.com; Howard, "Creating an Enchanted Land," 183–86.

29. U.S. City Directories, Los Angeles, 1908, Ancestry.com; 1910 U.S. Federal Census, Ancestry.com.

30. "An Impostor," *Red Man and Helper* (Carlisle PA), January 11, 1901; "Society's Pet Red-Man a Negro Painters Say," *San Francisco Examiner*, July 3, 1907; Beck, *Unfair Labor?*, 65; Pardue, "Marketing Ethnography," 107; Howard, "Creating an Enchanted Land," 160–61; "Antonio Apache Has Novel Project in California," *Albuquerque Morning Journal*, December 6, 1905.

31. Bold, "*Vaudeville Indians*," 44; P. J. Deloria, *Indians in Unexpected Places*, 13, 218.

32. "The Toona Indian Company," *Fort Wayne (IN) Journal*, April 16, 1911; "Madame Toona's Troupe from the Plains," *Harrisburg (PA) Courier*, November 12, 1911; "At the American," *East Liverpool (OH) Evening Review*, December 18, 1911.

33. King and Little, "George Byron Gordon," 25.

34. Hinsley, "Museum Origins," 134; Harvard, 1902–1903 Annual Report, 281; Browman and Williams, *Anthropology at Harvard*, 206–7; Pezzati, "Brief History of the Penn Museum," 16; G. B. Gordon to L. Shotridge corr., November 19, 1911, December 4, 1911, PU-Mu 0047, Penn.

35. Pezzati, "Brief History of the Penn Museum," 5–11.

36. Browman and Williams, *Anthropology at Harvard*, 206–7; Pezzati, "Brief History of the Penn Museum," 11, 16; King and Little, "George Byron Gordon," 39; "Penn Will Scour Alaska for Records," *Philadelphia Inquirer*, January 21, 1907.

37. Darnell, *And Along Came Boas*, 161; Browman and Williams, *Anthropology at Harvard*, 206–7; Witthoft, "Frank Speck," 7–8; King and Little, "George Byron Gordon," 38.

38. Madeira, *Men in Search of Man*, 40; King and Little, "George Byron Gordon," 42, 51; "The Origin of Language," *Philadelphia Inquirer*, May 8, 1902; "U.P. Summer School," *Philadelphia Inquirer*, June 28, 1914; Mason, "Louis Shotridge," 11; Milburn, "Politics of Possession," 54; Dauenhauer and Dauenhauer, "Louis Shotridge and Indigenous Tlingit Ethnography," 167; "University Museum Sends Man to Alaska," *Evening Public Ledger* (Philadelphia), June 2, 1915.

39. G. B. Gordon to W. Van Valin corr., October 24, 1912, PU-Mu 0047, Penn.

40. Williams, "Louis Shotridge," 66.

41. "Cultured Indians Make Home Here," *Philadelphia Inquirer*, February 11, 1912; Moses, *Wild West Shows*, 1.

42. "Explains Indian Life to School Children," *Philadelphia Inquirer*, November 28, 1912.

43. "Explains Indian Life to School Children," *Philadelphia Inquirer*, November 28, 1912; "A Little Chat with Katkwachsnea," *North American* (Philadelphia), January 2, 1912.

44. Education Lecture Booklets, Spring 1924, Autumn 1924, Autumn 1929, DR050, AMNH.

45. Margaret M. Bruchac has written of the silencing of women's voices and erasure of their work in her article "My Sisters Will Not Speak."

46. Wanneh, "Situwaka, Chief of the Chilcats," 283; Preucel, "Shotridge in Philadelphia," 44; Milburn, "Weaving the 'Tina' Blanket," 554.

47. Bruchac, *Savage Kin*, 140; A. L. Kroeber to F. W. Putnam corr., June 4, 1909, MS 999-24, Peabody; Fenton, "Frank G. Speck's Anthropology," 19.

48. F. Boas to L. Shotridge corr., February 24, 1915, MS B.B.61, APS; Boas, "Grammatical Notes," 5–8; L. Shotridge to G. B. Gordon corr., November 17, 1914, November 27, 1914, December 12, 1914, PU-Mu 0047, Penn.

49. "Former Alaska Resident Talks to Travel Club," *Lancaster (PA) New Era*, February 12, 1915; "Boy Scouts," *Evening Public Ledger* (Philadelphia), February 23, 1915.

50. Wanneh, "Situwaka, Chief of the Chilcats," 280.

51. "Cultured Indians Make Home Here," *Philadelphia Inquirer*, February 11, 1912; "Alaskan Chief Here on Visit," *Philadelphia Sun*, February 10, 1912; Wanneh, "Situwaka, Chief of the Chilcats," 283.

52. L. Shotridge to G. B. Gordon corr., June 14, 1915, PU-Mu 0047, Penn.

53. "Chilkat Indians Head Expedition," *Philadelphia Inquirer*, August 14, 1916; "Civilized Indians, Man and Wife, About to Explore Alaska Wilds," *Daily Ardmoreite* (Ardmore OK), September 20, 1916; Williams, "Louis Shotridge," 66–67; L. Shotridge to G. B. Gordon corr., July 1, 1915, PU-Mu 0047, Penn.

54. L. Shotridge to G. B. Gordon corr., February 22, 1917, June 13, 1917, PU-Mu 0047, Penn; G. B. Gordon to L. Shotridge corr., March 9, 1917, April 20, 1917, PU-Mu 0047, Penn.

55. L. Shotridge to G. B. Gordon corr., July 12, 1917, PU-Mu 0047, Penn; G. B. Gordon to L. Shotridge corr., August 13, 1917, PU-Mu 0047, Penn.

56. Milburn, "Louis Shotridge," 62–65.

57. L. Shotridge to G. B. Gordon corr., August 22, 1922, PU-Mu 0047, Penn; Williams, "Louis Shotridge," 67; Preucel, "Shotridge in Philadelphia," 45.

58. L. Shotridge to G. B. Gordon corr., January 27, 1923, PU-Mu 0047, Penn; Seaton, "Native Collector," 54–55; L. Shotridge to G. B. Gordon corr., August 7, 1924, PU-Mu 0047, Penn.

59. L. Shotridge to G. B. Gordon corr., January 18, 1918, PU-Mu 0047, Penn; Preucel, "Shotridge in Philadelphia," 45; L. Shotridge to G. B. Gordon corr., November 7, 1918, PU-Mu 0047, Penn.

60. Shotridge, "Visit to the Tsimshian Indians, Continued," 131.

61. McHugh to L. Shotridge corr., February 4, 1927, PU-Mu 0047, Penn; L. Shotridge to McHugh corr., February 17, 1927, PU-Mu 0047, Penn; McHugh to L. Shotridge corr., June 6, 1927, PU-Mu 0047, Penn.

62. Berman, "That Which Was Most Important," 191; Preucel, "Shotridge in Philadelphia," 51–53.

63. L. Shotridge to H. Jayne corr., July 28, 1930, PU-Mu 0047, Penn.

64. Milburn, "Politics of Possession," 229; "Native Play Shows Core Values Endure," *Anchorage (AK) Daily News*, June 22, 1992.

65. L. Shotridge to H. Jayne corr., July 24, 1931, PU-Mu 0047, Penn; L. Shotridge to H. Jayne corr., January 6, 1932, PU-Mu 0047, Penn; L. Shotridge to H. Jayne corr., April 5, 1932, PU-Mu 0047, Penn; H. Jayne to L. Shotridge corr., May 26, 1932, PU-Mu 0047, Penn.

66. H. Jayne to L. Shotridge corr., May 26, 1932, PU-Mu 0047, Penn; L. Shotridge to H. Jayne corr., July 23, 1932, PU-Mu 0047, Penn; Milburn, "Louis Shotridge," 54; 1920 U.S. Federal Census, Ancestry.com.

67. Milburn, "Louis Shotridge," 71–72.

68. Milburn, "Louis Shotridge," 72; L. Shotridge to McHugh corr., January 8, 1929, PU-Mu 0047, Penn; L. Shotridge to H. Jayne corr., December 19, 1930, March 16, 1931, PU-Mu 0047, Penn.

69. Milburn, "Louis Shotridge," 72; R. L. Wolfe to H. Jayne corr., August 16, 1937, PU-Mu 0047, Penn.

70. Milburn, "Louis Shotridge," 62–65.

71. Mason, "Louis Shotridge," 16; Preucel, "Shotridge in Philadelphia," 42; L. Shotridge to H. Jayne corr., July 21, 1931, PU-Mu 0047, Penn.

72. "Did Ju-Neau the Heritage of Klukwan," *Juneau (AK) Empire*, May 17, 1976.

Conclusion

1. Mary Catharine Martin, "After Almost a Century Absence, Sacred Objects Return to the Tlingit People of Hoonah," *Juneau (AK) Empire*, October 12, 2017; Williams and Starbard, "Woosh.Jee.Een," 231–32; Jonaitis, "Tlingit Repatriation in Museums," 56.

2. L. Shotridge to G. B. Gordon corr., January 12, 1925, PU-Mu 0047, Penn.

3. L. Shotridge to G. B. Gordon corr., January 12, 1925, PU-Mu 0047, Penn; Williams, "Woosh.Jee.Een," 219–25.

4. *U.S. Federal Register* 75, no. 239 (December 14, 2010): 77897–98; Putnam, "NAGPRA and the Penn Museum," 4–11; Williams, "Woosh.Jee.Een," 225–26; Jonaitis, "Tlingit Repatriation in Museums," 53.

5. L. Shotridge to H. Jayne corr., January 6, 1932, April 5, 1932, PU-Mu 0047, Penn; L. Shotridge to J. A. Mason corr., March 7, 1932, PU-Mu 0047, Penn; *U.S. Federal Register* 82, no. 84 (May 3, 2017): 20631–32.

6. V. Deloria, *Custer Died for Your Sins*, 86, 104.

7. "Smithsonian Forms Task Force to Develop Guidelines for Human Remains Collection," Smithsonian Institution News Desk Press Release, April 17, 2023, https://www.si.edu/newsdesk/releases/smithsonian-forms-task-force-develop -guidelines-human-remains-collection.

8. D. W. Adams, *Education for Extinction*, 64; National Native American Boarding School Healing Coalition, *Healing Voices*, vol. 1.

9. Meriam, *Problem of Indian Administration*; Holm, *Great Confusion in Indian Affairs*, 182; Child, *Boarding School Seasons*, 31–32, 36, 85; Coleman, *American Indian Children*, xii.

10. "American Indian Boarding Schools by State," National Native American Boarding School Healing Coalition, accessed April 21, 2023, https://boardingschoolhealing .org/list/.

11. Museums and the field of anthropology have undergone significant change in the past century. Anthropologists today are governed in their work by various codes of ethics and institutional review boards to keep themselves in check.
12. Apsáalooke (Crow/Absaroke) artist Wendy Red Star raised this important point to me during a conversation in November 2018.
13. Harrington, "Reminiscences of an Archeologist: VII," 30.
14. Eastman, *Pratt*, 196.

Bibliography

Note on sources: As there is little published material on many of these Native anthropologists and collaborators, extensive use was made of newspapers and census records, as well as archival sources in museums, universities, and federal repositories across the United States.

Archives and Manuscript Materials

American Museum of Natural History (AMNH), New York.
    Department of Anthropology Archives.
        Duvall, David Charles. Papers. D883.
        Jones, William. Papers. J664.
        Murie, James R. Papers. M875.
        Skinner, Alanson B. Papers. S5566473.
    Education Lecture Booklets. DR050.
American Philosophical Society Archives, American Philosophical Society (APS), Philadelphia.
    Boas, Franz. Papers. MS B.B.61, Correspondence.
Autry Museum of the American West Archives, Los Angeles.
    Oneroad, Amos. Papers. MS 201.4.7.
    Satterlee, John V. Papers. MS 201.4.8.
    Thunderbird, Chief, or Richard Davis. Papers. MS 641.
Beinecke Library, Yale University, New Haven CT.
    Pratt, Richard Henry. Papers. MS S-1174.
David R. M. Beck Private Collection.
    Satterlee, John V. Police Diaries, 1899–1907.
Field Museum, Chicago.
    Cummings, R. F. Expedition to the Philippine Islands.
    Department of Anthropology. General Correspondence.
Hodge, William H. "John Valentine Satterlee: A Tentative Analysis of a Menominee Informant." Unpublished manuscript, 1978. University of Wisconsin–Green Bay Archives and Area Research Center.
Milwaukee Public Museum Archives (MPM).
    Skinner, Alanson. Papers and Correspondence.
Missouri Historical Society Archives, St. Louis.
    Philibert Family. Papers, 1852–1930. A1212.

National Anthropological Archives (NAA), Smithsonian Institution, Suitland MD.
   Bureau of American Ethnology (BAE). Records, Correspondence.
   Fletcher, Alice, and Francis La Flesche. Papers. MS 4558.
   Tichkematse book of drawings. MS 7500.
National Archives and Records Administration (NARA), Washington DC.
   Bureau of Indian Affairs (BIA). Records. RG 75.
National Museum of the American Indian Archives Center (NMAI), Smithsonian
   Institution, Suitland MD.
   Churchill, Col. Frank C., and Clara G. Churchill Collection. AC.058.
   Museum of the American Indian, Heye Foundation Records. AC.001.
Peabody Museum Archives, Harvard University, Cambridge MA.
   Putnam, Frederic Ward. Papers. MS 999-24.
Penn Museum Archives, University of Pennsylvania Museum of Archaeology and
   Anthropology, Philadelphia.
   Shotridge, Louis. Papers. PU-Mu 0047.
Presbyterian Historical Society (PHS), Philadelphia.
   Oneroad, Amos. Papers. RG 414.
Pusey Library, Harvard University, Cambridge MA.
   Putnam, Frederic Ward. Papers. HUG 1717.2.
Smithsonian Institution Archives (SIA), Washington DC.
   Baird, Spencer F. Papers and Correspondence. RU 7002.
   Exposition Records of the Smithsonian Institution. RU 70.
University Archives, University of Wisconsin–Green Bay.
   Satterlee, John V. Papers. GB SC 77.

Published Works

Adams, Bluford. "'A Stupendous Mirror of Departed Empires': The Barnum Hip-
   podromes and Circuses, 1874–1891." *American Literary History* 8, no. 1 (Spring
   1996): 34–56.
Adams, David Wallace. *Education for Extinction: American Indians and the Boarding
   School Experience, 1875–1928.* Lawrence: University Press of Kansas, 2020.
"Agreement with Pawnees." In *Annual Report of the Commissioner of Indian Affairs,
   for the Year 1893,* 526–29. Washington DC: Government Printing Office, 1893.
Alexander, Hartley Burr. "Francis La Flesche." *American Anthropologist* 35, no. 2
   (April–June 1933): 328–31.
Alford, Thomas Wildcat. *Civilization and the Story of the Absentee Shawnees.* Norman:
   University of Oklahoma Press, 1979.
Allen, Chadwick. "Locating the Society of American Indians." *American Indian Quar-
   terly* 37, no. 3 (Summer 2013): 3–22.

Almazan, Tristan, and Sarah Coleman. "George A. Dorsey: A Curator and His Comrades." In *Curators, Collections, and Contexts: Anthropology at the Field Museum, 1893–2002*, edited by Stephen E. Nash and Gary M. Feinman, 87–97. Chicago: Field Museum of Natural History, 2003.

AMNH. "Museum Notes." *American Museum Journal* 14, no. 3 (March 1914): 119.

Anderson, Laura Lee. "More Dakota Texts: Collections of Alanson Buck Skinner and Amos Oneroad." MA thesis, Texas A&M University, 1993.

Apache, Antonio. "Address." *Proceedings of the Lake Mohonk Conference* 14 (1896): 38–39.

Armstrong, S. C. "Hampton Normal and Agricultural Institute." In *Annual Report of the Commissioner of Indian Affairs, for the Year 1884*, 182–202. Washington DC: Government Printing Office, 1884.

———. "Report of Hampton School." In *Annual Report of the Commissioner of Indian Affairs, for the Year 1880*, 182–85. Washington DC: Government Printing Office, 1880.

Auldridge, Edith. "The Story of Haines House." Owned and Operated by Board of National Missions of the Presbyterian Church in the United States of America. 1955.

Barrett, S. A., and Alanson Skinner. "Certain Mounds and Village Sites of Shawano and Oconto Counties, Wisconsin." *Bulletin of the Public Museum of the City of Milwaukee* 10, no. 5 (March 4, 1932): 401–552.

Bass, Althea. *The Arapaho Way: A Memoir of an Indian Boyhood*. New York: C. N. Potter, 1966.

Beck, David R. M. "Collecting among the Menomini: Cultural Assault in Twentieth-Century Wisconsin." *American Indian Quarterly* 4, no. 2 (Spring 2010): 157–93.

———. "Fair Representation? American Indians and the 1893 Chicago World's Columbian Exposition." *World History Connected* 13, no. 3 (October 2016).

———. *Unfair Labor? American Indians and the 1893 World's Columbian Exposition in Chicago*. Lincoln: University of Nebraska Press, 2019.

Berman, Judith. "That Which Was Most Important: Louis Shotridge on Crest Art and Clan History." In *Native Art of the Northwest Coast: A History of Changing Ideas*, edited by Charlotte Townsend-Gault, Jennifer Kramer, and Ki-Ke-In, 166–202. Vancouver: UBC Press, 2013.

Berthrong, Donald J. *The Cheyenne and Arapaho Ordeal: Reservation and Agency Life in the Indian Territory, 1875–1907*. Norman: University of Oklahoma Press, 1976.

Betts, John Rickards. "P. T. Barnum and the Popularization of Natural History." *Journal of the History of Ideas* 20, no. 3 (June–September, 1959): 353–68.

Boas, Franz. "Frederic Ward Putnam." *Science* 42, no. 1080 (September 10, 1915): 330–32.

———. "Grammatical Notes on the Language of the Tlingit Indians." *University of Pennsylvania: The University Museum, Anthropological Publications* 8, no. 1 (1917).

————. "William Jones." *American Anthropologist* 11, no. 1 (January–March 1909): 137–39.

Bol, Marsha C. "Collecting Symbolism among the Arapaho: George A. Dorsey and C. Warden, Indian." In *The Great Southwest of the Fred Harvey Company and the Santa Fe Railway*, edited by Marta Weigle and Barbara Babcock, 110–24. Phoenix: Heard Museum, 1996.

Bold, Christine. *"Vaudeville Indians" on Global Circuits, 1880s–1930s*. New Haven CT: Yale University Press, 2022.

Braun, Judith Elise. "The North American Indian Exhibits at the 1876 and 1893 World Expositions: The Influence of Scientific Thought on Popular Attitudes." MA thesis, George Washington University, 1975.

Browman, David L., and Stephen Williams. *Anthropology at Harvard: A Biographical History, 1790–1940*. Cambridge MA: Peabody Museum Press, 2013.

Bruchac, Margaret M. "My Sisters Will Not Speak: Boas, Hunt, and the Ethnographic Silencing of First Nations Women." *Curator: The Museum Journal* 57, no. 2 (April 2014): 151–71.

————. *Savage Kin: Indigenous Informants and American Anthropologists*. Tucson: University of Arizona Press, 2018.

Burleigh, Nina. *The Stranger and the Statesman: James Smithson, John Quincy Adams, and the Making of America's Greatest Museum: The Smithsonian*. New York: HarperCollins, 2003.

Canilao, Michael Armand P. "Ruination and the William Jones Affair: Regenerative Debris and Contested Narratives in the Archives." *Museum Worlds: Advances in Research* 9 (2021): 1–18.

Child, Brenda. *Boarding School Seasons: American Indian Families, 1900–1940*. Lincoln: University of Nebraska Press, 1998.

Cole, Douglas. *Captured Heritage: The Scramble for Northwest Coast Artifacts*. Seattle: University of Washington Press, 1985.

————. *Franz Boas: The Early Years, 1858–1906*. Vancouver: Douglas & McIntyre, 1999.

Coleman, Michael C. *American Indian Children at School, 1850–1930*. Jackson: University Press of Mississippi, 1993.

Conn, Steven. *Do Museums Still Need Objects?* Philadelphia: University of Pennsylvania Press, 2010.

————. *Museums and American Intellectual Life, 1876–1926*. Chicago: University of Chicago Press, 1998.

Cooper, John M. "Truman Michelson." *American Anthropologist* 41, no. 2 (1939): 281–85.

Cushing, Frank Hamilton. "My Adventures in Zuni." *Century* 25, no. 2 (December 1882): 191–208.

————. "The Nation of the Willows." *Atlantic Monthly* 50, no. 299 (September 1882): 362–74.

———. "The Nation of the Willows II." *Atlantic Monthly* 50, no. 300 (October 1882): 541–59.

Darnell, Regna. *And Along Came Boas: Continuity and Revolution in Americanist Anthropology*. Philadelphia: John Benjamins, 1998.

Dauenhauer, Nora Marks, and Richard Dauenhauer. "Louis Shotridge and Indigenous Tlingit Ethnography: Then and Now." In *Constructing Cultures Then and Now: Celebrating Franz Boas and the Jesup North Pacific Expedition*, edited by Laura Kendall and Igor Krupnik, 165–83. Washington DC: Smithsonian Institution, 2003.

Davis, Collis H., Jr. "Headhunting William Jones: 58-Minute Video Documentary." *American Studies Asia* 1, no. 1 (June 2002): 125–50.

———. *Headhunting William Jones: A Documentary by Collis Davis*. Manilla, Philippines: Okara Video Presentation, 2016. DVD.

Dean, Jonathan. "Louis Shotridge, Museum Man: A 1918 Visit to the Nass and Skeena Rivers." *Pacific Northwest Quarterly* 89, no. 4 (Fall 1998): 202–10.

Deloria, Philip J. *Indians in Unexpected Places*. Lawrence: University Press of Kansas, 2004.

———. *Playing Indian*. New Haven CT: Yale University Press, 1998.

Deloria, Vine, Jr. *Custer Died for Your Sins: An Indian Manifesto*. New York: Avon, 1969.

DeMallie, Raymond J., and Douglas R. Parks. "George A. Dorsey and the Development of Plains Indian Anthropology." In *Anthropology, History, and American Indians: Essays in Honor of William Curtis Sturtevant*, edited by William L. Merrill and Ives Goddard, 59–74. Washington DC: Smithsonian Institution Press, 2002.

DeMarce, Roxanne. *Blackfeet Heritage, 1907–1908*. Browning MT: Blackfeet Heritage Program, 1980.

Derus, H. K. "What Has the Indian Done to Deserve Misery and Privation at Our Hands?" *Wisconsin Magazine*, January 1929, 3–5, 20–21.

Dippie, Brian. *The Vanishing American: White Attitudes and U.S Indian Policy*. Middletown CT: Wesleyan University Press, 1982.

Dorsey, George A. *The Arapaho Sun Dance: The Ceremony of the Offerings Lodge*. Field Columbian Museum pub. 4. Chicago: Field Columbian Museum, 1903.

———. *The Cheyenne*. Vol. 1, *Ceremonial Organization*. Field Columbian Museum pub. 9. Anthropological series 9, no. 1. Chicago: Field Columbian Museum, 1905.

———. *The Pawnee Mythology*. Washington DC: Carnegie Institution of Washington, 1906.

———. *Traditions of the Arikara: Collected under the Auspices of the Carnegie Institution of Washington*. Washington DC: Carnegie Institution of Washington, 1904.

Dorsey, George A., and Alfred L. Kroeber. *Traditions of the Arapaho*. Field Columbian Museum pub. 5. Chicago: Field Columbian Museum, 1903.

———. *Traditions of the Arapaho*. Introduction by Jeffrey D. Anderson. Lincoln: University of Nebraska Press, 1997.

Eastman, Elaine Goodale. *Pratt: The Red Man's Moses*. Norman: University of Oklahoma Press, 1935.

Eggermont-Molenaar, Mary, ed. *Montana 1911: A Professor and His Wife among the Blackfeet*. Lincoln: University of Nebraska Press, 2005.

Emery, Jacqueline, ed. *Recovering Native American Writings in the Boarding School Press*. Lincoln: University of Nebraska Press, 2017.

"Employees in Indian School Service." In *Annual Report of the Commissioner of Indian Affairs, for the Year 1888*, 385, 400. Washington DC: Government Printing Office, 1888.

"Employees in Indian School Service." In *Annual Report of the Commissioner of Indian Affairs, for the Year 1890*, 356. Washington DC: Government Printing Office, 1890.

"Employees in Indian School Service." In *Annual Report of the Commissioner of Indian Affairs, for the Year 1892*, 865. Washington DC: Government Printing Office, 1892.

"Employees of Indian Service." In *Annual Report of the Commissioner of Indian Affairs, for the Year 1893*, 553. Washington DC: Government Printing Office, 1893.

"Employees in Indian School Service." In *Annual Report of the Commissioner of Indian Affairs, for the Year 1894*, 516, 549. Washington DC: Government Printing Office, 1894.

"Employees in Indian School Service." In *Annual Report of the Commissioner of Indian Affairs, for the Year 1895*, 520, 543. Washington DC: Government Printing Office, 1895.

"Employees of Indian Service." In *Annual Report of the Commissioner of Indian Affairs, for the Year 1899*, 598, 603. Washington DC: Government Printing Office, 1899.

"Employees of Indian Service." In *Annual Report of the Commissioner of Indian Affairs, for the Year 1900*, 685. Washington DC: Government Printing Office, 1900.

"Employees of Indian Service." In *Annual Report of the Commissioner of Indian Affairs, for the Year 1901*, 769, 778. Washington DC: Government Printing Office, 1901.

"Employees in Indian School Service." In *Annual Report of the Commissioner of Indian Affairs, for the Year 1902*, 701, 714, 724. Washington DC: Government Printing Office, 1902.

"Employees of Indian Service." In *Annual Report of the Commissioner of Indian Affairs, for the Year 1904*, 639, 649. Washington DC: Government Printing Office, 1904.

"Employees of Indian Service." In *Annual Report of the Commissioner of Indian Affairs, for the Year 1905*, 526. Washington DC: Government Printing Office, 1905.

Fenton, William N. "Frank G. Speck's Anthropology (1881–1950)." In *The Life and Times of Frank G. Speck, 1881–1950*, edited by Roy Blankenship, 9–37. Philadelphia: University of Pennsylvania, 1991.

Fields, Alison. "Circuits of Spectacle: The Miller Brothers' 101 Ranch Real Wild West." *American Indian Quarterly* 36, no. 4 (Fall 2012): 443–64.

Fisher, Margaret Welpley. Preface to "Ethnography of the Fox Indians" by William Jones. In *Bureau of American Ethnology Bulletin* 125, vii–ix. Washington DC: Government Printing Office, 1939.

Fitzhugh, William W. "Origins of Museum Anthropology at the Smithsonian Institution and Beyond." In *Anthropology, History, and American Indians: Essays in Honor of William Curtis Sturtevant*, edited by William L. Merrill and Ives Goddard, 179–200. Washington DC: Smithsonian Institution Press, 2002.

Fletcher, Alice C. "The Hako: A Pawnee Ceremony." Assisted by James R. Murie; music transcribed by Edwin S. Tracy. Extract from *Twenty-Second Annual Report of the Bureau of American Ethnology: To the Secretary of the Smithsonian Institution, 1900–1901*. Washington DC: Government Printing Office, 1904.

———. "Lands in Severalty to Indians; Illustrated by Experiences with the Omaha Tribe." *Proceedings of the American Association for the Advancement of Science* 33 (1885): 654–65.

———. *Life among the Indians: First Fieldwork among the Sioux and Omahas*. Edited by Joanna C. Scherer and Raymond J. DeMallie. Lincoln: University of Nebraska Press, 2013.

Fletcher, Alice C., and Francis La Flesche. *The Omaha Tribe*. Washington DC: U.S. Government Printing Office, 1911.

Fowler, Loretta. *Tribal Sovereignty and the Historical Imagination: Cheyenne-Arapaho Politics*. Lincoln: University of Nebraska Press, 2002.

Freed, Stanley A. *Anthropology Unmasked: Museums, Science and Politics in New York City*. Vol. 1, *The Putnam-Boas Era*. Wilmington DE: Orange Frazer Press, 2012.

———. *Anthropology Unmasked: Museums, Science and Politics in New York City*. Vol. 2, *The Wissler Era*. Wilmington DE: Orange Frazer Press, 2012.

Freed, Stanley A., and Ruth S. Freed. "Clark Wissler and the Development of Anthropology in the United States." *American Anthropologist* 85, no. 4 (December 1983): 800–825.

Frisbie, Charlotte J. "Frances Theresa Densmore." In *Women Anthropologists: Selected Biographies*, edited by Ute Gacs, 51–58. Urbana: University of Illinois Press, 1989.

Glancy, Diane. *Fort Marion Prisoners and the Trauma of Native Education*. Lincoln: University of Nebraska Press, 2014.

Gleach, Frederick W. "Cushing at Cornell: The Early Years of a Pioneering Anthropologist." *Histories of Anthropology Annual* 3 (2007): 99–120.

Green, Jesse, ed. *Cushing at Zuni: The Correspondence and Journals of Frank Hamilton Cushing, 1879–1884*. Albuquerque: University of New Mexico Press, 1990.

Greer, John T. "A Brief History of Indian Education at the Fort Shaw Industrial School." MA thesis, Montana State University, 1958.

Grinnell, George Bird. *Blackfoot Lodge Tales: The Story of a Prairie People*. New York: Scribner, 1892.

———. "A Buffalo Sweatlodge." *American Anthropologist* 21, no. 4 (October–December 1919): 361–75.

Hagan, William T. "Private Property, the Indian's Door to Civilization." *Ethnohistory* 3, no. 2 (Spring 1956): 126–37.

———. *The Sac and Fox Indians*. Norman: University of Oklahoma Press, 1958.

Hagenbuch, Mark O. "Richard Henry Pratt, the Carlisle Indian Industrial School, and U.S. Policies Related to American Indian Education 1879 to 1904." EdD diss., Penn State University, 1998.

Haley, James L. *The Buffalo War: The History of the Red River Indian Uprising of 1874*. Garden City NY: Doubleday, 1976.

Hardt, H. B. *Official Catalogue of the Lewis & Clark Centennial and American Pacific Exposition and Oriental Fair, Portland, Oregon*. Portland OR: Lewis and Clark Centennial Exposition, 1905.

Harrington, Mark Raymond. "Alanson Skinner." *Indian Notes* 2, no. 4 (October 1925): 247–57.

———. "Alanson Skinner." *American Anthropologist* 28, no. 1 (January–March 1926): 275–80.

———. *Certain Caddo Sites in Arkansas*. Museum of the American Indian, Heye Foundation, Indian Notes and Monographs. New York: Museum of the American Indian, Heye Foundation, 1920.

———. "Reminiscences of an Archeologist: VI." *Masterkey* 38, no. 3 (July–September 1964): 106–10.

———. "Reminiscences of an Archeologist: VII." *Masterkey* 39, no. 1 (January–March 1965): 30–35.

Herskovits, Melville J. *Franz Boas: The Science of Man in the Making*. New York: Charles Scribner's Sons, 1953.

Hertzberg, Hazel W. *The Search for an American Indian Identity: Modern Pan-Indian Movements*. Syracuse: Syracuse University Press, 1971.

Hinsley, Curtis M. "Anthropology's Organization Man: Reflections on Frederick Webb Hodge, 1864–1956." *History of Anthropology Newsletter* 32, no. 2 (December 2005): 3–9.

———. "The Museum Origins of Harvard Anthropology, 1866–1915." In *Science at Harvard University: Historical Perspectives*, edited by Clark A. Eliott and Margaret W. Rossiter, 121–45. Bethlehem PA: Lehigh University Press, 1992.

———. *Savages and Scientists: The Smithsonian Institution and the Development of American Anthropology, 1846–1910*. Washington DC: Smithsonian Institution Press, 1981.

Hinsley, Curtis M., and Bill Holm. "A Cannibal in the National Museum: The Early Career of Franz Boas in America." *American Anthropologist* 78, no. 2 (June 1976): 306–16.

The History of the Museum. Indian Notes and Monographs—Miscellaneous Series, no. 55. New York: Museum of the American Indian, Heye Foundation, 1964.

Holm, Tom. *The Great Confusion in Indian Affairs: Native Americans and Whites in the Progressive Era.* Austin: University of Texas Press, 2005.

Howard, Kathleen L. "Creating an Enchanted Land: Curio Entrepreneurs Promote and Sell the Indian Southwest, 1880–1940." PhD diss., Arizona State University, 2002.

Hoxie, Frederick E., ed. *Talking Back to Civilization: Indian Voices from the Progressive Era.* Boston: Bedford/St. Martin's, 2001.

Hrdlička, Aleš. *A Descriptive Catalog of the Section of Physical Anthropology: Panama-California Exposition 1915.* San Diego: National Views, 1915.

———. *Tuberculosis among Certain Indian Tribes of the United States.* Washington DC: Government Printing Office, 1909.

Immerwahr, Daniel. *How to Hide an Empire: A History of the Greater United States.* New York: Farrar, Straus and Giroux, 2019.

Jacknis, Ira. *The Storage Box of Tradition: Kwakiutl Art, Anthropologists, and Museums, 1881–1981.* Washington DC: Smithsonian Institution Press, 2002.

"James Mooney." *American Anthropologist* 24, no. 2 (April–June 1922): 209–14.

Jensen, Joan M., and Michelle Wick Patterson, eds. *Travels with Frances Densmore: Her Life, Work, and Legacy in Native American Studies.* Lincoln: University of Nebraska Press, 2015.

Jonaitis, Aldona. "Tlingit Repatriation in Museums: Ceremonies of Sovereignty." *Museum Worlds: Advances in Research* 5 (2017): 48–59.

Judd, Neil M. "Frederick Webb Hodge." *American Antiquity* 22, no. 4 (April 1957): 401–4.

Kalesnik, Frank L. "Caged Tigers: Native American Prisoners in Florida, 1875–1888." PhD diss., Florida State University, 1992.

Kidwell, Clara Sue. "Every Last Dishcloth: The Prodigious Collecting of George Gustav Heye." In *Collecting Native America, 1870–1960,* edited by Shepard Krech III and Barbara Hail, 232–58. Washington DC: Smithsonian Institution Press, 1999.

King, Eleanor M., and Bryce P. Little. "George Byron Gordon and the Early Development of the University Museum." In *Raven's Journey: The World of Alaska's Native People,* edited by Susan A. Kaplan and Kristin J. Barsness, 16–53. Philadelphia: University Museum, 1986.

Kroeber, Alfred L. "The Arapaho." *Bulletin of the American Museum of Natural History* 18, part 1 (September 1902): 1–150.

———. "Decorative Symbolism of the Arapaho." *American Anthropologist* 3, no. 2 (April–June 1901): 308–36.

———. "Symbolism of the Arapaho Indians." *Bulletin of the American Museum of Natural History* 13, article 7 (April 1900): 69–86.

Krupat, Arnold. *Boarding School Voices: Carlisle Indian School Students Speak*. Lincoln: University of Nebraska Press, 2021.

La Flesche, Francis. "Alice C. Fletcher." *Science* 58, no. 1494 (August 17, 1923): 115.

———. *The Middle Five: Indian Schoolboys of the Omaha Tribe*. Boston: Small, Maynard, 1900.

Lamb, Daniel S. "The Story of the Anthropological Society of Washington." *American Anthropologist* 8, no. 3 (July–September 1906): 564–79.

LaPier, Rosalyn R. *Invisible Reality: Storytellers, Storytakers, and the Supernatural World of the Blackfeet*. Lincoln: University of Nebraska Press, 2017.

———. "The Piegan View of the Natural World, 1880–1920." PhD diss., University of Montana, 2015.

LaPier, Rosalyn R., and David R. M. Beck. *City Indian: Native American Activism in Chicago, 1893–1934*. Lincoln: University of Nebraska Press, 2015.

Liberty, Margot. "Francis La Flesche: The Osage Odyssey." In *American Indian Intellectuals*, edited by Margot Liberty, 44–59. St. Paul: West, 1978.

Lindsey, Donal F. *Indians at Hampton Institute, 1877–1923*. Urbana: University of Illinois Press, 1995.

Loring, Stephen, and Miroslav Prokopec. "A Most Peculiar Man: The Life and Times of Ales Hrdlicka." In *Reckoning with the Dead: The Larsen Bay Repatriation and the Smithsonian Institution*, edited by Tamara L. Bray and Thomas W. Killion, 26–42. Washington DC: Smithsonian Institution Press, 1994.

Ludlow, Helen W. *Ten Years' Work for Indians at the Hampton Normal and Agricultural Institute, at Hampton, Virginia*. Hampton VA: Hampton Institute, 1888.

———. *Twenty-Two Years' Work of the Hampton Normal and Agricultural Institute at Hampton, Virginia*. Hampton VA: Hampton Institute, 1893.

Lurie, Nancy Oestreich. "Women in Early American Anthropology." In *Pioneers of American Anthropology: The Uses of Biography*, edited by June Helm, 29–81. Seattle: University of Washington Press, 1966.

Madeira, Percy C., Jr. *Men in Search of Man: The First Seventy-Five Years of the University Museum of the University of Pennsylvania*. Philadelphia: University of Pennsylvania Press, 1964.

Mann, Henrietta. *Cheyenne-Arapaho Education, 1871–1982*. Niwot: University Press of Colorado, 1997.

Mark, Joan. *Four Anthropologists: An American Science in Its Early Years*. New York: Science History, 1980.

———. *A Stranger in Her Native Land: Alice Fletcher and the American Indians*. Lincoln: University of Nebraska Press, 1988.

Maroukis, Thomas C. "The Peyote Controversy and the Demise of the Society of American Indians." *American Indian Quarterly* 37, no. 3 (Summer 2013): 161–80.

———. *The Peyote Road: Religious Freedom and the Native American Church.* Norman: University of Oklahoma Press, 2010.

Marvin, James. "Report of Haskell Institute." In *Annual Report of the Commissioner of Indian Affairs, for the Year 1885,* 228–35. Washington DC: Government Printing Office, 1885.

Mason, J. Alden. "George G. Heye, 1874–1957." *Leaflets of the Museum of the American Indian, Heye Foundation* 6 (1958).

———. "Louis Shotridge." *Expedition* 2, no. 2 (1960): 10–16.

McClintock, Walter. *The Old North Trail: Life, Legends and Religion of the Blackfeet Indians.* London: Macmillan, 1910.

McGee, Anita Newcomb. "The Women's Anthropological Society of America." *Science* 13, no. 321 (March 29, 1889): 240–42.

McGee, WJ. "Anthropology at the Louisiana Purchase Exposition." *Science* 22, no. 573 (December 22, 1905): 821–26.

McGee, WJ, et al. "In Memoriam: Frank Hamilton Cushing." *American Anthropologist* 2, no. 2 (April–June 1900): 354–80.

McMullen, Ann, and Maria Galban. "Lost and Found: Re-establishing Provenance for an Entire Museum Collection." In *Collecting and Provenance: A Multidisciplinary Approach,* edited by Jane Milosch and Nick Pearce, 229–42. Lanham MD: Rowman & Littlefield, 2019.

Mead, Margaret. *Blackberry Winter: My Earlier Years.* New York: Simon and Schuster, 1972.

Mead, Margaret, and Ruth L. Bunzel, eds. *The Golden Age of American Anthropology.* New York: George Braziller, 1960.

Meriam, Lewis. *The Problem of Indian Administration.* Baltimore: Johns Hopkins Press, 1928.

Michelson, Truman. "A Piegan Tale." *Journal of American Folklore* 39 (1916): 408–9.

Milburn, Maureen E. "Louis Shotridge and the Objects of Everlasting Esteem." In *Raven's Journey: The World of Alaska's Native People,* edited by Susan A. Kaplan and Kristin J. Barsness, 54–77. Philadelphia: University Museum, 1986.

———. "The Politics of Possession: Louis Shotridge and the Tlingit Collections at the University of Pennsylvania Museum." PhD diss., University of British Columbia, 1997.

———. "Weaving the 'Tina' Blanket: The Journey of Florence and Louis Shotridge." In *Haa Kusteeyi, Our Culture: Tlingit Life Stories,* edited by Nora Marks Dauenhauer and Richard Dauenhauer, 548–64. Seattle: University of Washington Press, 1994.

Miles, John D. "Report of the Cheyenne and Arapaho Agency." In *Annual Report of the Commissioner of Indian Affairs, for the Year 1875,* 268–71. Washington DC: Government Printing Office, 1875.

———. "Report of the Cheyenne and Arapaho Agency." In *Annual Report of the Commissioner of Indian Affairs, for the Year 1876,* 46–50. Washington DC: Government Printing Office, 1876.

Mooney, James. "The Indian Ghost Dance." *Proceedings and Collections of the Nebraska State Historical Society* 16 (1911): 168–82.

———. *In Sun's Likeness and Power: Cheyenne Accounts of Shield and Tipi Heraldry.* Vol. 2. Transcribed and edited by Father Peter J. Powell. Lincoln: University of Nebraska Press, 2013.

Morris, H. S. *Historical Stories, Legends, and Traditions: Roberts County and Northeastern South Dakota.* Sisseton SD: Sisseton Courier, 1975.

Moses, L. G. *The Indian Man: A Biography of James Mooney.* Lincoln: University of Nebraska Press, 2002.

———. *Wild West Shows and the Images of American Indians, 1883–1933.* Albuquerque: University of New Mexico Press, 1996.

Murie, James R. *Ceremonies of the Pawnee.* Edited by Douglas R. Parks. Originally published as *Smithsonian Contributions to Anthropology,* no. 27 (1981). Lincoln: University of Nebraska Press, in cooperation with the American Indian Studies Research Institute, Indiana University, 1989.

———. "Pawnee Marriage Customs of the Old Days." *Indian School Journal,* February 1915, 299–301.

National Native American Boarding School Healing Coalition. *Healing Voices.* Vol. 1, *A Primer on American Indian and Alaska Native Boarding Schools in the U.S.* Minneapolis: National Native American Boarding School Healing Coalition, 2020.

Oestreicher, Pamela Holcomb. "On the White Man's Road? Acculturation and the Fort Marion Southern Plains Prisoners." PhD diss., Michigan State University, 1981.

Oneroad, Amos E., and Alanson B. Skinner. *Being Dakota: Tales and Traditions of the Sisseton and Wahpeton.* Edited by Laura L. Anderson. St. Paul: Minnesota Historical Society Press, 2003.

"Opening of the Anthropological Collections in the American Museum of Natural History." *Science* 12, no. 306 (November 9, 1900): 720–22.

Palladino, L. B. *Indian and White in the Northwest; or, A History of Catholicity in Montana.* Baltimore: John Murphy, 1894.

Pardue, Diana F. "Marketing Ethnography: The Fred Harvey Indian Department and George A. Dorsey." In *The Great Southwest of the Fred Harvey Company and the Santa Fe Railway,* edited by Marta Weigle and Barbara Babcock, 102–9. Phoenix: Heard Museum, 1996.

Parezo, Nancy J., and Don D. Fowler. *Anthropology Goes to the Fair: The 1904 Louisiana Purchase Exposition*. Lincoln: University of Nebraska Press, 2007.

Parker, Arthur C. "Book on Secret Societies Written by an Indian." *Quarterly Journal of the Society of American Indians* 3, no. 2 (April–June 1915): 134.

———. "The Menace of the Fraudulent Wild West Show." *Quarterly Journal of the Society of American Indians* 2, no. 3 (July–September 1914): 174–76.

———. "The Perils of the Peyote Poison." *American Indian Magazine* 5, no. 1 (January–March 1917): 12–13.

Parks, Douglas R. "James R. Murie: Pawnee Ethnographer." In *American Indian Intellectuals*, edited by Margot Liberty, 74–89. St. Paul: West, 1978.

Patterson, Michelle Wick. "She Always Said, 'I Heard an Indian Drum.'" In *Travels with Frances Densmore: Her Life, Work, and Legacy in Native American Studies*, edited by Joan M. Jensen and Michelle Wick Patterson, 29–64. Lincoln: University of Nebraska Press, 2015.

Peri, David W., and Robert W. Wharton. "Samuel Alfred Barrett: 1879–1965." *Kroeber Anthropological Society Papers* 33 (1965): 5–11.

Petersen, Karen Daniels. *Plains Indian Art from Fort Marion*. Norman: University of Oklahoma Press, 1971.

Peyer, Bernd, ed. *American Indian Nonfiction: An Anthology of Writings, 1760s–1930s*. Norman: University of Oklahoma Press, 2007.

"Peyote Hearings before a Subcommittee of the Committee on Indian Affairs of the House of Representatives on H.R. 2614." Washington DC: Government Printing Office, 1918.

Pezzati, Alessandro. "A Brief History of the Penn Museum." *Expedition* 54, no. 3 (2012): 4–19.

Pokagon, Simon. *The Red Man's Rebuke*. Hartford MI: C. H. Engle, 1893.

Prado, Vickie Ann. "The History of the San Diego Museum of Man." MA thesis, University of San Diego, 1997.

Pratt, Richard Henry. "The Advantage of Mingling Indians with Whites." In *Official Report of the Nineteenth Annual Conference of Charities and Corrections*, 260–61. Washington DC, 1892.

———. *Battlefield and Classroom: Four Decades with the American Indian, 1867–1904*. Edited by Robert M. Utley. New Haven CT: Yale University Press, 1964.

———. "Catalogue of Casts Taken by Clark Mills, Esq., of the Heads of Sixty-Four Indian Prisoners of Various Western Tribes, and Held at Fort Marion, Saint Augustine, Fla., in Charge of Capt. R.H. Pratt, U.S.A." In *Proceedings of the United States National Museum 1878*, 201–14. Washington DC: Government Printing Office, 1879.

———. *The Indian Industrial School, Carlisle, Pennsylvania: Its Origins, Purposes, Progress and Difficulties Surmounted.* Carlisle PA: Cumberland County Historical Society, 1979.

———. "Report of School at Carlisle, PA." In *Annual Report of the Commissioner of Indian Affairs, for the Year 1893*, 448–56. Washington DC: Government Printing Office, 1893.

———. "Report of Training-School at Carlisle, PA." In *Annual Report of the Commissioner of Indian Affairs, for the Year 1880*, 178–81. Washington DC: Government Printing Office, 1880.

———. "Report of Training-School at Carlisle, PA." In *Annual Report of the Commissioner of Indian Affairs, for the Year 1881*, 184–94. Washington DC: Government Printing Office, 1881.

———. "Report of Training-School at Carlisle, PA." In *Annual Report of the Commissioner of Indian Affairs, for the Year 1890*, 308–14. Washington DC: Government Printing Office, 1890.

———. "Report of Training-School at Carlisle, PA." In *Annual Report of the Commissioner of Indian Affairs, for the Year 1891*, 588–97. Washington DC: Government Printing Office, 1891.

———. "Savagery Is a Habit." In *Annual Report of the Board of Indian Commissioners, 1890*, 170. Washington DC: Government Printing Office, 1891.

Preucel, Robert W. "Shotridge in Philadelphia: Representing Native Alaskan Peoples to East Coast Audiences." In *Sharing Our Knowledge: The Tlingit and Their Coastal Neighbors*, edited by Sergei Kan, 41–62. Lincoln: University of Nebraska Press, 2015.

Prucha, Francis Paul, ed. *Americanizing the American Indians: Writings by the "Friends of the Indian," 1880–1900.* Lincoln: University of Nebraska Press, 1978.

Putnam, Jennifer L. "NAGPRA and the Penn Museum: Reconciling Science and the Sacred." *Concept* 37 (2014): 1–21.

Ramirez, Renya K. *Standing Up to Colonial Power: The Lives of Henry Roe and Elizabeth Bender Cloud.* Lincoln: University of Nebraska Press and the American Philosophical Society, 2018.

Redman, Samuel J. *Prophets and Ghosts: The Story of Salvage Anthropology.* Cambridge MA: Harvard University Press, 2021.

"Report of Agents in Wisconsin." In *Annual Report of the Commissioner of Indian Affairs, for the Year 1882*, 172–73. Washington DC: Government Printing Office, 1882.

"Report of Indian School Superintendent." In *Annual Report of the Commissioner of Indian Affairs, for the Year 1885.* Washington DC: Government Printing Office, 1885.

"Report of Indian School Superintendent." In *Annual Report of the Commissioner of Indian Affairs, for the Year 1886.* Washington DC: Government Printing Office, 1886.

Rideout, Henry Milner. *William Jones: Indian, Cowboy, American Scholar, and Anthropologist in the Field.* New York: Frederick A. Stokes, 1912.

Rosaldo, Renato. *Ilongot Headhunting, 1883–1974: A Study in Society and History.* Stanford CA: Stanford University Press, 1980.

Rosenthal, Nicolas G. *Reimagining Indian Country: Native American Migration and Identity in Twentieth-Century Los Angeles.* Chapel Hill: University of North Carolina Press, 2012.

Rydell, Robert W. *All the World's a Fair: Visions of Empire at American International Expositions, 1876–1916.* Chicago: University of Chicago Press, 1984.

Seaton, Elizabeth P. "The Native Collector: Louis Shotridge and the Contests of Possession." *Ethnography* 2, no. 1 (March 2001): 35–61.

Shotridge, Louis. "The Kaguanton Shark Helmet." *Museum Journal* 20, no. 4 (December 1929): 339–43.

———. "A Visit to the Tsimshian Indians, Continued." *Museum Journal* 10, no. 3 (September 1919): 117–48.

Simmons, Leo W., ed. *Sun Chief: The Autobiography of a Hopi Indian.* New Haven CT: Yale University Press, 1955.

Skinner, Alanson. "Exploration of Aboriginal Sites at Throgs Neck and Clasons Point, New York City." *Contributions from the Museum of the American Indian, Heye Foundation* 5, no. 4 (1919).

———. "John Valentine Satterlee." *Wisconsin Archeologist* 19, no. 4 (November 1920): 209–13.

———. *Material Culture of the Menomini.* Indian Notes and Monographs. New York: MAI, Heye Foundation, 1921.

———. *Medicine Ceremony of the Menomini, Iowa, and Wahpeton Dakota, with Notes on the Ceremony among the Ponca, Bungi, Ojibwa, and Potawatomi.* Indian Notes and Monographs. New York: MAI, Heye Foundation, 1920.

———. "Recent Mound Explorations in Shawano County." *Wisconsin Archeologist* 18, no. 3 (August 1919): 105–7.

———. "Recollections of an Ethnologist among the Menonimi Indians." *Wisconsin Archeologist* 20, no. 2 (April 1921): 41–74.

———. "Social Life and Ceremonial Bundles of the Menomini Indians." *Anthropological Papers of the American Museum of Natural History* 13, part 1 (1913).

Standing Bear, Luther. *My People the Sioux.* Lincoln: University of Nebraska Press, 2006.

Stocking, George W., Jr., ed. *A Franz Boas Reader: The Shaping of American Anthropology 1883–1911.* New York: Basic Books, 1974.

Stoner, Barbara. "Why Was William Jones Killed?" *Field Museum of Natural History Bulletin* 42, no. 8 (1971): 10–13.

Stowe, Harriet Beecher. "The Indians at St. Augustine." *Christian Union* 15 (April 18, 1877): 345.

Temkin, Andrea S. "Alice Cunningham Fletcher." In *Women Anthropologists: Selected Biographies,* edited by Ute Gacs, 95–101. Urbana: University of Illinois Press, 1989.

Thunderbird, Chief. "Two Boys from El Llano Estacado." *Masterkey* 50, no. 1 (1976): 68.

Tooker, Elisabeth, and Barbara Graymont. "J. N. B. Hewitt." *Histories of Anthropology Annual* 3 (2007): 70–98.

Trafford, Emily. "Hitting the Trail: Live Displays of Native American, Filipino, and Japanese People at the Portland World's Fair." *Oregon Historical Quarterly* 116, no. 2 (Summer 2015): 168–75.

Trafzer, Clifford E., Jean A. Keller, and Lorene Sisquoc, eds. *Boarding School Blues: Revisiting American Indian Educational Experiences.* Lincoln: University of Nebraska Press, 2006.

Trenholm, Virginia Cole. *The Arapahoes, Our People.* Norman: University of Oklahoma Press, 1986.

Trennert, Robert A., Jr. "A Grand Failure: The Centennial Indian Exhibition of 1876." *Prologue* 6, no. 2 (Summer 1974): 118–29.

Vigil, Kiara M. "The Death of William Jones: Indian, Anthropologist, Murder Victim." In *Indigenous Visions: Rediscovering the World of Franz Boas,* edited by Ned Blackhawk and Isaiah Lorado Wilner, 209–30. New Haven CT: Yale University Press, 2018.

Viola, Herman J. *Diplomats in Buckskins: A History of Indian Delegations in Washington City.* Washington DC: Smithsonian Institution Press, 1981.

Vuckovic, Myriam. *Voices from Haskell: Indian Students between Two Worlds, 1884–1928.* Lawrence: University Press of Kansas, 2008.

Wallace, Kevin. "A Reporter at Large: Slim-Shins' Monument." *New Yorker* 36 (November 19, 1960): 104–46.

Wanneh, Gawasa. "Situwaka, Chief of the Chilcats." *Quarterly Journal of the Society of American Indians* 2, no. 4 (October–December 1914): 280–83.

White, Richard. "Frederick Jackson Turner and Buffalo Bill." In *The Frontier in American Culture: An Exhibition at the Newberry Library, August 26, 1994–January 7, 1995,* edited by James R. Grossman, 6–65. Berkeley: University of California Press, 1994.

Wilcox, U. Vincent. "The Museum of the American Indian, Heye Foundation." *American Indian Art* 3, no. 2 (Spring 1978): 40–49, 78–79, 81.

Williams, Lucy Fowler. "Louis Shotridge: Preserver of Tlingit History and Culture." In *Sharing Our Knowledge: The Tlingit and Their Coastal Neighbors,* edited by Sergei Kan, 63–78. Lincoln: University of Nebraska Press, 2015.

Williams, Lucy Fowler, and Robert Starbard. "Woosh.Jee.Een, Pulling Together: Repatriation's Healing Tide." In *Unsettling Native Art Histories on the Northwest Coast,* edited by Kathryn Bunn-Marcuse and Aldona Jonaitis, 218–39. Seattle: University of Washington Press, 2020.

Winnie, Lucille Jerry. *Sah-Gan-De-Oh: The Chief's Daughter*. New York: Vantage Press, 1969.

Wissler, Clark. *The American Indian: An Introduction to the Anthropology of the New World*. New York: Douglas C. McMurtrie, 1917.

———. "Ceremonial Bundles of the Blackfoot Indians." *Anthropological Papers of the American Museum of Natural History* 7, part 2 (1912).

———. *Indian Cavalcade, or Life on the Old-Time Indian Reservations*. New York: Sheridan House, 1938.

———. "Man as a Museum Subject." *Natural History* 23, no. 3 (May–June 1923): 245–57.

———. "Social Organization and Ritualistic Ceremonies of the Blackfoot Indians." *Anthropological Papers of the American Museum of Natural History* 7 (1912): 1–320.

———. "The Sun Dance of the Blackfoot Indians." *Anthropological Papers of the American Museum of Natural History* 16, part 3 (1918).

Wissler, Clark, and D. C. Duvall. *Mythology of the Blackfoot Indians*. Anthropological Papers of the American Museum of Natural History 2, part 1. New York: American Museum of Natural History, 1908.

———. *Mythology of the Blackfoot Indians*. Introduction by Alice Beck Kehoe. Lincoln: University of Nebraska Press, 1995.

Wissler, Clark, Alice Beck Kehoe, and Stewart E. Miller. *Amskapi Pikuni: The Blackfeet People*. Albany: State University of New York Press, 2012.

Witthoft, John. "Frank Speck: The Formative Years." In *The Life and Times of Frank G. Speck, 1881–1950*, edited by Roy Blankenship, 1–8. Philadelphia: University of Pennsylvania, 1991.

"The Woman's Anthropological Society." *Science* 13, no. 312 (January 25, 1889): 60–61.

"The Work of Clark Wissler among the Sioux." *American Indian Magazine* 5, no. 4 (December 1917): 265–67.

Yellow Robe, Chauncey. "The Indian and the Wild West Show." *Quarterly Journal of the Society of American Indians* 2, no. 1 (January–March 1914): 39–40.

———. "The Menace of the Wild West Show." *Quarterly Journal of the Society of American Indians* 2, no. 3 (July–September 1914): 224–25.

Young, S. Hall. *Hall Young of Alaska: The Autobiography of S. Hall Young*. New York: Fleming H. Revelly, 1927.

Zemanek, Alysha Danielle. "Indiana School Days: Native American Education at St. Joseph's Indian Normal School and White's Manual Labor Institute." MA thesis, Indiana University, 2017.

Zitkala-Sa. "An Indian Teacher among the Indians." *Atlantic Monthly* 85 (March 1900): 381–86.

———. "The School Days of an Indian Girl." *Atlantic Monthly* 85 (February 1900): 185–94.

Index

assimilation (*cont.*)
85, 264; William Jones on, 77. *See also* citizenship; cultural erasure; identity; Indian boarding schools; language erasure

BAE. *See* Bureau of American Ethnology (BAE; Smithsonian)
Baird, Spencer, 10, 25, 27, 32, 36–38
baptism, 31, 47, 87
Barnum, P. T., 100
Barrett, Samuel A., 165, 166, 168, 212
Battice, Walter, 101
Battle of Cibecue Creek (1881), 41
Battle of the Greasy Grass (1876), 26
Battle of the Little Bighorn (1876), 26
Baxoje (Iowa), 168
Being Dakota (Oneroad and Skinner), 221
BIA. *See* Bureau of Indian Affairs (BIA)
Bible Teachers' Training School, 210
Big Plume, Louise, 113
Black and Yellow Buffalo Lodge, 119
Blackfeet Reservation, 111, 113, 117–19
Blackfoot Confederacy, 112, 119
Blackfoot Lodge Tales (Grinnell), 122
blacksmithing, 114, 115
Black Tail Deer Dance, 119
Bliss, Zenas R., 44
Bloomfield, Leonard, 166
boarding schools. *See* Indian boarding schools
Boas, Franz: anthropological career of, 58, 59–61; Chicago World's Exposition and, 37; mentor of, 60; process of, 118; as professional mentor, 16, 59, 64, 66; work of, with Alfred Kroeber, 185; work of, with Alice Fletcher and James Murie, 145. *See*

also American Museum of Natural History (AMNH)
Bonnin, Gertrude. *See* Simmons, Gertrude (Zitkála-Šá)
Borneo, 147
Bourassa, Rosa, 197
bows and arrows, 25
Brinton, Daniel Garrison, 60
Brown, Charles E., 173
Bruchac, Margaret, 14
Buffalo Bill's Wild West shows, 100, 241. *See also* Wild West shows
Buffalo Head ceremony, 142
Bugkalot (Ilongot), 71–76
Bull Bear, 81, 83, 84, 85, 96
Bull Bear, Jack, 198
Bull Bear, Young, 196
Bunch, Lonnie, III, 258
Bureau of American Ethnology (BAE; Smithsonian): establishment of, 3, 38, 195; John Satterlee's work with, 166; leadership of, 2–3, 36, 38–40, 58; linguistic project of, 35, 43, 64; Native staff at, 4, 67–68. *See also* Smithsonian Institution
Bureau of Indian Affairs (BIA), 2, 17, 29, 146–47, 161, 264
burial grounds. *See* grave robbing
Burns, Robert, 195

Caddo, 22, 48
Cadzow, Donald, 214
California film industry, 105–6
Calumet ritual, 142
Carlisle Indian Industrial School: Cleaver Warden at, 179–81, 187; establishment of, 32, 179; Eva Rogers at, 187–88; founder of, 2, 7, 17, 21, 28; military discipline at,

28, 84, 87, 90, 132, 137, 180; outing
system at, 85–87, 180, 187, 259;
Richard Davis at, 9, 82–87, 89–91;
student recruitment for, 57, 82–83,
141, 179–80, 236
Catholic boarding schools, 113, 114, 160.
See also mission schools
Catholicism, 6, 113, 125, 157, 158. *See also*
Christian conversion
*Ceremonial Bundles of the Blackfoot Indi-
ans* (Wissler), 119
Chamberlain, A. F., 59
Chaticks si Chaticks (Pawnees), 16, 31,
56, 129, 131, 139, 142–43
Chaui, 131
Cherokees, 182
Cheyenne and Arapaho Reservation,
88, 91–92, 178–79, 185
Cheyennes, 15, 19–20, 21, 22, 26, 34, 42
The Cheyenne series (Davis and
Dorsey), 98
Chicago World Columbian Exposition
(1893), 37, 51, 58, 59–60, 67, 90–91,
146, 166, 235
Chillkat Tlingits, 68, 237, 245, 247
Chilocco Indian Boarding School, 114,
202
China, 70
Chinquilla, Princess, 242
Chippewas, 167
Christian conversion, 6, 31, 113, 135,
157, 158, 206, 210, 218, 221. *See also*
Catholicism
Christian naming practices, 1–2
citizenship, 102–3, 139, 258, 264. *See also*
assimilation
Cody, William F. "Buffalo Bill," 100. *See
also* Buffalo Bill's Wild West shows
Cole, Douglas, 61

Cole, Fay-Cooper, 71
Cole, Mabel, 71
collaborator as term, 12–13
collected narratives, 119–20, 170, 247,
262. *See also* cultural heritage materials; *and specific books*
Collier, John, 225
Columbia University, 52, 116
Columbus Day celebrations, 90–91
communal ownership: of cultural
objects, 121, 171, 255, 256; of land, 88,
92, 139, 207
Courts of Indian Offenses, 79, 223
Coutts-Johnstone, Mathilde A.
"Madame Toona," 103–4, 106,
237–38
Crow Creek Reservation, 225
Cuba, 70
cultural erasure, 1–2, 6, 10–12, 261–62,
264–65. *See also* assimilation; identity; Indian boarding schools; language erasure; salvage anthropology
cultural heritage materials: at AMNH,
64, 66, 117; of Bugkalot, 73; collected by Alanson Skinner, 169; collected by Amos Oneroad, 214–16;
collected by Antonio Apache, 235;
collected by Cleaver Warden, 187–
91; collected by D. C. Duvall, 111,
120–22, 250; collected by Frances
Densmore, 167; collected by George
Gustav Heye, 213; collected by John
Satterlee, 165, 169, 171–74; collected
by Shotridges, 227, 245–49, 255;
commodification of, 189–90, 262;
complexity of Indigenous anthropologists collecting, 224, 227, 260–
65; at Field Museum, 60, 75, 79, 98,
144, 189; James Murie on,

cultural heritage materials (*cont.*)
142–43; and newly made objects, 65,
120, 245–46; repatriation of, 255–
57, 260; salvage anthropology and
collection of, 10–12; at Smithsonian
Institution, 26, 33–34, 36, 40, 48,
148–49; from Sun Dance ceremonies, 98, 189; at world's fairs, 36–38.
See also collected narratives; grave
robbing; medicine bundles; sacred
ceremonies
culture area as term, 116–17
Cushing, Frank Hamilton, 17, 19, 36–43,
130
Custer, George Armstrong, 26
Custer Died for Your Sins (Deloria), 257

dairy farming, 88, 89
Dakota, 117
Dakota Missionary Society, 221
Dakota War (1862), 222
dance performances at Fort Marion, 25
dances. *See* sacred ceremonies
Davis, Elsie, 83, 91, 97
Davis, Emma, 83, 97
Davis, Henry, 97
Davis, Mary, 88, 97, 108
Davis, Mary Johnstone, 106, 108
Davis, Nannie, 87, 89, 97, 105, 108
Davis, Oscar, 83
Davis, Richard, 79–81, 108–9; advocacy
work by, 106–8; anthropological
fieldwork of, 94–98; as Carlisle
School student, 9, 82–87, 89–91;
Cleaver Warden and, 179, 180; early
life and schooling of, 81–82; Field
Museum work of, 67; film work by,
105–6; land allotments and, 91–93;
as performer, 16, 81, 99–105, 238;
West Grove life of, 87–89

Davis, Richenda, 88, 108
Davis, Roy, 97
Dawes Act (1887), 140
Deloria, Ella Cara, 243
Deloria, Vine, Jr., 257
Densmore, Frances, 153, 166–67
Diné (Navajo), 42, 48, 213
Dixon, Roland B., 52
Dog Soldiers, 81
Dorsey, George A.: anthropological
career of, 58, 67; Cleaver Warden
and, 194; fieldwork collaborations
of, 17, 144–47, 185–88; Richard
Davis and, 79, 95; William Jones
and, 68–69, 70, 74
doubling, 30, 89, 138–39, 223
Dousman, Rosalie, 158
Dumaliang, Romano, 73
Dunlop, John, 44
Duvall, Charles, 112–13
Duvall, D. C., 111–12, 127–28; anthropo-
logical work by, 111, 116–20, 122–
24; death of, 124–27; early life and
schooling of, 9, 113–14, 276nn5–6;
objects collected by, 111, 120–22, 250;
work of, at Fort Shaw and Browning, 114–16

Eagle Child, James, 125, 127
Eastern Band of Cherokee, 182
Eastman, Charles, 197
Elk Dance, 149
emotional abuse. *See* abuse
erasure. *See* cultural erasure; language
erasure
Esau, Mary, 138, 151
ethnographic work. *See* anthropology
ethnomusicology, 166
Exposition of Indian Tribal Arts, 107
expositions. *See* world's fairs

The Falcon Out West (film), 106
Field Museum of Natural History:
    Antonio Apache's work at, 235;
    cultural heritage collection of,
    60, 75, 79, 98, 144, 189; leadership
    of, 58, 67; transition of priorities
    at, 99; William Jones's work at,
    68–70
fieldwork. See anthropology
film industry, 16, 105–6
First Americans (organization), 106–7
Fletcher, Alice C., 3, 14, 140–44, 166
Folsom, Cora, 55, 63
forced removal, 7, 22, 35, 141. See also
    Indian boarding schools; land theft
Fort Berthold Indian Reservation, 144
Fort Hall Indian Boarding School, 113,
    276nn5–6
Fort Laramie Treaty (1851), 20, 81
Fort Leavenworth, 22
Fort Marion, 23–29, 43, 48, 137
Fort Reno, 44, 181
Fort Shaw, 45, 114–16
Fort Shaw Indian Boarding School, 45–
    46, 113–16
Fort Sill, 21–22
Fort Supply, 44, 45, 181
Fort William First Nation, 67
Francis, David R., 95
fraud, 233–37
Fred Harvey Company, 235
Freemasons, 218
Free Museum of Science and Art, 243

Gacad, 73, 75
Gago-gam-dzi-wust, 248
Garfield, James, 134
Gatschet, Albert Samuel, 35, 63
Gauthier, Joseph, Sr., 159
Gauthier, Mary, 158

gendered labor, 114, 242–43. See also
    women
Geronimo, 146
Ghost Dance, 182–84, 190, 191, 199
The Ghost Dance Religion and the Sioux
    Outbreak of 1890 (Mooney), 184
Gila Crossing Day School, 108
Gilmore, Melvin, 219
Glancy, Diane, 25–26
Goodwill Presbyterian Church, 206,
    210
Goodwill Presbyterian Mission School,
    207, 219
Gordon, George Byron, 17, 58, 238, 240,
    241, 246, 249
Goyathlay, 146
Grabowskii, Arthur, 137
Grant, Ulysses S., 36
Grass Dance, 119
grave robbing, 10; by Amos Oneroad,
    216, 250; James Murie and, 149;
    by John Satterlee, 164–65, 250; by
    Louis Shotridge, 250, 256, 257; by
    Richard Henry Pratt and Spencer
    Baird, 25, 27, 28, 32. See also cultural
    heritage materials; repatriation
Great Depression, 130, 250, 253
Grinnell, George Bird, 122, 219

Hairy Face, 43, 44
Hako ceremony, 142
Hampton Institute (formerly Hampton
    Norman and Agricultural Institute):
    on assimilation, 29–31; James Murie
    at, 31, 56, 132–35; as model for other
    schools, 160; student recruitment
    for, 55; Tichkematse at, 29–32, 55–56;
    William Jones at, 9, 31, 55–57, 66
The Handbook of American Indians
    North of Mexico (Hodge), 148, 182

In the Critical Studies in the History of Anthropology series

To order or obtain more information on these or other University of Nebraska Press titles, visit nebraskapress.unl.edu.